ALLY
OF THE
ENTREPRENEUR

*The Rise of Banking in the South
and the Fall of Wachovia*

By,

Carlos Elbert Evans

Published by Salem Books, LLC
Charlotte, NC

Library of Congress Control Number: 2024910814
ISBN: 979-8-218-45064-9
Printed in the United States of America

"Carlos Evans was the best Corporate Banker I have ever known. He was conservative in his underwriting, creative in his loan structuring, and he was always available for his clients. They depended on his skills and his judgment and they loved the respect he showed to them and their companies. So I repeat, he was the best."

–Ken Thompson,
former CEO and Chairman of Wachovia

"Carlos Evans is a Banker's banker."

–Charlie Way,
former Chairman of the Beach Company, Developer of Kiawah Island

"Carlos Evans is a Banker who helps his clients build their business. Throughout the history of our relationship, he has become a good friend, a valued advisor whose counsel has enabled us to become successful."

–George Dean Johnson,
Chairman of Johnson Management

"Carlos Evans is a man whose life has been conducted on the altar of trust, partnership, respect for others and fundamental values. As a leader of people in business, in a community, and in other endeavors, Carlos consistently advances and inspires everyone he encounters by his example. He sets the gold standard in how he pursues his life. For me, he was a client, is a friend and is an example to emulate."

–David Fox,
Managing Director, Greenwich Associates

Dedication

To my family, my departed mother and father, my departed mother-in-law and father-in-law, my brother and sister, and last but not least, my beloved wife Lisa and son Blake, who are both my rock and my inspiration. They, above all else, give life meaning and make the journey so extra special!

Carlos, Lisa, and Blake Evans
Picture from the American Diabetes Association
2014 Father of the Year Awards

Table of Contents

Introduction 7

Chapter 1   The Early Years 15

Chapter 2   My First Memories 19

Chapter 3   Evans Grocery 23

Chapter 4   My Life in Salem 27

Chapter 5   My Life in Florence 45

Chapter 6   Puttin In Tobacco...............................57

Chapter 7   Newberry College.................................67

Chapter 8   Donald Pee Wee Gaskins 75

Chapter 9   Bankers Trust My First Big Break 83

Chapter 10   Bankers Trust Just Getting Started....................89

Chapter 11   Sidetracked or So I Thought............................93

Chapter 12   Back In The Training Program........................103

Chapter 13   The Great American 109

Chapter 14   Dentsville My First P&L 113

Chapter 15   Lisa, My Life Partner.......................................125

Chapter 16   The Platform Finally Arrived 131

Chapter 17   Hilton Head Island "Camelot".......................141

Chapter 18   From Bankers Trust to NCNB 173

Chapter 19   Charleston First Time......................................179

Chapter 20   Columbia S.C. Second Time 193

Chapter 21   The End Of A Decade
                The End Of Banking As We Knew It..............227

Chapter 22   The Start of a New Decade
                The Start of a New Job 241

Chapter 23   On To Charlotte
                The NCNB Culture 251

Chapter 24   Interstate Banking Arrives
              Along With A Personal Crisis 267

Chapter 25   A New Name A New Boss..............................279

Chapter 26   The Night of the Long Knives,
              The Lewis Purge 293

Chapter 27   New Team, New Uniform, Same Game..........301

Chapter 28   A New Name, Another Culture......................313

Chapter 29   The Wachovia Championship.........................325

Chapter 30   The Coming Storm 337

Chapter 31   The Weekend at the Adoption Agency............351

Chapter 32   The Death of Wachovia 361

Chapter 33   Wells Fargo A New Culture............................367

Chapter 34   Reflections on Banking
              and on Corporate Culture 381

Chapter 35   A New Career On The Back Nine 387

Chapter 36   The Last Chapter Or Is It?.............................397

Introduction

My name is Carlos Elbert Evans and while my name is somewhat unusual as it signals something different about my heritage, I have always felt there is absolutely nothing that unusual about my life. So you might ask why I wrote this book, well the answer is one I have pondered since my retirement 6 years ago when this small voice started in my head that grew ever louder and louder as the months went by.

Some time ago as I began to prepare for the effort, I met with my friend Rolfe Neil, the former Chairman of the Charlotte Observer, to get some advice. Rolfe is a great newspaper man but more than that, he is an incredible public servant who has been involved in every aspect of making my hometown, Charlotte, North Carolina, into the wonderful city it is today. To say I respect him a great deal would be an incredible understatement, and so he was one of the first people I would seek out for direction and advice.

Rolfe and I met for a cup of coffee down the street at Panera which is somewhat of a morning gathering spot here in the Eastover/Myers Park neighborhood in Charlotte, a neighborhood full of trees, churches, and sidewalks where people walk their dogs and still know each other's names. After a few pleasant exchanges Rolfe quickly got to the point, "Why are you thinking of this book?" My response to him was I wasn't sure. I told him about the small voice growing ever louder in my head. I thought he was going to tell me I was crazy but to my surprise he looked at me and smiled and simply said, "I guess that's as good a reason as any!"

Since that meeting, I have pondered the question over and over a thousand times. Was I writing this book to make money? Well, no. Early on I decided to donate most if not all of any earnings from the book to charity. Was I writing this book because I have a high opinion of myself? Again, no. I have never considered myself special nor have I considered my career to be anything exceptional. I do not see myself as a Saint, and I am well aware of my many flaws.

I was told once by Ken Thompson, the former chairman and CEO of Wachovia, that he considered me to be the "Forest Gump" of banking because I was in the background and around the hoop when many significant events that transformed the industry took place. I was Forest Gump in his mind not because I was shaping those events, but because I was there.

While not the primary reason for writing this book, I have tried to set the story straight on the demise of Wachovia and to give a sense of what that bank was really like. So while not the primary focus, there is much in here on the inside story of significant events that shaped the Banking Industry.

After my meeting with Rolfe, I began to ponder the question of motivation at a deeper level. Was I writing this book to make some sort of political statement, or to convey some type of thought-provoking message? To be clear, I have some strong opinions on the important role entrepreneurship plays in our free enterprise system and some equally strong opinions on corporate culture. I also have some conviction about the importance in business and in life of being comfortable with diversity. Additionally, while I am not necessarily a person who wears it on his sleeve, I do have strong beliefs on the importance of faith, family and friends. While my opinions on these topics are woven throughout this book with some of the common themes summarized at the end of this introduction, at the end of the day after much consideration I came to the conclusion that none of these in and of themselves are what drove me to tell my story. As I continued to think about my motives and after spending a lot of time discussing this with my editor, I have come to what I think is the answer.

While the answer is simple, getting there was not. There were many long walks in the neighborhood, walks on the beach, as well as paddling trips up at our mountain house at lake Summit where I pondered the question before I started writing. In the end, I kept coming back to the fact that I spent my entire career trying to help people be successful in business; therefore, shouldn't this book be a natural extension of what I spent my life doing? The answer to that question was a resounding yes, so therefore what is the one simple concept that I want the reader to take away? Something that they can build into their approach to business and life that will help them succeed or at least improve their odds of success.

Early in my life I learned that you do not need to take advantage of people to be successful. I learned that true, long-term success in business and in life comes when you work hard to create the win-win. In other words, you do things in a way that helps other people while at the same time helping yourself. The key here is balance, so that both parties equally benefit and the scales are in equilibrium, not tilted too much to one side or the other. I learned many of these lessons in my father's country store where he emphasized the importance of a fair price for products and services even when the demand/supply dynamic dictated he could have done otherwise.

I learned those same lessons again later from Hootie Johnson, Chairman of the bank where I started my career, when in the late 1970s the prime rate went to the high teens and he chose to cap Bankers Trust's prime rate at a much lower level to provide much needed relief to business owners. Those lessons and many others were reinforced later when I realized that while money or success or even revenge were powerful motivators, for me they weren't nearly as powerful as the purer motive of simply trying to help my customers.

Additional reinforcement came when I called on prospects in New York City, arguably one of the most cutthroat business environments on the planet, however also a market where I was most effective and at the top of my game in winning new customers. Now, some might say the New Yorkers did business with me because they knew they could take advantage of a slower, more genteel southerner. In fact, nothing could have been further from the truth because my golden rule was always to create the win-win. As a result, had the business not been fair and a good deal for the bank I simply would not have done it. I am quick with numbers, and I quickly identified deals the bank needed to avoid. In the final analysis, I believe the reason for my success in New York was because the New Yorkers could see or sense that I would be fair. This allowed me to establish bonds of trust quickly.

On this last point, if there is anything to take away from this book, it is this: In business and in life, trust is everything. While you may be the fairest person in the world if people do not have confidence that you will act in a trustworthy manner, you won't be successful. I have thought long on the question of building trust, and I am convinced that it is developed over a long period of time when you focus on the win-win and do right by people as part of everything you do. I believe that if you behave a certain way often enough, consistently enough, and long enough, it becomes part of your persona.

Going back to my early days in my father's country store, he emphasized over and over the importance of doing things right. To him, doing things right was not just sweeping the floors clean and washing the windows properly. It was a mantra to be incorporated into everything you did including how you dealt with people. It did not matter whether they were rich or poor, black or white, educated or not, they were all treated fairly and with respect. From his point of view, if you incorporated the spirit of fairness and the win-win into everything you did, people would pick up on it.

My father's training was immensely important in a banking career that dealt in large measure with entrepreneurs. Make no mistake, entrepreneurs tend to be extremely good at reading people, and while they may come in all different ages, colors, genders, and backgrounds, they all need that skill to survive. They are also a group of people for whom trust is paramount. While my father probably had no idea what I would end up doing, the lessons he drilled into me of treating people fairly helped me develop trust with my clients and made me ideally suited to be a banker.

Since a banker is often the primary capital provider to an entrepreneur or business, he or she is arguably one of their most important partners. While my skill with numbers was important, at the end of the day what my customers valued most was the belief that I would be fair and work to do what was best for them, not only best for the bank. That they could trust me to behave that way in good times, bad times and everything in between was critically important.

In the final analysis, I have tried to live my life focused on the win-win and helping others be successful. My hope is that in reading this book you will take away one lesson for business and life: that the chances for long term success and personal satisfaction grow exponentially when you strive to do business the right way and in so doing create the win-win. If something is not good for everyone involved, do not do it. If you hold to that often enough and long enough, it will become part of your persona and people will reward you with their trust. That ability to inspire trust will become your greatest asset in business and in life.

As to some of the other themes woven throughout my story, here are a few of my thoughts that are reinforced throughout the book. Entrepreneurship: I believe entrepreneurs are the key, most important and necessary cog in our free enterprise system. The title of this book, "Ally of the Entrepreneur," was taken from an article in a North Carolina business magazine that was written about me in the mid 90s. I did not come up with the title, and to be clear, I am not sure how the writer came up with it. But when I read the article for the first time, I thought it perfectly described what my job was and the role I was supposed to play in my work.

Specifically, I have always believed that no jobs get created until an entrepreneur invests capital, and in most cases that capital is paired with debt largely provided to small business by the banks. That ability to create leverage or debt has a multiplier effect on the transaction, allowing the entrepreneur to increase job creation and spending, which are the keys to creating economic growth. When companies prosper, per capita income also grows, and consumer spending increases, resulting in GDP growth, which is the ultimate measure of economic prosperity. But to be clear, none of this starts until an entrepreneur chooses to invest capital, and in this country, small businesses owned by entrepreneurs are still the largest providers of jobs.

One more point about entrepreneurs. They are a rare and special breed. Few people combine the necessary appetite for risk, willingness to take risk (and most of them risk it all), willingness to work long, hard hours, willingness to deal with bureaucracies and the many roadblocks government throws up, willingness to confront failure, willingness to face ridicule if they do fail, and last but not least the willingness to expose their families to all of those risks. Make no mistake about it, entrepreneurs are rare; they come in all different shapes and sizes, races, ages, genders, creeds, backgrounds, and political persuasions, and no two are alike. As rare as they are, our free enterprise system would grind to a halt without them.

Corporate culture: it is incredibly important to the success of any business and likewise, a breakdown in corporate culture can be fatal. In most cases, corporate culture starts with the founder or a key executive early in the life of a business, and it carries forward from there. In my career I have witnessed many different corporate cultures, both positive and negative, through my dealings with thousands of entrepreneurs. I also have first-hand experience in the corporate cultures that fed into the creation of two of the largest banks in the country. Specifically, NCNB which became NationsBank and later became Bank of America. Then later in my career, First Union which became Wachovia and is now part of Wells Fargo. Later in the book I will describe these different cultures in greater detail, explain how they evolved, and in some instances how that evolution led to significant problems. Suffice it to say, corporate culture is very important and while it usually starts with a person or personality it gets harder and harder to maintain as the company gets bigger and bigger and further away from that founding personality.

Diversity: as I have already mentioned, entrepreneurs come in all different shapes and sizes. No two are alike. In my experience being able to deal with different types of people is a huge asset in business and in life. While, in this age, much is said about diversity especially in the context of race and gender, little is said about the broader context of being able to relate to people who are from different socio-economic backgrounds, or said another way, the poor, the uneducated, the working class who have come up through the school of hard knocks. Thanks to my father's lessons about fairness and respect for everyone, I came up in a way that helped me relate to people who were very different. While early on I did not understand the value of this, later I came to see the value of that trait especially in business.

Faith, Family and Friends: nothing is more important. I have been blessed in my life with some measure of faith and a very strong measure of family and friends. At the end of this book, I will give thanks to my family and friends many of whom will be mentioned along the way. But make no mistake about it, aside from the fact that they give life meaning, faith, family and friends provide the support one needs to get through the tough times, and all of us will have tough times. In my case I have had a few, and it was that support that helped get me through.

One final comment about faith. For the record, I was born a Methodist but became Presbyterian through marriage. One of the things Presbyterians believe in is predestination. As I have already said, I don't wear my religion on my sleeve, but I know there have been many times in my life where it has been clear that someone was moving me in a certain direction or making me choose one path over another. Perhaps it was even that small voice in my head that grew ever louder until it finally pushed me to sit down and start this book on December 4, 2020, some three weeks before Christmas. Did I choose that date? I don't think so, because my belief is that it was not my choosing. Having said that, as I sit here and type away on this cold cloudy day, the thought occurs to me that the Holidays were the perfect time to start a book about a life that has been filled with so much that I have to be thankful for. And at no other time of year am I ever more thankful than I am in the glorious Holiday Season and all it embodies.

Carlos Evans

Chapter 1

The Early Years

My mother and father met during World War II. My father, like all his brothers, served his country during the war where he was an Army Air Corps navigator. This was back in the days when radar was a new technology, and navigation was handled with slide rules, charts and compasses. Navigation was a natural fit for my dad, who was good with math even though he did not have a high school education.

Dad was stationed in The Panama Canal Zone where he flew diplomatic and intelligence pouches to embassies all over South America and Latin America. Much of the intelligence concerned the German U Boats that were patrolling offshore and sinking many Allied ships. Over the course of the war Dad flew thousands of hours. On one of his many trips his plane stopped in San Jose Costa Rica for the night and that is where my dad met Mom, who had just finished her college degree, at one of the many social gatherings that were held for American Military personnel.

At that point, Dad was in his early 20s. Mom was a little younger, but she had already earned her college degree, having graduated at 18. While Dad was less educated, he was highly intelligent and being southern, he was very polite and a gentleman. My mom was very pretty and quiet and thoughtful. Despite the differences in their education, kindness was a trait they both shared. I think it is safe to say that both were very young and still evolving as the people they would ultimately become. However, at that point in their lives with World War raging, they fell into what they thought was love and were married.

After the war mother came with dad to live in the little farming community of Salem Crossroads where my dad ran my grandfather's small general store. Most of my father's brothers were farmers in the area as was my grandfather Roy. My grandfather Roy had excellent people judgment and knew his sons' strengths and weaknesses well. In the case of my father, Grandfather Roy knew he was ideally suited for the store which had been started by my great grandfather, Andrew Edward Evans, in 1924 as Salem Supply Company.

Moving to Salem Crossroads in 1946 must have been a shock to my mom since she had grown up in San Jose, the capital of Costa Rica. As I mentioned earlier, Salem was a simple crossroads where one paved road met up with three dirt roads. While my mother was fluent in English, the country dialect she encountered in Salem was very much like a different language. The people of Salem Crossroads were incredibly poor with most homes not having running water and outhouses being the norm.

Since air conditioning was still not much in use, at least in Salem, summers were unbearably hot and humid. The heat and the low, swampy land provided a very unappealing contrast to San Jose, which sat on a high mountain plateau with a mild and temperate climate due to its proximity to the equator. My mom talked constantly about Costa Rica's tall mountains with their lush green rain forests and how it was the Switzerland of Central America.

Aside from the obvious differences of geography and climate, there were many more subtle differences. The population in Costa Rica was highly educated. With one of the highest literacy rates in the world, Costa Rica supported no armed forces and thus spent the vast majority of their taxes on education and healthcare. Also, due to its stable government, Costa Rica had many Europeans and Americans living and doing business there. This urbane, highly educated and sophisticated city was a significant contrast to Salem Crossroads.

Also, due to the heavy influence of the Spaniards and the mixing with the indigenous peoples, Costa Rican's were mostly dark skinned; the major religion was Catholicism. There was no such thing as segregation in Costa Rica. Salem Crossroads on the other hand was full of uneducated Whites and African Americans, who lived separately from one another. The Whites tended to have Welsh and English backgrounds but no education. The African Americans were the descendants of enslaved people and often spoke in dialects of their own such as Gullah and other variations.

The South was segregated in 1946 and would remain that way for years. The White population harbored significant feelings of bigotry toward non-white people. Regardless of race, most people were either Baptists or Methodists. In fact, I wasn't even aware of any other churches in our area. This world provided a difficult contrast to my mother's Hispanic coloration and Catholic religion, and it was against this backdrop that my dad brought my mom to Salem.

Notwithstanding all the differences and the rigid social divisions of the time, my grandparents accepted my mom and welcomed her to the community. My Dad built a small four room, two-bedroom cinder block house just behind the store, with one bathroom and a small kitchen and small living room. All in, it was about 600 square feet, and it was into this home that my sister was born in 1947 and I was born on July 25 1951.

Soon after arriving in Salem Crossroads, my mom began teaching school in the town of Hannah, which was a couple of miles down the road across the swamp, while my dad worked in the store 6 days a week from sunrise to 9pm every evening. Also, despite the many difficulties mom must have encountered with both culture and climate in America, she also worked hard to get two of her sisters into the country. Although my mom loved Costa Rica she knew there were greater opportunities in the States and she wanted her sisters to be here. During this time she helped my Aunt Narda (Tita) move to Charlotte where she met and married a wonderful man named Clinton Wilkinson. My other Aunt, Adelita (the youngest), met and married a Dutch Shipyard worker named Adre Van Gent in New York City. My Aunt Sole moved to Mexico City where she obtained a job in the Costa Rican Embassy. My other Aunt Ameneida, married and stayed in Costa Rica with my Grandmother Mamacita as did Carlos, my mother's brother.

My Father was a strict disciplinarian, and while underneath all that he was a kind person, he had very conservative old school values of hard work from sun up to sundown and a belief in the traditional family where the wife stayed home, cooked three meals a day and tended to the children. Mom was also a kind person in the most gentle of ways, but underneath the gentleness was a strong will and an iron determination to continually improve her education and lot in life. She wanted to work and while she was a good mother and housekeeper, that was not her focus. She loved teaching and believed in continual learning in the classroom where she would go on to get her masters degree and pursue a doctorate. While the kindness was a trait they both shared it would not be enough. With time the differences would lead to constant arguing which with time would lead to their separation.

Chapter 2

My First Memories

I was born on July 25, 1951, at McCleod Memorial Hospital in Florence S.C. McCleod was the closest medical facility to Salem Crossroads some 30 miles away. At the time, Florence was a railroad town as a hub for the Atlantic Coastline Railroad. The population of Florence in 1951 was 20,000 which made it infinitely bigger than Salem Crossroads which may have boasted 50 people in the surrounding community. Obviously, during the first 5 years of my life there is little recollection. However, a few memories of different things did stick with me.

First, there was my sister Melba, who was 4 years my senior. Melba was always the athlete in the family. She was undefeated in High School Tennis, where she played #1 for three years. She was also the star player on both sides of the court in Women's Basketball back when women players were either offense or defense, with only two rovers on each side running the full court. Melba had many 30-point games back when there was no three-point line. With today's rules she would have scored even higher because many of her baskets were outside what would be the three-point line today.

Melba was a straight A student and also Homecoming Queen at McCleneghan High School in Florence her senior year. But more than her accomplishments on and off the court, what I remember most from an early age was her iron will. To say Melba was tough minded would be an incredible understatement. She could beat up farm boys twice her size, something she regularly did, and she was my protector. I can remember like yesterday seeing her with a cast on after she broke her arm. Most kids

19

would have seen the cast as a nuisance. Melba saw it as a badge of honor. Melba was special, and whenever she was around, I always felt safe.

Another thing I remember about those early years was the frequent presence of my mothers two sisters, Tita and Adelita as well as visits from Mamacita. I can still hear them as they rattled on in Spanish at 100 miles an hour. In fact, I spoke Spanish before I spoke English but ended up losing much of it in my later years. There was always much singing and playing the guitar which my mom always had close by. While we were an American family, and my mother would apply for and receive her citizenship, from a cultural point of view we were Hispanic. Rice and beans were a staple in our diet along with tortillas, and the adults drank strong coffee in the mornings. I can remember Mom dropping hunks of cheese or queso in the coffee to let it melt so we could put it on toast. The music we listened to was Latin, and English was never spoken in the house when Dad was not there. It was all Spanish.

We made many visits to Charlotte, where my Aunt Tita lived with her husband Clinton Wilkinson. Clinton was the one who originally taught my sister to play tennis and basketball. So, you might say, while I was born in the USA, Spanish culture was what I experienced most during my first 5 years. In addition to my aunts, I have early memories of Mamacita who struck me as a very stern lady. My biggest memory of her was during Hurricane Hazel in 1954 when she grabbed me up in her arms, raced me out of our wooden store and ran me back to the safety of our block-constructed house. Even today I can remember the terrible, screaming wind that uprooted the huge chinaberry that stood beside the store, but thanks to Mamacita, I was safe. I also remember Mamacita as someone who was strong in her faith. While my mom was not what I would call a "church person," Mamacita had instilled in her a very strong belief in God. Every wish was prefaced by "God willing," and her strong Christian sensibility caused her to be always aware of the needs of others. I can remember my mom often giving her last dollar to people in need of which there were many in and around Salem.

Despite mom's lack of "churchiness," we were regular attendees at Salem United Methodist Church which was across the road from the store. In fact, all the Evans clan were members, and our family comprised the largest part of the congregation.

Another memory that sticks in my mind was when I almost drowned at age 3 or 4. With my father running the store all day, my mother teaching school at Hannah and Melba in grammar school, I was often left to my own devices and would play in our small fenced yard that was a short distance from the store. On the day in question, a man named Mutt, whose last name I have forgotten, was cleaning out the septic tank for the house. For anyone who does not know what a septic tank is, all I can say it is not a very pleasant job. Mutt was an old African American man who did odd jobs at the store like burning the trash, keeping wood in the old wood-burning heater during the winter and various other things.

I remember him as a wonderful old gentleman who often let me hang around while he did his work, and on this day I watched him use a bucket with a rope tied to it to do his cleaning. Like kids often do, I tried to imitate by tying a string to my sandbox bucket, then proceeded to help Mutt with his work. When Mutt stepped away to empty his pail, I went over to the edge to dip mine and fell in. All I can remember was that the horrible mess was over my head. All I could do was sink to the bottom and push up to gasp for air. Aside from the horrible smell, I remember my terrible, intense fear that I was going to drown. As my small legs were running out of the strength to keep pushing up to allow me to get air, I remember Mutt's hand reaching down like the hand of God to pull me out. There was a water hose nearby, so he hosed me down then took me up in his arms and into the store to my dad. My memory tells me that Mutt died not long thereafter, but I have not forgotten him and often wish I had been old enough to thank him in some way.

In addition to Melba, my mother and her sisters, and my close call with death and being saved by Mutt, my earliest memories also involve the beginning of embarrassment over my Spanish heritage. As I said earlier, my mother and her sisters spoke Spanish all of the time. In addition to the constant difference in language there was also our unmistakable darker complexion. In fact, I remember a couple of occasions when we were refused service in restaurants because we were thought to be Mexicans. I remember cringing while we were sitting in restaurants as my mother and her sisters bantered in Spanish, which was totally out of the norm in the Deep South. Heads would turn, and I would find myself feeling very uncomfortable and anxious. At that early age, I was too young to understand right from wrong. All I knew was that I did not want to be different. Like most kids, I wanted to be like everyone else, and in the Deep South at that time, being half-Spanish with a name like Carlos made me definitely very different.

The last thing I remember from my early years was the fighting between my Mom and Dad. Much of the fighting was over the constant speaking of Spanish both in public and in our home. Dad viewed it as telling secrets because he could not understand what my mothers and her sisters were saying. He also viewed it as impolite since no one else could understand. In private, it was okay, but when others were around it made him terribly angry.

My father was a stern disciplinarian, and I remember many whippings with his belt. He had a special warning. Anytime he saw me doing something he did not like he would say, " Do that one more time and we will go round and round." What that meant was that he was going to take off his belt, grab one of my hands and give me a whipping as I tried to get away by running in a circle around him.

While whippings were prevalent and a fact of life in Salem Crossroads my mother didn't like them. In her mind they may have been symbolic of Salem itself. My mother hated the country and all its prejudices. Way before her time especially in a small farming community in the Deep South, she took great issue with the separation of the races. Dad on the other hand believed in segregation, even though from everything I saw, he was totally fair in his business dealings and treated people with respect whether black or white. Initially, I was torn between the two and would flip-flop back and forth trying to appease both parents, however, with time I eventually came over to my mother's point of view, which has been instrumental in me developing my own deep belief in diversity and faith.

My mother's hatred of the deep prejudices she encountered in Salem led to many, many arguments between my parents culminating in their separation when I was 5. Initially, my mother and sister moved to Charlotte to live with Aunt Tita and Clinton, while I remained in Salem with my Dad for a year. I have no memory about why I was the one who stayed. I just remember Melba and Mother were gone and it was just me and Dad.

This was a strange time in my life since I was not in school. I would rise every morning and go to the store with Dad.

Chapter 3

Evans Grocery

Started by my great grandfather, Evans Grocery had its beginnings as Salem Supply Company in the early 1920s . Early on, it was nothing more than a storage shed with a padlock where my great grandfather sold feed, seed and fertilizer. Since my great grandfather and his son (Granddaddy Roy) were both farmers being in the seed and fertilizer business was a natural extension of their livelihood as farmers. Around 1927 Salem Supply Company became a country store know as Evans Grocery. While today I pronounce my name the English way (phonetically EHVANS) in the country it was pronounced IVANS.

By the time I was 5, living in Salem with my dad while Mom and Melba were in Charlotte, Evans Grocery had become a community fixture. The store (as we called it) was an old wood sided building roughly 20 feet wide and 30 feet deep, with an awning and gas pumps in the front. The store was painted white with dark green trim and a Coca Cola sign on one side. The area around the gas tanks was not paved, just dirt, so the whole thing looked like a Norman Rockwell painting. Inside, the walls were lined with shelves, and a long counter ran along the left-hand side where dad stood behind the cash register. To his right, just inside the front window stood an old timey drink box where bottles hung from a rack in a pool of cold water. One inserted a nickel or dime, pulled the bottle along the rack then up through the release. Next to the drink box was freezer box with big tubs of ice cream, usually four different flavors.

Atop the long counter were big jars filled with loose cookies and candy, and the shelves along the walls were stocked with canned goods

23

like beans, peas, as well as bags of sugar, rice, flour, and the ever-present round Morton's salt containers with the pull out tin spout on the top for pouring. The wall across from the counter had hard goods and hardware with fan belts, tire tubes, tire patches, truck tires, tins full of bolts, screws, as well as car batteries, motor oil, etc. In the middle at the front of the store was an old wood stove with tin covering the wood floors underneath to keep them from burning. Surrounding the stove were four rocking chairs and a couple of pine half benches good for one person each. Just behind the stove , several small tables held blue jeans, overalls, flannel shirts and underwear (soft goods) with Brogan shoes and boots under the tables.

Behind the soft goods table was the meat counter where my dad had huge tins of cheese, liver pudding, hogshead cheese, chickens, fat back, bacon, stew beef, and fresh eggs which he obtained from my Aunt Julia who raised chickens. The meat counter also offered fresh produce, mostly lettuce, cabbage, and fresh tomatoes obtained from local farmers. Behind the meat counter were the scales as well as the ever-present roll of waxed paper that my father used to wrap meat. Above the meat counter a small half attic provided storage, and it was accessed with a movable ladder.

This store was my dad's life. He was there from sunup to 9 pm everyday all day except for Wednesday afternoon and Sunday. In addition to groceries, hard goods, soft goods, meats and produce, dad also sold crop insurance as referral source to a man named Mr. Billy Draughn in Johnsonville. In addition, he filed tax returns for people in the community and collected electric and gas payments for Carolina Power and Light Company.

The other interesting place in the store was the gun rack in the middle on the right hand wall where dad sold shotguns (mostly the Savage/Stevens brand) and shotgun shells. Also, there were Daisy Red Rider BB guns as well as hunting coats, vests and pants. Lastly, I remember Daddy had a 12-gauge shotgun that he always kept behind counter right beside the cash register. That served as an ominous reminder of the dangers of running a store in the middle of nowhere with long hours. As much as anything else, I think the shotgun was a deterrent because it was kept in plain sight. In the 55+ years that dad ran the store, he never had a robbery.

The absence of an attempted robbery might not seem unusual, but in the Salem Community there were some really bad actors. In fact, the worst serial murderer in S.C. history lived right down the road in Prospect. His name was Donald Pee Wee Gaskins. Later in life, I would have a bone chilling experience with Pee Wee.

For me as a small child, my father's store was bigger than life, but in truth it was a very small business. My guess is that Dad never made more than $8,000 in any given year over the entire 55 years he ran the store.

My Dad was also my first experience with an entrepreneur even though I did not know it at the time. In later years I would think about this more and more. I would think about the fact that he went to work from sunup to 9 pm every day except Sunday; that he had a family to support with no regular paycheck and no assurances that people would buy from him; that every single day his reputation and livelihood were on the line. While I wasn't aware at the time, my guess on looking back is that funding inventory and having enough working capital were constant pressing issues. Every day he had to think creatively about how to make his business better, and he had no one to look to for help other than his own brains and determination. For me, the year that Dad and I were alone in Salem while Mom and Melba were in Charlotte was an interesting time. I was only five years old, but I have many memories of dad and me together, with much of that time in the store. I didn't realize it at the time, but I was getting lessons in business every day. I learned to treat people with respect, to welcome them with a smile, to give a firm handshake, and to look them directly in the eye. I learned to be fair in all my dealings even when circumstances might have allowed me to take advantage of people. I learned to work hard and long hours.

In the daytime hours when I wasn't in the store, I was at Grandmother and Granddaddy's. They lived in a house down a dirt road near the church, a little way from the store. Some nights I would sleep at the house behind the store and some nights at Grandmother and Granddaddy's. As I said earlier, Dad and I were apart from Mom and Melba for almost a year. At the end of that time my parents reconciled, at which point Mom and Melba moved back, however, they did not return to Salem. As part of their reconcilement, Dad bought a small yellow brick house on Berkley Avenue in Florence. This allowed Mom to leave behind the country life she detested. She also started teaching Spanish at McCleneghan High School in Florence. Melba entered the fifth grade at Briggs Elementary

School, and I entered the 1st grade. Then, about a year after our move to Florence, my brother Andy was born.

While the move seemed to help my parent's marriage, things between them were still far from ideal. Dad was now commuting the 30 miles back and forth to the store, and he tended to stay overnight in Salem many nights since the store did not close until 9 pm. Mom, on the other hand, found a new life in Florence in a more city-like environment, and so their differences became even more pronounced. By the time I was 10, their marriage was done and they were finally divorced.

I was heartbroken by the split. I loved them both, and I knew that the split would force me to share time between the two of them, which meant that I would be with each of them less. As heartbroken as I was, even at the age of 10 I realized that all the fighting was not good, and that the marriage could not last.

Interestingly, despite their differences and their divorce, my mom never said bad things about my dad, and my dad never said bad things about my mom. However, for the next several years I was definitely pulled in two different directions, spending weekends and most of every summer in Salem with my dad, and weeks with my mom. Thus, the pattern of a split life was established until I graduated from high school. Aside from the differences in place, the cultural differences were huge as well. In the early 60s, Salem was the Deep South with all of its attendant prejudices. Florence, on the other hand, was as culturally different as another country. After the split, my mom spread her wings. Florence gave her the opportunity to stay active, meet new people and visit interesting places.

When I say I had a split life, it was true in both place and people. Salem Crossroads and Florence really were like two different worlds, physically, culturally, economically, and even down to the way language was used in each place. Also, my two parents were as different in every respect as two people could be. Certainly, the differences pulled me in two opposite directions. It was hard sometimes, but perhaps it also broadened me, taught me to see the world in less black-and-white terms.

Chapter 4

My Life in Salem

In Salem, everything revolved around the store. The town actually had two stores, Evans Grocery and Daniel Brothers. People tended to use one store or the other so the customers were different. However, my dad and the Daniels were friends, which meant they were definitely competitors, but not at all cutthroat. In fact, my Aunt Julia (Uncle Son's wife) had been a Daniels before marriage. The two stores would actually help each other from time to time. If one store ran out of a particular item, the other would sell it some of its inventory. They would constantly share information about the community—about who was doing what and who wasn't paying their bills. I didn't realize it at the time, but I was learning a valuable lesson on how appropriate cooperation with competitors could make both parties better, a lesson that would prove valuable later in life on Hilton Head Island when I got my first big break in banking.

The only other public or business entities in Salem were a small welding shop run by Gene Daniels across from Daniel Brothers Store, the Salem United Methodist Church which was directly across the street from Dad's store, and last but not least the skating rink which was 100 yards down on the right from Evans Grocery.

In the immediate community of Salem, there were only four families in what I would call a 1/4 mile radius around the two stores. The Harris family was to the right of the store headed to the skating rink where Mr. Harris ran a small outside sawmill. The Daniels lived behind their store. Then there was Mayo and Eva Poston and their 10 children who lived in the tiniest of houses with no running water between the Harris's and the skating rink. Then there were the Evans's. Granddaddy and Grand mama as I have said earlier lived down a dirt road just past the church and the graveyard. Two of Daddy's younger brothers, Uncle Punk and Uncle Cedric, also lived with Grand mama and Granddaddy. His youngest brother, Uncle Danny, lived in Charleston where he worked construction jobs for Bonitz Insulation Company. Up the road from our store and just past Daniel Brothers lived Uncle James and Aunt Fan as well as Uncle Son (Winfred) and Aunt Julia. Both couples had 4 children. Uncle Son had three sons Jerry, Nelson, and Wayne and one daughter Teresa. Uncle James had two daughters, Peggy and Faye, and two sons, Jimmy and Stewart. These were my cousins and constant playmates along with the Poston children.

In those days, the Salem community could be characterized as dirt poor. Our family homes had running water and indoor plumbing which made us feel like upper class. Most families had outhouses and outdoor hand pumps for water. The small homes were made out of wood siding with no insulation, tin roofs, and most were heated with wood stoves, their small chimneys sticking through patched tin roofs. Paint was either peeling or non-existent with most homes whitewashed instead of covered with real paint. Chickens ran free in most yards, which caused me as a young barefooted boy to always be conscious of where he was running and what I was stepping into.

A way further outside of Salem were other families. Many were "up the road," which in our local parlance meant toward Florence or "down the road," which meant the other way. An African American lady named Lila and her many children lived down the road as did Reverend Pendergraph (who may or may not have been a real preacher) and his family. Up the road was Mr. Reless Poston and his brother Phillip as well as an area we called the Luke Woods that held a large African American community and school.

Down the road and to the right was "over the swamp." The swamp was a dark foreboding place covered with water and full of ancient cypress trees with huge canopies that blocked out much of the light even in mid-day. This low-lying land lay just off a creek and was not unlike many similar areas that dotted the area. In fact, revolutionary war hero Francis Marion, aka "The Swamp Fox" was known to have resided several miles down the

Pee Dee River in a similar area that was totally dense and surrounded by water making it very difficult for pursuing British soldiers to find him. "The swamp" was full of water moccasins, alligators, and snapping turtles, and black bears were known to be in the area. The place had a dark, earthy funk, and everything smelled of fish, worms and reptiles.

As a young boy I was scared to death of the swamp, but I would go anyway because the fishing was good with large bream and catfish in abundance. I also enjoyed going with Uncle Punk who would often act as my guide and personal source of entertainment since he was the jokester in the family and always fun. Even so, it was a scary place where you had to watch carefully with every step, the kind of place you would not wander thoughtlessly because you could easily become disoriented and lost.

I remember one time Uncle Punk and I were fishing. We heard the soft sound of footsteps, and we yelled out. Old Mutt stepped out from behind a bush and said, "Mornin', dis is a great day for fishin'." He wasn't more than 15 yards from us, and he had been there the whole time but we had never seen him due to the thickness of the undergrowth.

Down the road and to the right was ''over the swamp '' where Mr. and Mrs. Deleon (pronounced Deleean) lived, along with my dad's sister, Aunt Marilyn and her husband Fred Stone. They had two children Randy and Terry, who were also playmates. Further down the road was Poston's Corner where a large number of Postons lived who were unrelated to the Postons in Salem.

Perhaps five or six miles up the road from Salem was Bazen Crossroads where many Bazens lived, and beyond Bazens crossroads lay the town of Pamplico perhaps 10 miles from Salem on the way to Florence. The population of Pamplico was about 1,000 people, which remains its size today. While small, Pamplico was a metropolis compared to Salem.

There was a bank there known as Pamplico Bank and Trust, owned by the Munn Family. My father's Salem Grocery banked with Pamplico Bank and Trust, and my Daddy borrowed money from the Munn Family. Interestingly, Mark Munn would work with me much later on. Mark is a fine banker and today heads Bank of America's offices in Charleston S.C.

Pamplico also had a large tobacco warehouse as well as a full-fledged grocery store and a movie theatre. My uncle Stoll Joye and his wife Amy ran the theater. They had six children: Chan, the oldest, then Mickey,

Steve, Greg, Kevin, and Karen being the youngest. Even though they were 10 miles away, the Joyes were frequent visitors to Salem. While Chan, Mickey and Steve were much older, Greg and Kevin tended to be my playmates especially Kevin, who spent the most time in Salem.

The Joyes were a wonderful family, and my Aunt Amy was particularly special. She had a very sweet personality, and even though my mom and Dad were divorced, she always asked about mom. While Aunt Amy and Uncle Stoll never made a lot of money, they raised their children well. Chan and Mickey received full ROTC scholarships. Chan became an accountant and was the CFO for the State Record Company, the newspaper in Columbia S.C. After The State was sold to Knight Ridder, Chan served as an advisor to the family that had owned it. He was also very successful in his own business dealings, buying and selling several companies over his career. Mickey became a Corporate Attorney and was also very successful.

All the Joyes achieved great success in life and in their marriages, and much of that success I attribute to my Aunt Amy's influence. Kevin, her youngest son, died at an early age of a heart attack, which broke all our hearts. He was a big guy, loved to eat, was full of life, played the guitar and loved to sing. He was one of my favorite cousins.

Down the road about 3 miles from Salem was Kingsburg where there was a Pure gas station. Because it also had a short order counter that served hot dogs, hamburgers, and fries, it was a hangout for young people. A pinball machine inside the station received lots of use because it "paid off," meaning that if you won extra games, you could redeem them for cash at 5 cents per game. In essence it was a form of gambling, which was of course illegal in S.C. at the time. From our perspective, we preferred to think of it as a game of skill, and we spent countless hours pouring nickels into the pinball machine.

Since Kingsburg was 3 miles and we were just kids with no drivers licenses (even though you could get your license at 14 back then), we would often catch rides from Salem or "thumb" to get there. Also in Kingsburg was Miss Gert's, a very small store where everyone went to buy liquor. Miss Gert would buy half pints and resell them, almost certainly illegal since she had no liquor license. My uncle Cedric, farmed Miss Gert's land for which he paid her rent and spent countless dollars buying liquor from her store. As far as my teetotaler grandmother and grandaddy were concerned,

Miss Gert's was off limits. They tolerated Uncle Cedric's patronage of her establishment because he could claim it was business since he was farming her land.

Beyond Kingsburg, another 7 miles down the road, was the town of Johnsonville which was about the same size as Pamplico. Johnsonville had many of the same things as Pamplico. There was a Bank, Johnsonville Bank and Trust where my dad did a little business, a tobacco warehouse, and also a Dairy Queen where people would ride around on Sunday afternoon to show off their cars. Round and round they would go squealing their tires at every opportunity! But my favorite place in Johnsonville was the American Legion Hut. "The Hut" as we called it was run by a man named "Sarge" who made the greatest hamburgers on the planet. Many evenings after the store closed Dad and I would go there for a late meal. Dad would have a few beers, and Sarge and Dad would swap stories of their time in the military. Even though Dad would sneak off to have a beer at "The Hut" now and then, Evans Grocery never sold beer as long as my grandmother and granddaddy were alive.

Thus, Salem became half of my life, a world apart from Florence. Before I became old enough to work in the tobacco fields and barns, my days tended to follow the same pattern. I would wake up around 7, at which point my dad would already be at the store because he got there around 6 am. If I was staying with grandma and granddaddy, there would be a huge breakfast of eggs, sausage, and bacon, also grits and my grandmother's homemade biscuits. The biscuits were always served with Log Cabin syrup, and I would put my thumb in the biscuit then fill the hole with syrup. My grandaddy would always have his eggs over lite, and he would mix the eggs with his grits, something I still do from time to time.

Also, when I was at Grandma and Granddaddy's, we would have squirrel pretty much once a week, either cooked in gravy or fried. My grandfather would sit at the head of the table and crack the skulls with big spoons because the brains were a delicacy and his favorite. I would sit dutifully and eat what was left, totally content with the legs since I never developed a taste for the brains.

After breakfast, whether at grandma and granddaddy's or at our house behind the store, I would head in to work. From a very early age, Daddy's rules were that before I could go play with my cousins I had to do any number of tasks at the store for him. First was sweeping the store, which I hated because dad had a big barrel of waxed sawdust that he would make me put down before sweeping. It made a mess and got into everything, but it did keep the dust down. After years and years of sweeping with the sawdust, the hardwood floors were worn smooth as a baby's skin and the wax gave the floors a soft brown patina.

After sweeping I would fill the drink boxes from crates of glass bottles dad kept in the back. This was a difficult job when I was younger as I was too small to stand up while reaching down into the box to feed the bottles through the hanging mechanism. I had to use a stool, and I would lean over the edge and down into the box trying hard to keep my balance while I fed the bottles through. Occasionally I would drop a bottle into the case, and if it broke, it would make a mess that I would have to clean up. I can still remember many of the drink brands: Coke, Dr. Pepper, Orange Crush, Tab (the first diet drink, and Mountain Dew.

After filling the drink boxes, I would stack canned vegetables and bags of essentials like sugar, flour, etc. Dad had a stamp that he used to price things with. The stamp had to be filled with ink, which would get all over me, but during this pricing process I learned a valuable early rule about business. Specifically, dad always marked up everything the same 25 %. The markup was always the same without regard to who bought it or the circumstances. Dad sold a lot of fan belts because in those days they would often break, and people whose cars had overheated from a broken belt would walk in, clearly desperate. It was easy to see that Dad could have charged whatever he wanted. When I questioned him on this one day, he simply said that 25% was fair and all he needed to run his business. To charge more would have been to take advantage of people, which was simply not right. He went on to say that if you treated people fairly and consistently did the right thing they would come back. When I pointed out that many of the people coming in were from out of state and we would never see them again, Dad's response was an abrupt "Doesn't matter, people trust me to do the right thing." I tried to follow this important and valuable lesson the rest of my life. In later years, it seemed to make a difference for me because the banking business was and is all about trust.

My other jobs besides sweeping, stocking, marking up goods and filling the drink cases were washing the windows, taking out groceries for customers, keeping wood in the heater during the winter and burning the trash, which I loved because it got me outside. Whatever my assigned task, Dad's other rule was that when you have a job, do it right no matter how menial the work. I cannot count the times I had to rewash the windows or resweep the store because in my Dad's mind I had not done it right the first time.

Unfortunately for me, while I accepted this rule as it applied to work, it did not extend to school, which I viewed as something you did before going into the real world to work. Because of this, I never did well in school despite my mom's constant stressing the importance of getting a good education. Nevertheless, when it came to work or a job, I worked hard and did the job as well as I could.

By the time I was in the third or fourth grade, Dad would let me sit behind the counter and check customers out as well as do certain accounting tasks. Like my dad, I had a good mind for numbers and could hold them in my head and add them up. I'm not saying I have a photographic memory, but I definitely have a gift with numbers. To this day, I can still pick numbers out of the air from years past.

Needless to say, this ability would come to prove very useful as I began my banking career. But at 8 or 9 when I was barely tall enough to look over the counter at customers, it would prove useful as well. I was able to handle a customer who would have 7-10 items, add it all up in my head, add the sales tax, then take their cash and make change. Later, to give me more credibility Dad got me a pine stool which would raise me up so I could be more eye to eye with the customers.

One of the other accounting tasks was to add up all the light bills (or power bills for Carolina Power and Light) that customers came in to pay every month. At the end of the month Dad had to add up all the paper bill's he had collected and remit a check to CP&L for the total. Every month there would be anywhere between 40-50 payments which I would add up in my head then do a reconcilement on a brown paper bag with a pencil. In later years, Dad got one of the newfangled adding machines with a tape and crank handle so I could add the numbers up in my head then check my math by running them through the machine.

One day after I had run all the numbers, I asked Daddy why he did all this for Carolina Power and Light. As far as I could tell he did not charge them anything for serving as a collection point, and so to me it seemed like a lot of work for nothing. Dad explained to me that he did it "because I get to use the power company's money for a month before remitting to them." I didn't realize it at the time, but my dad was giving me a lesson in working capital and the importance of having it. Besides he said, when people came into the store to pay their light bill they always bought something. Again, I didn't realize it at the time, but dad was giving me a marketing lesson and teaching me the importance of creating foot traffic.

One of my other favorite behind the counter tasks was tabulating and totaling the monthly charges in dad's Black Book, which was nothing more than a black plastic binder with lined paper and a rubber band wrapped around it. The Book as he called it was in a cubbyhole just under the counter, and it was on those pages that daddy kept track of balances for people who had charge accounts. Some were settled weekly, primarily people with jobs who had a payday every Friday. Some were settled monthly, primarily people on social security who received monthly checks. Then there were all the farming customers, primarily tobacco farmers, who would start charging in the spring during planting season and keep charging all the way through the fall until the crops came in and were sold.

Dad's black book was full of people of all races, creeds, economic status, backgrounds etc. He was indifferent about where you came from. His only concern was about your character. Again, I did not realize it at the time, but I was getting a useful lesson in how to grant credit. My dad was a banker of sorts before I ever thought about becoming one. Once I became aware of how much money was represented by the Black Book, I became concerned. I realized that not everyone had charging privileges, so I asked Dad, how he decided who got credit. Dad's response was simple: you ask around and pretty soon you get a picture of whether someone does what they say they will do. His mantra was, "Past behavior is the best indicator of future behavior." I didn't realize it, of course, but I was getting another useful lesson in the importance of doing ones due diligence.

While doing my store chores there would be a constant flow of morning traffic. Some customers would hurry in and out, but most would sit awhile, read the paper that dad had delivered to the mailbox, and talk about the issues of the day. By the end of the day the paper would be dog eared from use. While many topics were discussed, most revolved around the weather because most customers were involved with farming one way or another. Everyone had a rain gauge so the conversation would invariably turn to, "How much rain did you get at your place?" Everyone grew tobacco, and getting enough rain was critical. Since summer thundershowers tended to be site specific, there was always great variability from farm to farm. In the winter everyone sat by the wood stove and the conversation usually gravitated to hunting and fishing. These conversations took place over many cigarettes, and dad had cans filled with sand for the butts. Another of my daily tasks was cleaning out the homemade ash trays.

Among the group that liked to sit around the stove and talk were my Uncle Son and Uncle James, who were considered serious farmers since they each had about 14 acres of tobacco allotment. Both uncles had big families to care for, so while they stayed to swap information it was not for very long. To put 14 acres of tobacco into perspective, a good crop could produce about 2,500 pounds per acre, and if a farmer had quality curing process (which I will describe later on) they might get an average of $1 per pound. Thus, they could gross about $2,500 per acre before significant expenses which included fertilizer, chemicals, the significant labor need to gather and prepare the crop for market, the fuel to cure the tobacco, plus in many cases farmers grew tobacco on rented land where they had to pay the owner for the right to use their tobacco allotment.

Before 2005, allotments were controlled by the US agriculture department to maintain a stable supply which created a nationwide cap on the amount of tobacco grown. As a result, only farms with tobacco allotment were allowed grow your tobacco, and then only on a fixed number of acres. Renting tobacco allotment land could cost as much as $500 per acre in those days. Thus, while a farmer might gross $2,500 per acre, after expenses and rental costs, the net would be perhaps $500 to $700 per acre.

My guess is my uncles were lucky if they made $7,000 to $10,000 per year, which seems a very meager reward when one considers the huge amount of risk involved in tobacco farming. Would it rain enough? Would the price when it came time to market be enough? Would one of their tobacco barns burn down, which happened surprisingly often? Would a major thunderstorm blow all the tobacco down? Would it rain too much and expose the tobacco to rot? Tobacco farmers were serious entrepreneurs

35

who were subject to huge risks, and they had to work incredibly hard. That made my uncles serious entrepreneurs, and my dad was a serious banker since his little store had to carry them all the way from spring planting until the fall when their crops came in.

Often times, things would go wrong, and people would have to pitch in and help. Tobacco stalks would get blown down in a heavy rain and people would go help their neighbor stand the stalks back up. A tractor would break down and folks would loan their neighbor a tractor till repairs could be made. The biggest risk however was always drought. Without enough rain crops would not grow and so farmers were obsessed with watching their rain gauges and reporting in at the store what was going on. I can hear their voices to this day, "I had an inch at my place up the road, but only a half inch down the road."

Crop insurance was another thing my dad sold through his arrangement with Mr. Billy Draugn, but since most people could not afford it, a drought meant that an entire crop and year's worth of work was down the drain. Since many of these customers were in Dad's Black Book, he would have to work with them and in many cases carry over their accounts until next year's crop. Although I did not know it at the time, I was learning a valuable lesson about working with people to help them pay off their loans, which would again prove useful in my banking career. Dad's logic was simple: if he was dealing with an honest person who was a victim of circumstances not their own making, he would have better success working with them versus trying to put them out of business to get his loan paid. If he did that successfully he would keep them as a customer and get his debt paid. Whereas, if he got his loan paid, but in the process, put them out of business, he would forever lose them as a customer. Later in my banking career I would chafe when others wanted to come down hard on people just because they could when it was clear to everyone that the borrower's circumstances were not of their own making.

Aside from Uncle Son and Uncle James and the other farmers who came in to share their rain gauge news, the store was a gathering place for a group of regulars who would spend most of their mornings around the wood stove. There was Phillip Poston, a retired Navy mechanic. Phillip could fix anything and looked a bit like a thinner, older Gomer Pyle with no teeth. He always wore coveralls that were totally stained with grease.

Everyone in the area knew that Phillip would be there, and if some truck, tractor, car, race car or lawn mower was broken and not running right he could fix it.

Every morning, Phillip would come to the store, buy a Coke and a BC powder then settle into one of the chairs. I never knew if the BC powder was for headaches (Phillip did not drink) or something else, or if he just plain liked them. BC powders were essentially aspirin in powdered form. Bitter has heck but when taken with a coke it went straight to the blood stream providing relief for muscle aches and pains especially those that usually accompany arthritis. Since Phillip was a mechanic and constantly working with his hands, I suspect he suffered from arthritis and need the BC's to be able to do his work.

Usually about the time Phillip finished his Coke someone who needed something fixed would stop in. Phillip would either repair it right there beside the store or he would drive his truck to the person's farmhouse or barn. Of course, Dad would usually sell the fan belts, batteries or other parts needed to fix the machine, however there was an understanding that Evans Grocery was not a garage and Phillip was an independent contractor. In any case, Phillip Poston was a fine man. He had the most wonderful laugh and would slap his knee at the same time whenever anyone said something funny.

Another result of Phillip operating out of Dad's store was the steady stream of race car drivers who would stop by. They were dirt track jalopy drivers who would race at the track in Lake City every Saturday night. Oh, could Phillip make those race cars run! I can still hear the roar from the unmuffled engines as he would tune them up beside the store.

I remember one driver in particular, a man named Lee Edwards, who was the hometown favorite and drove a big old black Packard. While the Packard had a high gear ratio and was slow off the starting line, it was very fast once it got going. With the added advantage of size and weight, it could push other cars off the track and blast through the unavoidable jam ups that would occur. Lee worked at Wellman Industries, a company that is still in Johnsonville. Tall and an Elvis look-alike with a 28-inch waist and broad shoulders, Lee would often come by the store to compare notes with Phillip who was his chief mechanic and pit boss. Lee was always very kind to me, but the other men knew he had a short fuse. He was known as someone who didn't start fights, but who invariably finished them. Phillip would often take me in his truck to the dirt track in Lake City where we would cheer Lee on and secretly hope that someone would pick a fight with Lee because we always knew how it would end.

Aside from my two serious farming uncles Son and James, who were always too busy to spend much time around the wood stove, there were some less serious farmers who did hang around, such as my Uncle Punk and Uncle Cedric who each had 3-5 acres of tobacco. With no children to support, they were more carefree and tended to visit much longer. Both were heavy drinkers, but my Uncle Punk could usually hold his liquor better. One time that he didn't was when he had too much to drink down at the river and decided to tame a rattlesnake. Because he waited too long to see a doctor about the bite, he ended up losing his thumb. That missing thumb was a constant reminder of Uncle Punk's escapades of which there were many. Uncle Punk loved to joke around, and he also loved to go fishing so in my younger days he would often take me with him. Somehow he came up with a nickname for me which was Carzee. Everyone in Salem had nicknames and usually there was some basis for them, but in the case of Carzee, I had no idea where Uncle Punk came up with it. Uncle Punk was also great at telling jokes and he would hold court by the wood stove with Phillip laughing and slapping his knee.

Uncle Cedric, on the other hand was quieter, but unlike Uncle Punk he could not hold his liquor. Whenever he would drink his personality would change and he would become CC. Unlike quiet Uncle Cedric, CC was a wild man who would drive to the store in his pickup and not think twice about cutting a donut in the gravel. Then he would give his famous wave, which was more of a sideways salute, and tear off up the road to Miss Gert's for another pint of whiskey. Despite being crazy when he drank, Uncle Cedric was always very kind to me.

In later years, when Dad married a widow in Salem named Dorothy Hanna who had 5 children and there was no longer room in the little house behind the store for me, I moved in with Uncle Cedric and Aunt Edna, and I worked for him during tobacco season. Even though I was ultimately displaced by my stepbrothers and sisters, I never harbored any ill feelings about it. By then I was a teenager, and I understood the simple fact that the house was just too small for all of us. Since I was a "summer resident," staying with Uncle Cedric and Aunt Edna made the most sense. Besides, Aunt Edna was a great cook, and as a growing boy working hard every day in the tobacco fields I had a huge appetite! I can still taste the fresh vegetables with fried chicken and biscuits today!

Among other frequent visitors to the store were several people with large broods of children: Miss Lila and Rev. Pendergraph (both from down the road), as well as Eva Poston from down by the skating rink. Dad would always give the kids little brown paper bags of penny candy which was a huge treat because these were very poor people. In addition to the families, there were other interesting characters like Jimmy Poston, who lived down the road over the swamp but was no relation to our local mechanic Phillip. Jimmy spoke with something almost like a British accent. He was brilliant and word was he had gone to some big school up north like Harvard or Yale where he excelled but had suffered a nervous breakdown. Due to his condition, he could not keep a steady job so daddy would let him work part time helping fill out the hundreds of tax returns dad did for people in the area, many of whom were farmers running small businesses where dad was also keeping the books.

Jimmy had a vocabulary that was totally unusual in Salem, and Dad loved to sit and talk to him. While my dad did not have a High School Education, he loved words and would do the crossword puzzle and word jumble from the paper every day. Whenever he learned a new word, he would repeat it over and over, for example the word "bodacious" which I remember him repeating over and over. In Jimmy, Daddy had a soulmate because there was probably no one else in Salem with any interest in words or what was happening in the rest of the world.

For my part, during my morning chores, I would listen to the chatter and say little. It's funny how some things stick with you. In my case, it came from frequent trips to Johsonville with my dad where I would get my haircut at the barber shop while Dad would go next door to Mr. Billy Draugn's Insurance agency where they would discuss business. The barber would put a wooden board across the arms of the chair to raise me up so he could cut my hair without stooping down. Directly across from the chair was a sign that read, "A Wise Old Owl once sat in an Oak. The more he heard the less he spoke. The less he spoke, the more he heard. Why ain't you like that wise old bird?" I had taken that message to heart, so those mornings in the store was a great place for me to do my chores and listen.

After my tasks were done, I was free to run off up the road where I would play with my cousins who were uncle Son and Uncle James's children. As I mentioned before, they each had four. Uncle James's two girls, Peggy and Faye, were older, so I would play with Jimmy and Stewart. Uncle Son's three boys were my playmates, especially Wayne who was the youngest with Jerry and Nelson being older. In addition, Kevin Joye was a frequent visitor from Pamplico, and we were playmates as well. Back then, everyone had nicknames. Wayne was Biscuit, Jerry was Cotton, Stewart was named Rod 0, Kevin was called Dog Ration or Ration for short, just to mention a few. My nickname was Lus. I guess short for Carlos.

In any case, for us kids, Salem was an incredible playground. We went hunting, fishing, camping, and at night we went Yellow Hammer hunting. This was done by taking a flashlight in winter and climbing up into the rafters at the top of the tobacco barn where the Yellow Hammer bird would sit. The light would freeze them at which point you would grab them and rap their head on the tier poles that ran the length of the barn to hang tobacco on. If you were good, one rap would do it and you would avoid their sharp beaks. These birds would then be cleaned and barbecued on an open fire. They were tough eating but with barbecue sauce they could be okay. There would also be nighttime rabbit hunts where we would sit on the hood of the pickup truck with our uncles driving the dirt roads. The rabbits would jump out in the middle of the road and run so you had to be a quick, accurate shot.

When we were younger and on foot or using bicycles, we would roam all over. We would play half rubber next to Gene Daniels's welding shop for hours. It's a game with a cut-in-half rubber ball where there would be double batters on one team using tobacco sticks as bats, a pitcher and a catcher on the other team, after two outs you would switch sides. The welding shop was a perfect place to play as the batters would stand on the concrete in front of the outside grease pit and the catcher would be behind the grease pit up against the wall. It made a great place to play since the ball had no place to go except up against the wall or into the grease pit if the catcher missed. The half rubber ball could be thrown so that it would curve, rise or drop so it was hard to catch or hit. A single was to the pitcher on the ground. A double was past the pitcher on the ground and a home run was past some pre-determined spot in the air. The Holy Grail was a riser that would cause both batters to swing and miss. If the catcher caught it that was two outs. We would play this game for hours on end, always barefoot in the spring and summer.

For all of us, Sunday was a special day. First, we would go to the church service at Salem United Methodist, which was usually just our family with Uncle Son and Uncle James as the two deacons. A few other families like Phillip Poston's and his brother Mr. Reless's would be there. A traveling minister would give the sermon with Mr. and Mrs. Deleon doing the piano playing and leading the singing of old hymns like Old Rugged Cross and How Great Thou Art. The piano was terribly out of tune as were most of the voices, but the services were simple and at times moving.

I remember one time after my dad and mom were separated, Dad broke down in tears and had to leave the service. I felt sure he was thinking about his ruptured marriage and the loss of my mother. After these services we would all go over to my grandmother and granddaddy's for a huge Sunday dinner. In those days people cooked a lot of food and left it on the stove so that friends who dropped by during the afternoon would have something to eat. In Salem at the time, there was breakfast, dinner as the mid-day meal, and supper in the evening.

After the Sunday dinner we would always sit in front of the TV to watch baseball with Dizzy Dean and Pee Wee Reese as the announcers. I can still hear Dizzy's voice saying "Hand me another Falstaff Pee Wee! They would eat hot dogs, drink beer, and call the games much to the disdain of Grandmother and Granddaddy who did not drink. As our price for getting to watch the game, all of us kids would have to shell butter beans which we would do dutifully until the game was over.

After the game Grandaddy would let us go out to the grapevine behind his house where he kept watermelons resting in the cool shade. We would pick one which he would promptly cut, taking the heart of the watermelon for himself, and leaving the rest for us kids. What a treat on a hot summer day. After watermelon season, the grapevine would be full of ripening muscadine grapes. Grandaddy would warn us not to climb up on the vines which, of course, we always did.

After eating our fill of watermelon or grapes we would have great fun harrying the chickens and in particular, grandma's rooster which we viewed with much disdain. He was mean as a snake, had spurs that looked like switchblades and would chase us anytime we entered the chicken coop, which was his domain. Another thing that made Sundays wonderful was the constant stream of people who would stop by to have a bite to eat, including the Joyes from Pamplico and my Aunt Marilyn, Uncle Fred Stone and their two children Randy and Terry.

As we grew older and hit the age of 14, one by one we obtained drivers permits. Even though we were older, the other parts of our lives pretty much stayed the same with the only difference being how far we could roam. With a car we could take trips of our own to the creek in the summer to go swimming and we could go to Kingsburg to play the pinball machine. At night we could even go to the skating rink where there would be girls!

The skating rink was an old building that looked much like a warehouse with wooden floors, and it was owned by Mr. Sam Joe Turner. It would open in the evenings on Friday and Saturday and stay open till about 10pm. Loud music played constantly, and you could hear it easily at the store or at Grandmother and Granddaddy's if you were sitting on the front porch. The music was mostly country like Johnny Cash with rock & roll tunes like The Jersey Boys thrown in between. The skating rink was a gathering place especially as we got into our teens.

The skating rink brings back even earlier memories. The sound of that loud music had been comforting especially when I was 5 to 8 years old, back in the day when we lived in Florence during the week and stayed weekends with Grandaddy and Grandmother. Since I was still young and couldn't stay up much past 8 pm, I would leave the store alone to walk across the highway and down the dirt road to Grandaddy and Grandmama's to go to bed while Dad would stay at the store until closing.

The bad part of the trip was walking by the graveyard behind Salem United Methodist Church. The graveyard was dark and foreboding and so the music drifting in from the Skating Rink was somewhat of a comfort, but not enough of a comfort that I could make it all the way walking. In fact, I would always get about halfway past the graveyard, then break into a run as in my child's mind I would see things coming out of the grave and chasing me!

Ally of the Entrepreneur

Although I have far too many memories of my life in Salem to mention in this book, I should say that my favorite memories revolve around one of my favorite people, 'By George.' The truth is I never knew George's full name or whether his name was Brr George (as in Brother George) or By George. The reason for the confusion was that in 'Salem Speak' his name was shortened to BuGeorge or BGeorge. At this point I should mention Salem Speak. As I have stated earlier, Salem was like a different part of the world from Florence. The English spoken in Salem was totally different. Since I was driven by a desire to be like everyone else due to my concern with my heritage and name, when I would come to Salem, I would immediately convert over to Salem Speak. For example, "this here" in Salem Speak was "dis sheer." "That there" was "dat der." "I am not going anywhere" was "I ain't gwiyn nowhar." "Let's go to the creek" was "les go to da crik."

Salem Speak was used by everyone including the African Americans who had slight variations that made it even harder to understand if you were from anywhere else. But for me, Salem Speak was definitely my preference, especially when we were in the presence of BGeorge who took Salem Speak to another level. Visits to BGeorge took place almost every Saturday afternoon. He was a slim African American man in his 80s who had once worked for my grandfather and Uncle Son but was now retired. He lived up the road in a small wood frame house that had no running water, only a pump and an outhouse nearby. His heat came from a small wood stove, and he had a small barn for his mule and used a sled as a wagon.

BGeorge had a small garden, and he owned the roughly 20 acres his house sat on. Given BGeorge's long working relationship with my family, every Saturday we would go to his place and work to help him. We would go with him into his woods to cut firewood, and then we would split the wood. We would also help him plant his garden. All the while we would be entranced by his constant stories of times gone by as well as other wisdoms about life. We learned all sorts of things such as pouring kerosene on a crosscut saw to make the sawing easier, or how to use pegs instead of nails when we repaired the rafters in his barn. He also taught us the merits of drinking water mixed with a teaspoon full of vinegar every day swearing that this was the key to his health and longevity.

BGeorge was well into his 80s, but his skin was smooth as a baby's with no wrinkles. He was lean as a hickory sapling and could work the whole day long with us, sharing his wisdom along the way. BGeorge always wore bib overalls with a worn flannel shirt beneath. The wardrobe was the same whether summer, winter, spring or fall. After working all afternoon to help him we would then settle by his fire to barbecue a chicken and listen to more stories. As we grew a little older, BGeorge would even let us bring a few beers to drink when the work was done, and we always knew that our drinking would not get back to our parents. It's certainly possible that our parents suspected that certain things went on at BGeorge's, but they trusted him, and they also knew we were getting an education on many things about life. BGeorge died a few years after I graduated from college, and it was a sad day. He had been a wonderful man, and we learned many lessons sitting by his fire.

So, this was my life in Salem, totally compartmentalized from my life in Florence.

Chapter 5

My Life in Florence

After the year when Dad and I were alone in Salem, Mom and Melba moved back from Charlotte. My parents got back together, and we all moved to Florence. While their marriage was reconciled, Mom and Dad still had their differences, but for a short while things were okay. Dad would commute from Salem coming every Wednesday afternoon as the store was closed on Wednesday afternoons much like the Banks did in those days. He would return to Salem on Thursday morning then come back on Saturday night to be with the family on Sunday.

Later on, as their marriage began to dissolve again, Dad would just come to visit us kids on Wednesday afternoons and then again on Friday evening to take me to Salem for the weekend, bringing me back late Sunday afternoon. Melba stayed with Mom on the weekends because, by this time, she had become active in sports, and she had never had much interest in Salem anyway. Andy was still too small to be alone in Salem with Dad, so he also stayed in Florence until later years when he would make the regular weekend and summer trips to Salem with me. So for me, my life in Florence really revolved around the weekdays during the school year.

While my memories of those early years in Florence isn't nearly as vivid as my memories of Salem, I remember from a very early time being largely left to my own devices since Mom had all she could handle driving Melba to and from basketball games and tennis matches. In addition to sports, Melba was a straight A student, very popular and involved in all sorts of high school activities and clubs. Andy was a baby, and also required a lot of Mom's time and attention. That left me as the child in the middle.

Fortunately, I was very self-sufficient, and for some reason mom just let me roam, which I did.

In Florence we lived in a small yellow brick house which had three bedrooms, a living room and a kitchen. There was the master bedroom, a bedroom for Melba and then one for Andy and me. Our neighbors across the street were the Banks. Mr. Banks ran the pool hall in Darlington S.C., while Mrs. Banks was a waitress at the Gangplank Seafood Restaurant in Florence, which was owned by the Costas family.

Mr. and Mrs. Banks had three children, Keith being the oldest, then Ronnie, and the youngest being the daughter Kathy. My friend was Ronnie, who was my age. After school most days, Ronnie and I would strike out for the woods that surrounded our small subdivision. We would build forts, dam up ditches, and do all the things small boys did with their free time. Camping out became a favorite pastime, and we would cook Vienna sausages and pork and beans in the can over an open fire.

I remember spending so much time running through the woods that my face would often be cut and scraped from the branches. The two of us would later join the Boy Scouts where we would enhance our camping and outdoor skills. While I never excelled in the Boy Scouts, for me the outdoor part of it was a great experience, especially as a young boy with limited access to a father except on weekends. I remain a big supporter of the Boy Scouts today, and I'm excited that young girls now have access to this same experience.

Perhaps the thing I remember most was the constant exposure to Narda (Tita) and Adelita, two of my Aunts. As I said earlier, Tita had married a man from Belmont, N.C. named Clinton Wilkinson . They lived in Charlotte, and we were often together, either us visiting them or them coming to Florence.

When Adelita's husband, Adre Van Gent, passed away, she and her young son Paul Van Gent moved to Florence with Mother's help. Adelita was a tall and dark haired and very beautiful. Mother helped her get a job as a dance teacher at Vera Marchette's Dance School. There were also frequent visits from Aunt Sole who was working in the Costa Rican Embassy in Mexico City. I remember once going to visit her there when I was 8. We stayed for what seemed like a month exploring Mexico City and touring much of the country with trips to the pyramids, Xochimilco, and other places. Aunt Sole was dating a man named Victor Julio who was a character. I remember that he taught me magic tricks.

In Florence, my mother's relationship with her sisters was unrestrained by my dad's dislikes so rapid-fire Spanish was spoken all the time. There was constant singing and playing the guitar. One of their favorite fun songs was "La Cucaracha" which in Spanish means the cockroach of which there were plenty in Florence with its pine straw and hot summers. I was still embarrassed that so much Spanish was spoken in our house, but at least in Florence it seemed to be a little more tolerated. By this time my mom was also entrenched teaching school at McClenaghan High where she established a Spanish Club and taught Spanish on the side to make extra money.

With Dad's modest child support and Mom's small teachers' salary, there was never enough money to raise three children. All three of us kids had to do without certain things. I can distinctly remember wanting my own chest of drawer as I came into my teens because clothes became important to me. Unfortunately, I never got one, even during my college years. It wasn't until I graduated from college and moved to Columbia to start my first job that Mom bought me my first chest of drawers and a bed.

The other constant reminder of our lack of money was Mom's car, a late 40's Ford or Chevrolet that was a terrible brown color. The Brown Bomber, as we called it, had the gear shift on the wheel and was incredibly hard to drive with a stiff clutch and no power steering. The car was so old that one of the floorboards in the backseat area was partially rusted out and you could see the pavement while under the car. For Melba and me, the Brown Bomber was a terrible embarrassment. Whenever mom would have to pick us up or take us to school, we would cringe at the knowledge that our schoolmates would see it. It wasn't so bad in grammar school at Briggs Elementary, but by the time I got to Moore Middle School status was becoming an issue. For Melba, who was in McClenaghan High School, it was a big issue.

As I said earlier, in those early years we were going to Charlotte a lot, usually my mother and the three of us, along with Aunt Adelita and Paul. There would be much singing and speaking in Spanish along the way. We would play games. One of our favorites was seeing who could count the most cows, and Melba, who was proficient in Pig Latin, would regale us with this strange form of communication. In those same years, Charlotte was our safe haven. Clinton and Aunt Narda had a loving marriage, and Clinton was a loving, caring husband who took interest in all of us kids.

Clinton taught Melba and me how to play basketball as well as tennis. He was an accountant at Cornucopia Mills who would later start his own business called Belmont Textiles and become an entrepreneur. Clinton was a saint and actually put up a basketball net for us next to our house in Florence, and that was where Melba perfected her shooting.

While in Charlotte we also enjoyed day trips to the mountains for cookouts, and my Aunt Narda was constantly having parties. Mother, Adelita and Narda became members of something called the Pan American Club. There were lots of get togethers and social gatherings where only Spanish was spoken.

During this time, while much of Mom's attention was focused on Melba and Andy, she also did her best to exert her good influence on me. She was always after me to do better in school and to speak more Spanish. She often spoke about the need to share God's blessings with others and, in particular, people less fortunate.

Mom was also on a constant mission to better herself. She would work hard all day, come home and make dinner for us kids, sew dresses for Melba and still find time to practice her piano or take courses toward her Master's Degree. I can remember many nights going to sleep as I listened to her play Moonlight Sonata over and over as she worked feeling and emotion into the piece. She would often play late into the night long after I was asleep.

Another important relationship during this time was Tramp, my one and only pet as a child. Later in life our family would have a cocker spaniel named Chevy whom we loved but there will always be a special place in my heart for Tramp. Dad had a habit of picking up stray dogs at the store and Tramp was one of them. We named him after the movie "Lady And The Tramp." He was part Airedale and who knows what else. When we moved to Florence Dad let me take him along, we were inseparable.

Tramp had two specialties: chasing cars and fighting other dogs. Whenever a car would come by in Highland Park, he would take off like a rocket. As far as fighting went, Tramp was a little like Lee Edward's. He never started fights, but he always ended them. Tramp was not a house dog; we had a small doghouse outside for him. However, we were inseparable and wherever I went, he went. There were many loose dogs in the neighborhood back then, and they would often confront us kids when we were playing someplace away from our block. If any of those dogs made a move toward us, Tramp would be all over them until they ran away with tails tucked between their legs. He was a viscous fighter but once the aggressor dog backed off, he would leave them alone.

Tramp was definitely my protector. I distinctly remember a neighbor a couple of blocks over with two German Shepherds. I believe the owner was a retired Army sergeant. One day, the two German Shepherds started threatening Ronnie Banks and me. It was interesting because the owner could see what was happening and never called them off. My guess is Tramp's reputation had gotten around and the man wanted to see what Tramp would do. Well Tramp took on those two German Shepherds and sent them running. I could tell the man was mad when Ronnie and I cheered Tramp, who came back to us triumphant as soon as the German Shepherds ran off. After that experience, I could tell the owner was spoiling for another fight, so we stayed clear of his house from then on.

Unfortunately, Dad came to visit one Sunday and we went off for the afternoon to get ice cream. When we came back, Tramp was nowhere to be seen, which was strange because he would always come running whenever we came home. Right away, I had a bad feeling. It was almost surreal because even at a very young age, I had an intuition that something was wrong, and I made Dad help me look for Tramp before he left to go back to Salem. After much searching in the neighborhood, we finally found him under the house. His throat had been slashed apparently by another dog, and he was bleeding badly. Dad picked him up in his arms and took him to the vet on the way back to Salem. Tramp survived but would never return to Florence. My Dad kept him in Salem where he met his end doing what he loved, chasing cars.

The week after tramp left, Ronnie Banks told me what had happened. He said the man down the street came by our house in his car with the two German Shepherds. He sicked them on Tramp who was lying in his doghouse minding his own business. I never told Dad the story of what happened because, quite frankly, I was scared of what he might do. For me, it was my first realization that there are bad people on this earth and that if you allow them into your life bad things will happen. Better to just stay away. This was a rule I followed in high school and later in life, and it has served me well.

As I grew older my sister's athletic accomplishments and her popularity in school continued to grow. I guess I would say I lived in her shadow but proudly. I went to all her basketball games and many tennis tournaments at Timrod Park. Many times, in a close tennis match or basketball game when she would be behind, I would see that look settle on her face as she willed herself to victory. She might have been behind in a tennis match, but suddenly she would start serving up aces. She was never beaten even once in four years playing #1 on the high school tennis team.

There were basketball games where her team was behind with time running out, but she would somehow steal the ball and go in for a layup, or make an incredibly long shot at the buzzer to win the game. She was Homecoming Queen her senior year and a straight A student. Yes, I lived in her shadow, and I was proud of it. People would always come up to me and say "Are you Melba's brother?" And I would respond emphatically "Yes!"

Since I was not very accomplished at anything, I took up playing trumpet in the band in the 6th grade. I was pretty good at the trumpet, and it would later get me a partial scholarship to Newberry College, but compared to Melba, I was basically a nobody in high school. Most of my time was spent trying to be like the other kids, and in particular, to dress like them. We couldn't afford to belong to the Florence Country Club, I was determined to look like the kids who did. However, to do that, I needed money to buy clothes at places like Dick Ames which was where the popular boys went to buy their Gant shirts, khaki pants, and alligator belts with the silver belt buckles. Back then, everyone also wore alpaca sweaters and madras shirts, with the shirts and khaki pants so heavily starched you could almost stand them up in a corner. I learned to iron my own clothes as I began to buy them with money I earned working tobacco during the summers, but more on that later.

In 7th grade I played in the school band at Moore Junior High School. The band director was Allen Perry who was in his early 20's. By that time, Mom and Dad were divorced as was Mr. Perry. In addition to teaching at Moore, Mr. Perry also taught at McClenaghan where mom taught.

According to Mom, he started dropping by her class after work, but she thought he was interested in her graduate student since Mom was ten years his senior. Much to Mom's surprise, the graduate student said, "No, I actually think Mr. Perry's interest lies with you!" My mom was a beautiful lady at that time and was accomplished in her profession, so I can easily see how my stepdad fell in love.

They were married when I was in the eighth grade, and we moved out of the yellow brick house to a small three-bedroom home on Juniper Road, located in the Botany Acres neighborhood in West Florence. By then or shortly thereafter, Melba was off to College at Queens University in Charlotte. She even stayed the summers there working as a lifeguard in Gastonia where she lived with Tita and Clinton. That left me and Andy living with Allen and Mother in Florence during the week but spending every summer and most weekends in Salem.

In retrospect, I wasn't the best big brother for Andy, which is something I have worked to be better at in later years. I can remember the exact day when my feelings for my brother took a sharp turn for the better. It was early one morning, just before 6, when Andy and I were headed down the road for "puttin in tobacco." Evening rains from the night before had produced a heavy fog. I was driving in front in my uncle Sun's truck, while Andy was behind me on the tractor pulling a trailer behind him. To get to where we were going we had to cross highway 378 which back then was only two lanes but was the main road to Myrtle Beach. When I crossed, I realized that the fog was so heavy any oncoming traffic would have a hard time seeing us and would have little time to stop, and that on the slower moving tractor Andy would be a sitting duck. As soon as I got across, I slammed on the brakes and jumped out of the truck. As soon as I did there was a terrible noise as an oncoming car crashed into the back end of the wooden trailer and ripped it off the tractor. Fortunately, the tractor remained upright with Andy sitting there scared to death.

The driver of the car stopped and immediately started screaming at Andy to not move the tractor one inch. About that time Uncle Son came up in another truck and yelled at me to run up the road and slow oncoming traffic. He then told the car driver that the tractor and the car would be moved immediately out of the center of the highway because they were a deadly hazard in the fog. He also proceeded to tell the man he had been driving way too fast for conditions since he could see the length of the skid marks. I don't think I had ever seen my uncle Son mad, but on that day he was incredibly angry and the man knew not to mess with him.

The police showed up a short time later and ticketed the driver of the car for driving too fast for conditions. No one had been injured, but for me it had been a life changing experience, making me realize for the first time that all of our lives are so fragile, and we can lose a loved one in an instant. I made a vow never to take relationships for granted, especially family, and to constantly remind them how much I loved them and appreciated having them in my life. This is a habit I still carry today not only with family but with dear friends, as well.

About that time, in addition to my interest in clothes I also began to develop an interest in girls. I also kept up my friendship with Ronnie Banks even though we were now living on the other side of town. Ronnie was everything that I was not. He was a great athlete and was somewhat of a ladies' man. I was somewhat dumpy and had not yet built the muscles I would later from working in tobacco.

Ronnie was also tough as nails and had never been beaten in a fight. I think it was Ronnie's upbringing that made him that way since his dad ran the pool hall and was tough on the kids and his wife until Ronnie got big enough to put an end to it. There were also frequent fights between Ronnie and his older brother until it was clear that Ronnie could best him every time. Despite his family, Ronnie was the nicest guy in the world. Like Tramp and Lee Edwards, Ronnie didn't start fights but he always ended them. In fact, his reputation as a fighter was so great that young men in Florence would come looking for him, hoping to start something, but the end was always the same, with Ronnie on top. Years later Ronnie would work for the phone company, and I last saw him some 20 years ago at a class reunion. He looked just the same as he always had, and I would love to see him today.

In addition to his skill as a fighter, Ronnie was the best pool player I have ever seen. Years of working in his dad's pool hall made him a pro. I feel sure he could have been on the circuit had he wanted to.

Another thing that Ronnie and I liked to do in those early days of high school was roam around the state, especially to places where the girls were. We both had our driver's license by that time, so instead of wandering the neighborhoods and woods, we were heading to places like Myrtle Beach, Ocean Drive and Garden City, some 70 miles away. All the rich girls from the best Florence families had houses at the beach, so right after school let out for summer and before tobacco season we would go there.

At first, we slept in our cars and bathed in the girl's outside showers, but the summer after my sophomore year in high school, Ronnie and I decided we would use our skills on the pool circuit to make some money so we could stay at the beach longer and more comfortably. We found a small efficiency apartment in a lady's house that we could rent for two weeks for $50.00. It was a great deal, but we didn't have $50.00. Between the two of us we could come up with $10.00 so we decided to implement our pool shark plan.

Our first stop was a place called The Pad in Ocean Drive Beach. We knew about The Pad because it was a legend in that part of the country. It played music all night long and was the hotspot for dancing the Shag to popular Carolina beach tunes sung by people like The Tams, The Drifters, etc. In the back were several pool tables that were always in use since the place was always packed.

Unfortunately, at The Pad we had another problem. We were not 18, the legal drinking age, so we had to bribe the bouncer with $5 of our $10 dollars to let us in. Ronnie soon got on one of the tables and started playing, being careful not to show all his stuff but winning enough so that our $5 grew to $10 and then to $20. I was holding the money and being careful not to order any beer so we could steer clear of getting ID'd.

After some time went by, I found an older girl who would get beers for us using her ID. To say she had a crush on Ronnie would be a huge understatement. As the evening progressed, I noticed a guy at one of the other tables who was attracting a lot of attention. He was the coolest guy I had ever seen and had girls hanging all over him. He wore a black turtleneck shirt and no belt. His pants had no belt loops but were made out of a stretch material that held them way up high on his waist. He was clearly beating everyone at the other table and winning a lot of money in the process.

When I asked the girl getting our beers who he was, she said, "Oh, that's Go Boy, and you and your friend do not want to mess with him. He's the best at the beach." Shortly after that, Ronnie and I went to the bathroom and compared notes. Ronnie had been watching Go Boy as well. When I asked if he could beat him, Ronnie nodded, saying that the guy was good, but he could beat him. Ronnie then went on to give me my instructions on how to play it.

He said he would lose a few games, then slowly start winning every other game, and as our stash started to grow again, he told me to start making side bets with our winnings, laying more and more down as the odds escalated.

When we went back out to the tables, the game with Go Boy began. They played 9-ball, so the games went fast, and Ronnie could not have written the script better. He lost a couple games then slowly started winning with what looked like lucky shots. Sure enough, the table quickly became surrounded by a mob of people, and the betting escalated. I felt like a kingmaker holding all the money and backing my friend. The girl buying our beer came over and asked me, "Who is your friend?"

I don't know what came over me. Part of me was scared because we were underage and in the Pad illegally drinking beer. We were probably also breaking laws by gambling over pool. The other side of me was concerned with trying to properly represent Ronnie as his handler. Without a thought I blurted out "He's the Florence Kid."

The name stuck as well as did Ronnie's reputation as a pool hustler at the beach so we were done. His reputation got out so fast that despite our efforts to get other games no one would play against him. However, we did end up walking away with significant winnings, so we were able to pay our two weeks rent and buy a case of beer, and we spent our remaining time on the beach living like kings.

Aside from the thrill of the experience at The Pad with Go Boy, my high school time in Florence was totally unremarkable. I squandered what could have been a good education and the opportunity to participate in wholesome extracurricular clubs and things because McClenaghan was an excellent school. The only thing of value that happened to me in high school was a girl I dated in the second half of my junior year and all of my senior year. She was a cheerleader, and she was the sweetest thing on the planet. She was actually "the girl next door" since her house was just two away from ours. She, more than anything else, kept me out of trouble, and while it was puppy love, it was real.

Harriet wanted to get married, which scared me to death because I saw my whole life in front of me. We dated a couple times from afar during our first year in college because she was at Winthrop University in Rock Hill, and I was at Newberry some 100 miles away. After that freshman year, we both went our separate ways. Shortly thereafter, she got married, had a good career and a wonderful family. We never spoke again other than when my mom died, when she reached out to extend her condolences, and we exchanged a couple emails. So, as my life in Florence came to an end, the only thing interesting about it was that I was able to keep it totally compartmentalized from my life in Salem.

Carlos Evans

Chapter 6

Puttin In Tobacco

As mentioned, as I entered my teen years I became obsessed with making money so I could buy clothes and dress like the other popular kids. I tried to get a job in Florence at an ice cream shop but when that didn't work out, I talked to my Dad, who suggested I go to work for with my uncles helping with the tobacco harvest. The pay was $2.50 per half day or $5.00 per day. Over the course of the 8-week harvest I could make $100, which would buy the clothes I wanted for the school year. So began a pattern that would extend over 7 years, when I would come to Salem the second week in June and stay with Dad, then after 9th grade when Dad remarried, I would stay with my Uncle Cedric or with CC in the trailer he and Aunt Edna had next to my grandfather's house.

Before I describe the nature of the work, I want to make a point about how I viewed my situation, given the fact that I had been kicked out of my father's house to make room for my new stepbrothers and sisters and was living in a trailer with an uncle who would go on drinking binges. That might sound bad, but I never saw it that way. Aside from the fact that Uncle Cedric and Aunt Edna were incredibly good to me and treated me as if I were their own son, because of where I had been raised, I knew that there were many people less fortunate than I, and I always viewed myself as being incredibly lucky and fortunate. Also, my mom and my dad reinforced that understanding: Mom by the way she lived her life constantly reaching out to help those in need, and with Dad it began with a story he told me that I never forgot.

The story he told me came on Christmas Eve one year when I was maybe 7 or 8. The two of us were in the store all alone as things slowed down, and Dad started on this story about Kaylas and Boonya, two young boys both about my age, one from a very poor family and the other from a more fortunate family. On Christmas Day Kaylas woke up to presents under the tree which included a new bicycle. Boonya on the other hand woke up to nothing but a brown paper bag with too small pieces of candy. Kaylas, was upset because he didn't get a Daisy BB gun, while Boonya was happy and grateful for the pieces of candy. Dad told the story in a way that was beautiful and sad at the same time. It was only toward the end that I realized the story was about me and Junior Poston, one of my best friends. I was Kaylas, and Junior, with ten brothers and sisters in a dirt-poor family was Boonya. Outside of my cousins, Junior was one of the closest friends I had, and upon realizing the point of Dad's story, I became overwhelmed with guilt and cried.

Up until that time there had been occasions when I felt sorry for myself, but after the story, Dad let me take part in a ritual he did every year at Christmas. He would take all the remaining fruit in the store consisting of apples, oranges, tangerines, and grapefruits, personally box them up and deliver them to the poorest families around Salem, both African American and White. I can still see the smiles on the faces of the adults and children as we would arrive in the cold of the winter night and step into falling-down houses lit by kerosene lamps since many did not have power. Yes, my mom and Dad taught me many things and one of the most important was to realize that there would always be many, many people less fortunate than me and that I should never ever feel sorry for myself but instead, focus on helping those who needed it.

Putting in tobacco or in Salem Speak, "Puttin' in baccer," was hard work. First came the harvest, a process that was incredibly manual (but which did evolve over the 7 years I did it). Initially, the harvest was done by croppers, who would walk down the long rows of tobacco plants behind a mule or a tractor pulling what was called a drag. A drag was nothing more than a wood frame on sled runners with burlap tacked to the sides to hold the tobacco in. The croppers would start at the bottom of the stalk taking the first two or three leaves since the tobacco leaves would ripen from the bottom up.

Usually, there would be 4-8 croppers with half on each side of the drag. Every four rows of tobacco there would be an open row for the drag. This was called the drag row. The first cropping was called the sand lugs since the leaves lowest to the ground were the biggest. Each subsequent week we would make another pass over each field for the second cropping, then the third, and so on until the last cropping which was usually the seventh and which usually took place toward the first part of August.

When the drag was full of tobacco leaves, it would head to the barn while another drag would be hitched up to the mule or the tractor. In the barn there would be what seemed like an army of people, usually one stringer for each cropper and two handers for each stringer. There would also be a person responsible for taking the tobacco out of the drags and placing it on long benches for the handers and stringers. The stringers would take three or four leaves, and using tobacco twine, would tie them together then loop the tied bundle onto a tobacco stick. When the tobacco stick held as many bundles as could fit, the string was wrapped around the stick and knotted. A hander would then take the stick to the barn door where another person would grab it and start handing it up into the barn through a chain of usually three people.

The barns were usually about 30 feet high, crisscrossed by tier poles that would hold the tobacco sticks. The tier poles were set in rows usually 4 feet apart lengthwise and 3 feet apart from top to bottom. Handlers would hang the top of the barn first, with one person handing the stick up to the next person, which is why it usually took three people to reach the top rows. As the barn filled up and the handers moved lower, the work took less hands, at first three, then two, and finally one.

All of this was back breaking work especially for the croppers in the field walking down long rows in the hot sun all day long, stooped over for the first cropping. The hanging was tough work as well since the initial croppings were heavy with morning dew. After a big rain the sticks could easily weigh 75 pounds. Handing them up into the barn was also difficult when the hander had to straddle two tier poles in bare feet, unable to hold on with their hands since they had to be free to grab the sticks.

Usually, men were the croppers and the hangers with the women doing the handing and the stringing. It was dirty work for all involved since the tobacco tar would get on everyone's hands. Whether a cropper, hander, or stringer, by the end of the day a worker would be black with tobacco gum.

Most people wore long sleeve shirts to keep the tobacco tar off their arms. Inside the barn where it was hot as hell, the dress of choice was a shirt with the sleeves cut out.

Over time, the drags evolved into trailers that we would pull up to the barn under the barn shed and drop the sides with two poles in the middle to hold the sticks with two stringers on each side. This eliminated the need for a person to remove the tobacco from the drag and place it on a bench since the handers could hand directly from the trailer once the sides were down. Several years later harvesters came along that were nothing more than a big rig where the croppers had a seat close to the ground. With two on each side they would crop the tobacco then hand it up to a stringer seated just above them. Thus, the harvester eliminated the need for handers.

The harvester had a canvas top, so the workers were in the shade. There would be one additional person on the harvester platform grabbing and removing the sticks as they filled up, then placing them on a pallet at the rear. When the pallet was full, the harvester would come to the end of the drag row and raise the lift on the platform to drop the pallet. A waiting tractor would then give the harvester a fresh pallet, pick up the one just dropped and take it to the barn.

One of the keys to making the harvester model work were the new John Deere tractors that had a very low-end gear range that allowed them to crawl. My uncle Cedric never had a harvester because his farm was small, however Uncle Son and Uncle James shared a harvester between them in order to get the economies of scale. As I said earlier, they were viewed as serious and cutting-edge farmers.

Every week during tobacco season I would stay with Uncle Cedric but help Uncle Son and Uncle James "put in tobacco," which meant harvesting on Monday Tuesday and Wednesday. Those days I would eat dinner (lunch) with Uncle James and Aunt Fan on Monday, with Uncle Son and Aunt Julia on Tuesday and Wednesday, then with Uncle Cedric and Aunt Edna on Thursday and Friday, since on those days I would help Uncle Cedric "put in tobacco" on Thursday afternoon and Friday. However, before I could help Uncle Cedric "put in tobacco," I had to help him take out tobacco, so that's what we would do on Thursday morning.

Taking out tobacco was the reverse of putting in, and we would go to the barn and start removing the bottom rows of tiers, gradually working our way up into the barn to remove the higher rows last. Since the curing process took about 6 days, we had to clear out the barn to make it ready for the next cropping or day of putting in. In the case of Uncle Cedric, since he only had one barn it was critical to get it done on Thursday morning so the barn would be open to start "putting in" that afternoon.

The 6-day curing process, which took place in the days between croppings, was done with big furnaces that sat on the sand floor in each barn. The furnaces burned oil, and the process required great precision as well as constant monitoring. In the early days, curing was done with wood fires, and people would have to stay up all night tending the fire. If you ran your tobacco furnace too hot, it would dry out the tobacco too much. Over-dry tobacco was considered poor quality and didn't bring a good price at the market. Being too dry also reduced the weight, and since you were paid by the pound you didn't want it too dry. On the other hand, if you didn't run your furnace hot enough, the tobacco would be too green and of very poor quality. Even worse, it could mildew in the packing house and be almost worth nothing.

The packing house was where we would take the sticks of tobacco after "takin'out" the barn. We would get paid a penny a stick to "take off" tobacco when we were not "puttin' in." Later in the season, the packing house people would take the tobacco off the stick, tie it in small bundles and place it in baskets (bales) covered in burlap for shipment to the market where it would be priced. If the farmer didn't like the price he'd been offered, he could always "turn the tag" which was essentially refusing the offer. However, a farmer who did that would have to load up their tobacco and take it to another market, and for that reason it was rarely done. Since tobacco farming was a labor-intensive undertaking full of risks at every step, my work with tobacco farmers was my second experience with entrepreneurs.

Every week during "puttin in" season was the same. At 6 am in the morning the horn would blow outside my Uncle Cedric's trailer, and I would jump out of bed barefooted, pull on cutoff jeans and a shirt with the sleeves cutout and run to the truck. On Thursday's and Fridays, when working for Uncle Cedric, I would drive the truck to go pick up the hands. Hands was the slang expression for all the tobacco workers, including our uncles and cousins. I realize that today the term "fieldhands" has bad connotations but in those days it did not. Hands were absolutely critical to the process, and the best compliment one could receive was that you were a "good hand."

Today, some might also say that the farmers were taking advantage of their hands at $5 per day, but in those days people were happy to have the work because eastern South Carolina did not have the textile jobs available in the upstate. Without doubt, the people appreciated the jobs and my uncles appreciated the "hands" as well as respected them. Likewise, my dad depended on the farmers and the workers as customers, and they depended on my dad for the essentials of life and the credit to see it through the season to harvest.

Appreciation and respect flowed in both directions. My dad's busiest time of year was the harvest season when people had money to spend in his store as well as money to settle the accounts in his Black Book. I didn't realize it at the time, but this cycle was a microcosm of what went on at a macro level in our economy with the entrepreneurs being at the center because of their role in job creation. Years later I would earn a degree in Economics in College and reflect a great deal more on this basic model.

So, each morning we would pick up the hands at 6 am. We would first go to Miss Lila's house down the road then on to Reverend Pendergraph's. Next would be Reuben, who worked for my Uncle Son, and McKinley, who would later come to work for Uncle James. Last stop would be the Poston children, mostly the boys who were old enough—Junior (my good friend and playmate), Frankie and Jimmy. Later on there would be Terry (or Cookie as he was known) because he loved the cookies which dad would give him all the time for free. By the time we finished, the back of the truck would be full with 20 or so people, and it would be off to the fields and the barn.

Work started promptly at 7 am and we would go nonstop except for one break when my uncles would bring soft drinks and nabs (Lance crackers) to the fields. Sometimes there would be moon pies. I can honestly say that I have never tasted anything better than that cold drink and crackers after several hours of back-breaking work. Following break, we would work until noon then "knock off" for lunch (dinner). Afterward, we would pick everyone up again and work from 2 pm until 5 pm. These were long hot days interrupted only by periodic thunderstorms and lightning that would send us running to take cover under the barn shed.

Over the course of my 7 years working tobacco, I would "graduate" from hander to cropper and ultimately to the most difficult and physically demanding job which was a hanger in the barn. I took dad's lessons to heart, trying to do the best possible job no matter how menial the task. While the work was incredibly hard, there were fun times as well. The chatter in the field and at the barn was constant. There was much kidding and joking, and the African American hands would always have a radio blasting out the ever-popular brother James Brown who came from Augusta and was the hometown favorite. Then, at the end of the day sweaty and tired, my cousins and I along with Junior Poston and his brothers would load up my dad's car or my uncle's truck and go to the creek.

The creek, or Bartells Landing, was "down the road" about 5 miles or so in Postons Corner. The purpose of the trips to the creek was twofold 1) to cool off after a hot day in the fields and 2) to bathe with borax soap and wash off all the sweat, tobacco gum, and dirt from the day. The creek also was great fun! There was a wooden platform built in the trees on the other side. One of the trees leaned out over the creek, and a cable was attached to the end of one branch with a car steering wheel at the end. Holding the steering wheel, one could swing out over the channel and cut flips or simply drop into the cool jet-black water.

We would swim for an hour or so playing tag and seeing how long we could stay underwater. As a child, it seemed like the creek was big and wide, and it was actually a challenge to get over to the other side especially if the water was high and running swiftly. I have been back since and it is amazing how small it is, but at that time in my life it seemed big and perfect. After swimming for an hour or so in our perfect creek, cleaning up and cooling off, we would head back to Salem.

After swimming, I would help dad in the store by taking out groceries for customers as well as doing other chores. I would eat something for supper at the store, or if I was lucky I would take a chicken down to BGeorges to barbecue along with a couple of beers. Afterwards I would hit the sack and sleep like a baby before getting up in the morning to do it all over again.

While I loved all the people I worked with and enjoyed them

immensely, there were two characters I particularly appreciated. They were McKinley and Reuben, both African American men of roughly the same age. Mckinley was a full-time employee who worked for my Uncle James, and Reuben was full-time for Uncle Son. Both performed the exact same jobs, and they were both wonderful people. Despite having similar backgrounds, they were a total study in contrast. McKinley was quiet and ascribed to the wise old owl theory, while Reuben was jovial, a big dancer and big drinker. He loved to cut a rug listening to Brother James, and like my Uncle Cedric, he would go on binges. He was even known to drink Sterno out of a can when he could not get liquor.

Both men were very hard workers, but McKinley had accomplished so much more in life. He lived in a little house that he owned. It was always neat and tidy, and when I would go to pick him up, I always noticed his garden and his flowers. While his clothes were old and worn, they were always clean and neatly pressed and his brogans would be clean and polished. Reuben on the other hand lived in a shack and always looked out of sorts and disheveled. What one could easily discern was that McKinley had made the most out of what he had, and Reuben had not. I aspired to spend the rest of my life trying to be more like McKinley, even though I had to admit Reuben was more fun to be around.

As time wore on and I progressed to more and more difficult jobs, my pay increased as well, to where at the end I was making $8 per day. While the added money was good, I was also pleased to see that the work had changed my physique. Those 8 weeks of really hard work affected my appearance as well as my confidence. I noticed in gym classes at school I could run much faster, and I was better at intramural football and softball. Due to my greater strength plus the improvement of my hand/eye coordination through playing so much half rubber, as a softball batter I was consistently able to not only push the softball into right field, but often to get it over the short fence on that side of the field.

In gym, we had a rope that hung from the high ceiling. Other boys would struggle to climb it even using their legs. However, I could climb it in 10 seconds hand over hand without my legs. While I was only 5'8"" and about 135 lbs., I was very strong for my size.

The summer after my senior year at the end of tobacco season, just before going off to college, I would have an opportunity to prove how strong I was. By then, going to the skating rink on weekends had become a pastime. It was the best local hangout, and there were always girls and guys of all ages. As the rink closed one night at the end of the season, some guys in their 20s decided it would be fun to have a wrestling contest for some of the younger guys. I didn't realize it at the time, but I was being set up.

They decided there would be three classes based on age with the older class last. Beside myself there was only one other 18-year-old, so I was pitted against a big farm boy who was about 6'2" and seemed twice my size. As our match started the hometown boys were laughing and calling me City Slicker and College Boy, as for the first 5 minutes my opponent tossed me around like a rag doll. The more he would throw me around the more ragging I would get from the crowd, and it was then that I realized I was being gamed. Finally, I was able to jump on the guy's back, get him in a headlock as well as a scissor hold around his waist and twist him to the ground. I then proceeded to squeeze him so hard that he turned blue, and they called the match. After the match, I expected to be congratulated, but there were no congratulations as there had been for the others.

It was then I realized that as much as I tried, I could never be one of them, so I decided right then to stop trying. The next day, which was my last day before going back to Florence to get ready for school, I rode down to the creek by myself one last time , knowing that it was the end of an era for me. I would return to Salem one more time to work in tobacco the summer before my junior Year in college, and I would come back for a week every year until I got married in order to allow my dad and stepmother to take a week's vacation in the Blue Ridge Mountains. While those visits would be fun and fulfilling, for me Salem would never be quite the same.

Change is hard, and my remembrance of that day after the wrestling match was that I was full of melancholy and sad that I was leaving one chapter in my life and going on to another. I've had much the same felling each time I moved during my banking career, when leaving one home for another and one job for another. It was definitely a sad felling but also one of excitement for what the next chapter would hold.

That last day before I left to go back to Florence to get ready for college, Dad pulled me aside. He said, "Uncle Son came by to tell you goodbye while you were at the creek." He said Uncle Son had to go out of town and could not stay until I came back. He told Dad to tell me that I was his "Best Hand." I could tell my dad was very proud because Uncle Son was a special man who had worked hard all his life to provide for his family. He was my favorite and while later I would have some measure of accomplishment as a banker, I would never see my dad prouder of me than that day. For me, I would never be more fulfilled or satisfied, no matter my station in life, than I was with that simple compliment.

Chapter 7

Newberry College

In the spring of my senior year in Florence, I began to contemplate where I should go to college. By then, Melba had graduated from Queens University in Charlotte and was teaching school in Atlanta. Queens, at the time, was an all-girls school, so it was out of the question. As mentioned earlier, my stepfather, Alan Perry, was also the band director at McClenaghan High School and he happened to be a graduate of Newberry. I also had a very good friend in Florence, also a senior, named Tommy Poston whose brother Billy had gone to Newberry. Both Tommy and I applied and were accepted. In addition, since I had been playing the trumpet in the band and Allen knew the Newberry band director, I was awarded a partial band scholarship.

I will never forget arriving at Newberry as a freshman that first day. It was totally exciting to be turning a page in life and leaving Florence and Salem behind. At the time, Newberry had an enrollment of about 900, consisting of students from many small towns in South Carolina, Georgia, and Florida. Since Newberry was a Lutheran supported College about 40% of the students were Lutherans with a 50/50 male/female mix. The student faculty ratio was about 12 to 1, so classes very small and the professors took a real interest in each and every student. For me, it was a perfect fit and I liked it so much I almost never went home. In fact, I think all four years I may have gone home only 3 times each year at Thanksgiving, Christmas, and Easter.

The first few days during freshmen orientation were full of new people and new experiences. Since I was in a male freshman dorm, the first people

I met were also freshmen. Tommy Poston and I were rooming together, and it seemed to us that a large number of the guys on our hall were from Columbia. The Columbia boys seemed so much more worldly than Tommy and I, who were small town guys from Florence. While they had gone to high schools that were similar in size to McClenaghan where we graduated, it was obvious they had a much more cosmopolitan perspective than Tommy and I.

For starters, the high schools in Columbia had male social clubs with names like "The Horseman" and " The Cavaliers" which were totally foreign to me. Since the Columbia boys were familiar with social clubs, the conversation invariably got around to fraternities and sororities, something I also knew nothing about. In particular, two boys on our hall seemed to really be plugged in: James Douglas Seigler, a former Cavalier, and Harvey Lee Atwater, a former Horseman.

While Doug and Lee had their membership in high school clubs in common that was about all they shared. Doug was very preppy in his dress and quiet in his demeanor. Lee was a bit dumpy, with long hair, but he was clearly the most outgoing boy on the hall. Lee had been in a band during high school, played the guitar and would regularly hold court on the hall with his singing the blues. Despite their differences, they both seemed to know the ropes much more than I, and on the subject of fraternities they both said it was something Tommy and I should do.

As to the fraternities and sororities, at the time there were essentially four: KA or Kappa Alpha, and ATO or Alpha Tau Omega for the boys and KD or Kappa Delta, and AZD or Alpha Zeta Delta for the girls. Since all of this was very foreign to me, I relied on Doug and Lee for advice. Unfortunately, they were at opposite ends on which fraternity to rush. Lee was committed to rushing ATO while Doug was sold on KA. Since both were becoming good friends, this difference of opinion put me in a terrible position. Because I could not make up my mind on which fraternity to try and pledge, I rushed both.

While I liked both Doug and Lee, Doug was probably more similar to me with his preppy attire and low-key demeanor. Also, Doug and I were both majoring in Economics so we began to study together and compare class notes. Doug was also more active on the social scene, so we often double dated and shared a beer in the afternoons. At the time, the KA's seemed to be more social and this appealed to my desire to be accepted by my peers.

On the other hand, Lee was a wild man! Partying was his thing, and he would often binge drink and stay up all night singing and playing the guitar. Since at that point, Lee had not developed his interest in politics, he was exclusively and singularly focused on having a grand time. In many ways, he was exactly like the Bluto character John Belushi played in the movie Animal House. He had a cult-like following and was determined to create a reputation for himself on our freshman 4th floor in Brokaw Hall.

In those days, Newberry still celebrated rat week, where the freshman wore beanies and experienced some level of hazing from upper classmen. Lee decided to put a stop to it and set fire to some croaker sacks full of pig parts outside the door of an upperclassman who had done more than his fair share of hazing. Suffice it to say, there was no hazing of freshmen on the fourth floor of Brokaw for the rest of rat week. Lee was so singularly focused on holding court and partying that he almost never went to class. In fact, he flunked out his freshman year and had to go to summer school in order to be readmitted. In many respects, the personalities of Lee and Doug helped contrast the differences in the fraternities.

To complicate this contrast in styles, there was also the fact that my good friend from Florence, Tommy Poston was going to rush ATO. There were also two upperclassmen from Florence, Donnie Cox and Eddie Gunn who had befriended me and were ATOs. All of this made the rush process difficult. I would go out one night with the ATOs and come back decided it was ATO. The next night I would go out with the KAs and do a flip flop. In retrospect, it seems like a waste of energy to have been so consumed with trying to make the right fraternity decision. With age and maturity, I realize that more of my focus should have been on getting the most out of the classroom experience.

On the final day of rush when bids went out, I went to Smeltzer Hall to see if I had a bid hoping that it would be one or the other and not two as I did not want to have to make the decision. When I received the envelopes, I did have two so I sat in the corner to decide. At the end of the day, my longer standing friendship with Tommy Poston and the connection to the upper classmen from Florence helped make up my mind. In a nutshell I have always considered myself to be a very loyal person and the need to remain loyal to longer standing friendships was clearly what resulted in me pledging ATO.

At the time, the fraternities and sororities were on Carol Courts which were housing dorms built for married students after World War II. Lined up along the dead-end street were four large buildings, two for the girls (KD and AZD) and two for the guys (KA and ATO). Each building had 8 apartments with four guys or girls in each apartment for a total 32 Greek residents in each building. In one of the girls' buildings was a lady named Mrs. Estridge, or "Mom E" as we called her, who was the House Mother or rule enforcer for all the Greeks. So, on pledge day we took our offer letters (or bids) then ran down Carol Court to go meet our new brothers or respective sisters. It was a day full of much cheering, chanting, and excitement, and also the day we would pick out our new rooms and roommates for the apartments we would move into after Thanksgiving.

In my case, while I was excited, I was also somewhat melancholy over the status of my friendship with Doug and others I had met along the way. In particular, a guy named Bobby Kemp from Bamberg, South Carolina, who I played intramural football with and who had become a good friend. As much as I looked forward to my participation in ATO, I also had an unsettled feeling since it was a known fact that the KAs and ATOs did not like each other and did not socialize. Since this antipathy seemed stupid to me, one of the first things I did after the party broke up was to walk over and congratulate Doug and Bobby.

We made a pact that we would remain good friends and would not let our fraternity differences interfere with our friendship. And so, for our remaining four years we did remain good friends and in the case of Doug, one of my best friends. Early on as we remained close friends and socialized together, some of the other brothers frowned on this activity. But as they realized we were not going to change and that we also appeared to have a lot of fun, others began to do the same. As we maintained our friendship pact, more friendships flowered across fraternity lines, and I like to think that Doug, Bobby and I were the first to break down what had always been a barrier.

That first year of college was an incredible experience for me, full of new experiences and new friends. One thing that did not survive, however, was my relationship with Harriett, who was in her freshman year at Winthrop

University some 90 miles away. While we dated a few times, it didn't last. I wanted to date other people and Harriett also met the man she would eventually marry. While there was much excitement that first year and I could tell story after story of essentially living in "Animal House," the most important thing that happened to me was something unrelated to college. Specifically, the Selective Service System established the lottery to determine the order of call to military service in the Vietnam War.

On the night of the draft lottery, I remember my dad calling the pay phone in front of the ATO house. His first comment was, "Congratulations, son, you are number 3!" He was clearly proud since he and his brothers had served in World War II. My own head was spinning with the realization that I would be going into the military within days of graduation. In those days they were calling up through number 165 or 170 so there was no doubt that at 3 I was going to Vietnam. The only question would be how would I go and for how long. At that time, if you had a number like 3, you were certain to be drafted within 30 days of graduation. If drafted, you would serve for 2 years wherever they chose to send you, which at that time, in most cases was Vietnam.

As an alternative to being drafted, as a college graduate you could apply for Officers Training School in one of the branches of service. In that case, assuming you were accepted, the commitment was for 6 years, but you got to choose what you would be doing. In my case, I decided I wanted to be a pilot, because if I was going to be in Vietnam I wanted to be riding in something going real fast and not be a sitting duck in a rice paddy on the ground. Therefore, I decided to join the Air Force and go to flight school to be a pilot.

For the next three years I assumed this was my destiny. So, while I passed all my classes and graduated on time, I partied like there was no tomorrow and essentially squandered what should have been a great education given the size of the classes and the quality of the teachers. Looking back, I have always regretted not working harder on my academics not only at Newberry but in also high school. The realization of that mistake led me later in life to work extra hard in my chosen field as a banker and to focus on lifelong learning by reading as much as I could about all kinds of topics. In a good way, my regret helped make me better in later years.

One thing I would get out of the next three years is that I would learn how to sell! When I returned to Newberry for my sophomore year, the ATOs asked me to be Rush Chairman for the next three years. During those years, I worked hard to recruit the best pledge class each year, which involved convincing incoming freshman that ATO was the fraternity to join. I learned how to listen to people and show interest in what they wanted to achieve. I also learned how to pair people up with the right personalities to make them comfortable. I learned how to deal with different people from the eggheads to the athletes. And last but not least, I learned how to throw the best parties.

In the case of ATO, we had an old gas station that we had turned into a party house, known affectionately as "The Gas House." We had an old juke box with all the beach music tunes, and there was, of course, a pool table. It was a bit like The Pad at Ocean Drive. We also had a TV room we called the Teakwood Room, which I had fixed up so people could take their dates to watch football and basketball games. I even went so far as to spend the first two weeks after my freshman year painting The Gas House and fixing things up to have it ready for rush in the fall. It was our home away from home, and we could throw an impromptu theme party on a moment's notice. We even had our own built in entertainment source in brother Harvey Lee Atwater!

As already mentioned, throughout his freshman year and into his sophomore year, Lee was an absolute wild man. During that same time, the United States was undergoing a near revolution because of opposition to the Vietnam war. Protests were going on at every campus, and the use of recreational drugs was exploding, including marijuana, speed and acid.

The name "Flower Child" was coined during that time as was "Hippy." Bell bottom jeans became the standard dress as everyone aspired to look like Sonny and Cher. Since Lee always did everything to extremes, he went in full force, grew his hair out, as well as a mustache and basically stayed stoned that entire freshman and sophomore year. He flunked almost every class, and had it not been for summer school he would not have returned in the fall. However, over the course of the summer before his junior year something else happened to Lee. In addition to summer school, his mom got him an internship with Senator Strom Thurmond, and his life changed. He returned his junior year clean shaven, with short hair, and he wore khaki pants and navy-blue blazers. Espousing conservative politics, he suddenly had an incredible thirst for learning. The other thing that changed was that Lee became an avid runner logging 8 to 10 miles per day.

Lee went from making straight Fs to making straight As and from having no interest in politics to being heavily involved. The one thing that did not change was Lee's impromptu guitar/singing concerts at the fraternity house and being a constant source of entertainment for all of us.

In the process of his changes, Lee's body went from chubby to lean and mean. In short, he went from being incredibly undisciplined to being very disciplined with the one exception of Friday night. Every Friday night for the rest of his life until he died at the early age of 40, Lee would binge on beer and cigarettes partying late into the night and being great fun. Then the next morning the discipline would start again with daily runs, no smoking or drinking and lots of studying and work on politics.

Since I was more on the preppy side, this newer version of Lee Atwater fit more with my style. We became close friends and grew even closer after college; he would be in my wedding and I in his.

As Lee got more and more involved in politics, he dragged us at least partly into the game. In his senior year, he was head of the South Carolina chapter of Young Republicans. One of his responsibilities was signing up new members. Ever the promoter, Lee would dress a bunch of us at the fraternity up in rep ties and navy-blue blazers and we would go to all the girls' schools to sign new members. In exchange for the free labor, we would get the names, addresses, and phone numbers of the prettiest girls using red, blue and green pens as code for attractiveness. As you would imagine red was stay away, blue was okay, and green was full speed ahead. I feel sure that approach would break today's privacy laws, but at the time we thought it was great fun. Lee would likewise go recruiting workers at the girls' schools like Converse College and Columbia College and do the same thing with them.

Even today, I'm not sure how legal all of this was, but it worked. In that year Lee signed up more Young Republicans than anyone else in history. Lee was all about promotion and how to motivate people. Perhaps for that reason, one of his favorite pastimes was to watch championship wrestling. I would ask Lee, "Why do you watch this stuff since it is all fake?" He would say, "It may be fake, but look at the faces of the people. They're having fun and they don't care if it's fake."

Lee viewed politics in somewhat the same way: promote the hell out of your candidate and turn the opponent into the bad guy. Thanks to him, we even had staged wrestling matches in front of the fraternity houses. Lee had a championship belt made up with a big silver buckle. The participants would have stage names. John Riley was "Puba The Bear." Jimmy White, another brother, was nicknamed "Barabbas." It was crazy stuff and great fun, but with Lee involved you knew it would always be a show!

While all of this was going on, I became more and more aware that within 30 days of graduation I would report for duty. At that point, my life would be committed to the military for the next 6 years. The reports of young men being killed in the rice paddies and jungles of Vietnam were growing every day, so I was convinced that the decision to join the Air Force was the right one. It reinforced my mantra of "Live for Today," and that's what I did!

In the spring of my senior year, I completed my flight physical at Shaw Air Force Base, and I was all but signed up. The only thing I needed to do was sign the dotted line, which I intended to do, but then everything changed. President Nixon announced we were pulling out of Viet Nam, and the country was ending the draft. In one week, my sense of certainty was shattered, and I had no clue what I was going to do.

Chapter 8

Donald Pee Wee Gaskins

As mentioned earlier, Dad kept a shotgun in the store. In the mid-60's he built a new store out of cinder block on the same site as the old store. He moved the old store across the road next to the Salem United Methodist Church so he could operate from there for the 6 months or so until the new store was completed. This was during the period when I was heavily involved in "puttin' in tobacco" during the summers and spending weekends with Dad in Salem during the school year.

The new store's contents were just like the old store with the only difference being that the new store was more modern, had bathrooms and central heating versus the old wood stove. The checkout counter in the new store was right in front, surrounded by a counter that created a bullpen where dad could collect payments from customers as well as work on tax returns, insurance, and other services. The location of the bullpen was specifically chosen to give Dad an unobstructed view of the entire store and to see who was coming through the front door well before they got there.

During those days, I often ran the store to give Dad some time off, especially at the end of the summer so he and Dorothy (my stepmom) could go to the mountains for a brief vacation. I did this every year during college and even after starting my banking career until I got married. Prior to Dad's departure he would give me the keys along with a verbal checklist of the things to do immediately after opening and just before closing and locking up.

The last thing on the list was to take all the cash from the cash register along with the Black Book and lock them in the old Salem Supply safe. The safe was this huge black steel vault with a big combination and handle on the front. Always, in going through the checklist, Dad would give his speech on bad people in the area and that if I was ever confronted with a possible robbery to only go for the gun if I could get it well before the robbers came through the door. His mantra was not to take any chances and that I should not hesitate to give the robber the money including what was in the safe.

Salem, like most rural communities in that time had its share of bad actors. Clearly, they were in the minority as most of the people in the community were hard working, honest, law abiding folks. However, an element of really tough, bad people did exist. They were usually from broken homes, raised in loveless environments of neglect and child abuse. While there were some African American bad actors, the absolute worst were the poor Whites, and there were plenty to go around. A large reform school in Florence just 30 miles away was full of such young men from the area. Chief among those bad actors was a man named Donald Pee Wee Gaskins.

Pee Wee was raised (if you want to call it that) in Prospect, a small place in Florence County, some 3 miles from Salem "down the road and over the swamp" toward Lake City. Born in 1933, he was approaching 40 by the late 60's and early 70's, and by then he was a hardened criminal who had been in and out of reform school, as well as in and out of jail. By that point, he had also committed his first known murders and most certainly was well down the road to committing many, many murders that made him the worst serial killer in South Carolina history.

Pee Wee drove a black hearse with a skull and crossbones painted on the side. In the late 60's to mid 70's, he was out of jail and living someplace in the area, and the black hearse was frequently seen on the road. Little did anyone know that during this time he was committing most of his murders and that when finally arrested in 1976 he would lead authorities to a large number of graves in the area. Much has been written about Pee Wee, so won't go into those details, but suffice it to say he was a very bad person. My dad would constantly tell me that if I ever saw Pee Wee, I should head the other way. Little did I know at the time that circumstances would place me directly in front of him in a situation I could not easily get out of. But before I get into my meeting with him, I need to describe the circumstances that led me to that scary day.

In 1972 during the spring of my junior year before my senior year at Newberry, I was dating a girl from Charleston. I was also fast approaching graduation, and I knew I needed a car. Up until that time, I had ridden back and forth from Florence to school with my fraternity brother Tommy Poston. While getting back and forth from college had not been difficult, dating was a different story. I had two options: double date or borrow someone's car. Therefore, that spring I decided to buy a car, but to do that I needed a job because "puttin' in tobacco" didn't pay enough.

During Easter break, I ran into my Uncle Danny on one of my trips to Salem. The youngest of my father's brothers and the only one in the family that moved away, Uncle Danny was the handsomest and clearly my grandmother's favorite. He lived in North Charleston in a trailer in what I would call a pretty rough part of town and worked as a foreman for Bonitz Insulation Company hanging sheet rock and acoustical ceilings on commercial construction jobs.

I was aware that my grandmother constantly worried about Uncle Danny living away from the rest of the family, fearing that in North Charleston he would be subject to bad influences. In the mid 80's he died of a heart attack at an early age, and I served as the executor of his modest estate, where I worked to close up loose ends of which there were many.

One complicating note was that Uncle Danny had a child out of wedlock. My grandmother had left him the house she and my grandfather had lived in, and my job was to sell it. In the end, it took me years to locate his daughter, sell the house and remit her the proceeds. As part of that process, I had to sell his trailer and take care of all his belongings which were minimal. However, included in his belongings were years of letters from my grandmother appealing to him to come back to Salem. She never stopped worrying about the "bad influences" in Charleston and his pattern of making bad choices.

It turns out that there was a lot I didn't know about Uncle Danny when I made the decision to come to Charleston in 1972 to live with him while working on a construction crew (not his crew) at the then minimum wage of $1.60 per hour. All I focused on was that this job would allow me to accumulate enough money to buy a car and make enough payments to almost prepay the car loan by the time I graduated in the Spring of 73, when I planned to join the Air Force.

My plan worked perfectly with the exception of Uncle Danny's situation when I arrived in Charleston to start my summer job. While Uncle Danny was a loving, kind, and considerate man, to say that he made bad choices would be an incredible understatement. When I arrived, his trailer was a filthy mess, and it was clear that it hadn't been cleaned in a very long time. There was absolutely no food in the house, and worse, he was hanging around with all kinds of bad people who would show up at all hours of the night. So, in addition to working all day to save enough for my car, I found myself trying to straighten up Uncle Danny's life.

My first order of business was to wash and scrub the trailer from stem to stern inside and out. Next, I cut the grass and stocked the refrigerator. Since I was also trying to spend time with my girlfriend, I had to manage all these extra jobs in between work during the day and seeing her some nights. It took a couple weeks, but I was able to get all the work done around Uncle Danny's.

More importantly, I was able to save enough to buy my first car, a four-year-old Austin Healy Sprite painted British racing green. My stepfather, Allen Perry, was a car buff, and he helped me find it and co-signed the note. I remember how excited I was to get the car! I paid $900 for it putting $250 down and financing the $650 balance over two years at the South Carolina National Bank. The monthly payments were $33.12, and I calculated that over the rest of the summer I could prepay 7 or 8 payments, which would mean my summer job would allow me to make almost all the first year's payments. I planned to come back to Charleston over the two-week Christmas Holiday and make enough to prepay my way through to the following summer, at which point I would be in the military making regular money.

This was my first experience with a bank, and I learned that properly managed, a bank loan could help me get something now versus having to wait for it. At first things worked beautifully. I had my car and my girlfriend, and my relationship with Uncle Danny was good. At first, he seemed to appreciate all I had done to straighten things up around the house, however, as time went on, he began to slip into his old ways. He started drinking heavily again, and then all the bad characters started to come around.

It was when I came back to Charleston to work during the Holidays that the worst happened. My Charleston girlfriend had ditched me when we returned to Newberry for the fall semester in 1972. During Christmas vacation when I lived with Uncle Danny over those two weeks, I had nothing to do in the evenings when I got off work. Most nights Uncle Danny and I would have few beers and cook something on the grill, but one evening, he asked me to go with him to see a friend "from home." He didn't tell me who the person was but simply that they were living in the area and wanted to talk about getting a job at Bonitz.

We took Uncle Danny's truck and drove two or three miles to a run-down house in North Charleston. When we went into the living room, I saw a young woman and her daughter who must have been 12 or 13. What troubled me was that they appeared to be incredibly nervous and scared half to death. Their fear was so palpable it made the hair on the back of my neck stand up. Also, the place was filthy and reeked of spilled alcohol and stale food. Despite their obvious fear, the two women were very quiet and seemed glad to see us. However, nothing was making sense, and my instincts were on full alert.

After about 5 minutes that felt like an hour, a very short, wiry, swarthy man came into the room. Uncle Danny introduced him as "Pee Wee," and as soon as he said those words fear ran down my spine. They say wild animals can sense fear and that it's the same with certain humans. I could tell by Pee Wee's eyes that he knew I was scared, and right away he started in on me.

"Danny here tells me you're a college boy. Well, I want you to know that I don't like college boys worth a damn. In jail we used to use 'em for punching bags and other stuff."

I'll never forget the crazed look in his eyes. If I had to guess, I'd say he was either totally drunk or on drugs, maybe both. Uncle Danny tried to defend me by saying that I spent every summer back home in Salem working tobacco, which seemed to placate Pee Wee a little. However, having known for a long time that Uncle Danny was a terrible judge of character, I was still stunned at this new low, and I just wanted to get the heck out of there. Aside from my own fear, I now realized that both women were being abused. I could see it in the pleading looks they threw my way.

Unfortunately, there was nothing I could do, but I knew we needed to get out of there and quick. Uncle Danny said something like he would check at work to see if they were hiring on any new help. Taking my own stab at ending the conversation, I said I would be leaving my job very soon and it might be open. Somehow, we got out of there, but I will never forget how I felt about leaving those women. I asked Uncle Danny if we should call the police, but he told me we should leave well enough alone. I will never forget my fear from that day. While I would experience other moments of fear in later years, none would come close to what I felt that night with Pee Wee.

I continued to live with Uncle Danny for the rest of that Christmas break, but we would part ways when I returned to Newberry. I spent my spring semester contemplating my future in the Air Force and enjoying my Austin Healy. I only saw Uncle Danny one or two times when he was back in Salem. He died at 54 or 55 of a sudden heart attack, apparently due to years of alcohol abuse.

After Pee Wee's arrest and conviction in 1976, I read in detail about his indiscriminate killing of men and women, and in particular his frequent raping of very young women. Whenever I read those accounts, I would find myself thinking of the two young women in that house. Since I never learned their names, I would never know if they managed to get away from Pee Wee or if they were among the many innocents he sent to the grave.

In subsequent years I have also thought a lot about what kept me from becoming a troublemaker, or someone like my uncle Danny who led a sad life. I had plenty of opportunities to take the wrong turns because there were lots of tough people in and around Salem. Many went to jail and while they weren't as bad as Pee Wee, they stayed in and out of trouble all their lives.

As I have thought about this my answer always comes back to the same thing. First, my father and mother always instilled in me the belief that everything I did represented our family, and that if I did something bad, I was creating a poor reflection on everyone, not just me. Second, my dad always said that if you hung around trouble long enough you would get in trouble, and I had enough street smarts to understand and immediately recognize the trouble makers when I saw them. I have an old friend who says "If you lie down with dogs you will get fleas." You might say I took this mantra to heart and later in life my ability to stay away from doing business with people of sketchy character served me well. While my Uncle Danny was not a troublemaker himself and was a kind man, I believe it was his choice of friends that brought him down.

Carlos Evans

Chapter 9

Bankers Trust My First Big Break

In late January or early February of my Senior year at Newberry, Nixon announced that the Draft would end on July 1st, 1973, when the law that began the conscription process would expire. At first, that news seemed too good to be true, but as the days and weeks wore on it became clear that my number 3 was never going to get called. The Vietnam War was truly winding down, driven by Nixon's desire to curb the social unrest that had been tearing the country apart.

I had already taken my flight physical and was teed up to go to Air Force Officer Training School, subject only to me signing the papers. As I contemplated my future, I realized I had more options than previously. If I signed up for the Air Force and didn't like it, I would still be locked in for six years. If I chose to go into the private sector, however, I could try it for a couple years and the option to go into the Air Force would still be there. As much as I was enamored with flying something fast, rationality took over, and I decided the smart thing was to get a job, try it, and keep all my options open.

On the day of my graduation, my dad and stepmom, Dorothy, were the only ones in Newberry because my mom and stepdad were traveling. Dad was so proud of my degree. When I told him of my plans to try the private sector before enlisting, he was supportive. For me, my graduation was a melancholy day, like the day at the creek at the end of my last real summer in Salem when I knew I was leaving my old life and starting something new. Also, as I contemplated that change, I was aware once again that I had squandered what should have been a much stronger learning experience. Right then I determined that if opportunities for education came my way again, I would not waste them. However, the past was the past. It was now game time in the workplace, and I needed to go all out to be "The Best Hand" I could be.

I'm not sure why I chose Columbia as the place to start my job search other than it was the State Capital and at the time the largest city in South Carolina. I also had friends who were focused on Columbia, like my KA friend Doug Seigler, who had graduated with his economics degree but decided to pursue a law degree. There was also my friend Lee Atwater, who was already heavily involved with politics and planned to base himself in Columbia. So, Columbia seemed like the logical place for me to find a job.

I returned to Florence to live with my mom and stepdad and began commuting back and forth to Columbia for interviews. Mom was a big help because she bought me my first suit, so I looked appropriate. Not knowing anything about the process of getting a job, I took the advice of a fellow ATO graduate from Hartsville S.C. who was also targeting Columbia. He advised going through an employment agency, so I used the same one he was using which was in the Citizens and Southern Bank building headquarters.

The employment agency lined up multiple interviews, everything from a shoe store manager position at the mall to other kinds of retailing jobs. My friend landed a spot with a life insurance company but I knew that was not for me. After several weeks of fruitless interviews, I was very frustrated, but on one of my visits to the employment agency, I looked up at the bank, and a light bulb went off.

I had been an economics major, and banks were deeply embedded in our economic process. Thinking that banking might be a fit, I reached out to a fellow ATO named Gary Welchel, who had played quarterback at Newberry. I knew he was in the bond department at the Citizens and Southern (C&S) Bank, and he was kind enough to set me up with an interview with Bill Pherigo in the C&S personnel department.

Bill seemed like a decent fellow, but right off he gave me a 24 question psychological test. All the questions were strange and had nothing to do with banking or the economy. Questions like, what is your favorite color, red, green or blue? What is your favorite hobby and why? Who is the famous person you admire most? At the end of the test, Bill advised me that I was not cut out to be a banker.

This angered me to no end, and while I kept my cool, I resolved to prove him wrong. When I called to tell Gary Welchel what happened, he suggested I talk to a new upstart bank in town called Bankers Trust of South Carolina, which was totally separate and apart from Bankers Trust of New York. Gary called a fellow in the bank's personnel department named Charlie James, and his phone introduction led to an interview. Gary has since gone on to a great career in the investing business, but his simple act of kindness put me on the right path, and for that I will be forever grateful.

Bankers Trust of S.C. began as The Bank of Greenwood in Greenwood, South Carolina. Started by Mr. Dewey Johnson, the bank was subsequently turned over to his two sons, W.W. Hootie Johnson, who was the CEO when I joined, and Wellsman Johnson, who was the Chairman of the Board but not active in day to day administration. The Bank had many offices in western South Carolina in small towns like Greenwood, Aiken, Johnston, and Ware Shoals, but it did not have a significant presence in Columbia. Sometime in the late 1950s, the Bank purchased the Lower Main Street Bank in Columbia, and following that acquisition, the bank established its headquarters there in a low-slung office building at the corner of Lady Street and Main. Shortly thereafter, the Bank changed its name to Bankers Trust of South Carolina, and Hootie launched an aggressive growth strategy.

Hootie was incredibly well connected, having served in the S.C. legislature at a very young age. By the early 70s he was chairman of the South Carolina Ports Authority as well as a member of Augusta National. He was close personal friends with former S.C. Governor Robert E. McNair, who led one of the most powerful law firms in the state known as The McNair law firm. While the little Bankers Trust building on Lady and Main was dwarfed by the larger buildings of S.C. National Bank, C&S, and First National Bank, Hootie was known as a mover and shaker, and his little bank had the reputation of being on the move.

My interview with Charlie James went well. I can't remember much of it other than the more I learned about Bankers Trust the more I wanted to be part of it. Over the next week, I had a series of interviews. My second was with a man named Nelson Taylor followed by one with Tom Connor the head of personnel. Tom was a wonderful man and would later become a good friend and teammate, as well as a strong advocate for me later in my career. At the conclusion of my interview, he advised that my next meeting would be with Executive Vice President John G.P. Boatwright, in Tom's words "a real banker's banker." Mr. Boatwright proved to be exactly that. More than any other individual on the Bankers Trust management team outside of Hootie, who I would not meet for some time, John G.P. Boatwright was incredibly impressive. He was a Virginia blueblood who Hootie hand-picked to run his bank. Highly educated with an impressive pedigree, John Boatwright was a sign to the rest of the state that Hootie and Wellsman's little bank had arrived.

My interview with Mr. Boatwright would take place on the mezzanine of the main bank building on Main and Lady, whereas my other interviews had been across the street in the smaller Lady Street building I showed up there in my one and only suit and saw that Mr. Boatwright's office was right next to Hootie's. I remember that he was sitting behind a very large desk with a big window directly behind him facing east. It was a morning interview, and the sunlight was streaming in, and I could not see his face clearly due to the sun. It felt like I was interviewing God, and while Mr. Boatwright was a very fine man who I would come to know and respect, to say I was intimidated would be a huge understatement.

Mr. Boatwright read from my resume as he started the meeting out, "Hmmmm, Mr. Evans, I see you are an economics major. What do you think the impact of President Nixon's price controls will be on the economy?" I was frozen in fear. I had no idea what Mr. Boatwright's political persuasions were. If I said the price controls were bad and Boatwright was a Nixon fan, I was cooked. If I said they were good and Boatwright was an economics purest, I was cooked.

After stuttering, I remembered some old advice from my dad that, "The truth never hurts," so I simply told him what I believed, namely that price controls would not work long term because eventually the forces of demand/supply would take over. I said that price caps created disincentives for production and would eventually lead to shortages and worse yet, rapid inflation. Eventually time would tell that I was right but that was much later.

Fortunately, Mr. Boatwright must have liked my answer because the next week my mom answered the phone and it was Tom Connor. He offered me a job starting at $8,500 per year to join the management training program. My first day would be the Monday, July 9th, following the July 4th holiday that summer of 1973. I was elated as was my mom who thanked Mr. Connor profusely. In fact, she got so excited that I think half of her thank you was in Spanish.

With mom's help, I immediately went out and bought a bed and yes, my first chest of drawers, and I made arrangements to move to Columbia immediately with my fellow ATO brother Jimmy Burr into an apartment we rented in an area called St. Andrews. Since I only had the one suit, I also bought a reversible blazer which was blue on one side and black on the other so I could get by 3 days without looking like I was wearing the same suit. Jimmy and I found a truck, and we loaded our gear and off to Columbia we went. Little did I know that I was about to start a lifelong career in banking and that I would never have a single regret about not joining the Air Force. What I did know was that I had been granted an incredible opportunity, and I was singularly committed to working as hard as I could to make the absolute most of it.

Carlos Evans

Chapter 10

Bankers Trust Just Getting Started

I remember the excitement and promise of those early days like it was yesterday. The nation's economy had been booming and Columbia was no exception. Construction was exploding. Bankers Trust had a 20-story office building under construction called the Bankers Trust Tower that would be the tallest building in Columbia. In fact, the economy was booming so much that the Fed began rapidly raising interest rates with fed funds moving from around 6% in the summer to well above 10%. Clearly storm clouds were brewing, but I was naïve.

While I had an economics background, I was too excited about my new career to worry about anything. All I knew was that I had a great job with a company I was excited about. I was making $8,500 per year, more money than I had ever dreamed of even though after making rent payments and car payments there wasn't a huge amount left. To his credit, a dear friend and former ATO, Staes Clawson suggested we start saving, so out of my first paycheck I started putting away $50 every two weeks into a savings account.

Back then, the training program involved spending the first 30 days at the operations center on Greystone Blvd. where we read a giant pile of books on banking and credit. There was also a thorough review of the check processing center including bookkeeping and the computer system and learning how checks were processed. At the end of the 30 days, we turned in a white paper on everything we had seen and read. During that time at Greystone, I met three ladies who would later prove to be incredible resources: Mary Johnson, who was the head of bookkeeping, and her key lieutenant, Mary Hill, also Mozelle Boatwright (not related to John Boatwright), who was head of returns item processing.

I dove into the work in earnest, reading everything I could get my hands on, especially the Robert Morris Associates material on Credit. Back then, much emphasis was placed on the five Cs of credit: Conditions, Capital, Collateral, Capacity and Character. Of all the Cs, the most time was spent on Character and the belief that honorable people fulfilled their obligations.

There was also much discussion about past behavior being the best indicator of future behavior. I remember reflecting on my dad's Black Book and his lessons on who went in and who went out, and those lessons, too, had been all about Character. I remember vowing to myself that each and every loan I would ever make would be tested against those five C's with the biggest of the C's being Character.

After 30 days in the operations center, my next stop was a branch office where I spent 6 weeks serving as a teller, as well as learning how to open accounts and getting my first lessons in how to make consumer loans. Next, I spent 3 or 4 weeks in installment loan collections, with the final part of the program being a 6 month stint in the credit department in the bank's basement. There, I learned how to calculate credit ratios, spread financial statements and write credit analysis reports evaluating the merits of real situations. The management training process was somewhat flexible and would take about 9 months if a person was lucky, but usually closer to one year. At the end of their time in the credit department, the trainee would be placed wherever the bank had the greatest need. Usually, that would be in a branch, but the choicest assignment was to become a commercial loan officer on the commercial loan platform.

While I was at Greystone studying and writing my white paper, we had a meeting downtown with all the people in the management training program. I showed up early and sat in the lobby as I waited to go downstairs to the basement credit department where the meeting would be held. I remember watching the men on the loan platform, which was nothing more than three big, beautiful desks lined up in the open lobby with two guest chairs in front of each. I watched those men in suits as they talked with customers, the ones that didn't have customers dictating letters or credit memos then taking the cassettes over to the secretaries who were in a pool at the center.

I remember deciding right then and there that this was where I wanted to end up, making commercial loans. It was clear to me that the platform officers were the fighter pilots of the banking business and that making business loans was where the action was. Obviously, at that stage I knew nothing about making business loans, but that was what I wanted.

After watching for a few minutes, I went downstairs for the meeting, really just a question-and-answer session about the banking industry for our group of about 20 very young men all in suits. Since I was the rookie in the group, I decided to be like the "Wise Old Owl" and keep my mouth shut. Some of the men were already in branches and some were already on the loan platform. It was also very clear to me that Bankers Trust of SC was making a huge investment in very young people, particularly large for a bank its size. I remember one of the young men asking when Bankers Trust would go over 200 million in deposits. Mr. Herbert Upchurch who was executive vice president and the chief credit officer said, "Any week now."

I didn't fully comprehend it at the time, but Bankers Trust was actually a very small bank on the way up. All I could think about was that, as the junior man in the training program, all these people who had come before me had jumped ahead. I feared that maybe I joined too late. But again, I reflected on Dad's lessons in the store. "Don't worry about your station in life or where you are on the ladder. Keep your focus on doing the absolute best job possible in whatever you are asked to do." I resolved to follow his advice and work as hard as I could during my training and get all the knowledge I could. I wouldn't squander this opportunity like I had in high school and college.

Carlos Evans

Chapter 11

Sidetracked or So I Thought

After my stint at the operations center, there was a short visit downtown to meet with key bank executives—Jack Upchurch (Herbert Upchurch's son), the Columbia city executive; Murk Alexander, the senior lending officer; and Julian Turner the area executive. All three were in their late 20s or early 30s and were incredibly impressive.

In particular, Julian Turner impressed me. He was affable, funny, high energy, engaging and struck me as very bright. Julian had a way of taking something complex and making it simple. He described for me the difference between consumer lending and commercial lending as follows: He said a consumer loan was like selling a product off the shelf, a cookie cutter approach. Commercial banking was like selling a custom-tailored suit, each loan structured specifically for the client based on their cash flow and needs. While both types of loans were important to the business, selling tailor made suits would be infinitely more challenging. This sold me completely on my desire to ultimately find my way to the loan platform and be a commercial lender.

After the visit downtown, I headed to the airport branch in West Columbia where I would do my branch training. The airport branch was run by Bill Elmore, a very preppy guy who struck me as someone it would be very good to learn from. My initial impression turned out to be correct. Bill was very competent and one of the best branch managers in Columbia.

While I learned a great deal from Bill, perhaps the biggest thing I learned was how difficult it was to be a bank teller. The pressure of handling transactions quickly and accurately for customers and then balancing every day at 1 pm when we closed for lunch was heavy. When the lines would get long either at the drive-in window or inside the bank, the heat would be on to go fast, which unfortunately could lead to mistakes. Those mistakes would then have to be found before a teller could close their window, either after 1 pm each day or at 6 pm on Friday. Fridays were the worst because the volumes were heavy with paydays. At day's end on Friday, everyone was exhausted and wanted to go home. Unfortunately, if one teller was out of balance everyone had to stay until the mistake had been identified. That added to the pressure enormously because nobody wanted to be the cause of the problem.

When I had been in the branch for about 6 weeks, Bill Elmore came to me and said the West Columbia offices would be hosting the biannual officers get together. He needed someone to plan the event and execute it and asked me to take the project on. This was no surprise to me since trainees were often assigned odd jobs. Bottom line, whether it was running errands or washing cars, trainees did whatever they were asked to do.

In my case, hosting and executing a party was right up my alley since I had been doing this for 3 years as ATO rush chairman at Newberry. I set out to make the West Columbia officers party the very best ever and I succeeded. We had kegs of beer, people cooking hamburgers and hot dogs, a full bar with the best whiskey. All in all, a very nice affair. Several days after the party, Bill Elmore called me to say that Tom Connor, head of personnel, wanted to see me downtown immediately. He had no idea what it was about.

Reporting to Mr. Connor's office, I was introduced to Robert C. Gorham, the head of property management for the bank. It was a big sounding title, but at the time given the relatively small size of Bankers Trust, Mr. Gorham was essentially a one-man band. However, since the bank had a large construction project going on for the new tower, Mr. Gorham had been staffed with a full time trainee working on a special assignment to oversee the upfit of the five floors of bank space and also to plan and execute the move into the new offices. The person who had been in that role was a trainee named Bill Stevens, and since Bill had been at it about a year and wanted to get on with his career, they decided to let him go back to finish his training and replace him with me. For a second, the thought dawned on me that this assignment would delay my training, as well, but that thought only lasted a split second because I knew the only answer was to salute and ask when I would start.

The special assignment started the very next morning when I reported to Mr. Gorham's office on Lady Street across from the main bank, the same building where personnel was located. Mr. Gorham gave me a small office behind the water cooler. It was a very small office but all my own, which I thought was pretty cool. Mr. Gorham handed me Bill Stevens's files and told me to study them in advance of a meeting with Bill to review what had been done. The files contained pencil spreadsheets with budgets for upfit of each floor by department with numbers being plugged in to keep track by each budget line item as funds were spent. I quickly did the math in my head and realized that the total budget just for the upfit and furniture was $2.5 million. This was a staggering amount of money for me to comprehend at the time. I had absolutely no experience in construction or budgeting, so I asked Mr. Gorham how I was chosen to do the job. He simply said he'd been at the West Columbia Officers Party and seen that the party had been well executed so he asked for me to be assigned to do this job.

The next day I had the opportunity to meet with Bill Stevens and tour the construction site. I donned my hard hat which I would be wearing a lot over the next 12 months. The site was at the corner of Gervais and Sumter Streets, catty corner from the State Capital. The building was still very early stages, just a steel skeleton, and the floor slabs were being poured. There were no permanent elevators, only an outside construction elevator.

Stevens and I went to the construction trailer and met a man named Zan Kizer. Zan was the job superintendent working for the construction company, M.B. Kahn corporation owned by the Kahn Family of Columbia. Zan seemed to be a very capable guy. We would work very closely together over the next year and while at times there would be some tension due to the pressure of change orders, scheduling etc., he would prove to be a great person to work with and learn from. While I didn't know it at the time, later I learned that the building was owed by Central City General, a partnership with four investors: the construction company M.B. Kahn; the architects, a well known Columbia firm LBC&W (Lyles, Bissett, Carlisle, and Wolff); the McNair Law Firm; and BT Building Corporation, which was owned by the Bank.

My next stop with Bill Stevens was to go see Aubrey Parrot at Columbia Office and Supply Company (COS). Aubrey ran the design division of COS and was an incredibly interesting man. The best adjective I could use to describe him was that he was elegant. He was a very snappy, perhaps even cutting-edge dresser. For example, he often wore bow ties as well as ties that had texture and looked more like a sock. He also wore cardigan sweaters and sometimes smoked a pipe. His handwriting was wonderfully precise, and he would constantly send handwritten notes along with the bills I had to process for payment and plug into the budget spreadsheets. He loved to play tennis and we would later play a lot together.

Most of all, however, Aubrey Parrot and Robert Gorham were both very loving family men, who were great role models for me. They were very different in their own way and committed to their work, however they both knew how to strike the right balance between work and family life. Mr. Gorham had a love of antiques and would travel extensively to antique shows on the weekends. While committed to work during the week, on weekends it was all about his outside interests and family. Aubrey was much the same way, but his leanings were more toward tennis and having an active social life. Working with those two men taught me little about banking but a great deal about life. In particular, Aubrey taught me a lot about the finer things of life and trust me, I had a lot to learn.

As in most office buildings, the tenant receives allowances for the tenant upfit. At Bankers Trust Tower the tenants could elect to have 'building standard' carpet, wall coverings, acoustical ceilings, lighting etc., or they could customize and get a credit from the landlord (in this case Central City General) for 'building standard' allowances. In the case of the five floors of bank space it was as far from building standard as one could get since everything was customized and Aubrey was a design genius. The bank would have teak parquet on the floors, Italian marble and grass cloth on the walls, different types paneling in the offices including wormy chestnut, kevazingo, oak, and maple.

The lighting was also incredibly customized, especially the boardroom and main lobby where a huge marble wall was backlit to bathe the space in a warm glow. The travel department (Bankers Trust was one of the few banks with a Travel Dept.) had backlit colorful batik panels of modern art.

Throughout the five floors, the style would be a combination of traditional and modern. The boardroom's huge table was topped with a slab of Italian marble that sat atop a curved teak base. Above the table, an elaborate cluster of backlit gold pipes resembled a sunburst, which was the bank's logo. Mixed with the boardroom's modernity was a beautiful antique breakfront that Aubrey had found in Atlanta. The breakfront had originally been owned by the Middleton Family in Charleston, and Arthur Middleton had been one of the original signers of the Declaration of Independence. Aubrey's ability mixed the bank's existing furniture along with the new in a way that made it all hang together. Aubrey's artistry combined antique oriental rugs, Greek statues, paintings by modern artists like Jasper Johns and fabric wall hangings from other cutting-edge artists. As the month's rolled by and the project slowly came together I began to see just how stunning the final product was going to be.

There were other subcontracts in addition to the tenant upfit and furnishings. For example, a big contract with the Mosler Safe Company dealt with the vault, the safe deposit boxes in the vault, the TV drive up windows, which were cutting-edge at the time, and the entire security system for the bank. Another contract with Millen Moving and Storage in West Columbia dealt with the move out of the old buildings into the new one. The move was complex as all the existing furniture had to be tagged to say exactly where it was going on the day of the move. The furniture that was not going to be used was tagged to go into storage. The plan for moving the safe deposit boxes out of the old bank was troublesome as it had to be done in one night with heavily armed security personnel and auditors watching the process every step of the way. Mr. Gorham reminded me that the liability was infinite because we had no way of knowing what was in those safe deposit boxes. Millen Moving and Storage proved to be an incredible partner, and they would ultimately move me and my family four times over the course of my career.

While my tower job was certainly busy and fulfilling, I also enjoyed my travels with Mr. Gorham. He was kind enough to allow me to see other aspects of managing the bank's buildings and leases even thought that was not totally within my job description. Having come to Columbia from Greenwood as part of the original Bank of Greenwood management team, he knew the bank inside and out.

Mr. Gorham took me to offices all over the state, in Charleston, Aiken,

North Augusta, Greenwood and all the little towns in between. In the early fall of 1973, Bankers Trust announced the acquisition of the People's Bank of Greenville, which effectively doubled the size of the Bank to over $500 million in total assets, so we began to visit those branches as well. However, even though I loved my work, there was always the constant reminder that I was getting behind my peers who were coming off the training program to sit on commercial platforms or run branches.

In the fall of 1973, the economy really began to slow. The oil embargo created shortages in gasoline, and lines at filling stations became the norm. When people would stop in to fill their tanks, they would often also fill portable fuel containers. The combination of higher interest rates and limited travel was taking a huge bite out of the economy. Bankers Trust was not immune. We had grown rapidly and had significant exposure to a number of large real estate deals, mostly in Columbia. As we entered recession, bank failures began to pop up around the country, and while I was not in a mainstream banking job I could sense the pressure mounting; there was definitely an element of tension in the air. Sometime during 1974, the $138 million American Bank and Trust in Orangeburg went under. It was a very large bank failure in a small state like South Carolina.

Since I was coordinating tenant upfit for every department in the bank, I had regular meetings with the key executives in each area to monitor progress. Along the way, they all wanted tours of the building—people like Virgil Duffie, head of the trust department; Gary Page, head of planning; Jack Weeks, vice chairman and head of audit; Jim Finch, head of operations; Winfield Sapp, head of correspondent banking; Bobby Morman, head of travel; Bob Isbell, head of marketing; and even Hootie Johnson, the CEO. I didn't realize it at the time, but I was making valuable connections and creating relationships or at least name recognition with the leadership of the bank, something my peers did not have.

Since I was still a trainee, and since I sat a stone's throw from Hootie's office, I got calls from time to time to do special things for Hootie, perhaps give a tour to some important person or run an errand. Some of those tasks were menial, but I didn't mind a bit; in those days it was "Yes, sir!" to anything and everything. One day Hootie's secretary, Margie Shelly, called and said, "Mr. Johnson wants you to pick up some very important people at Owens Field." (Owens Field was the private downtown airport.)

She said they were coming in for a very important meeting, but before I went to get the men, Hootie also wanted me to run out to his Spring Valley home to get his glasses. She added, "Mister Johnson wants you to take his car."

I saluted and said, "Yes, ma'am!"

Margie ended by reminding me that the meeting was time sensitive, and I needed to be punctual.

When I hurried down to get in Mr. Johnson's car, I saw that it was a big black Lincoln Continental. It had one of those new telescoping steering wheels that allowed you to adjust both height and depth. When I got in the car it was stuck in a position far forward of my short reach. I was running short on time, so I didn't waste time trying to figure it out. I made it to his house and got his glasses from his wife Pierrene, who was always incredibly nice to me, then I raced as fast as I could all the way across town to Owens Field. I made good time until I got to the Rosewood section of Columbia where I got to a train track just as a very long, very slow train stopped the traffic. I was about to have a heart attack because time was running short, so I raced away hoping get ahead of the train and find a parallel street where I could cross.

The steering wheel was still sticking straight up in the air outside my reach, which compounded the problem as I frantically raced up and down the streets of Columbia, running out of time. Fortunately, I found another crossing and was able to get through it before the arm came down. I managed to get to Owens field just as the visitors plane was landing so I was safe, but unfortunately I was soaked with sweat.

When the visitors got to the car, I realized that it was Federal Judge Falcon Hawkins and one of his lawyers. Judge Hawkins, whom I had met on a weekend trip to Charleston, was the father of Rick Hawkins, one of my KA friends who was one year behind me. Judge Hawkins took one look at me and said with a smile "Sir, you shouldn't let things get to you that bad." Then, with a smile he added, "By the way you can push this button here and stop trying to drive this thing like it's a Mack Truck." The steering wheel dropped to a normal place, and I was very relieved.

In late summer or early fall of 1974, the big day came for the move into the new building. We were going to do it over a weekend starting on Friday after the bank closed with everything in place to start business in our new home on Monday morning. We planned to work pretty much around the clock, starting with the safe deposit box move on Friday night, as well as taking the executive offices from the mezzanine of the old bank to the 19th floor of the Tower. Since we were getting the furniture loaded faster than the boxes, Mr. Gorham and I decided to split up. I would go to the new building and supervise unloading the executive floor, while Mr. Gorham would remain at the vault until all the boxes were loaded sometime early Saturday.

Everything had started well, but when I came up the elevator to the 19th floor my heart broke. An inch of water shimmered on the floor, and the ceiling had caved in places from all the water coming through. When I opened the stairwell door, I could see the water cascading down from the 20th floor so I knew the problem had to be coming from the Summit Club, the new private dining club on the top of the building scheduled to open in about a month.

I immediately called Zan Kizer, who fortunately was at home and able to come right away. The problem was that one of the plumbers working in the Summit Club kitchen had broken a pipe, but not realizing it was broken he had left for the day. Overnight, the leak had grown bigger and bigger until it became a raging flood. Fortunately, Zan Kizer was able to turn off water, then called the acoustical ceiling company, my former employer Bonitz Insulation Company . They promised to have three crews on the job the next morning to replace all the damaged ceiling squares on the 19th floor.

That left us with the water on the floor, and we needed to get rid it of very quickly or risk losing the teak parquet floors, which would buckle if the water stayed on them too long. I was able to get my old fraternity brother, John Paul Whitaker, on the phone that night. His family owned Whitaker Floor Covering in Newberry. John was a godsend, and he sent their whole crew at 12 pm that night complete with vacuums for sucking all the water off the floors and out of the carpet, as well as big heaters to dry everything out.

Mr. Millen sent his entire three crews to assist, helping with anything and everything whether it was in the moving contract or not. Mr. Gorham and I did not sleep that whole weekend, but by 8 am on Monday, we had everything put back together, all the old furniture in place, all of the new furniture in place, all the files in their proper cabinets. Hootie and the executive floor moved as planned. Other than some rumors about a water problem, they had no idea what had happened.

One of the benefits of the move was that Mr. Gorham and I relocated to a small suite of two offices and a conference room on the second floor along with personnel and marketing. My office even had a window overlooking the capital next to Mr. Gorham's corner office. Offices were rare in those days for junior officers and nonexistent for trainees, so it was perceived as a real benefit.

Once we were moved and settled, our next task was to complete and close out all the expenses for each department, also to help marketing plan the grand opening, which would be a huge affair and the highlight of the fall in Columbia. It would take place after the Summit Club opening. Bob Isbell, head of marketing, had been planning this event for some time. The plan was to have five nights of parties—one night for all the correspondent bankers, and then a separate night for each region in the state, culminating with a huge final blowout for the Columbia Region.

The quest list was a Who's Who from every corner of South Carolina and beyond. There would be young girls in full evening attire to give tours of each floor of the building with the tours ending up on the 20th floor in the Summit Club for a full-blown cocktail party complete with a band and dancing. The trainees would serve as parking boys, and they dressed us up in the most ridiculous lime green tuxedos full of ruffles for cuffs and ruffles where the studs normally go on the front of a tuxedo shirt. It was almost comical. With our long hair and sideburns (worn in the 70s style), we looked like a bunch of guys going out for an evening at Joe Namath's Bachelors III Club in New York. Aside from the horrible clothes the trainees had to wear as carhops, the week of the parties were the talk of the town, and the building and offices were absolutely stunning in every respect. Aubrey Parrott had people oohing and aaahing, and he was Hootie's guest of honor every night, as he should have been.

For me, I felt a lot of satisfaction during that week, knowing I had played a minor role in helping put together a first-rate event for the bank. The new headquarters would be a suitable home from which the bank could capitalize on the growth about to come into the state as we emerged from the recession. Everyone in Columbia knew that Hootie and his bank had arrived, and the fantastic new building was the talk of the town if not the State. Although I never asked, I suspect that was exactly the reaction Hootie had wanted.

However great the parties and celebrations, they had also been a time when I had watched my peers entertain their lending customers, and thus they had reinforced my need to get on with my banking career. Mr. Gorham asked me to stay and assume a permanent role in his properties division. He even offered me more pay. As much as I loved the man, I wanted to be a banker; telling Mr. Gorham that I could not accept his offer became quite emotional. This was a man that had been by my side every step of my career up to that point. He had never been critical and had always been there when I needed support or advice, and he had even helped me buy my first suits other than the one my mother helped me buy. It was truly one of the most miserable things I ever had to do. When I finally summoned the courage and told him no, he made it easy for me. He simply smiled and said he'd expected me to refuse.

At that point, I had been in the training program 18 months, and by the time I went back and finished my credit training it would be almost two years since I had joined the bank. All my peers were already well along in their careers. I thought my assignment with Mr. Gorham had caused me to drop behind the pack, but later on I came to realize that on several levels, maybe I had actually gotten ahead.

Chapter 12

Back In The Training Program

Sometime toward the end of 1974, I returned to what was supposed to be an accelerated program to finish my training. Before I talk about that, I should clarify several points. Several times I have mentioned my concerns about dropping behind my peers. These concerns stemmed from the fact that I had been working 18 months and was not even close to being an official banker. It was not about being in some type of competition with my peers but about getting on with my career. Due to my dad's early advice, I had always been a proponent of focusing on doing my job in the best possible way and not just trying to climb the ladder. I believed that if I did a great job, then that hard work would create the next opportunity, and that belief never wavered.

I should also note that the whole time I was working on the building project I was reading everything I could get my hands on about all types of lending—construction lending, receivable lending, inventory lending and the nuances of working capital. So, on one level my training never stopped, however, the formal piece remained in limbo.

At this point I should add that while the building project somewhat removed me from the mainstream, during that year and a half I met many of my teammates who became great friends and remain so today. People like Tom Anderson, Joel Smith, Roger Whaley, John Crabtree, Frank Knox, Frank Chisholm, Bob Howard, Ed Kesser, Mark Johnson, John Riddick, and Richard Rabb, just to mention a few. This was a great group of very fine young people the bank had recruited. In retrospect, I can see now that one of Hootie's recipes for success was to bring in energetic young people, empower them early, and give them lots of room to sink or swim. That was part of the corporate culture Hootie created. I didn't know it at the time, but further north in Charlotte, North Carolina a man named Hugh McColl was using the same recipe at North Carolina National Bank (NCNB). The fact that both Hootie and Hugh McColl were pursuing their progressive, high growth strategies in the same region, at the same time, added a tremendous dynamism to banking in the Southeast in the last quarter of the 20th Century, and I was lucky to be part of it.

To be given such latitude and flexibility at a young age and so early in my career was a huge motivator. That opportunity to have significant responsibility when we were still young made all of us feel important and part of something extra special. I made a mental note that going forward I would always try to pay special attention to bringing younger people along.

When I returned to the training program, I first did a few weeks in consumer lending, then moved to the basement in the credit department where a lot had changed. For one thing, we were no longer housed in the low slung non-descript building on Main Street but now in a glorious new building where the interior was essentially a work of art. The other thing that had changed was we now had a female management trainee by the name of Alice Holler.

Alice was a beautiful young lady, smart, quick, elegant, and she became a good friend during my stint in credit. I believe that she left banking and went on to become a doctor. She was one of the first females to come into a bank officer training program in what traditionally had been a male dominated environment. Aside from being a visionary in bringing in young people, Hootie also championed diversity before it became a national focus, bringing in women as well as African Americans like Clente Fleming and Tony Grant, and just like he did with the rest of us, giving them lots of responsibility.

On this last point, years later when Hootie ended up in the national spotlight over the Martha Burke situation at Augusta National when he was the club chairman, I found it interesting how he was portrayed by the media. The facts are that Hootie Johnson all his life worked hard to help disadvantaged people. He worked hard to ease race relations along with Governor Bob McNair after the horrible killings in Orangeburg in the late 60s. We were among the first banks and public companies to have an African American board member. Hootie was on the board of Benedict College, a Historically Black Institution of Higher Education at a time when a White serving on such a board was unusual.

While Hootie was neither a Democrat nor a Republican, his views on social justice were definitely progressive. For Hootie, the central issue at Augusta National was his belief that a private club had the right to admit who it wanted at a time of its choosing. He was not a man who liked being told what to do or when to do it. I believe his comment was, "We will not succumb to the point of a bayonet." In the end, one of the first women admitted into membership in Augusta was Darla Moore, a close ally of Hootie's. While Hootie was a very private person he was someone I knew fairly well, and I believe that when he felt the time was right, he would have been very supportive of female members.

After a quick tour of duty in consumer lending on the first floor of the new main office, it was down to the basement for intensive credit training. This is where I would learn how to break down financial statements, and to compute credit ratios like debt-to-worth, current ratio, inventory and receivable turnover, just to mention a few. I also learned how to write credit review memos, annual reviews and prepare books of loans to be reviewed by the various committees. Mr. Herbert Upchurch was the senior credit officer and a young University of South Carolina (USC) MBA. His chief lieutenant, W. David Rhodes was in charge of the trainees. David would later become a dear friend and would teach me a lot about credit. These were busy days full of learning new things and comparing notes with the other trainees like Alice Holler.

Some of the concepts were hard to grasp and talking to someone like Alice who was very smart was always very helpful. The credit department was in the basement right next to the vault, and it included a huge file room with four huge, electronic, state of the art, revolving file cabinets that I had installed as part of the move to the new building. These fireproof cabinets would hold duplicate credit files for every commercial borrower in the system complete with financial statements, spreads, annual reviews and credit memos from the officers themselves that read like mini novels.

I found all this information incredibly interesting, but I also knew it was very useful in giving lenders a deep understanding of each customer, their history with the bank, also their individual habits, quirks and management styles. I decided right then and there that I would try to write the most complete memos possible to make sure that whoever followed me had the benefit of all that history. The memos would give the background of the customer, what business they were in, current challenges as well as opportunities. The memos were the product of all that dictating done on the lending platforms. All the memos were initialed at the bottom by the officers who created them in order to authenticate them. I can still remember all the initials. NWS for N. Winfield Sapp; JGPB for John Boatwright; JBT for Julian Turner; RBW for Roger B. Whaley; JAS III for Joel Smith; TPA for Thomas P. Anderson just to mention a few.

One of the things that became clear to all of us was the important role the bank played in economic and business development in the communities where it operated. This was a hallmark of Mr. Dewey Johnson's State Bank and Trust and was carried forth by his two sons Hootie and Wellsman. In the early days of the bank, Mr. Dewey Johnson was a heavy supporter of the agriculture industry because that was mostly what existed in his market. As a byproduct of that, many of our customers were farmers producing a wide range of products: cotton, soybeans, corn, cattle, dairy, peaches, poultry, and eggs, etc.

Then with the Peoples Bank Merger came a heavier mix of industrial borrowers like textiles. I would read through the credit files for hours, sopping up everything I could about our customers and their businesses. However, one thing from all that information was clear: South Carolina was a very poor state. Millionaires were a rare commodity and mostly concentrated in the textile Industry. Almost all the bank's customers were very small undercapitalized businesses that were hanging on by a thread.

This might have been the current state of things, but the message was clear from Hootie and Wellsman: As had been the case with their father, Dewey Johnson, the bank's mission was to help improve things for the communities where we did business and for the customers we served. While that mission was deemed to be the right thing to do and constantly preached within the bank, there was also an element of self-interest because if our customers and communities did better, the bank would do better.

In this way, Bankers Trust would be the source of desperately needed capital for borrowers throughout the state. Unlike the more established

SCN, First National and C&S, we would be more innovative, more willing to take risk with the lesser known names, and essentially a better partner for individuals and companies. We were people on a mission, and we thrived on it. Also, as I was beginning to learn, there was a man in North Carolina named Hugh McColl who was also feeding his troops that same cocktail for success.

Carlos Evans

Chapter 13

The Great American

Along with my banking career, my personal life was moving along as well. Sometime in the spring of 1975, I took the big step of buying my first house. 1561 Brockwall Drive had a small kitchen, living room-dining room combination, a small den, 2 bedrooms and 1 bath, and it was about 1200 square feet. It cost $ 29,000, and I was able to buy it with a 95% FHA loan. The $2,000 or so down payment came from the money I had been saving every two weeks. I believe the payments were about $250 per month, which I could hardly afford but was able to swing by having two roommates move in. Each paid me $75 per month for rent.

One of those roommates was Ralph Turnage an ATO fraternity brother. The other was Larry Tyler, a transplant from Tyler Texas and also a trainee/branch manager. Owning my own house was a big deal for me, as well as a big step. But the even bigger impact would be from getting to know my next-door neighbor, who would become one of my best friends and who at 95 still is today.

Elden Walker lived to my right, in a small, white brick house with black shutters. His yard was immaculate, perfectly manicured, with beautiful plants and shrubs. Elden and Harriett Ann had three children all in their very early teens: David, Bruce and Betsy with David being the oldest. When I moved in, Elden was taking down a huge pine tree all by himself. He was hard at work, having rigged a system using a car jack with a nylon strap wrapped around the tree. I realized that, because the tree was leaning toward his house, what he was doing was clever.

The strap was anchored to another tree with the jack in between. Elden would chop a little, then jack a little, increasing the tension and slowly, ever so slowly, pull the tree away from his house, so that when it finally came down, it would be toward the street rather than onto his house. When it fell as intended, he was able to cut it up into small pieces and carry them off.

Obviously, Elden was very busy that day as was I, and we had little time to talk. I remember thinking that this 49-year-old family man must have thought I was his worst nightmare, and that he was about to be tormented by a fraternity house with 3 single men in their early 20s moving in next door. My concerns turned out to be totally wrong. Elden, his wife Harriett Ann, and their entire family would become dear friends. Elden was the plant manager at Shakespeare which was a fishing rod company.

He was a do-it-yourselfer, and he would teach me all I would ever need to know about fixing things and doing stuff around the house, such as how to root and replant azaleas, camellias and other plants. He taught me how to enjoy my free time with Crown Royal, ginger ale, and a teaspoon of lemon. He even taught me how to buy stocks. But more than all of that, he would be a wonderful role model on how to be a good family man and a loving father and husband. Elden was like a second father to me, and in many respects, he was the best example I can think of on how to be the best family man possible. Elden was an ex-marine, had a Purple Heart, and as I would later learn, had been a hero. He was a Great American, and I would later nickname him that when I would speak of him with family and friends. He truly is the Great American and the epitome of that generation that built this country after saving us from Hitler and Imperial Japan.

As the summer of 1975 waned, I finished the training program and was anxious for my first assignment. By now, I had been with the bank over two years, and I was hoping for a job as a commercial lender on the loan platform, however the then city executive, Jack Upchurch, told me I was going to be the branch manager at the Dentsville branch in Northeast Columbia. Clearly, it was a little bit of a disappointment.

I asked Jack if they would let me make commercial loans in Dentsville if I found them in my market. Jack conferred with Joel Smith, who was the senior lender in Columbia at the time, and they both agreed to let me make business loans. More than that, they encouraged me to do so.

As a parting comment, Jack smiled and said, "Carlos, you know the Dentsville Office takes care of our customers in Spring Valley, which is where Hootie lives. Remember, a lot of your customers will be friends of Hootie and Pierenne. Don't screw up."

So with that reminder and piece of advice, off I went!

Carlos Evans

Chapter 14

Dentsville My First P&L

The Dentsville office was on the northeast side of Columbia in a growing area that was soon to have a large new mall. When I arrived in the Summer of 1975, a recent ex-trainee named Ed Kesser was the branch manager, and the assistant manager was a long-term employee who had worked her way up in the bank. Ed was being promoted and moved to the loan platform downtown, which was a path I hoped to follow.

Back in those days, we had profit center accounting down to the branch level, although the accounting was rough and not fully loaded for funds transfer pricing. (A fully loaded accounting system gives the branch credit for the loans they make over the bank's cost of funds, and the branch earns further credits for the deposits the branch generates.) In any case, the branch was the first actual business I got to run that had a profit and loss statement for which I was fully responsible. The branch had 5 tellers: 3 on the front counter in the branch, 2 on the drive-in window. There was also a new account representative to open accounts and order checks, as well as the assistant branch manager for a total of 8 employees including me.

One of the first things I did upon arrival was to reorganize the filing system and read all the files. This was a crash course on the history of every customer who had borrowed from the bank and was a process I would repeat every step along the way in my career. I believed learning as much as I could about every account would save time in the long run, so I read every file and made new file folders with a clasp for financial information on the left and credit information like credit reports and credit memos on the right. Very early on I decided that being proactive with customers would allow me to respond to their loan requests immediately or a short period of time after we met in person.

For example, when a customer would call for an appointment to discuss a loan I would ask them if anything changed since their last application, and I would go ahead and run the credit report before their arrival so I would have everything I needed to say yes or no when they were there. As the storehouse of everything about my customers, the files would be critically important just like the ones downtown that were duplicates for all commercial customers.

I also determined that I would put into practice the 5 C's in their order of importance. Character, Credit (prior history), Capital (equity or skin in the game), Conditions (of the loan) and Collateral. Also, from the very beginning, I made the decision to spend a lot of time outside the office calling on business customers and getting to know the market for the little community surrounding my branch. Lastly, in keeping with Mr. Johnson's desire to give back to the community, in addition to supporting the local United Way through payroll deduction I joined the local Optimist Club which donated money to local causes by selling Christmas trees.

On the last point, I think it is worth saying that community involvement has always been part of the role bankers were expected to play. This was especially true for the Johnson's bank going all the way back to Mr. Dewey and the belief he instilled that the bank would rise or fall based on the overall health of the places it did business. One of the precursors to having economic health was to be a place where people wanted to move to and live. To be such a place, a community needed a very strong health and human services infrastructure, something that required more than just tax dollars. The participation of the community, or "People Doing Good" was critical to creating the right environment for growth. While somewhat self-serving, we called it "Doing The Right Thing While Doing Good Economically."

Since my retirement, I have often thought about how banking has changed. While I feel sure that in many banks this is still part of the mantra, in others it has clearly been replaced by too much focus on bottom line profits and keeping the regulators happy. Clearly, management has played a role in this shift, but the regulators bear part of the responsibility as well.

In addition to getting the monthly profit and loss statement (P&L),

which showed we were making about $2,000 per month, there were 8 other reports that evaluated all the branches in the Bankers Trust system and ranked them from top to bottom. The reports tracked both the number and dollar volume of account openings across checking accounts, saving accounts, installment or consumer loans and finally commercial loans.

Tracking the number of new accounts measured the velocity of new business, while tracking the dollar volume measured the quality of what was being opened. These were both very important measures and were reports I would follow for the rest of my career. Much later on, I would attribute the problems at Wells Fargo to the failure of one of the biggest banks in the country to understand the importance of tracking not only quantity but also the quality of new business.

In addition to the regular monthly reports that came out the first week of every month, a balance sheet came out daily. Roughly speaking, at the time I took over the Dentsville office, we held about $2 million in deposits and about $1 million in loans. Given my desire to do the best job possible and become one of the best branch managers in the Bankers Trust system (i.e. one of the "Best Hands"), I resolved to work hard to get the Dentsville branch results to the top of each of the 8 Velocity/Volume and Volume/Quality reports. Over time I managed to do just that. In the process the branch became more and more profitable, so that when I left after three years the branch was making about $10,000 per month or $120,000 per year, something I could barely comprehend when I started.

During the first 6 months things were going extremely well, business was starting to boom and the Dentsville office was near the top, if not at the top of all eight of the Velocity/Volume reports. By building the branch's balance sheet by growing loans and deposits, it was clear that we were starting to become more profitable, and the branch was getting busier and busier. It was also becoming clear that my strategy of doing all my due diligence up front and having great files to help me make decisions quickly was paying off. My reputation was getting out into the community that we were the place to do business whether you were a consumer or a business. My time outside the bank and my time helping do good in the community selling Christmas trees for the Optimist Club were also helping, so things seemed to be going well.

Other than the fact I was working my head off either outside calling on prospects or strapped to the desk, everything seemed great. Unfortunately, this meant I was spending very little time with the tellers. I was about to learn a very valuable lesson in management and of being responsible for employees which, after a very painful experience, would help me later on.

One of the most stressful things for tellers is when their account doesn't balance because everyone has to stay until the problem is found or written off and chalked up to teller error. This could be caused by a number of things like a miscount and/or giving a customer too much money. This could happen anytime but tends to be most common on Fridays or during holidays when volumes are heavy. In the case of the Dentsville office, we had been experiencing a number of these situations and the write offs had been large—$1,000 here and $500 with seemingly no particular pattern or individual teller. To say this was creating tension would be a huge understatement. Often, I would come back to the office after making calls and find that we were out of balance. All the tellers would frown at me, and it seemed that the tension and hostility was directed toward me. I was too stupid and naive to ask what was wrong, so the environment continued to worsen until one day the new accounts representative and I were staying late to do some work, and she gave me the shock of my short business career.

Sandra Bryan was a wonderful person. While her title was new accounts representative, she was eager to learn and do more. For example, she learned how to type, and she also learned to use the dictating machine as I began to make more and more commercial loans. By expanding her own skills, she made it possible for me to dictate the credit memos versus having to write them longhand. She also wanted to learn how to make consumer loans and was rapidly gaining the necessary knowledge. Bottom line, she was wonderful, and aside from the head teller, Jeanine Hill, she was a critical employee.

On that night we were working late, she asked me why was I sending memos to personnel saying that everyone in the branch needed to be fired because of all the times we had been out of balance. I was totally flabbergasted because there was no such thing going on! I pointed out to Sandra that by this point she was typing all my memos, and she knew I had never written anything like that. She responded that she had been told the memos to personnel were handwritten. I asked who told her, and she said it had been the assistant branch manager.

I was totally blown away. I asked Sandra who else knew about this, to which she replied, "Everyone." Right away, the light bulb went off. I was being undermined by the assistant who no doubt wanted my job and was disgruntled that she had not been promoted. I assured Sandra that there had been no such memos, to which she responded, "I thought so."

I asked her to keep quiet until I could talk to Jeannine Hill, the head teller, and determine what to do. The next morning I spoke to Jeannine ,a wonderful lady who confirmed everything Sandra had told me the night before. As with Sandra, I asked her to say nothing as well until I could decide on my course of action. Next, I called Hennie Dawson, the branch coordinator and then had a conversation with Jack Upchurch, the city executive. I told them both that the assistant manager had been an exemplary employee, however, she had broken my trust, an act that had been confirmed by two of my key employees. My announcement set off a number of issues. Personnel had to be brought in, and my managers encouraged me not to overreact. My response was that banking was a business based on trust, and that the lie had not been a small one. It had been a big lie, and I would no longer work with this person. Either she went or I would go, simple as that.

The next day, Hennie called to say that she would be transferred to another office. I asked how fast, and he said it would be done that week, to which I responded fine.

After this employee left, things at the branch improved markedly. Every week I would spend lots of time helping the tellers, and I even ran a teller window on busy days. I would never again allow myself to become so removed from my employees to the extent that I didn't know what was going on. Interestingly, with the assistant manager's transfer, the out of balance conditions became much less frequent, and things began to run much more smoothly as the branch became a wonderfully cohesive team.

A year or so later, I learned that my former assistant manager had been fired for "audit issues." This set off several alarms in my mind, so I went back and looked at all the days when our tellers had been out of balance. On the days preceding most out of balance conditions, the teller who'd had the problem had been given a surprise audit by the assistant manager.

Surprise audits are common in a bank. Essentially, they are a way to keep the tellers honest since no one knows when they will occur. When a surprise audit takes place, the auditor steps into the window, closes it, and does a count to see if it balances. The teller has to stand away from the window so if something is missing, there will be an immediate out of balance condition. While I have no proof of what took place, my conclusion was that the assistant manager was taking money during her surprise audits but reporting that the window was in balance. This would cause an out of balance condition to occur the next day when the teller balanced.

I was very thankful that I had drawn the line and asked for the person to be removed. Even though my reasons had nothing to do with the audits and everything to do with basic honesty, I was relieved to know I had made the right decision. However, at the same time I had learned several valuable lessons 1.) Never become distant from my people. 2.) If I had a bad apple, I needed to take it out of the barrel! Fortunately, I would experience only one other time when I would have a trust issue with an employee and be forced to act.

By mid 1976, things were really starting to roll at my little branch in Dentsville. So much so that we were initiating plans to open a branch of my branch in the new mall. I was working on this project with my old boss, Mr. Gorham, as well as my friend, Aubrey Parrot, at Columbia Office Supply. The economy was recovering from the recession, and this was providing a tailwind to everything we were doing. Bankers Trust was continuing to make acquisitions—one in Florence, and another in Beaufort/Hilton Head. On a personal level, I was enjoying my home at Brockwall Drive and especially enjoying my growing relationship with The Great American, Elden Walker. However, I did not have any kind of female companionship and that really bothered me. I'd had a serious relationship my junior year in college back in 1972 but none since. Back in those days people would often get married in college or shortly thereafter, but I was nowhere close.

Fortunately, about that time my teammate at work and roommate on Brockwall, Larry Tyler from Tyler Texas, reintroduced me to regular Sunday church. Although, we were not regular members anywhere, the Sunday services at different places reinforced in my mind that God had a plan for me and that somehow, some way, that plan would play out as long as I put my trust in Him. That return to worship proved to be a great comfort then, and it continued to be a continual source of comfort and strength for the rest of my life.

As time went on, I continued to make more and more commercial loans as I built a book of commercial loan business with entrepreneurs. During that time, there were two critical lessons I learned involving consumer loans that would relate to how I approached lending for the rest of my career.

The first one involved a young lady in early 1976 who came into the branch to apply for a car loan. She was a single mom and working mother who desperately needed to be able to buy a used car because the one she owned had totally broken down. She had terrible credit, which she said was due to her ex-husband. When married, she had signed several loans for a car he had purchased, as well as a boat. She explained that his spending habits and the fact that he had constantly gotten over his head in debt had been a big part of their marriage problem. Given the fact she had signed the loans, all of those problems were showing up under her credit history. She also had unpaid medical bills and credit cards debt.

Until that point, I had followed the 5 C's almost like they were some sort of religion. The thought of doing something out of the box and going against my 5 C policy concerned me. However, the more I talked to the lady, the more convinced I became that she was honest and well intentioned. Besides that, it was clear to me she was desperate and that she needed the car to continue to work and care for her children. The more I thought about it the more I kept coming back to the fact as lenders we were indoctrinated on the need to use good judgement in every loan we made. I also kept coming back to this notion of the big C for Character. I told the lady I would do a little more research and call her back.

The more I dug the more I became convinced the lady was telling the truth. I spoke directly to her employer who said she was an A+ employee. I spoke to some of the creditors who confirmed that it was the husband's car or boat and that the lady had tried to separate her name from the history. Ultimately, I decided that while the credit history was terrible there was an explanation and the other C's of Collateral, Capacity and Conditions were good and the big C of Character was very good. I went ahead and made the loan, even though it was only $2,000 it would be one of the most gratifying I would ever make.

Over the remaining two years I was in the branch, I would continue to watch this woman improve her station in life. I watched her progress in her job, do well for her family, and later become a bigger customer when she bought another car. More importantly, I would file away in my mind that I needed to rely on my God given judgment to make decisions that would benefit the bank and our customers even if they did not fit squarely within all of the boxes. I would also begin to fully understand the power of what I was doing, how it could change people's lives for the better, and how the bank could benefit as our customers succeeded.

The second lesson involved a small entrepreneur who owned an Exxon filling station in Downtown Columbia. Let's just say his name was Mr. Smith. He applied for a $5,000 second mortgage to do some repairs on his home. He had a previous car loan that was only 4 months old but was paying as agreed. I had tax returns on file, and they showed his business was making good money. His home had good equity so I made the loan and in the interest of time I did not pull a new credit report since the one I had was less than 5 months old. Almost from day one the loan was a disaster, and Mr. Smith became a slow pay borrower. After about 3 months, I ran the credit bureau report and was horrified to learn that Mr. Smith had obtained two other loans in short order just before the one I made him. I saw my career going down before my eyes. I had been in the branch just a little over 6 months, and a $5,000 charge off beside my name would have been a disaster. I could not sleep at night and so I resolved to make it right.

To my great benefit, Mr. Smith in the end turned out to be a man of good Character. I am not sure what caused his problems, whether living above his means, gambling, or what. While I had to go see him to collect payments each month, he paid. Also, by going to his place of business I made sure that we got paid before the other lenders. I even figured out that Mondays after paydays were best because those days his business had the most cash in the bank. My experience with Mr. Smith taught me two valuable lessons. First, I would never again short circuit due diligence. I should have run the new credit report even though we had one 5 months old. I would also learn that the best time to get paid is when the customer has lots of cash. This lesson would prove useful several years later on a much bigger scale.

In addition to the above two very practical lessons about banking, I was also making progress learning how to make commercial loans. I was learning by doing because I was beginning to make a lot of commercial loans in the branch. I also made a big effort to continue my reading as well as attending any and all training the bank would give me access to through the South Carolina Bankers Association or any other organization. I was becoming more convinced than ever that commercial banking was my future and that I had a particular knack for it. I could hold numbers in my head and make calculations on all the ratios without needing the spreadsheets. I was also rapidly understanding the power to do good that came with helping a business expand.

It was one thing to help a consumer, like the lady who needed the car loan. However, when I made a business loan to help a company expand, I was also helping all their employees by creating more opportunity for them. It was also clear to me that these businesses were giving back to the Dentsville community. My branch sponsored a little league baseball team as did many of the businesses around us, and that was one way it was easy to see that if the business boats were rising, all boats in the community were rising.

I can still remember many of my old customers and entrepreneurs. Bill Elliot owned a truck stop restaurant in a leased building, and we financed him buying property and building his own very successful family style restaurant. Homer Yandle owned a garbage service and tree service, so we financed more trucks and equipment. Gene Cone owned several trailer parks as well as two convenience stores. I financed a new restaurant called Applegate's Landing, owned by several PEPSICO executives where we used their PEPSICO a stock as collateral. Lee Atwater's political consulting business called Baker and Associates was flourishing, and he was a customer as well. Harold Hutchins was a wonderful man who owned Sportsman's Repair and Hardware. We financed their expansion to a new location in the Columbia Mall to provide for a much bigger store and the inventory needed for the expansion. These are but a few of those early customers, and my dealings with them only served to reinforce my notion of a win-win. In fact, when making a business loan before I ever got to the 5 C's and the numbers, I would ask myself if the transaction was good for the customer and the bank. If it was not good for both, we would not do it even if I was 100% sure we could get paid.

One transaction where the outcome would be good for both and where the answer was yes, was the transaction for Harold Hutchins, a transaction that would also teach me another valuable lesson. Harold was in his early 50s at the time, as lean as a hickory stick. He wore thick glasses and always had a pen and notepad in his shirt pocket. A fine man and good businessman, his hardware store had grown through the years through conservative, capable management. The store was profitable and had a strong capital position through years of building up retained earnings. In addition, Harold was an accomplished gunsmith with a healthy recurring revenue stream from the repair of shotguns and rifles for hunters in the area.

In the overall scheme of things Harold's loan was not huge, but for me it was substantial. In keeping with the reputation I was trying to create as a different kind of banker, I decided to have the closing at Harold's place and take the check and all the paperwork to him. I clearly remember going to meet Harold in his old building with my folder full of documents and the check. His office was in the middle of the store, not really an office but a bullpen much like my dad's in his store. Harold welcomed me and we signed papers, so I gave him the check and went back to the bank. It wasn't until the next day that I was able to review all the documents prior to booking the loan, and to my great chagrin realized I neglected to get the personal guaranty signed.

To say I was horror stricken would be a huge understatement because the personal guaranty is the most important document for a loan to a closely held business. I grabbed the paperwork and rushed over to see Harold. From his usual spot in his bullpen, he saw me coming through the front door. As I approached, he said, "You forgot something didn't you." I said yes.

"And what you forgot was very important, wasn't it?" I said yes again. He then said, "And what are you going to do if I don't sign it?"

The look on my face must have said it all because Harold immediately smiled, and said, "Hand it over. I am happy to honor our original agreement."

For me it was a lesson in two things. First, it was a reminder that most people are honest and good for their word. Second, it emphasized the fact that banking is a business where it is critical for bankers to focus on the important details. I would never again make that mistake of being careless.

By early 1977, business at Dentsville was booming and the branch was getting close to doubling its loans and deposits. I was at or near the top in all the categories that measured performance and my reputation as a banker, at least in Dentsville, was growing. The connections with senior management I had made during the year and a half of my special assignment were also proving helpful. If I needed help from travel, I could call Bobby Norman; if I needed help from marketing, Bob Isbell; trust, Virgil Duffie; and Bob Gorham helped me do the branch in the new mall. Most importantly, my relationship with Hootie grew as he would often call to ask me to help someone in Spring Valley where he lived. These calls were always directly to me and not through the chain of command. Yes, life was pretty good. I had now been with the bank for four years and a banker for two of those. Little did I know that my life was getting ready to change in the most profound way!

Carlos Evans

Chapter 15

Lisa
My Life Partner

1977 was shaping up to be a good year. The economy continued to improve, and business was booming at the branch. I was 26 years old, nowhere close to getting married, and I was starting to think myself a bit long in the tooth for a bachelor, especially since young people back then got married much earlier than today. When I became anxious about it, I gained comfort from my faith. I knew that the right person would eventually come along according to God's plan. My faith also kept me from fretting too much that I was nowhere close to my goal of getting on the loan platform. I knew that was in God's hands, so my focus remained fixed on making Dentsville the best branch bank it could be.

Aside from the fact I did not have a serious relationship, my social life was actually very good. Larry Tyler moved back to Texas and another fraternity brother, Roscoe Green, moved in. Two other fraternity brothers, Mike Ussery and John Riley, rented a house down the street. Lee Atwater's political career as a campaign strategist was blossoming, and he was always around and making things happen. We would have parties at one house or the other on my street, with Lee on the guitar and plenty of female quests. Even so, given my respect for Elden next door, we kept things in line. As to my relationship with Elden, by this time we were fast friends.

When Elden and Harriett Ann would leave town, he would ask me to watch out for David, Bruce and Betsy. I was somewhat like the chaperone next door. Elden would say, "We're leaving town, and I know they're going to have a party. Please keep an eye out to make sure they don't get into trouble." As he suspected, Elden and Harriett Ann would barely get around the corner before the cars and coolers would start rolling up. Even so, David, Bruce and Betsy were always well behaved. While they would have fun, things never got out of line.

On weekends, Elden and I would work in our respective yards. I took great pride in my house and wanted it to be more like his, so he was constantly helping me learn to be a better gardener. One day in the spring of 1977, we decided to take on a major project, and on that day I would learn a secret about my friend next door.

The idea for the project started when Elden mentioned that he knew where we could get some free railroad ties. We would get them from a site where railroad tracks had been torn up, and we could use them for landscaping. The catch was we had to go pick them up and haul them off ourselves. Elden had a small trailer so off we went. The day was warm, and we had to carry the ties a good ways from where they were to where we could load them onto the trailer. Railroad ties are soaked in creosote, which makes them much heavier than ordinary wood of the same dimension. As a result, it wasn't long before we were both soaked with sweat and pulling off our shirts. When Elden removed his, I couldn't help but notice some scars. When I asked what caused them, Elden responded that we would talk later, maybe over a drink. We went home and were able to place all the ties in my yard and his. They are still there to this day after some 43 years.

After we finished our work Elden suggested we have a drink, our traditional Crown Royal and ginger ale with a splash of lemon juice. That was when Elden's story began.

He had served in the Marines in World War II and been stationed in the Pacific Theater. More to the point, he was part of the first wave to hit the shores at Guam in a landing craft with 50 other Marines. The LST got hung up on a coral reef just offshore and suffered from heavy mortar fire. Roughly half the group made it to shore only to be cut to pieces by machine gun fire. Of the 25 that made it to shore only 10 to 15 would make it past the machine gun nests for the next phase of combat, which was to root out the enemy and take the island. As Elden slowly told the story I could not even begin to imagine the Hell he must have endured. If that experience was not enough after Guam he was in on the first wave to Hit Okinawa.. Somewhere along the way Elden was badly wounded from grenade shrapnel. He blacked out and had to be taken to one of the offshore hospital ships. When he awoke, he asked to be released back to his platoon, to which the doctor responded "Son, you have had and seen enough. The only place you are going is back home."

As Elden told the story I teared up, embarrassed by the staggering sacrifice that he and others had made on our behalf. Although I already held Elden in the highest esteem, from that point forward our relationship would have a special meaning. Elden was and is one of those Great Americans who sacrificed so much for our country. From my perspective, anyone who would choose to dishonor our flag dishonors them. While I would always totally support people's right to express their political and social opinions, I draw the line when it comes to our flag, because it represents the men and women like Elden who gave so much. Later in my career I would face a difficult predicament involving Elden and the bank, but more on that later.

As 1977 wore on, the political excitement was heating up and Lee Atwater was in the thick of it. Senator Strom Thurmond was running for reelection against a strong Democrat contender Pug Ravenel, who had run for governor in 1974 and would have won except for a technicality involving a residency issue that caused him to withdraw. Pug had been born in Charleston, but he had been living in New York working at the investment banking firm of Donaldson Lufkin and Jenrette. The residency issue surfaced near the end of the primary, causing Pug to be disqualified. Later, Pug would become a dear friend as would his chief political strategist David Rawle.

Even without Pug's candidacy and taking into account Strom's popularity, the Senatorial race was hotly contested, Lee Atwater was right in the middle as Strom's chief strategist. Mike Ussery, my neighbor up the street, also got involved in the campaign, so the political scene was a beehive of activity. Mike would later become ambassador to Morocco under Bush Sr, and I will say more on him later on.

One particularly memorable political event occurred when Bob Hope came to Columbia to take part in a fund raiser for Strom. Nancy Thurmond, Strom's young wife wanted the event at the Coliseum, which was new and would hold 12,000 or so. Lee was adamant about doing it at Ovens Auditorium, a much smaller venue but one Lee knew he could pack. He said political events were like wrestling matches. The last thing you wanted were empty seats! Eventually, Lee got his way, and the event was held at Ovens.

Strom's reelection campaign was successful, and that really helped put Lee's career on the launching pad. Also, by this time Lee had become somewhat of a visible personality in the state. He still held to his highly disciplined old ways, reading 10 to 15 newspapers from all over the country daily, running every day, but binging on beer and cigarettes on Friday nights. His favorite haunt was Bullwinkle's Bar over near Fort Jackson. I asked Lee one day why he went there. He said if you wanted to know how the common working man or woman thinks, Bullwinkle's was the place. You would learn nothing about mainstream America at the country club or some preppy bar, he said. In any case, while I didn't see myself as a political person, the events were fun and great places to meet girls.

In a nutshell, life was good. I was rolling along and having fun with lots of dates but none serious. I was still working hard, but things were a little easier because I had a great assistant branch manager named John Riddick. John was fresh off the training program and married to Debbie, a Winthrop University graduate. We became good friends, and one afternoon after work we were having a beer at the Steak and Ale when Debbie suggested I meet her friend Lisa Hudson who she had gone to school with. I'd already had a few beers and suggested we call her right then to see if she could come out.

We stepped over to the pay phone where Debbie called Lisa then put me on the phone with her. When I asked Lisa to come join us, she refused saying she had to do some chores at home. When I asked if I could call her another time, she said yes. For some reason, the fact that here was a girl who did chores resonated with me. It implied that she was responsible and had her priorities right, quite unlike most of the girls I had been dating to that point.

The next week I called her back and asked her out. July 25 was my birthday, and I was having a few people over to my house including my roommate and friend Ralph, his date and soon to be wife Anita, as well as my Sister Melba and her husband Jimmy. It proved to be a very nice evening, and when I returned Lisa to her parents' home in Spring Valley, I asked if she could join me the following Saturday for a day trip to the

Biltmore House in the Western N.C. mountains near Asheville.

Lisa said yes, so I planned what I thought would be a very romantic trip where I would impress her with my knowledge of the house, its artwork, furnishings and gardens. However, despite my best intentions, the trip turned out to be a disaster. As I quickly discovered, Lisa was not a morning person, however my plan had required that we leave at 7 am. Another difficult discovery was that Lisa got carsick on curvy roads, and I made the mistake of taking her up to Mt. Mitchell, which is the highest peak east of the Mississippi, on the curviest of roads. She, of course, got sick, and we barely spoke all the way home. Despite our difficulties, the day did have a decent ending as Lisa's parents had me over to barbeque steaks when I brought her back. Joyce and Walker were delightful, but my vision of what I hoped would be a perfect trip had been destroyed.

As I was leaving, I told Lisa that I'd had a nice time, but it was obvious we were different kinds of people who liked different things. Maybe best that we just ended on that note, which she said was fine by her.

Four or five weeks went by, and I was back in the mode I had been in before I met Lisa Hudson. However, fate or perhaps the man upstairs was about to cause me to change directions, and it happened when I was asked to attend the Heart Ball as a representative of the bank. There were a number of girls I had been seeing from time to time, but none seemed right for this kind of event, so I broke down and called Lisa Hudson. When she answered the phone and I asked if she could come she said, "What's happened? I thought you didn't want us to see each other anymore."

I responded, "Well, I have to go to this Heart Ball to represent the bank, and you're the only respectable woman I know."

Someone was looking after me because she thought for a minute and said, "Well, I can take your answer two ways. One is bad, and one is good. I'll choose to take it in a good way and as a compliment."

So, we went to the Heart Ball and something clicked. We held hands that night. Since that night when we first bonded, I have often thought about how my life was changed, and I have often wondered what things would have been like without her. To say that my life was forever enriched and made whole would be a vast understatement. From that night onward, we started seeing each other every weekend and often during the week. There were many cookouts with her parents as we drew closer, and I drew closer to them as well. I took her to meet my mother and stepfather as well as my dad and stepmom in Salem. On Thanksgiving night, we decided to get engaged and on Christmas Day I asked her dad and mom for her hand in marriage. Our wedding took place on May 13, 1978, and it was the most important and best day of my life, equaled only by the day our son Blake was born some 5 years later.

Lisa was not only my wife, but also my best friend and life partner. She was everything I had hoped for and more. We became a team in the truest sense, and while she was a housewife for most of our marriage, in reality she deserves as much or more credit than I for my success. She raised our son, became the spiritual leader of our home, spent countless hours by my side entertaining customers, as well as attending many, many bank functions, meetings, and events. Most importantly, in my darkest hours which were yet to come, she was my rock and the one thing I could hang my hat on in an otherwise stormy sea. With Lisa by my side, my life was forever changed for the better!

Chapter 16

The Platform Finally Arrived

In early 1978 Lisa and I were heavily into wedding planning, and I was consumed with making my house suitable for my soon-to-be-wife. There was painting to be done, along with furnishing and lots of little things to try and make it feel like a home rather than a fraternity house. Lisa's mom would be a big help as we undertook this effort. Also, Elden next door would be my constant advisor and helper whenever I needed advice.

About this same time Lee Atwater decided to marry Sally Dunbar, a woman from Union, South Carolina, who would become a dear friend. I would be in Lee's wedding, and I asked him to be in mine along with a number of my fraternity brothers and my KA friend Doug Seigler, who was now practicing law in Columbia. These were fun times with all the wedding parties and the excitement of all of us getting on with our lives. Things were good at the branch as well. My business was running smoothly, the growth continuing, and John Riddick was turning out to be a great assistant capable of running the branch by himself.

Shortly after the wedding, I received the call I had been hoping for from Joel Smith, the senior credit officer for the Columbia office. At that time each city office had two principal officers, the city executive who functioned much like a city president responsible for all the branches in the area, and the chief credit officer who was responsible for both the consumer and the commercial loan portfolios. In Joel's role as chief credit officer, the platform reported to him. Needless to say, I was very pleased; however, I was also melancholy at the thought of leaving Dentsville because all of the employees had become dear friends. I especially hated to leave

Jeannine Hill, the head teller, and Sandra Bryan, the customer service representative. Regardless of my lingering sadness, I left and reported to that shiny new downtown office that I had helped build and open three years earlier.

Thus, the summer of 1978 began my commercial lending career in earnest. I was taking Tom Anderson's portfolio of customers and his old position on the platform since Tom was being transferred to the loan platform in Charleston where he would be a commercial banker as well as our chief trade finance person in the Charleston market. By then, Tom was already a close friend as we had been in the bank's training program at about the same time.

Prior to coming downtown, I did my usual due diligence and ordered all the credit files for the customers in Tom's portfolio, so by the time of my arrival I was familiar with all the relationships. Thus, the transition from Tom amounted to 3 or 4 days of personal introductions to insure a clean handoff. Back in those days, commercial bankers didn't specialize so Tom's portfolio consisted of all types of loans: operating companies, real estate loans, even loans to individuals of the type that would be in private banking today. It was a hodgepodge with the common denominator being that the customers were entrepreneurs of different shapes and sizes, all trying to either grow a business, start a business, or invest in a business someone else was starting.

The portfolio I inherited totaled about $5 million (about $40 million in today's dollars) and had everything from a specialty chemical manufacturer, Hardwicke Chemical owned by Jim Hardwicke, to American Development Corporation or ADCOR, a defense contractor. ADCOR was owned by Melvin Brown who would shortly be on the board of directors at Bankers Trust and one of the first African American board members of a public company in South Carolina. Melvin's boardship was another example of Hootie being a progressive thinker and ahead of his time. Aside from those two larger operating businesses was Brittons, a great retailer owned by Arnold Levinson which is still in business in Columbia today, and Ducane Heating Corporation in Blackville, South Carolina, that made gas furnaces and was getting into the barbecue grill business in a big way. Ducane was owned by the Ducate family that had relocated its business in 1972 from New Jersey to Blackville where they had become one of the largest employers in Barnwell County.

While South Carolina was still a very poor state these people wanted to grow profitably, create jobs, and assist in creating a better life for their employees and the communities they served. My role was to help them by providing much needed capital as long as it met my golden rule of being a good investment for the bank and good for the customer.

About that time an incident took place that reminded me of how truly poor the state was. It took place at one of Lee Atwater's political functions in Charleston, a reception for Carroll Campbell who was beginning to lay the groundwork for a successful run for governor in 1982. The reception took place at the home of a prominent family in the best area of downtown Charleston called 'South of Broad Street.' Today, all these homes have been immaculately restored but in the late 70s many were in a horrible state of disrepair. I remember walking over to a large, beautiful oriental screen and out of curiosity, looking behind it. Incredibly, the screen was being used to cover a rotten area at the rear of the house where the wall almost seemed to be falling in. For me, it underlined the fact that while conditions in South Carolina were improving, in almost every category of economic health, we were at or near the bottom. In keeping with the Johnson family's mandate to help change all of that, Bankers Trust was clearly on a mission to provide the capital to raise all boats.

As I began the next phase of my career, I developed some additional business principles on top of the ones I had learned in the branch. These were disciplines I thought would be good for business and in the long run help the bank.

1) I would always answer my phone personally when I was at my desk. Many of the officers had the secretary pool answer the phones to insure they would not be interrupted when dictating memos and so forth. However, I would be different. I wanted people to feel they could get straight through to me every time.

2) I would spend a lot of time outside the office at the customers' places of business. I thought I could learn more about my clients that way. Also, the thought occurred to me that customers would be a lot more comfortable meeting on their own turf rather than in my office. In some respects, bank buildings symbolize money and power where the bank is in charge. I wanted to send a message of partnership.

3) I would continue to do as much up front due diligence as possible so I'd be in a position to commit on the spot when I could. When I could not commit on the spot, I would buy a little time by saying something like, "Let me go back and think on all this." I would never say something like, "I have to go back and talk to the committee." I wanted customers to know that I was in charge not some obscure person behind the curtain. On this last point, it should be noted that by then my individual loan authority was about $200,000 (roughly $1.5 million in today's dollars). It had been increased every year I was in the branch and then increased again upon my promotion to the platform. Back then, we called "your pen" the amount you could sign the bank up for by yourself with no one else's involvement. Anything above that had to go to someone with a higher pen, or for very large transactions, to one of the committees.

4) I would continue to work hard to improve my listening skills. Like the wise old owl, I learned that the less I talked the more the customer talked and the more I would learn about their business. Entrepreneurs loved to talk about their business. My favorite question was, "How did you start your company?" Their stories were incredible tales of overcoming obstacle after obstacle and many near death experiences. Clearly, entrepreneurs loved what they were doing, and they loved talking about it which provided a great learning experience for me.

5) I entertained a lot with Lisa's help. Even though our house was very small we had cookouts, drinks before football games, and we took customers to dinner. While these relationships were professional, I wanted to get to know my customers personally and for them to know me.

6) Last but not least, I worked to build the reputation as someone creative, who could find ways to do things other people could not. Simply put, if I thought an idea was good (Conditions) and the numbers provided a path to repayment (Capacity) and if the borrower's Character was unimpeachable but the deal was short on Capital and Collateral, I viewed it as my role to figure out a way to mitigate the additional risk imposed by the lack of those two C's, which are there primarily to protect the bank if a loan went south. These simple rules and habits would stay with me for the rest of my career.

Given my economics background, the logic appeared obvious. Every good entrepreneur with a great plan or deal that I could not find a way to facilitate was a missed opportunity for Bankers Trust, and a missed opportunity to create jobs in my community. I also worked very hard to give people a quick no if the answer was not going to be positive. It was clear to me that bankers were notorious for stringing customers out, asking for more and more information when the reason for the no was clear on day one. I would often hear stories about competitors down the street who would say no after weeks of information gathering, and the reason given for the no was "The loan was against policy." Well, a decent banker should have known what the policy was on day one and saved the customer a lot of time and energy. Prospects who had been put through that sort of ringer by the guys down the street were easy pickings as far as I was concerned. Entrepreneurs wanted a yes, of course, but they preferred a quick no versus a long turndown that involved much wasted time and energy.

Many times during my stint on the platform, I thought of Julian Turner's comment about commercial lending being like custom tailoring suits versus selling suits off of the rack. I concluded that I would work hard to become the best tailor in town, and if I succeeded, business would come to me. My supposition proved correct, and over time, slowly at first but then faster as time went on, the business did come.

One important point is that part of the tailoring involved delicate discussion and negotiation concerning loan covenants. Loan covenants are stipulations with the borrower that they agree to meet certain financial tests. There are negative covenants which are "Thou Shalt Nots" and the affirmative covenants which are "Thou Shalts". All covenants or tests are usually date specific and, to be blunt, are hated by most entrepreneurs. For example, negative covenants can include limitations on capital expenditures, officers salaries and/or dividends. Affirmative covenants include such things as net worth step ups, current ratio tests (measures of liquidity), which are basically current assets compared to current liabilities. There are many others because all loans are different and require different structures.

Suffice it to say that most entrepreneurs view the covenants as the bank trying to tell them how to run their business. One time, a borrower told me that I was trying to strangle him with covenants that were creating a "Turtle Neck." I responded that I wasn't strangling him, rather I was trying to keep him from freezing in the winter when the recession came.

Covenants were always testy discussions, but if the borrower truly felt you had their interest at heart then you could usually work through them. As I was quickly learning, banking was all about trust and I strove to be a banker people could trust.

Aside from my efforts to get better at the tools of my trade, I also benefitted from the contacts I had made during the almost two years of my special assignment. Hootie would call from time to time and ask me to go see a prospect, as would John Boatwright, Virigil Duffie, Jack Weeks, Bob Morman, and the other executives on the 19th floor. I also got calls from time to time from people asking for my opinion on certain things.

One day I got a call from Bob Isbell, Head of Marketing saying that he and Hootie wanted to have lunch with me to ask about a new product they were considering. The lunch was at noon in the Summit Club in its very formal, beautiful dining room, and they wanted my take on a new checking account product they were considering to bring more young people into the bank. I felt sure they were asking for my opinion because at the time I was only 28 years of age and could relate to the group they were targeting, but I think my answer surprised them. Essentially, I questioned why they were targeting young people rather than seniors, the group with the greatest wealth. I had just read an article on the amount of bank deposits and liquid assets controlled by seniors versus younger generations, and it was compelling how much wealth the seniors controlled.

It was interesting to watch their reaction because I could see their wheels turning. A few years later Bankers Trust introduced a Money Manager Account similar to the Merrill Lynch CMA. It was designed as a means to gather liquid assets and combine money market funds with brokerage accounts. Although I was not involved in designing the product, I would like to think that I had some input in the genesis of the idea, which ended up being a good one both for the company and our customers.

As far as my meetings with senior management are concerned, I remember an other meeting in early 1980 that was not so comfortable. As everyone at the bank knew, Hootie was an imposing figure physically, being a former blocking back on the USC football team. He had presence when he entered a room. He was a man of few words, but when he spoke, everyone listened. He was also known to have a short temper and no patience for any failure to follow orders.

On this particular day, I was down on the platform tending to business when Margie Shelly called and said Hootie wanted to have lunch that day with me and Governor McNair, the senior and founding partner of the McNair law firm and also a partner in Central City General. While Margie didn't explain the reason for the meeting, I had a sneaking suspicion, and it wasn't good! For some time those of us on the platform had directed quite a bit of business to an attorney named John Lumpkin Jr., a young partner at Boyd Knowlton Tate and Finlay. John was a Princeton graduate, smart as a whip and a fine lawyer. Unfortunately, in addition to his firm being the McNair firm's key competitor he was also the son of John Lumpkin Sr, the CEO of South Carolina National Bank the largest bank in the state and Hootie's chief rival.

The moment I got the call, I knew I was screwed. They were going to ask why we were doing so much business with John Lumpkin Jr. given the bank's relationship with Governor McNair and his law firm. Aside from all the business connections, everyone knew that Bob McNair was a very close personal friend of Hootie's. What was I going to say? I toyed with possibly trying to minimize what we were doing, but then I remembered two of my dad's old sayings, "The truth never hurts," and "There is no antiseptic like the light of day."

Almost as soon as we were seated Hootie cut to the chase. "Carlos, knowing our banks relationship with Governor McNair and his firm, why are you and your teammates using John Lumpkin Jr? I know you're not the only one, but the Governor and I thought you would give us a straight answer."

I understood why I had been chosen. In addition to getting to know Hootie through the building process, I had come to know Governor McNair, as well .Over the years, I have often thought of another important aspect of that lunch: whether Hootie already knew what my answer would be. Was it possible he just wanted the Governor to hear it straight from me? In any case, I took a big gulp and said, "Governor, with all due respect, we have found your team to be slow to respond in situations where speed was critical. We have also found your team to be very expensive and we often find ourselves at odds with customers when having to explain why the bank's legal fees (paid by customers as part of the closing cost) are so high. Lastly, we find that your team seems to work in a way that makes it difficult to do deals while Mr. Lumpkin works in a way that makes it easy."

Hootie didn't bat an eye. He looked straight at Governor McNair and said, "Governor, given our relationship with you and your firm we have a real problem. In my estimation, there are but two solutions. Either teach your people how to do business like Mr. Lumpkin or go out and hire Mr. Lumpkin, however, I suspect that you should try the latter rather than the former."

Hootie then turned to me and said, "Carlos, what do you want to eat?"

That was the end of the discussion about that topic, and we went on to have a nice lunch. Shortly thereafter, Governor McNair hired John Lumpkin Jr., who went on to do many transactions for us including one of the most important transactions of my career some 8 years later.

By the late 70's the Fed began rapidly raising rates to try and stamp out inflation. By early 1980 the Fed Funds rate (what banks charge to lend to one another) hit 20%, and by the later part of 1980 the prime rate (the rate we charged our best customers before the introduction of LIBOR) also hit 20%. The rise in rates was so sharp and so sudden that Hootie decided to cap our prime rate at 14% to give our business customers a break, which they sorely needed. Hootie's position was that we would rather make less money and help our customers survive to fight another day. I don't feel many Bank CEO's today would make that same call.

As I have said before, over the years much has changed in the banking industry, and I believe not all for the better. While the banks are much bigger today and can do so much more, the lack of focus on helping entrepreneurs succeed and grow is not a good thing for our communities or our economy. Much of this is due to how the banks are being led, but I also believe the regulators are part of the problem. While Hootie's decision to cap our prime rate definitely affected profits in the short term, it was a long-term enhancement to the bank's future growth and profitability. I believe that banks and communities are better served managing for the long term.

By early 1980 Lisa and I were coming up on our second anniversary. Life was good, and I was enjoying my work and achieving good success. In just two short years my portfolio had doubled to about $10 million. Lisa had a part time job teaching tap dance for little girls which, as a prior dancer, she loved. We enjoyed spending time with her parents, and every

Sunday after church we would dine with them. We were also enjoying Harriett Ann and Elden and their entire family, our wonderful next-door neighbors. I was playing lots of tennis with my friend Ralph from school. Lee Atwater was gearing up to back Ronald Reagan's bid for the Presidency, which was an interesting turn of events.

At that time, Lee was to some extent a protege of Strom Thurmond and Carroll Campbell, who was soon to be the next governor of South Carolina, and both were supporting Texas Governor John Connolly for the party's nomination. Lee broke with them when he concluded that Connolly could not win the general election, but Reagan could. In hindsight he was clearly right. Leaning on our friendship, Lee even talked me into being the treasurer for Reagan's primary campaign in South Carolina. Lee's consulting firm, called Baker and Associates, was a bank customer; how could I refuse? Once I asked Lee why he had chosen the name "Baker and Associates." Lee said he'd done it because it sounded better than Atwater and Associates. Lee was ever the promoter and by that time was making good money that he was shrewdly investing in rental property, which of course, I financed.

Yes, these were good times! Everything was lovely as far as Lisa and I were concerned; we could not have been happier. I was making a little more money which meant we were able to do a few things to the house such as adding new curtains and a new sofa. Professionally, I was totally content, doing the best job that I could in Columbia, my new hometown. Then, in the blink of an eye, all of that changed!

Carlos Evans

Chapter 17

Hilton Head Island
"Camelot"

In the Spring of 1980, we took a group of customers and prospects to the Heritage Golf Tournament on Hilton Head Island, an event that had become an annual affair our customers and prospects enjoyed. The bank rented a small twin engine plane that would take a different group of 8 down every day. The clients and the bankers would stay overnight in a house the bank rented on the golf course. The next day that group would leave, and another group would come down.

I was there for one night with Jim Hardwicke, CEO and owner of Hardwicke Chemical Company. I was somewhat familiar with Hilton Head as I visited there in 1974 for a weekend with a date and two other couples. I also attended a Young Bankers convention in 1979 with Lisa and our friends Ann and Tom Anderson. During all those trips my impression of Hilton Head had been very positive.

Everyone knew that the island had gone through a rough recession in '74 and '75 that almost bankrupted the area's largest employer, Sea Pines Company. In fact, there was supposedly a sign placed at the drawbridge that connected the island with the mainland saying "Last One Off Turn Off The Lights." Back then, in addition to the recession, the fuel embargo had made it very difficult for people to vacation in places they had to reach by car. However, based on my visual observations from my two previous trips, things seemed to be coming back despite the high interest rates of the late 70s and early 80s. I saw signs of new construction and activity everywhere.

The brilliant master plan that Charles Fraser (founder and major shareholder of The Sea Pines Company) put in place had created an environment full of green trees and huge areas of open space that, when combined with the use of wood and earth tones in construction, created a wonderful setting. Charles's masterpiece was Harbour Town, which looked like a Mediterranean fishing village complete with the now famous candy stripe lighthouse. The town was incredibly functional and offered the right blend of restaurants, retail, bars, docking facilities, music for the kids under the Liberty Oak Tree, all of it interspersed with homes, condos, bike and jogging trails, and, of course, the beach, tennis and the golf. Harbour Town was extremely appealing, and it literally hummed with activity during Heritage week.

It was also very clear that Hilton Head Island was very different from the rest of South Carolina. Hilton Head Island aligned itself economically more closely with Savannah Georgia due to the closest major airport being in Savannah, even though Hilton Head had its own small strip. Also, many of the vacationers, home and condo buyers were from Georgia and places much further north like Ohio, Pennsylvania, New Jersey and New York. On top of this, things were very expensive compared with the rest of South Carolina. A typical starter home in Sea Pines would be 3x what my home was worth in Columbia.

In any event, we had a great time during the brief visit for the Heritage Tournament, and my guest, Jim Hardwicke, seemed to appreciate the quality personal time. Jim's company, Hardwicke Chemical Company was in the middle of a major expansion that we were financing so the trip gave us some time to discus his plans in more detail. Upon returning to the office, things got back into rhythm with customer meetings and new loan discussions. Hilton Head Island was the last thing on my mind other than the memories of a nice visit.

However, in early June Joel Smith, my boss on the loan platform, called me into his office and told me the bank wanted me to move to Hilton Head as the senior lender for the combined Beaufort and Hilton Head portfolios. At that time, the Beaufort area had a main office and two branches. There were two commercial lenders on the loan platform. Total deposits were about $20 million, and the total consumer and commercial loans were about $15 million. Hilton Head had one branch and a main office with two commercial lenders on the loan platform. Total deposits were about $25 million with about $20 million in total loans both consumer and commercial.

At the time Hilton Head was not an incorporated city but had a population of about 8,000 while Beaufort was incorporated with a population of about 8,000 as well. If I took the job, I would take over responsibility for a combined $35 million loan portfolio with 4 commercial bankers reporting to me. In turn, I would report to the city executive, an experienced banker from the upstate who had been with the bank a long time. Along with a modest raise, I would be promoted to senior vice president. At that point, I had been with the bank 7 years; I had been promoted first to assistant Cashier, then to Cashier, then to Vice President. Back then, titles were important so the jump to SVP was attractive along with a little more money. My boss Joel thought it was a good opportunity. However, I had some serious reservations.

First was the cost of housing which was easily 3x what it was in Columbia when comparing cost per square foot. Secondly, John Crabtree the current senior lender wanted out, and he had only been there about 18 months. John said he wanted to join the real estate lending group in Columbia and work for a man named John Walker, who was building up real estate specialty lending at Bankers Trust. Although I trusted John Crabtree, I wondered if there might be other reasons why he wanted to leave. There was also the whole issue of the island being almost like a different world from the rest of South Carolina, and we would be leaving a very comfortable situation in Columbia.

Early on, I got a commitment from Tom Connor in personnel to give me a housing allowance separate and apart from my pay to cover the difference in debt service for my home loan which would be much larger than my mortgage in Columbia, assuming I was to buy a comparable home. When I voiced my other concerns, Joel suggested Lisa and I make a visit to the island to check it out.

For the entire three-and-a-half-hour drive to Hilton Head, I tried to convince Lisa that the move was a good thing. My primary argument was the benefit to my career since everyone knew the place was growing very rapidly. Lisa's concerns were that she would be leaving her parents and to some extent, the known for the unknown. Her father, Walker, was also weighing in as he did not want us to leave. He kept saying that with the added cost of living the whole thing did not add up.

Upon arrival we checked into the Sea Crest Motel, and I went directly to the bank while Lisa went and looked at houses with a young realtor named Jeff Wilson. I told Jeff to find a traditional styled house with shutters which he said would be almost impossible. As Lisa and Jeff rode off and I went to see what I could learn about the portfolio.

It was no surprise to me that there were very few operating company loans other than a large revolving credit facility to the Sea Pines Company and line of credit to a big furniture retailer named Hilton Head Interiors. There were also lines of credit to contractors and sub-contractors and a large number of real estate loans to very rich people to finance either the construction of new homes or purchase of existing homes on the island, many of them with unusual repayment structures. For example, one very large loan to a Norwegian couple that owned a pizza chain in Norway had repayment provisions tied to them bringing back Krone from Norway and converting them to dollars. Another large line of credit had been granted to Robert Graves to build custom sport fishing boats on a presold basis. Finally, as I thought natural for a coastal resort location there were many loans to restaurants and local shrimpers. To put it simply, it was a very different loan portfolio from what I was used to in Columbia.

That evening, Lisa and I went to dinner with the city executive and his wife, who will remain unnamed for reasons I will get to later. We went to "The Gaslight Restaurant," owned by a bank customer named Serge Pratt. The food was outstanding, and the place was much more sophisticated than anything we had ever experienced in Columbia. Over dinner we learned that the city executive and his wife were short timers like the Crabtrees. They reportedly wanted to return to their hometown of Anderson, SC. This made me nervous all over again and suspicious of the undisclosed problems I might be stepping into. In any case, we had a nice dinner and stayed overnight at the Sea Crest which was a lovely small hotel on the ocean.

On the way back to Columbia, Lisa and I flip-flopped and reversed our previous roles. I suddenly sounded like Lisa's father, saying that the whole thing, "didn't add up." Lisa, on the other hand, took the position that it might be a good thing for us to leave "the nest" and have an adventure on our own. From her perspective, Hilton Head Island would be an adventure because it was totally unlike anything we had ever experienced.

I remember the drive back like yesterday. I had a small Fiat sedan I had purchased used for $500 when I sold my new car to buy her diamond engagement ring. The little Fiat had a four-speed stick shift and it purred along. We debated for the entire 3 1/2 hours on our way back. To give credit to the potency of Lisa's argument, by the time we got back to our little house on Brockwall drive, I had decided to take the plunge. We would immediately transfer to Hilton Head and stay in the Sea Crest Motel until we could sell our house and we could buy something in Sea Pines. I didn't realize it at the time, but an exciting new chapter was about to begin that would effectively launch the next stage of my banking career. Our lives were about to be changed in the most dramatic ways, but all for the better!

As was my habit, during that last week we remained in Columbia while I handed off my job on the loan platform, I ordered all the credit files for the portfolios on Hilton Head and in Beaufort and stayed up every night reading those files from cover to cover. I wanted to hit the ground running and know everything there was to know about each customer when I arrived. I also, did a crash course on the history of Hilton Head/Beaufort. I learned that Hilton Head Island consists of about 25,000 acres with about 12 miles of beachfront. Originally settled by Native Americans thousands of years ago, several shell rings on the Island that date back approximately 4,000 years provide evidence of these early settlers.

A Spanish Explorer, Francisco Cardillo, was the first European to explore the Island in 1521. Years later in 1663 Captain William Hilton sailing on the Adventure from Barbados identified a headland near the entrance to Port Royal Sound. He named it after himself and it became Hilton Head Island. By the late 1700's there was much farming on Hilton Head, and the entire area experienced economic prosperity through the planting and growing what became known as Sea Island Cotton.

During the civil war Union troops occupied the Island. The population surged to about 40,000 because it was the center of operations for the Union blockades of Charleston and Savannah. During the Union occupation, many African American slaves came to the island, and they were immediately made free men and women. After the war, the population dwindled with the downward spiral accelerated by a terrible hurricane that struck the Sea Islands and Lowcountry of South Carolina in 1893. By the early 1950's Hilton Head's population was down to less than 300, mostly African Americans with small farmsteads. The balance of the island served as timberlands for the tall pine trees that grew in abundance. One of those timber men was Joseph B. Fraser from Hinesville, Georgia, whose son, Charles E. Fraser, was a Yale educated lawyer. In 1956 the island was connected to the mainland through construction of the James F. Byrnes bridge, and in that year, Charles would begin to develop the Sea Pines Resort. Following Charles's blueprint, similar gated communities like Hilton Head plantation, Palmetto Dunes, Port Royal Plantation, and Shipyard Plantation sprang up and imitated Sea Pines architecture and covenants.

Beaufort some 30 miles northwest of Hilton Head was South Carolina's second oldest city. Founded in 1711, the area was first discovered by European explorers in 1514 when it became the site of the second landing on the North American continent by Europeans. What followed were many failed attempts at colonization before the British founded the city in 1711. Initially, the city grew slowly. There were many attacks from the Native American tribes and threats from the Spanish Empire to the south. Later, in the 1700's and early 1800's, the city began to flourish as a center for ship building and the growing of Sea Island cotton. A huge setback came in 1893 from the same hurricane that struck Hilton Head. In the 1900's the area began growing again, helped by two large Marine Corps installations notably Paris Island and the Marine Corps Air Station.

When Lisa and I moved to Hilton Head in the summer of 1980, we set up our temporary home at the Sea Crest Motel. It would take about 2 months to sell our Columbia house and purchase a new one in Sea Pines. During that time, I was working long hours in the office while Lisa was talking slow walks on the beach and doing house searches with Jeff Wilson. Every evening we would have a nice dinner to compare notes at the Sea Captains Table, the wonderful restaurant at the Sea Crest. Since we yet didn't know anyone on Hilton Head there was little socialization, but the quality time we spent together was important. By August we moved in our new home at 44 Wagon Road in Sea Pines, four blocks from the beach on a quiet street.

As we began to meet more and more people, one thing became

very clear: the people we would become friends with and do business with were incredibly diverse and far different from what we were used to. First, there were the professionals who were permanent residents: lawyers, accountants, realtors, and the executives of the island's four major developers and the resorts. In addition to the professionals, there were entrepreneurs who owned businesses ranging from restaurants to publications, to small contractors. Many of these entrepreneurs came from interesting backgrounds in other places and had moved to Hilton Head to start new lives.

Of the 8,000 permanent residents the professional workers like Lisa and I numbered 300-400 so in a short period of time we met most of them. In addition to the working people, there were about 7,000 retirees, mostly 'captains of industry' who had retired from Fortune 100 companies but were still very active and eager to get involved in making this new place into something special. There were also descendants of the original African American islanders. They were small in number but very respected and involved in all aspects of community, and they are still so today. While these groups were incredibly diverse, they all shared a commitment to the island and a desire to make it a better place to live and to work.

Geographically, the island was defined by its several major developments. Hilton Head Plantation stood at the north end. When Lisa and I arrived, it was owned by Citicorp, having been taken back from the Sea Pines Company in a major restructuring during the 1974 recession when Sea Pines got in serious trouble. Moving south, next came Port Royal and Shipyard plantations, initially developed by the Hack family led by Fred Hack Sr., but subsequently sold to Josh Gold, a Philadelphia investor who owned the Hilton Head Company. Next was Palmetto Dunes Resort owned by Greenwood Development Corporation. Greenwood Development was a subsidiary of Greenwood Mills in Greenwood, SC, which was owned by the Self family, who were very close to our Bank. At the south end of the island was Sea Pines, the grandaddy of the island developments, which was owned by a publicly traded company. As an indication of how important and dynamic Sea Pines had been, in 1973 the company hired more Harvard graduates than any other Fortune 500 company.

Back in those days, Bankers Trust had a local advisory board in each city made up of leaders in the business community who could serve as the bank's eyes and ears for what was going on. One of their key roles was to help Bankers Trust keep up with the competition. When I arrived, there were three banks operating in Beaufort/Hilton Head: Bankers Trust, Citizens and Southern Bank and the Bank of Beaufort, which was the largest. The environment was extremely competitive, and the advisory boards were a source of great insight. Even though they were not fiduciary boards, being invited to participate was prestigious, and the members received small stipends of $1,000 per year. The boards met monthly, one in Hilton Head and one in Beaufort, and one of the first things I did was attend the meetings with the Beaufort city executive. .

In Beaufort we had a very strong board made up mostly of big farmers, realtors, lawyers and Willie Scheper, the former CEO of the People's Bank of Beaufort, which Bankers Trust had purchased to gain access to the two markets. They were delightful people and I remember some of them quite clearly. Two of the big farmers were Neil Trask and Beanie Trask. At the time we had a lot of loans to the agricultural industry notably tomato farmers and other row crop growers as well as a large watermelon distributor, Melons Inc. In addition, there was Colden Battey, a very influential attorney, as well as Helen Harvey, married to the former Lieutenant Governor Brantley Harvey and clearly the most successful realtor in town. Willie Scheper was one of the most beloved people in Beaufort and over time proved to be a great ally and source of help.

We also had a very strong board in Hilton Head. Three board members were attorneys: Richard Woods with the McNair firm, Jim Herring with Herring and Meyer, and Ed Hughes who owned his own firm. On the real estate side, we had Peter Parrot, a successful developer, Ed Spears who ran Hilton Head Plantation for Citicorp, and Joe Fraser Jr, Charles Fraser's brother who was essentially a chief operations officer for Sea Pines. Both Ed Spears and Joe Fraser would become great friends and allies, as well as candid critics. In fact, shortly after my arrival both confided in me by saying that Bankers Trust was getting its clock cleaned by The Bank of Beaufort and Citizens and Southern (C&S). While our Bank was showing okay growth numbers because of the growth of the island, the other banks were putting up stunning numbers and leaving us in the dust.

This was especially true of C&S, which had arrived on the island two years earlier by acquiring the failed Hilton Head National. Both Ed and

148

Joe spoke very highly of the C&S local city executive, Harold Chandler. Harold had been a little All-American quarterback at Wofford College in Spartanburg. I knew of Harold because Newberry played them in football, and they beat us mercilessly every year. In addition to being a great athlete, Harold was a scholar—straight A student who graduated Summa Cum Laude and was class valedictorian. In short, Harold was smart as a whip.

One of the first things I did as the new banker in town was to go down the street and meet with Harold. In many respects, he was the Golden Boy at C&S. Even at this early point in his career he was viewed as the next generation CEO after a man named Hugh Chapman and his bank president, Bob Royal. In short, in the banking world of the Lowcountry, Harold was somebody, and I was a nobody. When I went to see him, Harold could have blown me off, but quite the opposite occurred. He spent a lot of time with me sharing what he had learned about Hilton Head.

He was also quick to point out that there were some people on the island of suspect character who played fast and loose and I should be careful with them. Because of his openness, Harold and I made an agreement to cooperate and share credit information in accordance with RMA (Robert Morris and Associates) standards. We also agreed to work together for the betterment of the island community when it involved things like the chamber of commerce and United Way. In short, Harold and I became good friends. Little did we know that our paths would cross several more times later in our careers.

One of the things I learned from Harold was that the lawyers and realtors were essentially the traffic cops in referring business. Aside from controlling huge escrow deposit balances because of all the real estate activity, they were also the first people anyone would meet when planning a move or purchase on the island. Given the volume of activity and the size of the transactions, the deposits were very important. Many home purchases were north of $1 million, and upon signing a purchase contract, it was customary to put 10% of the purchase price in escrow until closing. If you were a real estate firm and had 20 contracts in process, you could easily have in excess of $2 million in your escrow accounts.

Deposits were also very large with the lawyers. A lawyer could easily close $20 million in loans in a month. The checks would be written on the day of closing to pay off the old mortgage, remit taxes to the county along with any proceeds to the prior homeowner. Sometimes it would take weeks for all the checks to clear so the balances in the attorney escrow accounts were huge. There were also the rental management companies who would collect 40% as an advance deposit for the rental of a house or a condo. This money would be escrowed until the renter arrived and paid the balance. At that point, the management company would write checks to pay all the cleaning expenses and remit the homeowner's share after the rental commission. Several management companies were renting over 200 houses, and the advance deposits would pile up over the winter and early spring. In consequence, the island was awash in cash deposits and Bankers Trust was not getting its share !

Aside from the huge deposits generated by lawyers, realtors and management companies, the people who provided those agent services also told out-of-town buyers and real estate owners where to get their insurance, which bank to use, and in the case of the realtors, which law firm to use. At that time the prize consumer customer was the person moving down from the North to build a second home with a plan to ultimately retire on Hilton Head Island. These were not your average bank consumer customers. They were very wealthy relative to the rest of the state, and once they moved to the island permanently, they would have very large savings and deposit balances.

In almost every case, the cycle started with the person buying a lot in one of the communities. Almost immediately, I realized the best way to capture the people moving down was to finance their lot purchase and let that evolve into a home construction loan and then a full blown banking relationship. At the time, on Hilton Head we had two bankers making these kinds of loans, a wonderful young man named Stewart Hull from Augusta and a banker from Columbia named John Poole. With John and Stewart's help we revamped the lot lending program which had previously been limited to loans with a 5-year amortization and requiring a 25% down payment. We decided to offer a 7-year amortization to make the payments more affordable. Since the lots held their value well, we were comfortable with that. The other thing we decided was that if the realtors would deliver us a contract, we would get all the closing papers to the lot buyers attorney that same day. We would even deliver them by hand rather than sending them through the mail.

That one alteration totally changed our flow of business because human nature is a powerful thing. I knew realtors and attorneys did not get paid until the day of closing, and therefore if we became known as the bank that was able to get transactions to closure faster, we would become the provider of choice and the place realtors and lawyers would send their customers. We became just that.

At that time, there were a number of realty firms on the island, but two very large firms dominated: Sea Pines Real Estate, owned by Sea Pines Company, and Lighthouse Realty, an upstart owned by a group of former southeastern Bible salesman. Jeff Wilson, the agent who helped Lisa, was with Lighthouse, as was a young man named Herb King. Both became good friends and sent us lots of business. Both also became serial entrepreneurs and went on to very successful business careers outside real estate brokerage. In addition to Herb and Jeff, Lisa and I did lots of entertaining with the other successful real estate salespeople and real estate attorneys. Many became customers and great friends.

One of our favorites was Lottie Woodward, a single mother of two young daughters who became a highly successful salesperson. Clearly, people liked to do business with people they knew and trusted, so Lisa and I invested a lot of time in getting to know these folks. Since there were annual publications touting each firm's top salespeople, it wasn't hard to identify them. Aside from all of the one-on-one entertaining, we also did a lot of things around the Family Circle Tennis Tournament where we had bank box seats. We also had a hospitality house on the course during the Heritage Golf Tournament.

Every year in early fall the Beaufort Office would have a large function known as the Beaufort Office Shrimp Boil where all of the customers and prospects would be invited. The event was outside at the waterfront park behind the bank, where we served frogmore stew, a combination of boiled shrimp, sausage, corn and potatoes. Hootie Johnson would always fly down from Columbia. It was a time of great fun and conversation, but most importantly, an opportunity to thank our customers. In later years on Hilton Head, we hosted a big outdoor oyster roast as another way to say thanks.

Almost immediately upon making those few changes (longer

amortization, quicker document delivery) to how we were doing business, the bank started to grow at a much faster rate. The one area where I was still failing to meet my goals was in persuading retirees who were already on the island to move their accounts to us. Lisa and I became very involved in our church where we met many of them personally. Also, I became very involved in the United Way and the local chamber of commerce where many retirees were involved, and it underlined for me that while these people were retirees they were very active and community-oriented.

Finally, an opportunity presented itself, but it was one that carried some risk. Two young developers, Joe Webster and Wes Wilhelm came to see me about financing a non-profit retirement community named The Seabrook. The developers were working pro bono. The 501C3 would be run by a board of directors, and the board chair would be Bob Killingsworth, a retired Fortune 500 executive. The project would be built on land donated by the Fraser Family. While Mr. Killingsworth was a wonderful man and what they were doing was a good thing for the community, there was no equity or capital in the entity doing the project. Both Joe and Wes were aware that it was a tough deal, but they worked hard to sell me, explaining that people had been moving to Hilton Head in earnest since the early 60's when they were in their early 60's. Those people were now in their early 80's, and they needed a place to live that would allow them direct access to great healthcare, also several different levels of care as well as independent living. Joe and Wes told me that if I could figure out a way to finance the project, Bankers Trust might well become the bank of choice for the older retirees on the island who desperately wanted this project.

I thought on how the deal stacked up against the five C's. On Character and Credit, there was no issue because Bob Killingsworth was a saint and incredibly well-regarded. From my standpoint Capacity was there to repay since I thought the project would sell. What gave me pause was Collateral and Capital, but I determined I could mitigate the bank's risk with the right Conditions for the loan. What I did was base the loan on achieving 80% presales of the condominium units with 20% deposits up front. This was a stiff presale requirement for the time, since most deals required only 50% presales. In addition, the 20% deposit requirement was stiff because at that time most contracts only required 10% down.

With my loan offer, the math worked a little like this: Project cost was about $15 million with $10 million allocated to 100 condos (of all different sizes) at an average of $100,000 each. The remaining $5,0000,000 was allocated to the dining, support and healthcare facilities. Since the units were selling for an average of $150,000, an 80% presale requirement would produce approximately $2,400,000 in deposits (80 X $30,000 = $2,400,000). These funds could be used to fund construction so the loan amount would be $12,600,000 ($15,000,000 - $2,400,000). Once the 80 presold units closed (and the $30,000 forfeitable down payments made the likelihood quite high), then the loan balance would reduce by $8,100,000 (80 X $150,000 = $12,000,000 - $1,500,000 realtors commissions - $2,400,000 down payments = $8,100,000).

At that point the loan would have a balance of $4,500,000 secured by the 20 remaining condo units having a total value of $3,000,000 ($150,000 X 20) plus the health care and ancillary facilities which cost $5,000,000. That gave the bank a total of $8,000,00 in collateral value for the $4,500,000 loan or a loan-to-value ratio of slightly over 50%. Furthermore, the projections showed that the healthcare facility by that time would generate cash flow to pay the interest on the loan until the remaining 20 units could be sold, at which point the debt would be further reduced by another $2,700,000 (20 X 150,000 = $3,000,000 - 10% commissions or $300,000 = $2,700,000). At that point the loan balance would be $1,800,000 ($4,500,000 - $2,700,00 = $1,800,000) a level that could be easily supported by the cash flow of the 48 bed health care facility revenues.

Before I came to a final decision I met with Joe Fraser Jr to get his input. I had great respect for Joe, in addition to him being my strongest board member. Joe and his wife Becky had become dear friends along with the entire Fraser family of 4 sons and a daughter who were all close to our age. Joe told me the project was desperately needed and while he recognized the lack of capital, he thought my plan would work. When I next laid my plan out with Joe Webster, Wes Wilhelm and Bob Killingsworth, they were very concerned about the size of the presale requirement and the size of the 20% deposits; however, they agreed to the deal.

My next step was to get the loan approved. By that time my loan authority had been increased to $1 million so I would need to go to Columbia to get approval for $15 million. By that time W. David Rhodes had replaced Mr. Upchurch as the chief credit officer. Fortunately, David had a lot of confidence in me and while there were many questions, he ultimately approved the deal.

Thanks to the great project skills of Wes Wilhelm, The Seabrook was built on budget and on schedule. Bob Killingsworth became a strong advocate for the bank, and we opened new accounts for almost all the new residents. We also offered mortgage financing for the units, but since most of the residents were paying cash for their new home not many mortgage loans resulted. However, the buzz in the community was that Bankers Trust had stepped up to do something good for Hilton Head, and that led many people to open accounts. The bank and our one branch on the island rose to the top of all the activity reports which measured the number and dollar value of account openings. Mary Catherine Plowden, the bank's business development officer, did a great job of capitalizing on the exposure we got from making The Seabrook loan.

At completion, as the units started to close quickly, the loan paid down rapidly exactly in accordance with the plan. However, there was one big problem: no one at The Seabrook was getting sick and going into the health care facility. All of the projections and studies had been done on national averages, and it was becoming crystal clear that the retirees on Hilton Head were healthier. There was zero revenue from the healthcare facility, and while interest rates were off their earlier highs set at the beginning of 1982 when the prime rate hit 21%, they were still in the mid-teens. With a $4,500,000 loan balance at 15%, the interest meter would run almost $600,000 per year, and there was no cash flow to support the interest.

The good news was that while the original presales of 80 sopped up most of the initial demand, the units were still selling, so I made what would turn out to be a good decision. Essentially, I decided to take 20% from the remaining 20 sales ($30,000 per unit) and put it into an interest reserve. Assuming the remaining 20 units sold this would generate about $600,000 to help carry the project until the health care facility filled up and could carry the balance.

What I proposed to David Rhodes was that we give $600,000 of our remaining collateral value of $3,000,000 in the remaining unsold 20 units to The Seabrook. I wonder if banks today would do something like that, and I regret to say that I don't think they would! Today, bankers have so much fear of regulators that giving up collateral in a problem loan situation would be almost unheard off. In addition, besides being worried about regulators, managers today would most likely not give local leaders the latitude to make these kinds of decisions. While short term one could say a collateral give up hurts the bank, there is no doubt in my mind that long term the bank benefitted on many different levels.

Fortunately, David Rhodes approved my recommendation, and that is what we did. Bob Killingsworth and I met every month to review the status of the interest reserve as well as the operations of the healthcare facility. Slowly the remaining 20 units sold and created $600,000 for the interest reserve that was being consumed every month. At the same time, the loan balance was being reduced by the remaining $105,000 ($150,000 - $15,000comissions - $30,000interest reserve = $105,000 pay down). As each of the remaining units was sold, $105,000 was applied to reduce the debt. Eventually all 20 units sold, and the loan was paid down another $2,100,000 to bring the balance to $2,400,000. At the same time this was going on, the residents were beginning to use the healthcare facility. It began to generate revenues, and within 6 months or so, there was plenty of cash flow to pay interest and principal.

A year or so later, I would take everything I learned from The Seabrook and finance a similar, larger, much more elaborate project at the north end of the island called The Cypress of Hilton Head Plantation. It would be a huge success as well, just like The Seabrook and would later be replicated in Raleigh and Charlotte N.C.

As we approached the second half of 1982, life was good. The bank on Hilton Head had more than doubled in size, and we were making progress in Beaufort as well. My little bank on Hilton Head, which had been making about $200,000 per year when I arrived, was now making in excess of $1 million per year, a fivefold increase in earnings. My boss relocated to Anderson, and I was named the Beaufort County city executive. In reality, I had been running the bank for the most part anyway, but formalizing my role was a big promotion.

In addition, we were in the final planning stages for a new, much larger main office as well as two additional branches on the island, one in a new project being developed by Greenwood Development at mid-island called Shelter Cove, the other in a new specialty shopping center in Sea Pines called Sea Pines Center developed by my board member Joe Fraser Jr. and his partners.

I hired a great group of young bankers to staff the loan platform—Randy Dolyniuk, Phillip Bell, Roger Cleveland—and I brought in a very experienced banker named Richard Rabb to take my place as the senior lender. All these people went on to have long, successful careers in banking. Meanwhile, I was getting very involved in all facets of life on Hilton Head and in Beaufort. At the same time, I was meeting and trying to help new entrepreneurs every day. While I could write volumes about all these great people, at this stage I will only mention a few to give a flavor for the wonderful mix of people we had on the island many of whom are still there today.

Berry and Ruthie Edward's had moved to Hilton Head in the 70s. Ruthie was a fabulous decorator and Berry was a textile executive. They visited one weekend and made the decision to go all in, buying a very small landscape company and nursery called "The Greenery." Today, The Greenery is one of the largest employers in the Lowcountry with thousands of employees. They maintain grounds for condominiums and other commercial properties all up and down the South Carolina coast.

Brian and Gloria Carmines picked up lock stock and barrel in the 70s to move to the island. Brian, a successful corporate banker in Atlanta, gave up a promising career to make the move. They bought Hudson's Seafood, the largest restaurant on the island and a tourist destination in and of itself. Rainer and Olga Gerngoross came from Austria and purchased Cafe Europa under the lighthouse at Harbour Town. Abe Grant, a local African American owned a great restaurant mid-island. I went there every Friday in the early days to buy lunch for all the tellers to make their life a little easier on what for them was a hard working day.

Wally Seinsheimer left a very successful real estate business in Cincinnati to come to the island and develop with his partner Bob Albright. Wally, ultimately moved to Charleston and had a successful run there, as well. All these people and others like them were incredibly different but they had two things in common. 1) They risked it all to open businesses on the island and 2) They got very involved in the community and gave back.

Two other people, both serial entrepreneurs, were added to my board of directors at the bank and were a great help to me in building the bank. While the people I have mentioned are still dear friends today, J.R. Richardson and Jim Bradshaw as well as their families have remained especially close over the past 41 years. While different from each other, Jim and JR are the very best of friends, God parents to each other's children, and live next door to each other on Caliboque Cay on the intracoastal waterway in Sea Pines. Both have built their lives on the island and given back in so many ways. Both have gone on to serve with me on different nonprofit boards that I have chaired like the Spoleto Festival USA board in Charleston, as well as the Medical University of SC Foundation board in Charleston. They are Renaissance men from humble beginnings with wide interests and have friends all over the world. Both have been very involved in the Young Presidents Organization and now the WPO (World Presidents Organization). Both have wonderful supportive wives who are also dear friends of Lisa and me. Because both married at the end of my time on the island, they were bachelors in those early years. I could devote a whole story to some of their escapades, but in the interest of preserving my relationships with their wives I will leave that alone.

JR or Jimmy as his close friends call him, moved to the island in 1955 before the drawbridge opened. His parents, Norris and Lois Richardson built a small grocery store at the south end of the island near what is now Coligny Circle on a dirt road in the midst of wild hogs and huge mosquitos. The Richardsons had a daughter and two sons with JR being the middle child. At the time, the Richardson children would be the only white children in the public school system since the island population at the time numbered around 150 most of which were African Americans.

One of the Richardson's first customers was Charles Fraser who started developing Sea Pines in 1956. At the time Charles was selling lots and running the business out of his car, and he noticed that Lois kept the books for their small store. Charles hired Lois and she kept his books for 14 years. He also hired JR as his janitor, and they became close friends. In some respects, I think JR was like a son to Charles because he married later in life and had two daughters and no sons. No one ever told me this, but when I arrived on the Island in 1980 it was clear they had a special relationship. JR would learn many things from Charles who was incredibly well educated and whose knowledge covered a wide range of topics including a love of cartography (collecting old maps) and sailing.

JR would pick up on many of those refinements, most unusual for a boy living on a wild, uninhabited island.

After returning from military service in Viet Nam, JR went to work for Charles and the Sea Pines Company in the early 70s and learned a great deal about marketing and architecture. By the late 70s, JR was running the family business, which by the early 80s was a small specialty shopping center known as Coligny Plaza. By the time I met JR in the early 80s, he was a serial entrepreneur buying into a travel business, the local radio station, in addition to having a number of real estate investments.

While JR has had many successes, perhaps his best was Windmill Harbor which was owned by an Argentine investor named Andy Deutsch. Charles Fraser did the original master plan and advised Andy to adopt a Dutch architectural scheme around an inland Harbor that would be accessed by a lock system to raise the boats up much higher than the surrounding waters. While the Harbor design was sheer genius, making it one of the most protected harbors on the east coast, the architecture was not successful because the design was much too modern for the early 80s. JR ended up taking over the project and completely repositioning the architecture to more of a Charleston townhouse approach, which immediately took off. JR also developed the South Carolina Yacht Club at Windmill Harbour which he and his wife, Leslie, own and operate as one of the most successful private clubs in the state.

JR and Leslie, who is a dynamo unto herself, would become valued customers and dear friends, and JR would join our board of directors. JR and Leslie went on to compound their success, starting restaurants, a local bank, and building apartments just to name a few of their ventures. In addition, JR and Leslie supported everything good on Hilton Head Island from schools, to the arts, to their church.

Jim Bradshaw was from modest means in South Boston, Virginia, the son of a tobacco auctioneer. His strong intellect earned him a scholarship to the University of Virginia where he lived in one of the small rooms on the lawn that UVA reserved for the best and brightest students with the highest GPAs. Jim graduated with honors and went to work for his friend, Jim Chaffin, also a UVA graduate, as a real estate salesman in 1971. By that time, Jim Chaffin was executive vice president of Sea Pines, and his friend, Jim Light, a Duke graduate, was president.

I later became good friends with both Jim Light and Jim Chaffin through Jim Bradshaw. By the time I got to Hilton Head in 1980, both men had left to purchase the Snowmass resort in Colorado which they successfully developed. As Jim Bradshaw tells the story, he arrived in Harbor Town, which was under construction in 1971, in a broken down car that was on its last legs. He met Jim Chaffin, who gave him a resort credit card and the keys to a shiny new condo. The instructions were, here are the keys to your new house and a card that is good at all of the resort restaurants and bars. Your job is to go out and show clients and prospects a good time and sell a lot of real estate.

Jim, who looked like a young version of John Denver, took his marching orders to heart. He went on to become one of the most successful realtors in Sea Pines history. In 1973 when Sea Pines started a new development in Puerto Rico called Palmas Del Mar, they sent him there. At first Jim was wildly successful, but when Sea Pines got into financial trouble in 1974, the Palmas Project also began to suffer from delays, cost overruns, and permitting issues related to the difficult government. To Jim's credit, he saved many of his customers by talking them out of closing on condo purchases even though it cost him significant commission income in what would eventually be a problem project.

When the Palmas Development shut down in 1974, Jim was without a job. However, having saved a lot of money through the good times, he started looking around for opportunities. During a trip to Haiti, he discovered he could manufacture wicker and rattan baskets and furniture in what was a cottage industry, ship the stuff in containers to the states and then sell them to companies like Pier One Imports. By the time I met Jim in early 1981, his import business was booming, and he was operating a large retail business on the North end of the Island named The Wicker Warehouse.

As was my custom, before going to call on Jim I did my homework and due diligence. First, I learned that he had been an exceptional salesperson and that he had done a very honorable thing at his personal expense by treating his customers fairly. In addition, I learned that he was developing a Wal-Mart Shopping center at the North End of the Island with some other investors including Wally Seinsheimer. I also learned that Harold Chandler's team at C&S Bank was providing the financing and had issued two or three loans.

When I went to see Jim that day, I started out with my standard opening question, "How did you get in business?" After telling me how he got into the wicker and rattan business, he asked if I wanted to examine his books. Taking him up on his offer, I met with his bookkeeper, and I could immediately see that he had a good business with excellent margins and that C&S was making lots of money issuing import letters of credit to bring his goods on shore.

I was also able to compute the interest rate he was paying C&S because I could see the monthly checks for interest on his loans. Doing a quick calculation in my head on the rate he was paying, I met with Jim again and told him on the spot that I would replace $500,000 of his C&S loans and save him 1% on the rate or $5,000 per year. I could have a letter to him and all the papers delivered by courier to his lawyer that afternoon so he could start saving interest right away. Anyone who knows Jim knows that he likes to save money so we made a deal on the spot, and we went on to become great friends. Later, I financed Jim's entry into the retail business as the wicker and rattan trade began to wane. Today, Jim owns six retail stores that operate under the Camp Hilton Head brand. Jim's shopping center at the north end of the island ended up being a huge success. As time went on, he also acquired a lot of real estate as well as other businesses including a travel agency, three car washes, a theatre, a flower farm in Argentina, a Ranch in Patagonia, and a property management company just to mention a few.

Eventually, after clearing the bank's conflict committee, I became Jim's partner in a successful mini warehouse business. Jim, like JR, did many good things for the island getting involved in his community's property owners' association and doing other good works as well. He also created a scholarship fund at the University of Virginia for needy students from his South Boston home.

In short, the people Lisa and I were meeting were incredibly interesting, and we were learning and growing with each interaction. Another example was a customer named Robert Graves. Robert was a local boy raised on his father's farm, Pepper Hall. He went to South Carolina on a basketball scholarship but quit after several years because he really wanted to build houses and farm. When his father refused to help him start his building business, he sold the 4H pigs and cows he had been raising since childhood in order to get the cash needed to build his first house. By the early 70s, easily the largest builder on the island, he was over $10 million in debt when the recession hit in 1974. For the next six years he worked to liquidate his holdings and pay everyone back.

By the time I came to the island in 1980, Robert was starting to recover. I financed several very successful projects for him, but what I most enjoyed helping him with was his boat business. Robert built custom sport fishing boats for the very wealthy. Despite coming across like a country boy (he spoke Gullah, the native language of African Americans in the Lowcountry), he was a skilled craftsman and employed highly skilled workers.

One day Robert asked if I wanted to fly with him to Palm Beach to visit a client at the Rybovich boat yards. At the time, Rybovich was like the Mercedes Benz of sport fishing boats. When we arrived it immediately became obvious that Robert Graves was something on the order of a rock star. If Rybovich was a Mercedes, then a Graves Boat was a custom-made Aston Martin. We had a great time and I left with a much greater appreciation for Robert. Robert was a God-fearing man who became a good customer and good friend.

While Lisa and I were meeting so many new and interesting people, I met one who was an entrepreneur but in a different way. Frank Harrington was from Georgia where he had been the minister at Charles Fraser's Presbyterian church in Hinesville before the Frasers moved to Hilton Head. Joe Fraser Jr. was a member of the First Presbyterian Church on Hilton Head where Lisa and I worshiped. I chaired the finance committee at the church and our bank was in the middle of financing an expansion. Joe suggested I meet Dr. Harrington since he spent a month there every summer and had been involved with a number of church expansions.

By that time, Dr. Harrington was the senior minister at the Peachtree Presbyterian Church in Atlanta, which had over 10,000 members and was still growing rapidly. Frank Harrington was a force unto himself. He was chairman of the board of Presbyterian College and more than any other person had helped raise a large amount of money for the school. A kind man with a country sense of humor, he was obviously very bright and energetic. When we met for lunch at the restaurant in Harbor Town, he softly asked that we bow our heads in prayer.

That small request became a formative moment for me. I had joined the Presbyterian church right after Lisa and I married due to my father-in-law's influence, but I was somewhat self-conscious about religion, and I felt embarrassed because· 1 noticed that we were being watched by some tourists. However, my experience with Dr. Harrington made the lights come on, and I realized there is nothing wrong with thanking God before a meal for all our blessings in life. From that point forward, the simple act of giving thanks before a meal became a habit for our family regardless of where we were.

Another thing I gained that day was meeting Frank Harrington, who would become a good friend. Lisa and I enjoyed spending time with him when visited the island each summer for his 30 days of supposed rest and relaxation. The truth was, he spent that time writing 48 sermons, enough for the entire year. I asked him one time why he spent his vacation that way. He said that with 10,000 members he needed all his energy during the year for the care and nurturing of his membership. Writing his sermons in advance was the only way he could get everything done. As I thought about all the weddings, funerals, sickness and counseling in a congregation that large, I was humbled. I could tell he poured his life and soul into those people. Frank Harrington died in his mid-fifties having accomplished enough good works for several lifetimes.

If Hilton Head was Camelot, Charles Fraser was King Arthur and Merlin all wrapped into one. A Yale graduate and lawyer, he had written his college thesis on the use of restrictive land use covenants to protect property in perpetuity. He started developing Sea Pines in 1956 when his father Joseph B. Fraser sold him a 6,000 acre timber tract at the south end of Hilton Head Island where he could test his theories. Charles had great design instincts and hired the Sasaki firm to help with the master plan even though he was operating on a budgetary shoestring.

Sea Pines struggled in the early years but began to pick up steam in the 60s as word of mouth began to gather steam and with the advent of the Heritage Golf Tournament in 1969. In 1971 when Sea Pines went public, the company had a number of projects underway notably Hilton Head Plantation at the north end of Hilton Head, Kiawah Island resort outside Charleston, Amelia Island in Florida, Palmas Del Mar in Puerto

Rico, Wintergreen in Virginia, River Hills near Charlotte, and Big Canoe in Atlanta; however with the 1974 recession, Sea Pines got in serious financial trouble.

A young banker I would eventually work for named Buddy Kemp at North Carolina National Bank (NCNB) chaired the creditors committee when Sea Pines went into a debt restructure.. Buddy was a genius and figured out that the best path to resolution was for every lender to take title to whatever assets they held as security in exchange for the debt. This left the Sea Pines Resort Company and Travelers Insurance Company which had been the lender to Sea Pines Plantation intact and free from all other claims. By the time I arrived on the Island in 1980, the restructure was complete, and Sea Pines had become more of an operating company than a development company.

Organized as a number of separate and distinct businesses, Sea Pines included The Hilton Head Inn; a real estate brokerage business; a villa and home rental company; the golf course operation which ran three public courses including the renowned Harbor Town Golf Links; the private club course and members club; the tennis facilities; the yacht basin at Harbor Town; and the commercial real estate portfolio (generally leased to third party tenants for restaurants, bars, and retail shops). The stock while publicly traded was only selling for about $2.00 per share. While Charles was the CEO and chairman, the day-to-day running of the company was left to his brother Joe and Phil Lader, the president of Sea Pines who would leave in the early 80s to pursue a political career and end up as ambassador to the Court of St. James under Clinton.

Charles was perhaps the most interesting person I had ever met. His office was a huge space in the old Sea Pines executive offices that overlooked the forest preserve. One wall was floor to ceiling bookshelves crammed with books and the opposing wall was floor to ceiling window overlooking the preserve. There were old maps scattered everywhere as well as globes, well-worn antiques and rugs. Charles greeted each visitor with their full name which made them feel like the most important person in the world. In my case, he would say, "Welcome Carlos Evans," then he would spend an incredible amount of time talking about a variety of interesting topics, skipping from subject to subject with no concept for time. I was Charles's personal banker for much of my 6 years on the island, as well as the primary operating banker for Sea Pines Co. As a young 30-year-old banker still wet behind the ears I was mesmerized.

In addition to our business relationship, Lisa and I spent social time with Charles and his wife Mary. We were invited to many wonderful parties at their home, and we often cruised on his sailboat "The Compass Rose," which would leave Harbor Town every Sunday afternoon with a large group. Charles was a family man and everything about Sea Pines was designed with family activity in mind. These sailing trips were full of discussion on wide ranging intellectual topics with Charles as the ringleader stimulating the conversation. Since I was a sailor, having a small sunfish myself, Charles would often give me the helm while he held court. He was incredibly creative and well read on so many topics, so the conversations were always stimulating. Unfortunately, as history would reveal, Charles was not a great businessperson, and his primary focus never seemed to be on making a ton of money. As a result, he made some terrible financial mistakes. Nevertheless, everything that Hilton Head, Sea Pines, and many other communities have become are testaments to his creativity and entrepreneurial drive.

While I could write volumes about Charles's exploits as an entrepreneur, there is a book written by Charlie Ryan called, "My Life With Charles Fraser," which perfectly captures the man. It consists of stories written by people who worked with Charles over his career. Unfortunately, in December 2002 Charles died in his early 70s in a freak boating accident. He will forever be remembered as a pioneer in planned community development.

On February 21, 1983, I had a life changing event second only to my marriage to Lisa. The birth of our son Blakeley Hudson Evans took place in Beaufort because the Hilton Head Hospital did not have a birthing facility. I jumped the gun about 36 hours early, insisting we leave at 1am in the morning the day before because I was so worried that the drawbridge to the mainland might not be open. (At that time the new fixed span bridge was not there.) In any event, the birth of our son was an experience I will never forget, and to see him come into the world was a blessing. I know of no other time when I have felt the power of God as much as I did that early morning in the delivery room.

Lisa's parents, Joyce and Walker Hudson, came to Hilton Head the day she and Blake were released to come home and, they were a big help that first week. I should note that when Lisa and I moved to Hilton Head, it felt like we had gone quite far from our families. While we would come home to visit our respective families for the big holidays like Christmas, Thanksgiving and Easter, the rest of the time we were on the island pretty much by ourselves. Her parents were frequent visitors, which we greatly enjoyed along with occasional visits from my side of the family. As Lisa had foretold, the whole experience was a great adventure for us to be off on our own, and with Blake's arrival we were now a family. While I continued to work hard and long hours during the week, my weekends were full of family time.

One of my good friends was another young banker, Sterling Laffitte. His father, Monk Laffitte, was on the Bankers Trust board, and the Laffittes owned and ran a small family-owned bank in Estill S.C. They also owned a beach house on Hilton Head, since Estill was only about an hour away. Sterling married his lovely life Linn during our last two years on the island, and we took ski trips together in the winter. Sterling would often say in jest that he envied all the action we had at the bank on Hilton Head compared to his family bank in Estill. I would counter with yes, but you will live much longer than me because you get to go home every day for a fresh tomato sandwich lunch and a long nap. Sadly, Sterling died at 60 from throat cancer even though he never smoked a day in his life.

After Blake's birth the last two and a half years on Hilton Head passed in a blur. The island incorporated in 1983 and became a city. It was growing by leaps and bounds such that by the time I left in 1986, the population had more than doubled to 17,000. Beaufort continued to grow as well, although not as fast as Hilton Head.

Through that last two and a half years, I put into practice what I had learned about resorts through my financing experience with Sea Pines as I extended credit to new customers. For example, three young entrepreneurs—Jim Coleman, Bob Kolb and Steve Kiser—were able to purchase Hilton Head Plantation from Citicorp, and I was able to help them with several financings. One loan was for the water and sewer facilities that were part of the purchase but were a separate entity from the actual development and which had their own revenue streams from monthly resident water bills as well as sewer and tap fees.

By then we had opened our new main office on Pope Avenue as well as new branches at Shelter Cove and Sea Pines center. For the new branch in Sea Pines, which opened in 1985, Blake cut the ribbon along with the new Mayor, Ben Racusin. For the celebration I commissioned a painting of Harbor Town by a young artist named West Fraser. West was Joe Fraser's son, and he has since become one of the finest coastal landscape painters in the South. We gave customers prints of the original. West and I became good friends, and several years ago he gave me the study he had done for the painting. I now have a number of his paintings.

Part of the reason the last few years became a blur is that I became very involved in the community. I chaired the Beaufort County United Way Campaign, was chair-elect of the Hilton Head Chamber of Commerce, chair of the accommodations tax advisory committee that established ground rules for how the bed tax dollars would be allocated. The early funds were used for the promotion of tourism, and we were able to beautify the median in the new four lane road that ran the length of the island.

Given the growth in the island's population, the economy was booming, and the recession in 1981/82 at the end of Jimmy Carter's term was in the rearview mirror. Ronald Reagan was the new President, and Lee Atwater's stock had gone through the roof given his role in running Reagan's southern strategy. Atwater was now a partner with the consulting firm of Black, Manifort, Stone and Atwater. He was making a lot of money and was beginning to achieve his rock star political campaign strategist status.

Sometime in 1983 or 1984, Lee attended Renaissance Weekend, a four-or-five-day New Year's Eve event hosted by Phil and Linda Lader at the Hilton Head Inn. I'm not sure why Atwater was invited since he was pretty much the lone Republican at the event. Lisa and I were friends with Linda and Phil, so we were invited to several of the functions, and at one of them, along with Lee, we met Arkansas Governor Bill Clinton and his wife Hillary. While I am sure the Clintons had no idea who Lisa and I were, they definitely knew Lee. I distinctly remember Lee pulling us aside to tell us that the Clintons were people to watch, and that as a Republican, they worried him.

Lee was obviously seeing into the future. He would go on to run George W. Bush's successful campaign in 1990, but given Lee's untimely early death, he wasn't there to help President Bush's unsuccessful reelection campaign against Bill Clinton.

For me, 1985 was our best year. The bank's assets on Hilton Head alone exceeded $100 million, and we were four times the size we had been upon my arrival in 1980. Also, we earned in excess of $2 million, a tenfold increase over the $200,000 we had been making when I got there. My senior lender, Richard Rabb, had been promoted back to Columbia where he took a senior job in credit reporting to David Rhodes. I selected John Riddick to replace Richard. I felt he was someone who could succeed me as the city executive.

I was named Outstanding Young Man of the Year by the Jaycees and was given the award at a big, seated dinner. All my teammates were there. Even Julian Turner, now President and head of banking operations, came down from Columbia for the event. I so appreciated him taking the time to attend because he was an affable and wonderful man. It was also one of the last times I saw Julian because he died shortly thereafter from cancer.

The island was on an absolute roll. Josh Gold had sold the Hilton Head Company a few years earlier to Marathon Oil, and they were pouring money into redoing Port Royal as well as developing a very high-end inland harbor community called Wexford. Jim Coleman and his team were doing great things at Hilton Head Plantation after purchasing it from Citicorp. Even Sea Pines was booming after being purchased from Charles by Heiser Corporation. At the end of the summer of 1985, the island was hitting on all cylinders, but then all of that changed.

Since my arrival on the island, we had been doing business with Bobby Ginn and his company Ginn Development Corporation. Bobby had several very successful projects, the most notable being Turtle Lane in Sea Pines. Bobby was a self-made man from the small community of Hampton, South Carolina. He was also good friends and a customer of former governor Bob McNair, who was on our big board. Bobby could sell ice cream to the Eskimos, but he was also known to be capable of outrunning his headlights from a financial point of view. I loved Bobby, and Lisa and I had a social relationship with he and his wife Marty.

Bobby's CFO was Kumar Viswanathan, a very bright young Indian. Kumar was someone I trusted, and as long as he was around, things seemed to stay on track. When Kumar left to go out on his own, Bobby hired Earl

Hewlette from Columbia as his chief counsel and operating officer. Earl was a very smart lawyer who was also very good at financial engineering. While I liked them both, I always took great care to ensure that we were well secured with solid assets and repayment sources for our loans. It wasn't that I didn't trust Bobby and Earl, it was just that they were involved in so much stuff there was no way I could know what might be going on around the corner that might affect my loans.

At that time, the savings and loans around the country were making crazy loans, and word was they were financing Bobby. In late summer, Bobby purchased the Sea Pines Company from Heiser, paying cash and assuming all Sea Pines debt, which included our big line of credit. Within a very short time, he also purchased the Hilton Head Company's assets from Marathon Oil with the total purchase price of both companies being in excess of $100 million, all with debt from a small savings and loan. I was shocked! While I knew these were great assets, there was just no way the cash flow could support the debt, and Bobby simply could not sell assets fast enough to reduce the burden. Worst of all, we were headed into the winter, and I knew what that meant.

The first thing I did was call David Rhodes in Columbia and tell him I was going to call our loans and that he needed to tell Hootie so he could be prepared for a call from Governor McNair. David asked if I was sure it was necessary, because it was going to cost us a big customer. I responded that I had never been surer in my life. David called back almost immediately and told me to go ahead. My next call was to Bobby and Earl. It was a very cordial conversation. I congratulated them on the purchase and then asked to get paid. They asked why, and I told them that according to my calculations they would not have enough cash to get through the winter. They said, "You realize we are now the largest landowner on the island and a big customer." I told them, "I love you guys- but I have to do what's in the best interest of the bank."

The whole time I was talking to them, I was staring at the cash balances in their accounts, and I was prepared to offset for payment if I had to. To their credit, they said they would send me over a check that day to pay us in full and they did. As soon as I paid off the balance, I thought back to the problem loan I'd had to the service station operator 10 years earlier, when I would go to his store on Mondays because I knew it was the best time to get paid. The same principle applied: it was summertime, and I knew there would be problems ahead, so it was best to get paid off while Sea Pines had the cash.

As soon as that problem was resolved I turned my attention to the next one. Charles Fraser had become a good customer and friend. When he sold Sea Pines to Heiser Corporation in 1983, part of the consideration was cash and part was a debenture or unsecured note for the other half. The note was governed by a loan agreement that precluded Sea Pines/Heiser from levering the company without Charles's consent. Charles had a large line of credit with me secured by his Heiser note, and he was using it to invest in a variety of telecom businesses, notably cellular towers that were being sold through a lottery arrangement where the buyer had to escrow a large nonrefundable sum for each market they wanted to vie for.

Charles's idea was to bid for 5 or 6 key cities like Nashville, Charleston and Atlanta with the idea that if he got one or two it would be a winner. The odds at the time were essentially one-to-three, giving him a 33% chance of getting what he posted for. By posting for six key markets, it should have been a sure thing. Charles was way ahead of his time because he could already see that cellular was going to be big. He was right about cellular but not about his odds. He did not win a single city, so the primary source of repayment on my loan was now the note from Heiser, which had been assigned to me as collateral.

As part of the assignment agreement with Charles, the Sea Pines Corporation agreed that as assignee they would agree that the bank as well as Charles would have to sign off on any covenant waivers. When Bobby purchased Sea Pines from Heiser, he got Charles to sign off, but either he didn't know about my assignment or in the heat of battle just decided to go ahead and close and try to get me to sign off later.

If I had been concerned about Sea Pines paying off my secured line of credit, I was even more concerned about them paying off an unsecured note. After speaking to Bobby and Earl about paying off Sea Pines line, my next call was to call Charles to tell him that he needed to immediately get Sea Pines to post collateral for his loan or risk me suing him, Heiser, Sea Pines, Bobby Ginn and anyone else involved for a direct breach of the assignment agreement.

Charles became very upset because he had been talking to Bobby about being an advisor to his new company, among other things. He wanted more time to work it out, but I stuck to my guns and told him I wanted it done that week. Bobby was able to free up some very valuable land to secure the note, and Charles and I eventually got paid. However, by late fall Bobby, Sea Pines, and the Hilton Head Company were in serious financial trouble. Bobby tried to file bankruptcy in Judge Sol Blatt's court (a dear friend who recently passed) but would be denied. The companies would be sold to an entity called the Cuyuhoga Wrecking Company.

In the end, the whole thing went into Bankruptcy, and my good friend John Curry who was a great islander and good man was the trustee. Interestingly, all the assets would eventually be sold out of bankruptcy in pieces for an amount well in excess of $100 million. So in the end, Bobby's idea and strategy was a good one; he just didn't have enough cash to see it through.

Because of the protective actions I had taken, by 1986 when everything was a mess, I was sitting on the hill high and dry with no exposure to any of the troubled companies. Our bank would skate through with not so much as a scratch. I was able to salvage something for Charles as well by making sure he got collateral for his note.

In January of 1986, Hootie Johnson and Hugh McColl announced that NCNB would buy Bankers Trust in a cash and stock deal. In early summer I was promoted and moved to Charleston as the south coastal area executive responsible for the bank's offices in Beaufort County and all of Charleston. I was melancholy as our time in "Camelot" was over. However, I was very pleased that Beaufort and the island would still report to me.

In June of 1986, 1 was presented with a resolution from the Hilton Head Chamber of Commerce that read:

CARLOS E. EVANS

Whereas it is with a sincere sense of gratitude, and respect that we honor an individual who has made unique contributions to many aspects of the Island Community, and Whereas through his enthusiasm, resourcefulness, dynamism and positive attitude of "let's get it done," he has accomplished outstanding results, and Whereas by his service as an Officer of the Chamber of Commerce he arranged financing for its new award-winning building; organized the government/legislative affairs program and provided wise counsel for its ongoing operations, and Whereas under his leadership the towns Accommodations Tax Advisory Committee has won state-wide recognition and praise for its precedent setting method of developing methods and procedures for evaluating applications for funding, and Whereas his Church, United Way, and numerous other community organizations have benefitted from his dedicated guidance, and Whereas his bank has grown and prospered under his direction, and Whereas the Hilton Head Island Jaycees acknowledged his contributions to the community by naming him their Young Man of the Year in 1984 Now Therefore, the Board of Directors, Officers and Staff of the Hilton Head Island Chamber of Commerce take great pleasure in recognizing his outstanding achievements and thanking him for all his selfless efforts.

Presented this 20th day of June, 1986.

Angus Cotton Chairman

As I thought about the life changing experience Lisa and I and now Blake had enjoyed over the course of our 6 years on the island, I thought of my dad back in Salem and the lessons he had taught me. I found comfort in knowing that we had done the best job we could possibly do.

Carlos Evans

Chapter 18

From Bankers Trust to NCNB

When it was announced that NCNB would purchase Bankers Trust in 1985 it was no surprise. Even as the purchase was consummated in 1986 it was essentially a nonevent. For years there had been a close relationship between the two banks because NCNB was our primary upstream correspondent bank for check clearing and loan participation's when a loan became too large for us to handle by ourselves. They were to us what we were to the downstream smaller correspondent banks like The Exchange bank of Estill which was owned by the Laffitte family.

Everyone also knew that Hootie and Hugh McColl were great friends. In fact, every year our management played NCNB's management in a softball game. Many of our policies and forms were the same as NCNB's, and culturally there were many similarities with the most notable being that both banks were full of young people who had been given lots of responsibility at an early age and a chance to sink or swim .

However, there were several key differences. First, the NCNB culture was a reflection of Hugh McColl from top to bottom. Hugh was an ex-Marine, and he ran the bank like it was the Marine Corps. Everything was couched in military terminology like, "Full Speed Ahead," and when he was trying to buy C&S Bank, he described it as, "I am going to launch my missiles." Hugh also gave away crystal hand grenades every year to top performers. He clearly led from the front lines, and while his President, Buddy Kemp, was the person running the bank on a day-to-day basis Hugh was very visible and always out front talking it up with the troops.

Every meeting was like locker room talk before a football game but more in military terms. Hootie on the other hand was somewhat of an enigma inside the bank. While all the senior management team knew him, people at my level really didn't. I'd probably had a little more exposure to him through the work I had done on the building. In truth, most people were afraid of Hootie and tried to steer clear. Having said that, our culture at Bankers Trust was solid, built around a core set of values like teamwork, doing the right thing, helping build up the state. As I would learn later, cultures that rely too much on a person or singular personality have a very hard time surviving after that person leaves.

That was the case when Hugh McColl retired and the NCNB culture, in my opinion, actually became a liability. The same thing happened at Wells Fargo after Dick Kovasevich stepped down, resulting in problems that endured long after his departure.

With respect to Bankers Trust and NCNB, while there were differences in leadership style, the two cultures were compatible. Part of what made it work was Hugh's deference to Hootie which resulted in a gradual transition. There was no chain of senior executives coming down from Charlotte to tell us how to do things, which meant we were essentially left alone to do our jobs and run the bank. The only thing that really changed was our lending capacity, which increased substantially because we were now part of a bank with about $20 billion in assets, and that was 5 or 6 times bigger than Bankers Trust had been.

We also knew that there was an end game playing out in the industry, and we were positioning to survive and thrive as part of NCNB. Hootie wrote a moving personal note to the senior executives the week the merger closed. He told us it was the end of one era but the start of a new and exciting one where, as part of NCNB, we were in a better position to help ourselves personally as well as to help our state. He expressed deep pride in what we had accomplished together. At the time I had joined Bankers Trust, the net worth of the bank was about $23 million. Just 13 years later, the bank sold for about $50 per share or $500 million in cash and stock. Hootie was very proud that much of that money stayed in South Carolina where most of our shareholders lived. I suspect that for many years Hugh and Hootie had known we would eventually have interstate banking. The only question was how it would play out.

Before the 80's banks were limited to doing business in a single state, and in some states they were further restricted to specific counties. Many of our laws were borne out of the Great Depression and were specific to the USA. This meant that banks abroad were growing faster and getting much bigger than the U.S. banks. NCNB was one of the first banks to break out when they were able to acquire a bank in Florida through a loophole in Florida law that basically said if you owned a trust company you could own a bank. The law was tested in court and NCNB won.

What Hootie and Hugh both wanted was for the banks in the Southeast to be able to get bigger before the banks in the North got into the game. The truth was that the South had been capital starved since the Civil War. There is no doubt that reconstruction was economically debilitating to the South. In many respects, much of the South was like a third world country with very little in the way of economic benefit from rest of the USA. The South had no big banks after the war, and all the money and economic power lay in the North. Hugh and Hootie wanted to change that.

Both men knew that we needed bigger banks and more capital to fuel growth and prosperity for the region, and they wanted to maintain control of that capital. They lobbied legislatures and were successful in getting something called the Reciprocal Banking Act passed. This basically allowed certain states to use old trade laws and pass legislation to allow the banks in one region to merge and grow while keeping everyone else out. My guess is that Hugh probably had a clearer picture of the end game from his seat in Charlotte, but Hootie was very powerful politically because he sat on a number of large corporate boards and had strong political connections.

Both men were very focused on doing what was best for the Southeast, and probably held some resentment toward the big banks in Northeast to whom they had played second fiddle for so long. While I don't know Hugh McColl as well, I can state with certainty that Hootie was never driven by desire for personal gain but, like his father before him, was driven by a desire to do well for South Carolina and the southeastern region.

Hootie's values, what some might even call 'old school,' were reflected in other ways, as well. Hootie absolutely did not allow any intercompany dating or mixing business in a social setting. An example would be one year when our annual Bankers Trust/NCNB softball game took place in Charlotte. There was an NCNB keg party at one of the apartment complexes after the game, and they invited the Bankers Trust bus to stop there on our way back to Columbia. We arrived at the party where there were kegs of beer, an open bar, and lots of secretaries and young women in scanty bathing suits. Hootie took one look and said, "Men, we need to load up and head back home." We were all disappointed; we wanted to stay!

Another time, a group of us were invited up to Charlotte for one of Hugh's pep rallies on the 40th floor of the old NCNB Tower. Hootie wasn't with us, so we stayed for the whole thing. Rusty Page, head of investor relations, was MC, while Hugh held court, saying, "We're going to do this, and we're going to do that," all expressed in military terms. It was exciting and we were all drawn into what seemed almost a cult-like following. When we left, we all said we'd been at "Animal Bank," because the whole thing had been just like being in a big fraternity house and we'd liked it!

Buddy Kemp, NCNB's president, was very different from Hugh, although the two men loved each other. They were the perfect compliment. Buddy was taller, light skinned, a little heavy and had a sort of professorial preppy look. Hugh was darker and always tanned, short and lean with close cropped hair, always looking like he had just stepped off Paris Island.

Buddy's eyes burned with intellect, and he was an operator with tons of bandwidth for facts, figures, and budgets. He watched every penny and was famous for his budget meetings with all the managers where he would drill down into minute detail. He could remember numbers from prior years and call them up instantly. Buddy was also the best lender and credit guy I have ever met. He had that rare blend of caution, but also a willingness to take risk, and enough confidence in his own judgement to take those risks when he thought the scales were in balance. Buddy and Hugh were the perfect Mr. Inside and Mr. Outside, although, like Hugh, Buddy was great with people.

I was one of the people won over by Buddy Kemp. Even before the merger was consummated, he would come by the Hilton Head office when he vacationed with his family in Sea Pines. He knew Charles Fraser as well as many of the other Sea Pines executives since he had been chairman of the creditors committee in the Sea Pines workout. In fact, many people inside Sea Pines said that Buddy Kemp was the person who saved Sea Pines by getting the other banks to go along with a restructure. Buddy's kind of gravitas was unusual, especially in an environment where he was telling the much bigger Citicorp bankers and others what they should do. In any case, Buddy would drop in unannounced, and we would just talk banking. Although I do not know this for sure, my guess is he was part of the reason I was promoted to area executive and moved to Charleston.

I would note here that even though I was promoted to Area Executive, I still reported up the chain of command to John Boatwright, a longtime Bankers Trust executive, who with the merger became the South Carolina president of NCNB.

Buddy came in one day in the Spring of '86 when it had already been announced that I was going to Charleston. Most of our conversation revolved around what would I do when I got there. I told him about my theories of certain people being "traffic cops," but fortunately I had enough sense not use that term because I was beginning to understand the need to be politically correct. I called them "centers of influence"—the lawyers, realtors, and insurance people who could be in a position to send us business—and I would meet them first. I also explained my intention to read all the credit files before my arrival, so I would know the customers cold and be able to hit the ground running.

Buddy liked my plan. He asked how long it would take for me to do in Charleston what I had done in Hilton Head. I said it should not take as long. I wasn't trying to be arrogant, just stating that I had learned much in my time on the island and could put that knowledge to work in a way that would make things happen faster. I said that Charleston was easily 9 times bigger market than Hilton Head, but the two banks were roughly the same size, each with $100 million in total assets, which should make Charleston a more fertile hunting ground. Buddy agreed with my assessment so in the summer of 1986 Lisa, Blake and I went to Charleston where we rented at first while we tried to find a downtown house to buy.

Carlos Evans

Chapter 19

Charleston First Time

One of the things that helped make the Bankers Trust/NCNB merger successful was the competitive culture that had been fostered by both CEOs. In the case of NCNB, there had been an obsession with overtaking Wachovia and in later years a constant battle with First Union as well. Hugh McColl used to say that the banks in North Carolina were honed and hardened in a cauldron of competition. In the case of South Carolina, it was the same. At the start of my career, we had been tiny compared to South Carolina National (SCN), C&S, and First National. Later in my career we began to overtake them, but when I arrived in Charleston, we were third rate in that market at best.

In particular, the competition with SCN, the largest bank in the state, was keen, and for both SCN and C&S, Charleston was in many respects their power base even though both were headquartered in Columbia. In fact, both SCN and C&S Bank had been founded in Charleston. Also, the Lane family, the original founders of C&S, were still in the city, but with another bank they started.

A year or so earlier, Hootie had tried to buy First National Bank. The buyout attempt had been backed by Hugh McColl, who purchased Bankers Trust's mortgage company, Bankers Mortgage, for over $100 million, which gave us the capital base to make our unfriendly offer. Hootie had called me as the process unfolded and asked me to hand deliver a package to Francis Hipp, whose family-owned Liberty Life Insurance Company in Greenville, and who sat on the First National Bank board.

Hootie's instructions to me could not have been clearer. "I am having someone drive a package from Columbia to Hilton Head to place it directly in your hands. You are to take the package directly from your hands to Mr. Hipp at his beach house in Sea Pines. Do not involve anyone else."

I had heard rumors about a possible offer, and I knew Mr. Hipp was on the First National board. Francis Hipp was an icon in the South Carolina business community, but I knew him personally because he was a frequent visitor to First Presbyterian Church on the island, and he had recently made a large gift to our capital campaign. When I arrived at his house, he could not have been more cordial. He invited me in for a drink and set the package on the coffee table in front of us. We had a great conversation about the growth on the island, the church, and business in general. However, as we talked, I found myself staring at the package wondering what was in it. I think Mr. Hipp could sense my nervousness and maybe even found the whole scene amusing with me trying to talk as I struggled to keep from staring at the package.

Hootie did end up making his unfriendly offer at a significant premium to the price at which First National had been trading. This prompted First National to run to SCN to escape Hootie's offer. Many people expected Bankers Trust to top the SCN offer, but unfriendly takeovers did not seem Hootie's style so we backed down. Many of us thought First National was our last chance to stay independent but my feelings were that the combination with NCNB had been part of the plan all along and that Hugh was simply trying to kill two birds (Bankers Trust and First National) with one shot.

In any case, while competition in Charleston was quite keen, it was especially hot between our newly merged entity, now NCNB, and South Carolina National, which would be bought by Wachovia in 1991. When I arrived in Charleston in the summer of 1986, I was especially focused on trying to put a dent in SCN's customer base.

To some extent the move to Charleston was tough on Lisa. We found an old house south of Broad Street on Little Lamboll, a very quiet one-way street at the lower end of the peninsula between Meeting and King Streets. The house was about 200 years old and needed an incredible amount of work. There was rotten wood everywhere, and the un-landscaped back yard was filled with trash and debris. Due to the age of the house, there were no closets because at the time the house was built people used armoires. I had to get creative and close in a porch to create closet space.

All the bathrooms needed to be redone and the house was dark, so we added a skylight on the third floor in the middle of the stairwell which rose up through all three floors. We added a big bay window in the kitchen to let in more light as well, and we paved the driveway with tabby, a combination of oysters and concrete, then we edged it with old Savannah brick. Also, we totally redid the back yard, installed a fountain and extensive landscaping. It was a lot of work but very gratifying because we could see the improvements almost daily.

We were fortunate because some good friends, Doug and Marsee Lee, who we knew from Hilton Head, had moved to Charleston several years earlier where they had purchased and renovated a beautiful townhouse on King Street. Their work showed us what was possible with an older home, and they were also kind enough to introduce us to their contractor.

Later, Doug also helped make introductions for me at Kiawah Island, where he was a very successful salesperson. At the time, Kiawah was owned by the Kuwait Investment Company and was being developed in accordance with a master plan put together by Charles Fraser and the Sea Pines Company. For all practical purposes Kiawah was like Sea Pines, only better, with many enhancements Charles had learned along the way. I immediately implemented the same lot lending program at Kiawah Island and Seabrook Island that had proven so successful on Hilton Head. When we combined it with great service and speedy closure, we got out of the box fast, and Doug Lee's introductions were a big help.

In addition to the stress of renovating the house in under five months so we could be in for Christmas, there was also the work of moving around from place to place. I think we rented three separate spots before finally moving into Lamboll Street. Even when we moved in, the house was far from complete, and we had to live in the midst of a construction project for several months.

When the time came for us to move, despite the house not being totally finished, we used our old friends at Millen Moving and Storage who had done the move to the Tower in Columbia. They had also handled our move to Hilton Head and were the best at making it easy. Even so, Lisa was so exhausted after our move-in just a couple of days before Christmas that she didn't have the energy to put up a tree.

When she went out to buy groceries to stock up for the Holidays, Blake, who was approaching three, and I went out and bought a tree. I think I paid $2 for it the day before Christmas. Blake and I put it up, and had it decorated by the time she returned. It was the sweetest little tree, and Lisa was so excited that we could at least have the house feel like Christmas even though it was still a construction zone. Aside from the stress of the move, I was having to make frequent trips back and forth to Hilton Head and Beaufort. John Riddick was proving to be a very capable successor to me in that office, but there were still plenty of loose ends that required my attention.

One of the loose ends was a problem loan I had made for roughly $3 million (maybe $20 million in today's dollars) on an Island called Callawassie roughly halfway between Beaufort and Hilton Head. The island had been purchased from South Carolina Electric and Gas by Dr. Wilhelm Stein, a wealthy Swiss entrepreneur. In early summer just before my move, Dr Stein had come in out of the blue, saying he had a falling out with his minority partner, who had been my primary contact and had been developing the island up to that point, and that he planned to give me the island back. At the time, Callawassie already had a great Tom Fazio 27-hole golf course, and there were plans for a very nice clubhouse. The island also had about 600 lots, many with either marsh views or waterfront perimeters, but only 200 or so had been sold.

Aside from having a loan on the island itself, I was also aware that Spring Island was right next door and that by working with the owners of Callawassie, Spring Island's owners could possibly get a bridge permit that would provide an economical way to get to Spring. Around 1985, Charles Fraser had owned an option to buy Callawassie from Dr. Stein but had been unable to close. Bridging to Spring from Callawassie had, in fact, been Charles's plan and his reason for trying to buy Callawassie.

I had visited 3,000-acre Spring Island in 1982 when two Columbia developers, George Flynt and Ed Robinson had a plan to buy and develop the island. They took me over by boat for an overnight stay, tour, and quail hunt since the island had been a hunting plantation for many years, owned by Elisha Walker, a New York investment banker. Following Mr. Walker's death, the island was being sold, the transaction handled by Nelson Adams, a New York lawyer. On my tour in 1982, I met Mr. Walker's caretaker,

Gordon Mobley, who had lived on the island for many years with his three daughters who he took to school every day by boat. A very interesting man who knew every inch of the place, Gordon toured us around, and what a tour it was. The island was stunning.

Everywhere we looked, massive live oaks towered over the island with Spanish moss dripping from every branch. In fact, Spring Island held the largest standing live oak forest on the East Coast. There were beautiful ponds, both small and large, as well a great salt pond at the west end of the island that Gordon had built, and a shrimp pond near the Walker's house at the boat landing. A massive Tabby ruin was all that remained of the old plantation house that had been built in the 1700's when the island grew Sea Island Cotton, the house having been destroyed by the Union Army during the occupation of Hilton Head and Port Royal. Tabby was a mix of oyster shells and sand that, when fired and combined with lime, would become like concrete. At the end of the live oak allée that led to the tabby ruin stood a giant statue of St. Francis of Assisi that Mr. Walker had erected in front of a fig vine wall. The spot was both magnificent and very spiritual. At the east end of the island a beautiful gazebo with a huge fireplace sat beside a large pecan orchard where the Chechessee and Colleton Rivers came together. We took a break from hunting there and had a shrimp and crab boil.

To top it all off the island's average elevation was about 20 feet above sea level, which made it pretty much the highest piece of land in Beaufort County. To put that in perspective, Sea Pines had an average elevation of about 6 feet, which meant the whole place would be underwater if a hurricane came along with a 15-foot storm surge like the one in 1893. Thus, from the moment I set foot on Spring Island I knew it was special.

That being said, I never considered making the loan to Flynt and Robinson since their plan was to bridge Spring from Lemon Island at a cost about $20 million. I didn't know it at the time, but the bridge from Callawassie would ultimately cost about $1.25 million when it was built in 1991 since it went over marsh and would only need to be several hundred yards long. In any case, I thanked Flynt and Robinson for their time and filed away in my mind everything I had seen during the tour. Spring Island was an impressive place in every respect and one of the most beautiful places I had ever seen.

Now, four years after my Spring visit, I did not want to have a problem loan at Callawassie; however, my biggest concern wasn't the bank's money but Doctor Stein's. He had invested about $8 million of his own money in Callawassie, which meant my loan to value was incredibly low, by design. While I knew there was absolutely no way I would lose any money, I did not want him to lose all of his.

I told him, "Dr. Stein, if you will give me through the weekend, I believe I can find someone who will buy your Island and assume my loan. You will not get all of your money back but you will get some, and it will be worth waiting around a little longer before going back to Switzerland."

He agreed, and so the first call I made was to Jim Chaffin in Snowmass Colorado. I told him about Callawassie, but more importantly, I told him about Spring. To Jim's credit, he dropped everything and immediately got on a plane to come East. I had known Jim Chaffin and his partner, Jim Light, for about four years. I'd met them through Jim Bradshaw and had financed an oceanfront house for them in Sea Pines where they vacationed with their families every year.

Jim Chaffin and Dr. Stein met over the weekend and made a deal. An entity owned by Light and Chaffin, as well as Dr. Peter Lamotte of Hilton Head, Jim Bradshaw and JR Richardson would buy the island by assuming my loan, paying Dr. Stein some up-front money as well as several prime waterfront lots and a profit interest going forward. In my opinion, Light and Chaffin were very fair with Dr. Stein because the lots and the profit interest were a gift to someone who had been willing to walk away for nothing.

Bradshaw and Richardson would later drop out of the partnership due to the risk involved with developing Spring Island. Light and Chaffin, on the other hand, immediately started planning to option and buy Spring once the Callawassie purchase was consummated. Peter Lamotte would remain an investor and later would move to Spring Island. Dr. Lamotte was a wonderful man having moved to Hilton Head from New York City where he had been the chief physician for the New York Mets in the late 60s and early 70s. He founded the Hilton Head Hospital and had been a partner with Light and Chaffin on several deals.

From the very start Light and Chaffin focused on Spring Island. My loan on Callawassie paid off quickly as the lots were sold. Jim Chaffin and his wife Betsy moved to Spring Island and lived in one of the tiny cottages they had renovated to show the island to potential buyers. Betsy came to have a major impact on how the island was developed, reflecting the Chaffins' shared conservationist ideals, and the two of them commuted back and forth to the mainland by boat for 5 years until the bridge was built. The development of Spring was a labor of love for both, and they became dear friends of Gordon Mobley and his family.

For my part, I helped Light and Chaffin devise a founding member plan which would provide the $10 million or so in equity needed to make the down payment with the balance of the $20 plus million purchase being financed by the Elisha Walker Trust. The founding member plan was simple, involving the sale of 30 plus memberships at roughly $350,000 each, which generated the $10 million needed to close.

Each founding member received a membership in the Spring Island Club, a waterfront lot of their choice and collectively 6% of gross sales before expenses as lots were sold. The founding member program ended up being a good deal for the founding members as well as Light and Chaffin. One of my most memorable visits to the island came right after Light and Chaffin had acquired their option. They held a planning charette on Spring where they brought in land planners and marketing people as well as other successful developers like Harry Frampton an old friend from Sea Pines. At that charette they made the monumental decision to downsize the density of the previously approved master plan from thousands of units to only 500.

I thought they were crazy to give up that much value, but I was totally wrong because that one thing made the island distinctive. Later on, the property owners would downsize that number even more by buying back roughly 100 lots from Light and Chaffin. Chaffin kept saying that, "he wanted Spring to be a community within a park and not a park within a community." That is exactly what they created.

They built a fabulous Arnold Palmer golf course that wove through the magnificent moss covered live oaks and along the marshes of Port Royal Sound. Reflecting their great care and attention to the environment, they directed a percentage of every home and lot sale into something called the Spring Island Trust, which helped to fund the island's many environmental programs. They also instituted strict control over the architecture, and

Betsy insisted on major setback requirements and the maintenance of nature curtains to hide the homes.

Today, Spring Island remains a very special place and a total departure from everything else in the area. A visitor could ride around the island by boat or drive its winding roads by car, passing through live oak allées that date back nearly 300 years, and hardly see any of the houses. Everywhere, ancient live oaks drip with Spanish moss, their massive limbs covered with resurrection ferns, which are brown in the dry season but become lush and green with the rains. Several ponds pocket the island, all of them full of white herons, egrets, and other waterfowl, and of course, ubiquitous alligators basking on the banks. With only 350 houses on the 3,000-acre island, huge areas of open space remain protected in perpetuity by conservation easements. Homes are understated and hidden from view, and many of the island's roads are dirt.

Lisa, Blake and I purchased a lot there in 1996, some 10 years after Light and Chaffin became involved. We visit there frequently, and it has become a family tradition to spend every Thanksgiving there. For me, it remains a special and spiritual place, where I cannot help but think about the perfection of God's creation.

At this point, I was in a good position to make my professional transition. Fixing the situation at Callawassie had taken very little time, and my prior responsibilities on Hilton Head were in John Riddick's capable hands. While I would often travel to Hilton Head and Beaufort to meet with customers and employees, my focus and attention would turn to Charleston. I began to work out of the third floor of One Broad Street, our main Charleston office and a very historic building. My office windows overlooked Charleston Harbor and Fort Sumter where battles had raged in both the Revolutionary War and Civil War. In fact, in the Board Room next to my office, a cannon ball remained wedged in the rafters where it had been exposed by the decorator who designed the interior. I even had a small coal fireplace in my office to keep things warm in the winter.

My loan authority had been increased to $5 million which gave me lots of firepower to do business, and I intended to use it to help Charleston grow. In addition to setting up the lot lending programs at Kiawah, Seabrook and Wild Dunes on the Isle of Palms, I worked to grow our existing customer relationships as well as develop new business. Some existing customers were the Piggly Wiggly grocery chain and the Asten Johnson Group, an international manufacturer of various items used in paper making. Charleston/Summerville was a good spot for Asten Johnson given all the paper companies in the Southeast.

Outside of a small number of big businesses, however, Charleston was still very poor and lacked key economic vitality. Mayor Joe Riley, who would end up serving for over 40 years as one of America's longest running mayors, was doing some interesting things to bring the city back. Mayor Riley was a dynamo and would ultimately do more for the city than anyone to put it on the map. Best of all, he would do it in a way that would create prosperity for everyone without regard to race, creed or color.

Unlike many politicians who tend to cater to one demographic or class, Mayor Riley strove to be the people's mayor, and he struggled to ensure that Charleston would be a great city to live in for everyone. Under Joe's guidance, Charleston's tourist business boomed, and it was named the Best Place in the world to visit by Conde Naste. During his long tenure building a world class city, Joe won many awards for urban land planning.

He oversaw the construction of city parks with fountains where children of all classes could play and a huge waterfront park on what was arguably the most valuable land in the city, complete with beautiful live oak trees and their drapes of Spanish moss. Riley also pioneered the use of tax increment financing bonds to fund public infrastructure projects, all for the betterment of the community with no negative impact to the city's credit rating or general operating budgets.

One of his pivotal projects, the new Charleston Place Hotel, had just opened about the time I arrived. It was a sign that things were starting to improve, but the pace was very slow. Since the Charleston economy was still awakening from over a century of hibernation and the overall US economy was turning in the slowest GDP growth numbers of the Reagan years, it was clear to me that if we were going to grow the bank, we needed to take business away from others.

In addition to the opening of Charleston Place, another bit of good news was that oil prices were dropping as they started heading down to some of the lowest levels in the 80's. This was good for Charleston because it was a tourist destination often or even usually accessed by car. It was also good for car sales, and I kept noticing that the local Chevrolet dealer, a young well-spoken man named Tom Parsell was advertising heavily on TV. It just so happened that Tom and his family lived right down the street on Lamboll so I did my homework and went to see him at Parsell Chevrolet west of the Ashley on the strip where all the car dealers were located.

Tom was a tall, attractive fellow a shade older than my 36 years. Originally from Flynt, Michigan, where he'd worked in his dad's dealership, he came south for college at SMU, where he met his wife Suzi, who was a Dallas girl. After they were married, they went back to Flynt where Tom worked in the family dealership learning the ropes. However, Tom and Suzi wanted to come back south, so he searched the country for the ideal place. Based on the outlook for growth and other demographic data, Charleston seemed to be the right spot, so they put it all on the line and moved to Charleston in the 70s. While the early years were tough, they built the business with drive, determination, and marketing. Suzi was very much involved because she had a great mind for business, especially the marketing side.

By the time I walked into Tom's office their business was well established, and they were selling a lot of cars. I also noticed the service area was humming with activity. Tom was clearly very busy, so while he was polite, I could tell he had better things to do and was simply giving me the appointment out of courtesy since he was my neighbor.

As always in these situations, I asked him how he came to get in the car business. Like most entrepreneurs who love to tell their story, he opened up. My next question really caught his attention. I said "Tom, I've already done my homework on you, and if I'm right about how well you're doing, I'm prepared to save you a lot of money. Would you mind showing me your last years financial statement?"

The saving money part really got his attention, so out came the financial statement from a file behind his desk. By that point in my career, I could rifle through an audited financial statement in minutes. I knew exactly what to look for and where. I could see that Tom and Suzi were making a sound profit, at least over the past two years, since statements always display the current year compared to the previous year. I could also see they were retaining money in the business by the increase in owner's equity or capital. Furthermore, I could see exactly what they owed their current bank and what the interest rates were because that information is always disclosed in the footnotes in the back. Finally, and perhaps most importantly, I could see that Tom was running a tight ship and that all his departments were profitable including service, repair, parts sales, new car sales as well as used car sales.

I knew everything I needed to know in order to make a decision along with the prior due diligence I had already done on him. I leaned back in my chair and said, "Tom, you have two loans here that total close to $5 million, one on the building and one on your equipment package for the dealership. When I get back to my office, I will have hand delivered to you a commitment letter for both loans. If you give me the green light, I will have the closing papers sent to your lawyer the same day. The terms, covenants, and structure will be the same as your current loans, however, the interest rate will be 0.5% better, saving you $25,000.00 per year. You can take the extra money and buy Suzi a beach house."

He looked at me and said, "We already have a small beach house at Kiawah, but I can sure find something else to do with the money. We have a deal."

I walked out of there with a great new customer. Tom would go on to have a second successful career in an altogether different business (more on that later), and in one shot I grew the assets of the bank by 5%. More importantly, while I didn't realize it at the time, Tom would become a dear friend, one of my best friends, until he died in a tragic car accident some years later.

The situation described above or some variation of it would be replicated over and over in 1987. With the help of Marc Johnson, my Chief Credit Officer, we did a version of it with an investor named Gordon Darby to help him buy two apartment projects in Mt. Pleasant called Crickentree and Thicket which are still there today. Gordon is a wonderful businessman and a generous philanthropist. He was also, like me, a graduate of Newberry College, and we would serve on the Newberry College board together in later years. Marc and I also financed the construction of a new golf course called Charleston National for an investor from the North. By this point in my career, I still carried a loan portfolio myself because I believed in keeping my hands dirty with the paperwork and the process; however, many transactions were handled by others on the loan platform and overseen by Marc Johnson, the senior lender, who reported to me.

Marc, who was there when I arrived, was the son of Wellsman Johnson and Hootie's nephew. Marc was a couple years behind me, having started the training program about the time I came off special assignment on the Tower to finish my training. Although he was Hootie's nephew, he worked twice as hard as the rest of us in order to prove himself because of his name. He was a great thinker, had a sharp credit mind, and would be someone I could regularly consult with to keep me out of trouble. Marc would go on to have a very successful banking career with NCNB/Bank of America and later with First Citizens. He would also become a close friend.

Since Marc had been in Charleston before my arrival, he was incredibly helpful in introducing me to people. One particular introduction would prove to be very important. Capital South was a holding company with two principals, Pug Ravenel and Chuck Eiserhart. While Pug and Chuck were the principals, there were many other investors, mostly other prominent South Carolinians. Capital South's mission was to provide much needed capital to help South Carolina grow, a most noble cause and similar to what we had been doing at Bankers Trust and now NCNB.

Pug was a South Carolinian who had played quarterback at Harvard where he was given his nickname due to his combination of small stature and competitive drive. After Harvard, Pug would have a very successful investment banking career with Donaldson, Luffkin, Jenrette in New York before coming home to Charleston. Pug almost became South Carolina's Governor in the early 70s, and he also ran an unsuccessful campaign for Strom Thurmond's Senate seat in 1978.

Chuck Eiserhart was a bright, energetic real estate entrepreneur, and he and Pug were taking Charleston by storm. Capital South had businesses in real estate, brokerage, property management, insurance, subordinated lending to businesses, and they also owned a small savings and loan, Citadel Federal. Citadel later created a huge problem for Pug personally, leading to a criminal conviction that sent him to prison for a short sentence. In later years, I became somewhat aware of the circumstances surrounding his conviction, and I always felt that the sentence had been far too harsh for the circumstances.

Marc and I began lending to Capital South, but we were very careful to pick our spots. Not that we thought Capital South was a bad business, we just knew there was a lot of leverage and Pug and Chuck were risk takers. We advanced real estate loans secured by income properties and we financed their purchase of Heffron Ingle, a large insurance brokerage company. I had prior experience financing insurance agencies on Hilton Head where I financed the acquisition of Carswell of Carolina by the three principals. They were essentially loans backed by a very consistent and predictable cash flow.

Marc and I continued ramping up our loans outstanding to Capital South, and at one point we may have had $15 million in exposure. However, we stayed away from subordinated debt lending. Many of these loans were made to shaky businesses, and Marc and I worried about the consequences of being in a second lien position, in some cases behind large first lien lenders. The problem with being behind a first lien is that if there is a problem you have to be able to pay off the first lien to protect your position. In order to do that, you must have enough liquidity to pony up the cash. Marc and I never believed Capital South had sufficient liquidity to be in that business, and thus, while we would often be asked to lend into some of these transactions, we stayed away.

Ultimately, our caution was rewarded when several years later Capital South experienced big problems related to this activity. The company lost most of its capital on several large second lien loans, which resulted in Capital South being broken up and the pieces sold to repay creditors. We ended up collecting most of the interest and principal on our loans to Capital South, and we were able to escape with minimal losses.

By late 1987, in just a little under two years, we had grown the bank over 50%, and we were beginning to put a dent in the more established SCN and C&S. Lisa, Blake and I were happy in our Lamboll Street home, which by then was perfectly renovated and furnished, and we were enjoying life in Charleston. I walked to the office on Broad Street every day, and we walked around the corner to First Scots Presbyterian on Sundays where we were members. We enjoyed frequent visits by Lisa's parents, Joyce and Walker, and even my dad came to visit from Salem.

There were day trips to the beaches at Sullivan's Island on weekends and for two summers Lee and Sally Atwater came to Charleston for their family vacation where they rented homes at Isle of Palms. Lee's career as a strategist was booming, and it was clear that he was going to run George

Bush's election campaign when Reagan's second term ended. These visits by Lee and Sally were always great fun, and we spent many hours in the beach house with Lee entertaining Blake and his girls on the guitar. We often dined at local restaurants where Lee entertained us with all the goings on in Washington. Lee asked a number of times if I wanted to do something in Washington, but I always told him that I just wanted to be a banker not a politician.

On a personal note, these were wonderful years. In addition to spending time with family and old friends, we made many new friends in Charleston who remain friends to this day. There is something about having kids the same ages that helps bring people together, and people often forge relationships that last a lifetime. In our case there were many: the Lees, David and Kate Latimer, Hal and Shannon Ravenel (Pug's brother), just to mention a few. Yes, life was good, but little did I know that it was about to get turned upside down again but all for the better in what would be the most exciting part of my career with NCNB, soon to be NationsBank and then Bank of America!

Chapter 20

Columbia S.C. Second Time

Sometime in late fall of 1987, John Boatwright, president of NCNB South Carolina, hosted a management meeting for the South Carolina bank. At the conclusion, Joel Smith pulled me aside to inform me that the bank was being reorganized into a functional structure versus the old geographic structure. Until that point, every market had a city executive who functioned like a bank president with responsibility for everything that happened in that market to include consumer lending, branch activities, commercial lending as well as corporate lending.

Joel explained that John Boatwright was moving from Columbia to Charlotte to take a new job and that he would be assuming responsibility as President of the SC Bank. Three functional business heads would report to Joel, one person over statewide consumer banking including the branches and small business, one person over statewide commercial banking and one person over statewide corporate banking.

This change was a total shock to me since we had only been in Charleston 15 months, and we were just starting to get traction. I had gotten involved in the Charleston United Way as well as the Chamber of Commerce and was essentially executing the same plan that helped me be successful in Hilton Head and Beaufort. The Bank had already started to grow much faster and Lisa, Blake and I were finally settled in our newly renovated home on Lamboll street.

However, I totally understood the importance of aligning the bank functionally because it had been clear for some time that being all things to all people was not the optimal way to run things since most managers naturally gravitated toward one business or the other. Some were great consumer bankers but terrible commercial or corporate bankers and vice versa. Over time things had become more complex, and specialization through a functional organization structure definitely seemed the way to go. There was just one problem: Joel was asking me to be the corporate banking head.

At that time corporate banking was defined as all public companies and private companies with sales over $100 million. As time went on, this line of demarcation would move upward. For example, by the end of my career corporate banking would be all public companies with sales greater than $1 billion and commercial banking would be all private companies regardless of size and public companies with sales less than $1 billion.

I would also note that since corporate customers were bigger, that job was generally viewed as the more glamorous position. Also, it was not lost on me that most of the senior management team at NCNB in Charlotte had come out of Corporate Banking. There was one rub, however: I thought my skill set was more suited to commercial banking where the borrowers were smaller, the CEO or founder typically made all the decisions and usually didn't have a highly skilled CFO. In that smaller environment, the advice and counsel from a company's banker was highly valued, and loan structures tended to be more specific to the situation (i.e., tailor made suits).

In the corporate banking world, many of the customers were investment grade, had access to the capital markets, CFO's or corporate treasurers were responsible for dealing with the banks, and the CEOs had little involvement in financings. Aside from those differences, there were few true corporate customers in South Carolina and far more commercial customers. Thus, in South Carolina, while perhaps less glamorous, the commercial banking job would have a much larger balance sheet, more lenders, and a bigger P&L. Also, being commercial banking head would allow me to stay in touch with many of the relationships I had developed in Hilton Head, Beaufort and Charleston.

My dilemma was that my new boss wasn't asking me which job I preferred. He was asking me to do the corporate job, and back in those days a person generally saluted and asked when they should report for duty. Fortunately, Joel Smith was someone I had previously worked for and was very comfortable with, so I made a snap decision to express my opinion, diplomatically as best as I could.

"Joel, while I am flattered and honored by the promotion, and at the end of the day I will do whatever you and the bank want me to do, I really feel I am better suited for the commercial job." I went on to explain the reasoning behind this feeling and why I felt my skill sets were more aligned with one versus the other.

To Joel's credit, he came back with, "I thought you might say that which is why I asked you first." He then explained that he needed to discuss the change with John Boatwright and Buddy Kemp and he would get back to me. The next day Joel called and said the commercial job was mine. To say I was elated would be a huge understatement for all the reasons I will mention below.

First, the job meant Lisa, Blake and I would be returning to Columbia, and while we had been away for about 7 ½ years, Columbia in many ways was still home. Lisa's parents were there and we had grown even closer to them during our time away . I would likewise be closer to my own family in Florence and Salem, as well as my sister who was now married and living in Columbia.

Blake was turning 5 in February and would soon be starting school, so the timing was good from that point of view. From a selfish perspective, I would be returning to the building I helped create and best of all, moving to the Executive Suite on the 19th floor right down the hall from Hootie. I couldn't help but think back to the opening in 1975 when I was wearing a lime green Ban-Lon tuxedo and parking cars. How things had changed in just 12 years!

Joel asked me about my office preference. He would occupy John Boatwrights old office on the corner across from Hootie. There were two larger offices beside his and a smaller visiting office that had been set aside for Wellsman Johnson, Hootie's brother. I chose the smaller of the three offices because I wanted to stay under the radar, and that office was right next to the board room away from the others in a very private space. I knew I would be talking on the phone a lot approving loans. (With the new job my loan authority was increased to $20 million.) Also, there would be frequent meetings with customers so being close to the board room made sense. Roger Whaley, head of the consumer bank, would occupy one of the larger offices next to Joel ,as would Bob Howard, head the corporate bank.

About that time, a big article appeared in The State newspaper about NCNB's new management team for the 80's. As I made the move, I hired a new administrative assistant, Mary Willa Roper, who was a great help to me as I undertook my new responsibilities. I started working in Columbia almost immediately, while Lisa and Blake remained in Charleston. I rented a hotel room during the week and went back to Charleston on weekends, unless we were in Columbia house shopping.

We quickly found a home we liked very much in an older part of town at 11 Heathwood Circle. Lisa fell in love with the house, but the situation was complicated because the current owner was in financial trouble and making a deal with him was impossible due to the number of creditors involved. The more Lisa looked at the house, the more she fell in love with it, and her father even started drawing plans for the renovation since being something of an architect, he had an excellent eye for scale and finish details.

Given the legal complexity of the situation, I called my old KA friend Doug Seigler, who was an attorney. Doug advised that the existing first, second and third lien creditors were going to foreclosure in hopes of getting some of their money back. The only way to get title to the house would be to go to the foreclosure sale and bid. Doug and I ran the calculations on what we thought the house was worth and what the renovations might cost.

By that point, I was headlong into my new job and traveling all over the state. Because of my schedule I sent Doug to bid in my stead on the day of the auction. The auction had been set for a Friday afternoon, and I remember clear as a bell the call from Doug as I was driving back to Charleston to spend the weekend with Lisa and Blake. Doug told me that there had been two ladies at the auction, and the bidding had taken off like a rocket significantly outstripping the top end of what we were willing to pay. When I got to Charleston and told Lisa, she was distraught because she had really been looking forward to making the house on Heathwood Circle our new home.

The house was a handsome brick Georgian-style, and unlike our house in Charleston, which wasn't really functional for modern family living, the house on Heathwood was perfect. It had a big yard with a fenced in back for our cocker Spaniel, and there was even enough room to add a pool. Huge magnolia trees covered the property. While we would have been renovating again if we'd bought it, we were nonetheless very deflated because we had gotten our hopes up.

I tried to console Lisa and said we would immediately start looking for another house in the same general area...hopefully we'd be able to find one. From our prior two moves, I knew that getting our family settled as quickly as possible was important to me getting fully engaged in my new job. As I departed for Columbia early that next Monday morning, I thought about how disappointed Lisa was and how I needed to find something she'd be happy with as soon as possible.

Later that same day, Lisa called. "You won't believe what happened," she said. "This lady from Columbia called asking if we were the people who wanted to buy the house on Heathwood Circle."

Lisa said we were but somebody else bought the house away from us. The lady replied that she and her friend had been high bidder, but now it was a big problem because they didn't want the house! It seemed the two ladies were blooming entrepreneurs who decided to go out and buy a house to renovate and sell without speaking first to their husbands. They had gone to the auction without an attorney, and they didn't fully understand the rules, especially, the very key point that bids were in excess of the first mortgage balance. For example, if the first mortgage on the house was $100,000, a bid of $150,000 meant that the buyer was actually paying $250,000 for the house.

Not having understood how much they were truly bidding, the ladies were beside themselves. They had gone to the judge hoping back out, but the judge told them to be in his chambers that coming Friday with the full purchase price or they would lose their deposit. The situation was complicated by the fact that their husbands were unaware of their mistake. Telling them about it was not going to be fun. Lisa gave me the lady's number and said she hoped something could be worked out.

By then I knew I needed to do whatever I possibly could to get the house. I called the lady, and even though the price was more than I wanted to spend, I thought I could make it work. I agreed to step into their shoes and buy the house at their price refunding them their deposit. Needless to say, they were relieved, but I was also relieved because Lisa was happy. It was good for all of us, because we could get on with planning our move, and I could get focused on work! And it was an especially good deal for the two ladies who had just learned a valuable business lesson about doing their homework. This was a mistake they would never make again.

As I began to get into the rhythm of my new job, it was clear that there was much work to be done. I divided the state into 4 regions, Coastal, Central, Piedmont and Western. Each region was headed by a regional executive who had teams of commercial lenders from each city in their region reporting to them. The loan portfolio was about $1.2 billion, and earnings were about $15 million after taxes, so this was a far bigger business than anything I had ever run.

The economy in South Carolina had evolved from primarily agriculture at the start of the century to textiles and manufacturing as we neared the end of the century. While textiles were still king, there were already rumors that the industry in the USA would soon be displaced by countries where labor was far cheaper. Also, tourism was booming, on its way to being by far the largest industry in the state. The tourism was concentrated in Myrtle Beach, Charleston and Hilton Head, all markets that I knew well. Everyone was betting that tourism would be the catalyst to help pull South Carolina out of its historic economic privation to a state of greater prosperity.

I decided to place my bets on tourism as well, and in keeping with the culture ingrained in us by the Johnsons, I would do all I could to help our state and economy grow. I knew that helping the entrepreneurs in every location where NCNB did business would be the key to making that happen. I also knew that from my new seat on the 19th floor in Columbia, I was in a great position to be their "helper of choice."

As the summer wound down and fall rolled in the economy was doing just fine. Interest rates had ticked up into the 9% to 10% range, but they weren't nearly as high as the 20% rates we had seen earlier in the decade. I was settling into a ritual that involved lots of travel around the state by car and sometimes in small airplanes. While I maintained my old habits of doing my homework in advance so I would be in a position to commit on the spot, I also began to develop some new habits. One was to spend as much time in the field as possible so I could get to know the customer and they could get to know me. As the person with the "Big Pen" customers wanted to know who I was. I also made it a point to read everything that hit my desk that day so I could be responsive to my people.

In those days there were few desktop computers and no laptops, so the loan approval reports were in paper called CARs for credit approval reports. Copies would come in advance of loan approval for discussion, then an original would be circulated for everyone to initial as evidence of final approval after the loan was booked. With $20 million of lending authority, I was usually the last to sign, other than for those really large deals that had to go to Charlotte. Since the loan officers had to spend a lot of time putting the CAR's together, I considered it my responsibility to read every single one and be knowledgeable in advance of every credit discussion. I remember getting angry when someone would ask a question that was clearly addressed in the writeup which made it clear that the person asking the question did not read the material and was therefore wasting everyone's time. The CARS would come in waves every day, since the field generally had $2 million in authority, so that anything between $2mm and $20mm in total credit exposure (existing and proposed) came to me.

Since my quick response time and my habit of answering my own phone were hallmarks for me, I used this strategy in my new role. However, now my responsiveness was in support of my people instead of the customers, since the loan officers in the field were the ones doing the calling. To keep up with this constant flow of information, I had daily mail packages follow me around wherever I was using the bank's couriers who went to every office every day to deliver interoffice mail.

Also by then, cell phones were starting to be used although the coverage was spotty. I had a phone installed in my car with a little antenna on the roof. I wanted my people to be able to reach me any day, any time. Mary Willa Roper was proving to be a valuable partner who always knew how to track me down when people would call my office.

I also made it a point to learn everything I could about all our major customers—details on their family life, where they went to school, their hobbies. To get this information I spent a lot of time reading the credit files which were, of course, down in the basement in those big fireproof files I had installed 13 years earlier. Armed with this information, I found that when I was out calling on customers I could relate to them more effectively, and the customers realized that I was aware of all aspects of their relationship and history with us.

These calls were incredibly interesting because they included plant tours, site tours, and learning how the entrepreneur started their business. As I had learned, the best question was always, "Tell me how you got started?" When I would return to the office, I would immediately dictate a string of letters to the customers and prospects I had met thanking them for their time and commenting on their business. By then I had become proficient with the dictaphone and could bang out 10 to 15 letters in short order. Mary Willa Roper was equally proficient in getting them typed and in the mail that same day.

In addition to my general rules around responding quickly and always being up to speed on things, I developed one more rule. Invariably, in the lending business there were occasions when we had to say no. Sometimes it was an easy no, and I knew the customer was expecting it. Other times it was a tough no, where the decision was close, and the no had significant impact on the entrepreneur's business. In many cases jobs were at stake, there were impacts to a local community when an expansion couldn't get financed, and worse, impacts to people's livelihoods and families. Just so people understood that I was in the trench with them, my rule was that whenever there was a tough message to deliver, I would go in person to be with our lending officers. I didn't want my people to think I was sitting in an ivory tower in Columbia safe from where all the bullets were flying.

As things began to heat up, we were starting to grow. I was spending a lot of time in the field, and I remember one trip to Greenwood, SC, where Bankers Trust had been founded. It was in October of 1987, and we were calling on customers and prospects. In those days each bank main office had a stock quote machine, and I remember looking at the machine in the Greenwood bank and seeing that the stock market had dropped 22% in one day. Today, that would be the equivalent of the Dow dropping over 6,000 points. It was incredible.

I remember asking someone if there was something wrong with the machine. The person said what I was seeing was real and was going to get worse. I remember thinking the world as we knew it was coming to an end! My drive back to Columbia took me through a number of small towns, and I stopped along the way curious to see the impact the market fall was having.

Interestingly, life was going on as usual; in fact, most people were totally unaware of what had happened. It was then that I realized Main Street was a long way from Wall Street, and while the happenings there would eventually have an impact on the macro economy, for everyday Americans it was essentially a nonevent. I remember thinking that disconnect was a good thing and we would be okay. Fortunately, the circumstances that created the precipitous drop were related to computer trading and were technical in nature, so the effects were short lived.

As we entered 1988 business was starting to hum, and I was really enjoying my work. I was learning to be a general manager and doing things through people versus doing them myself. I was often in the field, and every week would take me on travels throughout the state. The customer base was very diversified from textiles and manufacturing in the upstate, to the peach farmers and chicken growers in the middle of the state, to the tourism businesses on the coast, and everything in between. There were sawmills and lumber companies, car dealers and heavy equipment dealers, a big pecan sheller in Florence, beer and soft drink distributors, convenience store chains, just to mention a few. A number of nonprofits and government entities were also commercial customers. Cities and counties were mostly cash management customers, along with water districts, special purpose entities like the SC Ports Authority and electric co-ops. There were higher education customers like the state supported colleges and universities, as well as the small private schools like Newberry, Converse College, Wofford and Presbyterian. We were lending to all of them and taking care of their cash management needs. I loved reading the constant flow of numbers, updates on financial performance, new transactions, etc. Fortunately, since I had a good head for numbers, it was easy for me to keep up, and customers seemed to appreciate that I was always available and current on their situation.

While I loved the variety of businesses in the midlands and upstate, there was a special place in my heart for the resort businesses on the coast. Aside from believing that South Carolina's future resided with tourism, many of our closest friends were in Hilton Head, Beaufort, and Charleston.

In my 8 years of living on the coast, I had acquired a deep understanding of those tourism related industries. In particular, I knew that golf was growing in popularity and the entire coast was rapidly becoming a golf Mecca. Myrtle Beach in particular was a hotspot, and the hotel operators were teaming with golf course owners to provide three-and five-day golf packages through a central reservation system. At the time, we viewed golf courses as operating companies as opposed to real estate companies, because their financial metrics were very similar to hotels. Instead of occupancy and average daily rate, which were the key metrics in hotel lending, golf courses had rounds of play as a proxy for occupancy and greens fees as a proxy for daily rate. As in all things there were different classes of facilities. There were championship courses that generated much higher greens fees and then middle of the road courses that were still successful but charged lower greens fees and, as a result, produced lower cash flow and value.

In those days, a good golf course could generate 50,000 rounds of play with $50 greens fees for $2.5 million in gross revenues. After expenses of about $2 million one could expect to generate about $500 thousand in cash flow, which at a 10% capitalization rate would produce an asset value of about $5 million. At the time, we would lend about $3 million per golf course for a loan to value of about 60%, financed over 15 years. The key was having good operators and a course design that drew the players. We thought we were pretty good at judging both, so we dove in. By 1988, we held loans on about 50 golf courses for a total of about $150 million, and it ended up being a great business for us.

All this activity had me traveling frequently to Myrtle Beach and Hilton Head, both over 3 hour drives from Columbia. Since I hated being away from home at night, this usually meant I would have to fly in a small plane so I could get back home most evenings. At the time, there were two flight options.

One was Bank Air, a small company that flew routes daily in the morning and afternoon to pick up checks for processing at the banks centralized check processing centers in Columbia. These planes were mostly single engine Piper Cubs with a jump seat behind the pilot that I could rent for short hops. The planes left daily out of Owens Field in downtown Columbia, the same airport where years earlier I had almost been late picking up Hootie's guests. I remember on more than one occasion during the summer being terrified at having to fly around thunder storms with lightning all around and the little plane being tossed around like some kind of toy.

In situations where I needed to stay later for a dinner meeting, I would charter a twin-engine Cessna. This was a much more comfortable plane but more expensive and only used when the Bank Air schedule wouldn't work. My habit was to board the plane after dinner and settle in with a gin and tonic for the flight back to Columbia. Since the planes flew very low, I would play a game trying to identify all the cities and small towns as I sipped my drink. I often thought about how each point of light was a home or business where people worked hard to survive and prosper .

I was well aware that I had the opportunity to help create an environment that made their lives better, just as early in my career on a much smaller scale I had helped the lady buy her car after her ex-husband ruined her credit rating. On every one of those lonely flights home, which were many, I would look at the lights and resolve to find ways to do things that were truly a win-win for the customer and the bank, things that perhaps other people could not figure out how to do. While I don't consider myself a genius, I knew that if I looked hard enough to figure out a way to do things, much more was possible. I thought about the Seabrook and other examples where finding a way had brought about much good.

As the winter of 1988 concluded, I received a call from Charlie Way CEO of the Beach Company in Charleston that would change my professional and personal life on many different levels. The Beach Company had been started by JC Long, the original developer of the Isle of Palms, and over the years the Long family had become large landowners and very successful commercial property developers in Charleston County. The Beach Company's ownership was now in the hands of Mr. Long's heirs—his two daughters (Charlie was married to one, Mary Ellen), their families, and the family of his deceased son.

Charlie Way was an attorney, and he had been at the right age to take over the company when Mr. Long passed away. While Charlie was essentially the CEO, his three nephews (Buddy Darby, John Darby, and Leonard Long) were also involved in management. I had called on Charlie Way and the three nephews during my time in Charleston, but they had been staunch South Carolina National customers while we, as Bankers Trust/NCNB, were relative newcomers to the market. While those calls were cordial, they never developed into anything since the Beach Company was entrenched with the more established banks. So, to say I was surprised by the sudden call from Charlie was a huge understatement.

Charlie was a tall, imposing figure with a booming Southern Gentleman's voice. Those that knew him could attest that he never minced words and his phone conversations tend to be very brief. Charlie, quickly relayed to me that they were trying to buy Kiawah Island from the Kuwait Investment Company and were dealing with the General Manager, Sal Alzaman. They were thinking of forming a partnership with an entity owned by the Beach Company as the major partner. The minority interests would be held by Lou Ranieri, a Wall Street investment banker, along with Frank Brumley and Pat McKinney, both Charleston Developers and former employees of the Sea Pines Company.

Charlie said they were talking to a number of savings and loans about long term financing since at that time S&Ls were doing a lot of real estate deals. I knew that many of these loans were not well underwritten, like the ones made to Bobby Ginn when he purchased the Sea Pines Company and the Hilton Head Company. Charlie said they wanted to be able to show Mr. Alzaman that they were credible buyers so they wanted a bank commitment in order to get his attention. They were offering to buy the island for $102.5 million and willing to pay $2.5 million up front. Charlie said he realized it was an unusual loan for a bank to make, but he figured if anyone could figure out a way to do it, I was their best shot given my knowledge of Hilton Head and master planned communities. After all, Charles Fraser had done the original master plan for Kiawah under a management contract with the Kuwait Investment Company. I told Charlie that I was prepared to move quickly and could come to Charleston the next day to start due diligence. It turned out that the trip to Charleston was quite convenient because Lisa and I were already planning to head down to Hilton Head for the weekend to visit friends.

However, I also told Charlie up front that a loan of this nature would have to be made under unusual terms, and that it would be expensive since they were essentially going to use our commitment to secure a contract and then try and obtain more favorable terms from another lender. Charlie said he realized that, but it was worth it if it enabled them to get a contract with the Kuwait Investment Company at their price and terms.

As soon as I got off the phone with Charlie, I walked down the hall to Joel Smith's office and explained what was going on to make sure he didn't think I was crazy. Both Joel and I knew that this was going to be a massive land loan for a bank our size. In fact, although we didn't know it at the time, it would end up being the largest real estate loan ever made in South Carolina. At the time NCNB a was only a $25 billion bank. So for us to make a loan this size relative to our $25 billion in assets (roughly 0.5% of total assets), it would be equivalent to today's $2.5 trillion Bank of America making a $12.5 billion land loan—something that would simply not happen.

To Joel's credit, he didn't throw water on the idea. He simply told me to go down there, get all the information, then write up my recommendation on what we should do and how we should structure it, assuming the loan was indeed doable. If we both agreed the idea had merit, we would make a joint visit, and after that if we still thought it had merit, we would need to get Buddy Kemp down there because he was the only person in the Bank who could approve such a loan. It occurred to me that Buddy was, in fact, the perfect person to approve a loan like this given his involvement in the Sea Pines Company restructuring in the early 70's. Although I didn't yet have any of the financial information when Joel and I were having our initial conversation, I knew that the basis of the loan would have to be a summary of the parts analysis of all the resort assets, including the golf courses, tennis facilities, Kiawah Inn, lots, water company, Kiawah Island Club, real estate brokerage company and future developable property.

During my short fact gathering visit to Charleston I was given an enormous amount of information by Frank Brumley and Pat McKinney, including details on all the assets, some sketchy past financial information, as well as future projections. The past financial information was of little or no value since the Kuwait Investment Company had essentially mothballed the island for the past couple years after deciding to sell it. There were golf courses where the greens were being cut every day that were not open for play. I was even told they buried all the rental bicycles on the island for fear of liability. While I was given financial information on the Beach Company, Charlie Way made it very clear that this would be a non-recourse loan, so the island and whatever else I asked for in the way of collateral would have to suffice.

After our meeting, Lisa and I departed for the 2 1/2-hour drive to Hilton Head. I asked her to drive since I had some very important work to do. As I studied the information, I began to formulate a structure in my head. While I could easily see that there was tons of collateral value in a number of completed oceanfront lots that I valued at roughly $500,000 each; there was also the inn; 4 golf courses; the site for a new, yet-to-be-built private course; the water company, which I thought was easily worth $10 million plus; the tennis facilities; the site for a new convention hotel; the site for a commercial shopping center development; the real estate company, which in good times made a lot of money because it was the only brokerage company on the island; and then a huge piece of stunning undeveloped land on the east end of the island with tons of ocean frontage; and chaneers on which lots could be created that would have unobstructed Kiawah River views.

The problem was that the resort operation itself was losing money at a substantial rate, and since it had been mothballed, it would take some time to start everything back up. On top of that, there was the interest expense on a loan this size which at 10% plus would run $10 to $12 million per year. As I thought through all this, I realized there were some similarities between Kiawah and the situation I had experienced with the Seabrook loan years earlier when I had found a way to fund operations out of condo sales until the health care facility could become cash flow positive. So, with all of this in mind, I picked up my dicta phone and started in as Lisa drove.

The first order of business in the memo was to summarize the history of the Beach company since its founding, as well as to provide a brief assessment of their financial wherewithal. Even though they would not be personally obligated on the loan, my position was that in a crunch they were capable of providing support to protect their position.

The second section of the memo detailed all the assets along with my assessment of their value both on a "normal" basis, and on a gross basis if we ever had to liquidate them in a fire sale . The last section of the memo was a proposed structure for the loan which was really pretty simple. I was proposing to lend the purchasing entity Kiawah Resort Associates $125 million which was essentially 100% of the purchase price plus $22.5 million for an interest and operating reserve. We would establish a 65% release price for all lots and assets sold. Essentially, that meant if they were able to sell 20 of the valuable oceanfront lots for $500,000 each year for the first two years, they would generate $20 million in proceeds which would reduce our loan by $12.5 million and fund approximately $7.5 million back into the operating and interest reserve. This, along with the reserve already in the loan, would basically give them 2 1/2 years of runway to cover interest and operations until things got turned around.

I thought my assumptions were very conservative and that things would actually sell a lot faster once people realized the island was back open for business and in capable hands. Little did I know that they would ultimately need every penny of the reserves I had structured into the loan. I also required a $25 million dollar letter of credit from an acceptable bank with NCNB as the beneficiary. The letter of credit would essentially be the equity in the deal and would give us additional collateral margin if things went wrong.

As I droned away on my Dictaphone, I began to notice that Lisa had grown very quiet. When we arrived on Hilton Head and I finally put the device down, she looked at me and asked, "Are you sure about this? Because if it doesn't work you're out of a job."

When I returned to Columbia the following Monday, Mary Willa Roper typed up my memo and I took it over to Joel's office. He quickly read it and then came back by my office saying "Your plan might work. Let's go down there and take a look and then if we're still positive, we'll schedule Buddy Kemp to come as well. A day or so later, Joel and I chartered a small plane and flew into Johns Island airport near Kiawah. While both of us had visited the island in the past the trip gave us both a fresh look and the opportunity to see things as a lender. What we found was a stunning island, beautiful in every respect with the best parts of the master plan yet to be realized.

The island ran 10 miles east to west, not north/south like most coastal barrier islands. Charles Fraser's master plan had set the oceanfront houses way back from the beach, even more so than the setbacks at Sea Pines. In addition, the sand dunes were massive, some as high as 30 feet which gave the Island another buffer of protection. The land at the east end which I had never seen before was stunning, with a dune field on the ocean side that made it look like Scotland. The back side of the east end of the island was every bit as impressive with fingers of high land reaching out into the marsh with unobstructed views of the sunset and Kiawah River. In a nutshell, the place was spectacular, and even though it was in a semi closed state, everything was being maintained in first class condition.

Joel asked if I still felt positive, to which I responded, "Even more so." I did point out that while the plan was for us to never have to close the loan, assuming they could find an S&L lender, we needed to be prepared to do so, especially given the flakiness of the savings and loan industry. With that final thought, we set things up for Buddy Kemp to come down along with representatives from the NCNB real estate lending group. In those days, real estate loans were joint undertakings with the so-called experts in the home office and the local commercial people in the field.

I don't remember the time lapse between the visit Joel and I made and the visit from Buddy Kemp. However, it couldn't have been too long because I remember when Buddy flew in on the NCNB King Air to pick us up to go to the island there was actually a light snow in Columbia . . .so it must have been March, only a few days after our first visit. On the plane were the two heads of real estate, Ralph Carestio and Larry Vogler, as well as Linda Fairchild their real estate lender for SC, and Fred Figge, NCNB's new chief risk officer. In 30 minutes, we were on the ground on Johns Island and 20 minutes or so later we were in a conference room on Kiawah Island that was full of maps, architectural renderings and marketing materials.

Charlie Way kicked of the meeting by saying that they had vehicles on standby to take us all on a tour. To which Buddy Kemp responded, "I don't need to see the island because I know it's pretty. Carlos has already briefed us in a memo on the transaction. You all go out on the tour. I'm going to stay here and visit with Charlie to see if we can do a deal."

I realized that Buddy wanted the time to visit with Charlie personally one-on-one to evaluate the big C or Character part of the equation. With that, the group went off, and Buddy asked me to stick around. We had a nice visit with Buddy asking tons of questions, not so much about the deal itself but more about Charlie's background as an attorney and the history and activities of the Beach Company. It was a nice conversation similar to many conversations I had held with customers when I would say,"Tell me about how you got started."

After an hour or so, someone came in the room and said, "Mr. Kemp, you have a call from Charlotte." Buddy left the room to take the call, but when he came back, I could tell he seemed distracted. He said the call had been from Hugh McColl, and he needed to get back to Charlotte immediately. Little did I know that there was a much bigger deal brewing as NCNB was about to make a bid to acquire First Republic Bank in Texas which would effectively double the size of NCNB, but more importantly move us one step closer to having interstate Banking.

We packed up and went back to the plane. Buddy asked that Linda and I sit in the back with him. He asked me to lay out the terms then asked about pricing. I said I thought the loan had a more than usual element of risk so we should price it at prime plus 2%. I also told Buddy the upfront fee should be 2% or $2.5 million. Furthermore, since they were going to use our letter as leverage to negotiate a good purchase price then shop the transaction with other lenders to try and get better financing, I suggested to Buddy that we charge $250,000 to be credited against the $2.5 million fee. Our offer would be good for only 24 hours upon receipt of our letter, and they would have to pay us the $250,000 upon the delivery back to us of their signed acceptance. This would ensure that we got paid something for delivering the commitment even if they found another lender with more attractive terms. There was one additional caveat, which was that every 15 days the commitment would need to be renewed, requiring additional payments of $250,000 with each extension. In this way we would get paid more and more as time went on for the risk of having our loan commitment outstanding. Buddy liked the plan and as we exited the plane in Columbia, he told Linda and me to draft the commitment letter and deliver it. It was just that simple and over that fast.

The next day Linda and I drafted the letter and engaged John Lumpkin Jr. (the attorney who had been the cause of the furor with Hootie and Governor McNair) to represent us. As mentioned earlier, John was now with the McNair firm, so using him was no longer a problem. Linda, who would eventually be in charge of managing the loan, was a great help in working through the drafting process. The letter was delivered, and the next day a signed copy was hand delivered to me along with a check for $250,000.

From that point forward Charlie Way and I started having what he called our bi-weekly "ante up" meetings reflecting the Beach Company's need to post another $250,000 every 15 days. On one of those visits, Charlie informed me that Lou Ranieri had dropped out of the deal but that one of his young lieutenants, Shep Davis, had remained to try and find another partner to replace them in the deal. Ranieri's withdrawal was a problem because The Beach Company did not want to put up the entire letter of credit alone. Without partners, they would not want to do the transaction.

Charlie asked for a respite from the ante ups and said that they were no longer shopping the transaction because it was clear they could not find anyone else to make the loan. On the strength of his word that we were no longer being shopped, I agreed to the break in the payments. Fortunately, Shep Davis was able to bring in Mabon Nugent to replace Ranieri, so on June 29, 1988 we closed the largest real estate loan in the history of South Carolina to consummate the purchase of Kiawah Island from the Kuwait Investment Company.

This transaction returned an important South Carolina tourism asset into the hands of a South Carolina family that was deeply committed to the state and the promotion of all things good for Charleston and South Carolina. On the weekend after closing the Beach Company held a grand function at Charleston Place to celebrate the purchase. It was a gathering of all the Beach Company stockholders, including Mrs. JC Long, her two daughters, the family of her deceased son as well as all the other children and grandchildren. I found it incredibly interesting that even the youngest of the Ways, Darbys and Longs had full appreciation of the risk they were taking to try and replicate what their entrepreneurial grandfather Mr. JC long had done with the Isle of Palms years earlier. It was a moving experience for Joel, Linda, and me, who attended on behalf of the Bank. The evening was a celebration with many kind words expressed for all those who had a part in the transaction, including NCNB. Little did I know at the time that there were storm clouds brewing on the horizon but not the economic ones we normally fear in a transaction of this nature.

Maria Eugenia Lopez, mother

Andrew Elbert Evans, father

Evans Grocery

New Bankers Building Board Room and Travel Department

Ally of the Entrepreneur

Lisa and Carlos Evans,
Wedding Day

First Home,
1561 Brockwall Drive

Second Home,
44 Wagon Road,
Hilton Head Island

Robert Killingsworth, left, seated, turned over the final payment on The Seabrook's construction loan to Carlos Evans, Bankers Trust executive vice president, last week. Enjoying the celebration were, left, standing, Richard J. Rabb, Bankers Trust vice president; Joe Webster and Wes Wilhelm, both of Development Associates, and Bob Allen, Seabrook's executive director.

Seabrook construction loan settled

Bankers Trust and The Seabrook of Hilton Head Inc. last week jointly announced the settlement of the construction loan of $6,150,000 applied to the first two residential buildings of the retirement community facility.

Robert Killingsworth, Seabrook board chairman, presented the final payment to Carlos Evans, the bank's senior vice president, thanking bank officials for the role they played in bringing The Seabrook to reality.

"They recognized its value as a community service," Killingsworth said of their participation.

The project spanned 18 months between the initial negotiations between Development Associates for The Seabrook and Bankers Trust and the termination of the construction loan.

"Because of the unique nature of this project, the financing involved was quite complicated...A number of obstacles had to be overcome. The fact that the loan is now satisfied is a tremendous tribute to Development Associates and the entire Seabrook staff," said Evans.

"Their hard work and cooperation ave given us a facility here on Hilton head that is second to none. Bankers Trust is proud to have played a part in helping to bring what was once a dream to reality as we feel that The Seabrook will be a great asset to the island now and in years to come," Evans added.

Following the presentation, Killingsworth announced that all but two of the 94 apartments have been sold. A few are available for resale.

A waiting list for reservations is growing, Killingsworth said.

Construction of a third building of 55 apartments is planned for this year.

Seabrook Loan Payoff Celebration
The Island Packet, January 6, 1983

Construction underway for townhouse project

Groundbreaking ceremonies were held Thursday for Westwind, a cluster of waterside residences in Windmill Harbour.

The first community development underway in Windmill Harbour, Westwind will consist of 36 two- and three-bedroom townhouses overlooking Calibogue Sound and the Intracoastal Waterway. The first residences will be complete by late summer.

"Each townhouse has been carefully sited so that every living room and master bedroom has a westward view across the waterway, the sound and the marshlands beyond," said project coordinator Don Furtado. "They are spectacular waterviews, some of the best on all of Hilton Head."

Westwind owners will be able to purchase boat slips in Windmill Harbour's 12-acre inland marina. Other features of the 172-acre residential community will include the Sports Center complex with six clay tennis courts, pro shop and swimming pool; miles of bike and cart paths; and a residents' dining, lounge and entertainment facility.

The townhouses were designed by Nichols Carter Seay/Grant Architects Inc. of Atlanta and have stucco exteriors, waterside patios and covered entrances. Each townhouse has a private garage, with a workshop area, and golf cart parking as well as ample guest parking.

"The firm of Nichols Carter Seay/Grant has designed a number of outstanding projects for communities in the Southeast," said Furtado. "Among their recent projects are villas and common facilities at Amelia Island Plantation and at Sawgrass."

Tile foyers and kitchens, fireplaces in living rooms, separate dining rooms and master bedrooms featuring six-foot marble whirlpool baths and twin lavatories are among the notable interior features of Westwind. The three-bedroom homes have three full baths while the two-bedroom residences have 2½ baths.

"In keeping with the energy conservation theme planned throughout the entire Windmill Harbour community, Westwind's residences have numerous energy-saving design features," said Furtado. "Among them are high ceilings, special wall and ceiling construction, insulated exterior glass, masonry common walls, energy-efficient heat pumps and quick-recovery hot-water heaters."

Furtado said private boat slips will be available to owners upon completion of the harbor. An owner operated navigation lock will control the water level. A 300-foot fixed mooring pier with a floating dock in Calibogue Sound will accommodate property owners in the interim. The pier is scheduled for completion in June.

According to Sea Pines Real Estate Co. Vice President Paul Franks, the homes will initially range in price from $199,000 to $259,000. He said a model residence, furnished by Plantation Interiors, will be open in August.

Austin Construction Co. is the general contractor for Westwind. The construction lender is Bankers Trust of South Carolina and Robert Marvin and Associates of Walterboro is the landscape architect.

On hand for Westwind groundbreaking ceremonies were, from left, Johnny McCauley, executive vice president, Austin Construction Co.; Furtado; Charles Fraser, chairman, Sea Pines Co.; Paul Franks; Jim Richardson, project manager; and Carlos Evans, Bankers Trust.

Groundbreaking at Windmill Harbour; Charles Fraser, third from left
The Island Packet, April 19, 1983

Camp Mondamin, Lake Summit, "On Golden Pond"

Lisa, Blake, and Dad on deck at Lake Summit

Back to Columbia, SC for the second time
11 Heathwood Circle

Bob Gorham, Hootie Johnson, Carlos Evans

Lee Atwater, Running With George Bush

Nations Bank, Teammates:
Pat Phillips, Loy Thompson, David Rhodes, Carlos Evans, Hugh McColl

Meeting with Greenwich Associates:
Ben Jenkins, Carlos Evans, Don Rafferty, David Fox

Bank of America losing its S.C. chief to Wachovia

S.C MARKET SHARE

Wachovia and Bank of America rank atop the list of banks with deposits in South Carolina

Bank	Deposits, in billions July 2003	Deposits, in billions July 2004	Market share July 2004
Wachovia	$8.3	$8.9	18.5%
Bank of America	$5.7	$6.3	13.1%
BB&T	$4.3	$4.5	9.4%
Carolina First	$3.6	$4.0	8.4%
First Citizens	$3.2	$3.5	7.3%

SOURCE: Federal Deposit Insurance Corp.

Gibson will direct commercial banking for firm in Carolinas

By BEN WERNER
Staff Writer

Stan Gibson, Bank of America's president for South Carolina, is leaving after 32 years with the company to work for rival Wachovia.

Gibson will run Wachovia's commercial banking group for the Carolinas.

Replacing him at Bank of America is Kim Wilkerson, a 24-year veteran of banks that eventually became part of Bank of America. Wilkerson also will be Columbia market president and middle market banking executive for the territory including South Carolina, western North Carolina, and Augusta.

Gibson said his base would be in Columbia, but his job would require him to spend a significant amount of time in various markets, such as Charleston, Greenville and North Carolina. Before, he was pretty much restricted to South Carolina.

Gibson, who is looking forward to having a renewed focus on commercial banking, said the appeal of his new job with Wachovia is the expanded territory — both Carolinas — to increase market share.

For Wachovia, commercial banking refers to companies with assets of more than $15 million.

He also liked the opportunity to work with a former associate at Bank of America, Carlos Evans,

SEE **GIBSON** PAGE A15

GIBSON

FROM PAGE **A12**

who is now the wholesale executive for Wachovia's General Bank.

"His ability to build key relationships with company owners and community leaders is going to help us build on our position as the — hands down — number one commercial bank in the Carolinas in both market share and customer service," said Evans, who is now Gibson's boss.

Wilkerson is a longtime member of the Columbia banking community. Before being tapped to head the bank's state operation, she was middle market banking executive for Palmetto region.

"She is a business leader with a long history of community involvement in Columbia," said Graham Denton, market president executive for Bank of America.

Wilkerson, who was attending a conference in Asheville, N.C., couldn't be reached for comment.

Wachovia and Bank of America battle each other in the Carolinas for banking dominance. Nationally, Bank of America, with $393 billion in deposits, has the edge over Wachovia, with $227 billion in deposits.

In South Carolina, though, Wachovia, with deposits of $8.9 billion, maintains an 18.5 percent market share to Bank of America's $6.3 billion in deposits and 13 percent market share.

The two also have battled for executives. In February, Wachovia picked off John "Jack" Goettee, at the time a top Bank of America executive in the state. Goettee left Bank of America, where he had spent two decades of banking, to become Wachovia's community banking president for Columbia.

"Having Stan (Gibson) on the team is a big win for Wachovia," said Walter McDowell, Wachovia's chief executive for the Carolinas banking group. "I've competed with Stan for most of my career at Wachovia, so I'm delighted to finally be on the same team."

Reach Werner at (803) 771-8509 or bwerner@thestate.com.

Headline of Stan Gibson, "Revenge Days"
The State, October 27, 2004

Carlos Evans

Two Great Entrepreneurs:
Wayne Huizenga and George Dean Johnson

City mourns Parsell's death

Charleston restaurateur's success was 'stuff of legend,' mayor says

BY KYLE STOCK
The Post and Courier

Charleston hospitality workers on Thursday began mourning Thomas Parsell, a renowned restaurateur and one of the main ingredients in the magic recipe that put the Holy City on the nation's culinary map.

Parsell, co-founder of Magnolias, Blossom Cafe and Cypress Lowcountry Grill, died Wednesday night when he apparently lost control of his classic silver Corvette. He was 63 years old. Police expect to spend the next couple days reconstructing the wreck.

Originally from Michigan, Parsell made his way in the Lowcountry by selling cars, running Tom Parsell Chevrolet Inc. from 1975 to 1989 and then running a Honda and Toyota dealership in Georgia. He also started the Bank of Charleston, which is now part of Carolina First.

Though he did not have the resume of a restaurateur, Parsell possessed an uncommon mix of entrepreneurial shrewd-

ness and social skills, and he was a wine connoisseur to boot.

"It's hard to find someone who's such a gentleman and such a good businessman," said John Edwards, a friend and general manager of the Mills House Hotel for 20 years.

Parsell and chef and longtime business partner Donald Barickman whipped up their first culinary creation in July 1990, opening Magnolias less than a year after Hurricane Hugo laid the city low. The ambitious Lowcountry restaurant became one of the first in Charleston to win praise from the country's most discerning food critics.

Please see PARSELL, Page 12B

Thomas Parsell

PARSELL From Page 11B

A string of successes have since popped up nearby, including Slightly North of Broad and High Cotton. Parsell's Hospitality Management Group Inc. tacked on the Blossom Cafe in 1993 and the opulent Cypress Lowcountry Grill in 2001.

Mayor Joe Riley said Magnolias served up a "wonderful vote of confidence" to a community ravaged by Hugo.

"It was a major restoration of a building and in a part of town that was emerging. It just gave the city a tremendous emotional boost," he said.

Riley called Parsell's success "the stuff of legend."

"We made a decision to do the best in Charleston that we or anybody else could do," Parsell told The Post and Courier in 2000.

Though Parsell's properties frequently served food writers and famous people from all over the country, they made a point of courting local business. Magnolias had one of the city's first reservation lines set up for area residents.

In recent years, Parsell was instrumental in keeping local kitchens stocked with affordable and talented cooks. When Johnson & Wales University announced plans

to move its local campus to Charlotte in 2002, he joined a small team of local business people and government officials who helped develop an expansion of Trident Technical College's culinary program and lure a campus of the Art Institutes to town.

Barickman said Magnolias, Blossom and Cypress will continue to operate as they have, though Parsell will be greatly missed.

"I really don't know what to say," he said. "Tom's legacy — these restaurants — speak for themselves."

Reach **Kyle Stock** at 937-5763 or kstock@postandcourier.com.

The Death of Tom Parsell, Another Great Entrepreneur
The Post and Courier, September 28, 2007

Ally of the Entrepreneur

SEVEN TO WATCH
SHAPING OUR REGION IN 2009

Carlos Evans
United Way board chair, Wachovia exec

Between United Way and Wells Fargo, he's got tall orders to fill

Sixth in a series

BY MARK PRICE
mprice@charlotteobserver.com

Two of the biggest stories of 2008 in Charlotte involved the sale of Wachovia to Wells Fargo and the CEO pay controversy at United Way.

Carlos Evans is connected to both. He is the chairman of the board of United Way of Central Carolinas and an executive with Wachovia.

The year ahead will be one of many challenges for him. Evans has accepted responsibility for rebuilding public trust in United Way, which saw a $15 million drop in campaign donations this year. As part of the Wachovia-Wells Fargo merger, he has been asked to assume a new role, as head of commercial banking for Wells Fargo's eastern franchise.

"There's an old adage that you must prune a tree to have robust growth," says Evans. "That's true for the economy...and the difficulties we're facing in the nonprofit arena. I hate the place that we're at with United Way and all the controversy, but a lot of positives will come of it."

THE VITAL STATS
Evans' background, what people say about him and why he'll make news. 3B

COMING SATURDAY
After she faced an attempted carjacking, Julie Eiselt formed an anti-crime organization.

GARY O'BRIEN – gobrien@charlotteobserver.com
Carlos Evans has accepted responsibility for rebuilding public trust in United Way of Central Carolinas.

Age: 57
Family: Wife, Lisa Hudson Evans, son Blakeley Hudson Evans.
College: 1973 graduate of Newberry College in Newberry, S.C., with a bachelor's in economics.
Job: Responsible for Wachovia's Commercial, Business and Community Banking segments, Wachovia's dealer business, and the Government and Not-For-Profit Healthcare groups.
Community affiliations: Chairman of the board, Winthrop University Real Estate Foundation and Winthrop University Foundation Board of Directors; also chairman of the board of United Way of Central Carolinas; chair-elect, Spoleto Festival USA; and board member, Medical University of South Carolina Foundation.

Early impressions of Charlotte: "It was a very different place in '91 (when he moved to Charlotte). Downtown did not have very many people living here and no restaurants. I was on the board at Discovery Place and I remember we'd have board meetings at 5:30 to 6 p.m., and it was frightening to walk from Trade and Tryon, north to Discovery Place. There was no nightlife, no people on the street. It was basically a very dark, kind of foreboding place."

Keeps him awake at night: "The economy. Obviously, in my job here at Wachovia, soon to be Wells Fargo, I have responsibility for a commercial and industrial loan portfolio that is reflective of the economy across the country. The more serious the situation gets with the economy, the more problems we have in that portfolio with customers.... The economy has also had a double whammy on United Way. It has affected the base of contributors and it has driven up the need for services, with more people jobless, homeless

Evans

and seeking counseling, creating a strain on families."

His background

A native Carolinian, Evans was born in 1951 and raised in the small S.C. farming community of Salem Crossroads, 30 miles east of Florence. His father ran a country store and his mother was a school teacher. Still, the family did not have a lot of money, so young Evans worked summers cropping and hanging tobacco. "It was tough work, but it taught me to focus on a job, no matter how menial."

Evans doesn't recall having a childhood ambition, but got a job after college in 1973 at Banker's Trust of South Carolina, which was later acquired by NCNB, the bank that eventually became Bank of America. A job transfer brought him to Charlotte 17 years ago.

Why he'll make the news

In January, Evans and the rest of the United Way board will gather for a one-day strategic planning session, which will likely remake many aspects of the agency. Among the recommendations being considered is cutting the size of the board in half, as well as provisions that could limit the powers of the next CEO, to be hired in March. All this will be done with a maximum of public exposure, which Evans believes is the way to regain public trust.

What's his approach?

"I'll ask a lot of questions. I'm a believer in gathering a lot of data before making a decision, and that means listening to what other people say. I believe the best decisions are made when you have different points of view at the table."

What others say about him

"There are a lot of folks in this world that will think of all the reasons why we can't accomplish a task. Carlos is the kind of leader that will think of the ways of how we can accomplish the task.... He is straightforward and he does what he says he will do."
— MARK TURNER, SCOUT EXECUTIVE, BOY SCOUTS OF AMERICA, MECKLENBURG COUNTY COUNCIL, WHERE EVANS SERVED AS VICE PRESIDENT OF FINANCE.

Story on The United Way
The Charlotte Observer, Friday, December 28, 2008

Doug Seigler's Last Duck Hunt

Two Great Entrepreneurs and Two Bankers:
Charlie Way, Jim Bradshaw, Joel Smith, Carlos Evans

Ally of the Entrepreneur

Elden Walker "The Great American" and his Grand Daughter, Ellen Walker

New Salem Capital Offices, Morehead Street

Success Story | La Tortilleria

Three Brothers Forge a Business in Winston-Salem

Dan, Nat and Phil Calhoun started out on their entrepreneurial journey as a landscaping company but have since redirected their focus to include food distribution, real estate, media and more over the past three decades.

Although the Calhoun brothers grew up in Mexico, they have always considered Winston Salem home. They finished high school and then theology degrees at Piedmont Bible College (now Carolina University).

In 1986, they started a lawn-care and landscaping company that provided service throughout Winston-Salem. In 1995, they founded La Tortilleria, which began as a tortilla factory but grew into something much larger.

"We started by making tortillas and along the way, we became a major Hispanic food distributor," said Dan Calhoun, chief executive and president of La Tortilleria.

In 2008, the brothers began another business venture by starting a B2B magazine called Abasto, which is the only Spanish language business magazine in the country. Their portfolio of companies in Winston-Salem now includes La Tortilleria, Abasto Media, and Purple Crow Investments, a real estate holding company.

"Winston-Salem is not a congested city; it still has a small-town feel to it. The economic climate here is great, the employee base is great. Winston-Salem is an ideal place for the family home," Calhoun said.

In 2018, the Calhoun brothers met Tom Teague whose company, Salem Leasing is another great Winston-Salem success story. Tom brought together a group of investors including Carlos Evans and Ken Langone, a founder of Home Depot. The new investment assisted with doubling the company's warehousing operations and opening new facilities in other markets.

"When we get this building finished in early 2021, we're going to be poised for a lot of growth and additional expansion," said Calhoun.

The future of La Tortilleria looks bright – Calhoun says that they are actively looking to acquire other companies in this space, having already acquired a food service company in March 2020. They also have plans for more distribution centers in 2021 and beyond.

According to the Calhoun brothers, another major factor in their success is their underlying philosophy to "treat others the way you want to be treated," which shows in their work and their company's mission. "Winston Salem has treated us this way and I know they will continue to do the same for others"

The advice that Calhoun has for anyone looking to start a company or relocate in Winston-Salem is to "knock yourself out" and really, just go for it. The Calhoun brothers have certainly proven that there's no limit to the incredible things you can accomplish here.

La Tortilleria Website

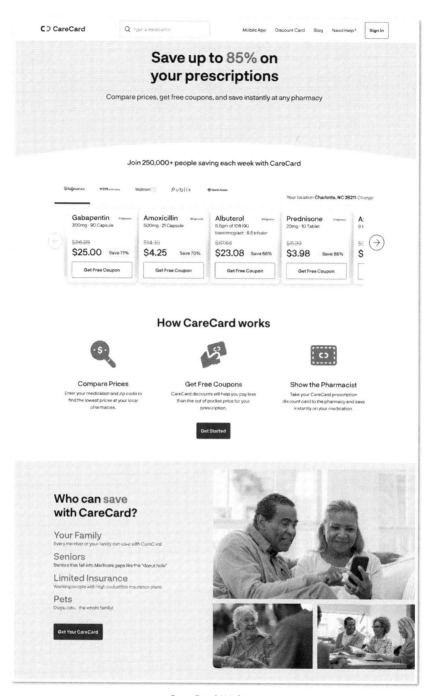

CareCard Website

Carlos Evans

Chapter 21

The End Of A Decade
The End Of Banking As We Knew It

After the Kiawah Loan closing, I refocused my efforts on developing new business. We were growing dramatically. In fact, the Kiawah loan all by itself had increased the loan portfolio by about 10% to $1.4 billion. The $2.5 million fee had been a nice uptick to the P&L. I was traveling continuously across the state meeting new prospects and customers every day.

Lisa and I were settled in our renovated home at Heathwood Circle and enjoying family life as well as frequent visits by parents, family, and friends. We also did a lot of entertaining when customers were in town. Lisa was a real trooper even though it was a lot for her to juggle with Blake and coordinating babysitters. Her parents were a big help since they loved keeping Blake as often as they could.

In the summer of 1986, we purchased a 1/3 interest in a cabin on Lake Summit along with two other couples, who were friends from Hilton Head. It was located in the mountains in the little town of Tuxedo near Hendersonville N.C. By the summer of 1988, we were enjoying trips to Lake Summit as often as we could. Summit is a small lake set in an idyllic setting surrounded by mountains with three camps on the lake, Camp Mondamin for Boys and Camps Greystone and Green Cove for girls. While the lake has only 200 homes, it is big enough to ski and sail on.

I had three lake kayaks down at the boathouse along with a Sunfish. Lisa and I used to joke that Lake Summit was our "On Golden Pond," and it was. Not only could we escape the summer heat there, but it was also a place to escape the hectic pace of business. Although at that point I had never really been negatively affected by the pressure of my work (that would come later}, it was a wonderful place to recharge my batteries. I would spend hours kayaking on the lake, riding bikes and taking hikes. The exercise and fresh air were rejuvenating.

Blake also attended Camp Mondamin under Lisa's watchful eye (she could see the camp from our deck which overlooked the lake). Every summer Blake and I went on a three-day father-son camping trip sponsored by Mondamin. These times with my son as he grew up were extra special.

We often had friends and family visit us at the lake, but in addition, we had many friends among the cottage owners on the lake, mostly people from Charleston and Spartanburg. In particular, Bill and Valerie Barnet became great friends. Bill owned a company called Barnet Manufacturing in Spartanburg, which happened to be a bank customer. Bill would later sell Barnet Manufacturing to the employees, a company which had been in his family for over 100 years having moved south from New England. Bill was on the board of Fleet Financial which would ultimately be acquired by the successor to NCNB, Bank of America. Bill would later join the Bank of America board as well as the boards of Duke Energy and the Duke Endowment . After selling his company, Bill would go on to be the mayor of Spartanburg for a number of years. In addition to being a great friend, he was and is a great example of how entrepreneurs give back not only to their companies and their employees but to their communities as well.

By the fall of 1988, Lisa and I were back in step with many old friends, in particular, Lee and Sally Atwater; my old KA friend and personal attorney, Doug Seigler; and my old next door neighbor Elden Walker, "The Great American." Lee Atwater was up to his ears in the 1988 election where he was running George H. W. Bush's successful campaign.

To say Lee was a ruthless master of negative campaigning would be a huge understatement. He was able to dig up an old video of Bush's opponent, Michael Dukakis, riding around in a tank wearing a silly looking hat with ear flaps that made him look like he was in the Mickey Mouse Club. Lee was also able to dig up dirt on a convicted killer and rapist named Willie Horton, who Dukakis had furloughed. The ad portrayed Dukakis as a liberal who was soft on crime, and while the ad was socially divisive and in some respects racially slanted, it was very effective.

Dukakis and his running mate, Lloyd Bentsen from Texas, never had a chance, and Bush and Quayle won by 8 points. Lee was credited with helping put him in office. On the night of the election on November 3, Lisa and I hosted a dinner at our house to watch the election returns. At approximately 9 pm the phone rang, it was Lee calling from the campaign victory celebration. He told me that it was the happiest day of his life and that George Bush had fulfilled his dream by telling him that he would become Chairman of the Republican National Committee (RNC). He was calling a few friends who had helped him along the way to share the good news.

Lee asked half-jokingly if there was anything in government I wanted to do. I told him that while I was always flattered when he asked me, all I ever wanted to do was be a banker and that I, like him, was in my dream job. At the time Lee and I were both 38 years old. Little did we know that Lee's life would last just a little over 2 more years, and while he would serve as Chair of the RNC, it would be short lived. I concluded our conversation by telling Lee that I was in a room full of people, some of whom were democrats but all South Carolinians. While everyone was not necessarily of his political persuasion, as South Carolinians we were all very proud of him and what he had accomplished. Lee and I would have one more adventure together before his life was cut short. At the end of his life, Lee would have a turn of heart and extend apologies to many people he had harmed with his rough and tumble politics.

As 1988 came to an end, there was much going on in the bank most of which was related to NCNB's purchase of First Republic. Essentially, Hugh McColl and NCNB's senior team had been able to acquire management control of the failing institution through a creative structure. NCNB had put 25% down and acquired the option to buy the remaining 75% of First Republic from the FDIC over 5 years at a predetermined price.

It was the deal of the decade, effectively doubling the size of the bank to over $50 billion. Best of all, we had the ability to put bad loans back to the FDIC in a "bad bank" entity that insulated NCNB from all the problems with the Texas economy. To add icing on the cake, NCNB General Counsel Paul Polking and a very sharp tax attorney, Frank Blanchfield, figured out a way to preserve the loss carry forwards in the Texas legal entity so the bank could use them to shelter future income. It was a home run by any standard and, in fact, was recognized as such by the market because NCNB stock started trading up almost immediately after the deal was announced.

While much has been said and written about this acquisition, for those of us in the bank it was another signal that the interstate banking laws were going to eventually come down. The protection afforded by the State Reciprocal Bank Pact had, in fact, worked as Hugh and Hootie had hoped by keeping the big northern banks out while allowing banks in the Southeast like NCNB to merge and get bigger. In the years following the Bankers Trust merger, NCNB had made a series of acquisitions in Florida, Virginia, Maryland and other places in addition to the big move in Texas which allowed us to "get out from under the tent" that had been thrown up around the Southeast.

Now that the State Reciprocal Bank Pact had served its usefulness, Hugh was lobbying full blast for interstate banking. His pitch, and rightly so, was that the United States was the only country in the developed world that did not allow banks to branch anywhere inside their respective country. Without interstate banking, we would fall behind the banks in Japan and Europe. Interestingly, no mention of China was made at the time.

While banking was changing and NCNB was at the forefront of that change, the merger had not caused any changes in the management of NCNB South Carolina. Whether the lack of merger-driven change was due to NCNB having made mistakes in Florida by moving too fast or whether it was out of deference to Hootie, it was good for those of us in Columbia because the old Bankers Trust management team was running the bank with very little outside interference.

As we moved into 1989, I was confronted with a problem that would deeply affect me personally. It had to do with Elden Walker "The Great American." Elden called me one day saying that in the high rate period of the early 80s he had purchased about $100,000 of tax free municipal bonds. The bonds yielded 8% tax exempt and were paying interest quarterly that he and Harriett Ann were living on in their retirement. Then very recently, our bank had sent him a check for the principal value saying that the bonds had been called. Elden said he had purchased the bonds under the assumption that they were non-callable. He had a lot of paperwork and none of it indicated that the bonds had a call feature. I explained to Elden that the brokerage business was outside of my area of control, but I would put in a word with the people in charge who were in Charlotte.

Ultimately it came down to Elden's word against the broker's. All I knew was that even if the broker had explained the call feature, he obviously had not done a good job because Elden was an experienced investor who would have known what a call feature meant. Not only did I know him well, but Elden was a good customer. His whole family had accounts with us including all the kids.

Since the bonds had been called, Elden would reinvest the proceeds at the much lower 4% rate that was then in effect. It was going to cost him about $4,000.00 per year over the remaining 8-year term of the bonds. It wasn't a massive amount of money; however I knew it was important in his retirement plan and I couldn't just write him a check for $32,000. The whole thing weighed on me because here was a man who had given so much to his country. Whether the Bank was right or wrong, he was being harmed because of our failure to explain, or at least properly disclose what he was buying. The whole thing was making me sick to my stomach because I felt powerless to help him, but then the light bulb went off!

I suddenly remembered years earlier during the high-rate period of the late 70s when I was on the loan platform in Columbia and I made an industrial revenue bond loan to a company. Industrial revenue bond loans were made by banks to foster job creation and since they were issued through a local authority known as JEDA (Jobs Economic Development Authority), the loan carried a tax-exempt interest rate of 10%. At that time in the late 70s, 10% was the market rate. Best of all, since a fixed rate 10-year taxable loan at that time was in the 13% range there was little likelihood of the loan prepaying.

So, to solve the problem I sold Elden a $100,000 participation in that 10% tax free loan which still had 10 years remaining. It was an elegant solution because not only was the rate better but the remaining term was 3 years longer than Elden's original bond, so he could enjoy the tax exempt yield for three years more. When I called Bob Welling, the account officer for my old IRB loan , and instructed him to do the participation, he asked what he should do if the auditors questioned him.

I told Bob to send them to me which in fact he did. When the auditors inquired about why I sold a participation in a perfectly good high yielding loan, I told them that the bank sold downstream participations to smaller correspondent banks all the time. I further told them that since Elden was a good customer just like the correspondents, I was simply allowing him to make a reasonable investment just as we did with correspondents. Besides, I said, it was my damn loan, and I would do with it as I pleased as long as it was consistent with the banks track record of taking care of good customers and doing the right thing. That was the end of the conversation. The loan went on to pay as agreed over its remaining life. Elden was happy, and I was happy to be able to find a creative way to right what I felt had been a wrong.

On September 22, 1989, disaster struck South Carolina. I remember the day vividly. I was in West Columbia that morning calling on The Farm Bureau headquarters at Hootie's request. We had a good visit, and I was excited because it was clear that the Farm Bureau network was extensive and there were many opportunities to do business especially on the cash management side. I remember sitting in the president's office, and he had his radio on. While I was very much aware of the hurricane in the Atlantic, it wasn't until that specific moment that I realized that South Carolina was going to take a direct hit.

At that time the forecasters were calling for a landfall at either Hilton Head or Charleston, and it was going to be a Category 4 hurricane or possibly worse. While Columbia is 120 miles inland, the bank had a lot invested on the coast with all the golf course loans and especially Kiawah, and it was suddenly clear that we were going to have a natural disaster. Reports were coming in that Interstate 26 was a parking lot and traffic was at a standstill.

I received a call from my good friend Doug Lee asking if he could spend the night with Lisa and me. He had evacuated Charleston early that morning heading to Anniston, Alabama where his wife Marsee was visiting her family, but he had already been in the car 6 hours and was making little progress. I had another call from Jim Bradshaw saying they were on the way from Hilton Head. I left work a little early and stopped by to pick up a bunch of Chinese food because I knew it was going to be a long night.

As I got out of my car to pick up the food, I remember the air being so humid that it was like nothing I had ever experienced. By then it was late afternoon. Heavy clouds were gathering, but the thing I remember the most was the moisture in the air, almost as if I was standing under a warm, wet towel and I could reach up and wring out the water. I took the Chinese food home and by then the Bradshaw's and Doug Lee were there.

We turned on the TV and watched with keen interest as the forecaster switched back and forth between Charleston and Hilton Head, talking about where the storm would make landfall. By 9:00pm the eye of the storm made landfall just north of Charleston near McClellanville, a small fishing community near what is known as the Cape Romain Wildlife refuge. The eye of the storm was huge, over 40 miles across, and hurricane winds were extending out 140 miles from the center. We knew it was doing an incredible amount of damage to the South Carolina coast. Little did we know that the damage would extend far inland and include Columbia as well as up into Charlotte and western North Carolina.

Just as the eye was about to make landfall, Doug received a call from John Ragsdale who had remained in her home on Broad Street in downtown Charleston. John told Doug that she was scared to death because slate shingles were flying around like missiles. She said the wind was shaking the house, and it sounded like a freight train. We knew John to be a strong, independent woman so for her to be scared spoke volumes about the ferocity of the storm. Midway through the phone conversation with Doug, the connection was cut off, and phones in Charleston no longer worked. By 11:30 pm we all went to bed with the wind picking up dramatically and none of us knowing what the next day would hold.

I awoke early the next morning with Blake yelling that the swimming pool was black. Sure enough, so many pine needles had blown off the trees that the water appeared totally green from all the debris. The yard looked like a bomb had gone off and a huge limb had fallen through the windshield of the Bradshaw's van. Trees were down blocking many streets in our neighborhood, although fortunately none blocked the way out to the main arteries. Power was out everywhere and would remain so for about a week. The Bradshaw's were elated that Hilton Head had been spared, and they headed back shortly after getting their windshield replaced. Doug Lee also left, heading to Alabama right after breakfast. After the last departure, I went straight to Owens field to board a King Air along with Joel Smith and the rest of the South Carolina bank management team to fly the entire coastline at 300 feet.

By then we were getting reports that all the islands were totally cut off. The Ben Sawyer drawbridge that connects Sullivans Island to the mainland was standing straight up, twisted like some kind of mangled toy. Flooding from the storm surge was everywhere, and roofs had been ripped off of many thousands of homes allowing the heavy rains to pour in.

As we boarded the plane on late that Friday morning, we decided to fly straight to Hilton Head, then head north flying as low as possible along the coast. Thankfully, all the clouds were gone, and we had great visibility. Aside from my concerns over our customers and the impacts to their businesses, I was also worried about my stepfather Alan Perry.

Alan had left the school where he and mom taught at 3 pm on Thursday afternoon to drive to Georgetown where he kept a trawler docked at the downtown city marina. He had planned to take the boat up the Waccamaw river and anchor behind Sandy Island in Thoroughfare Creek. I knew of Allen's plan to ride out the storm, but by now I also knew that the area where he'd been headed had experienced tremendous storm surge. I was incredibly worried. The fact that we had heard nothing from him by midday Friday gave me even more concern. I made a mental note to look for his boat as we went up the coast.

As we approached the north end of Hilton Head, we could see that the island was relatively untouched, and the same was true for Beaufort, Fripp Island, Hunting Island, and Edisto Island as we flew northward. However, as we got to Seabrook Island just south of Kiawah, we began to see some evidence of the storm. Coming over Kiawah, just north of Seabrook, we could see that there had been no visible damage to the beach because those huge 30 ft. dunes Joel and I had seen on our visit almost a year and a half earlier had done their job, along with the visionary setback requirements imposed in the master plan by Charles Fraser.

However, we could see tremendous tree damage just north of mid-island, apparently from a number of tornadoes that ripped through. In coming weeks, Kiawah would spend almost $1 million removing downed trees and debris. When we got to Folly Beach just South of Charleston, we began to see the impact of the storm surge which been approximately 12 feet at Folly. Many houses had been knocked off their foundations, and others had been wiped off the beach. In Charleston we saw standing water in parts of the city and blue tarps everywhere to cover ripped off roofs and protect the inside of homes from additional rains. Sullivans Island was a disaster as the storm surge had been higher as we moved toward where the eye had come ashore. The storm surge had peaked at roughly 22 feet near McClellanville where many residents rode out the storm in the attic of the schoolhouse because the rest of the school had been covered by water.

At Isle of Palms, parts of the Wild Dunes golf course had been totally washed away, and the Wild Dunes Marina had been completely destroyed with boats sucked out of the harbor and stacked like cord wood on Goat Island. I gasped at the sight since I knew it would keep getting worse as we moved north into the area where the northeast quadrant of the eye had struck. (Since hurricane winds move in a counterclockwise motion, on the east coast, the northeast corner of the eye brings the worst wind and storm surge.)

By the time we came over Georgetown, we knew we were witnessing the effects of the worst natural disaster in South Carolina's history. The town's two marinas were essentially gone. All we could see were dock pilings sticking up out of the water and the masts of sunken sailboats. Many boats lay strewn along the town's main street. At Debordieu Beach just north of Georgetown, many oceanfront houses had been wiped clean from the beach. At Pawleys Island there were beachfront homes sitting back in the marsh, and on its south end, the hurricane had breached the island, cutting it in two. At Garden City Beach, we saw much of the same, but we could see that the storm surge was now lessening as we went north, which gave me hope for our golf courses in the Myrtle Beach area and further north, many of which were well behind the beachfront and in many cases west of the intra-coastal waterway.

By the time we got to Myrtle Beach it was clear that the worst damage was south and relatively speaking Myrtle Beach had been spared. As we made the turn at Little River to come back, I asked the pilots to make a pass south down the Waccamaw River at the lowest possible level so I could look for the signs of Allen Perry and his boat. As we flew over the area, I asked them to make several turns because there was no sign of him but only devastation everywhere. I could see many sunken boats, but no sign of Allen. My stomach churned with a sick feeling knowing that I needed to call my mom and inform her that Allen might have been lost.

When we got back on the ground in Columbia, we went to the office. I called Mom and asked if she had heard from Allen. She said she hadn't heard a word, and by this point she was almost hysterical. I told her about the damage I had seen and most importantly, that there had been no sign of my stepdad or his boat. I could tell that Mom was exhausted, and I told her I would be in Florence the next morning. By that point the bank's aid network was shifting into high gear with truckloads of water, electric generators and chainsaws headed to Charleston and points north. Hugh McColl had also announced the formation of a special disaster bank to provide relief loans to the citizens and businesses in the affected areas of South Carolina. We all knew that in the days and weeks ahead we would be rolling up our sleeves to help with the recovery.

The next morning, I awoke to some good news when my mom called to tell me that Allen was safe. Several hours later Allen called to tell me that by the time he had gotten to Georgetown at around 4:30 pm, the storm was already moving in with lots of heavy rain and wind gusts between 50 and 60 knots. He'd been able to get into Winyah Bay, but by then the rain was so hard he couldn't see the bridge to get under it. He had turned to go back into Georgetown, but unable to see the mouth of the harbor, he'd made one more pass at the bridge and managed to get under. At that point he had headed north, away from where the eye had made landfall but still in the northeast quadrant where the storm surge and winds would be huge. When he'd reached Sandy Island there were already many boats anchored in Thoroughfare Creek just behind the island, so he had been forced to go further up the creek away from the protection of the high bluff. In the end, that turned out to be a blessing because the boats just behind the island had been pitted from the winds blowing sand off the bluff, essentially putting them in a sand blaster.

Once he'd found a spot, Allen put out two Danforth Anchors, one off the bow and one off of the stern. As the storm came in, he'd started to worry that with so much tension on the lines and so much whipping back and forth the constant chaffing of the lines might cause them to break. To make sure he was safe, anytime a lull would occur, he had crawled out on his belly to re-cleat the lines in order to minimize the wear. This process had gone on all night, first as the storm approached and then again after the eye went through and the winds reversed. As the storm surge had been peaking, Allen said the water level had risen almost 20 feet on top of an already high tide. He had been able to see the tops of the trees, and he'd known that if the anchors had broken loose, he would have been swept into the trees on what was normally dry land.

The next morning when the winds had dissipated, he'd been so exhausted from crawling around all night that he slept the entire day. On Friday, when he'd finally awakened, it had been early evening. He'd motored over to where the other boats were anchored and decided to spend another night and go back to what was left of the marina the next morning. It had been early afternoon when I had passed over Sandy Island, and since he'd been farther up Thoroughfare Creek I could not see his boat. When he called me Saturday morning, it was from the only working phone at what had been the marina. Even then he was still exhausted but ready to come home. When I asked him if would do the same thing again if another storm came, his the answer was an emphatic no!

In the aftermath of Hugo, we all dove into our work. Many of our customers needed accommodations on their loans and we did all we could to help. Since many of us had never experienced anything like this, it was hard to gauge the long-term impact. Short term it was devastating with all the damage, but as the weeks went by the picture became clearer with one exception.

At the onset of recovery, it became clear that the speed with which insurance claims were being processed would be a huge plus. Almost immediately after the storm, an army of insurance adjusters arrived along the coast and started settling claims and writing checks immediately. We could see it in our bank deposits which swelled almost 30% in the aftermath of the storm. The other obvious impact was the huge surge in construction activity as people immediately started building back in earnest, in most cases bigger and better than before. In fact, a running joke in Charleston was that it had taken Hugo to get all the old houses repainted in one fell swoop!

The more difficult question was how fast the resort activity would come back. There had been so much publicized about the devastation along the South Carolina coast, it seemed clear that people were not going to come back in earnest for some time. Even in areas like Hilton Head and Myrtle Beach that had been relatively unaffected, people were essentially staying away from what they thought was a disaster zone. While business interruption insurance would cover the downtime to rebuild, it would not cover the time it would take for people to return.

In particular, I was very concerned about Kiawah, which was experiencing zero real estate sales after good success in the fall of 1988 after our loan closed. It was clear that unless something changed there was going to be a problem. With no sales to replenish the interest and operating reserves built into the loan, the situation would run out of gas some time in 1990 if sales stayed in limbo.

Sometime between Thanksgiving and Christmas in 1989, I received a call from Charlie Way. "Carlos, I would like for you, Joel, Mark Johnson and Linda Fairchild to join me and our management team on a trip to Carmel California to visit a man named Gerry Barton, the CEO of LandMark Land Company."

"What for," I asked.

"He wants to purchase the resort assets at Kiawah including all the golf courses, the tennis facilities, the Inn, the second convention hotel site and the dune field at the east end of the island for a new golf course."

I asked how much he was proposing to pay, and Charlie said $45 million. I then asked why he needed our management team, and Charlie said that he wanted Mr. Barton to know that NCNB was behind The Beach Company, and we weren't scared. Charlie said that if Barton thought the bank was concerned, he would try to beat down the price.

I joked that the message was going to be hard to deliver because given that real estate sales were frozen I was scared as hell. I then got serious and told Charlie that if Barton really wanted to make that purchase it would be the deal of a lifetime since it would significantly reduce the debt, put some gas in the tank, and more importantly eliminate the drag from the operating assets which were running about $5 million per year in the red, before interest. Charlie concurred so we agreed to go.

Upon our arrival in Carmel, it was obvious that Gerry Barton and his team were rolling out the red carpet. We were given huge accommodations, and that evening had dinner in their private board room. Over the course of dinner, Gerry told us all about Landmark. They were the largest developer of high end golf courses in the US having more PGA Championship courses than anyone on the planet—PGA West, La Quinta, Mission Hills,

Carmel Valley Ranch, Palm Beach Polo and Oak Tree just to mention a few. Landmark Land Company's parent was an S&L named Oak Tree Savings Bank, which was their funding source. While I thought the structure unusual, it was clear that they were experienced and capable high-end operators and owners of golf assets.

At the conclusion of our dinner, a waiter came in with a bottle of 100+ year old port in what looked like a baby cradle. Mark Johnson and I still joke about the scene to this day as we coined the joke, "Nero fiddling while Rome burned." As the port was being served, I went into my little spiel about how much we respected and valued the relationship with the Beach Company and Kiawah Island, and that we stood ready to assist them with all their needs; all of that was true, except for the specifics of how and what.

Prior to toasting, Gerry Barton then informed us that not only were they planning on purchasing the resort assets, but they were going to build the greatest golf course on the East Coast in the dune field on the east end of Kiawah. Just as important, the 1991 Ryder Cup would be played there! We all gasped. Meekly I asked, how could that be since the Ryder Cup was only 1 year and 10 months away and no work had started on the course.

Gerry responded, "We have more pull with the PGA than anyone, and they have confidence we can do it. We have hired Pete Dye, the plans are already done, our due diligence is done as of today, and we are ready to close immediately so he can start his work post haste. We all toasted the transaction, and I was beside myself with elation! Not only would the transaction reduce debt, eliminate a huge operating drag, and replenish the interest reserve, but it would improve the island with the new golf course and bring thousands of buyers by virtue of the tournament itself and all the resulting publicity.

Upon our return to Columbia, I was still ecstatic, but there was one small problem. Fred Figge, the bank's chief risk officer was concerned about the transaction and asked to meet with me. Fred explained his concern about the sale given the tenuous financial position of Landmark's parent company, Oak Tree Saving Bank. I explained to Fred that while his concerns were legitimate, the master plan for Kiawah put in place by Charles Fraser and protected by restricted land use covenants would preserve the quality even through bankruptcy which is what had occurred on Hilton Head. We knew that Hilton Head, and Sea Pines in particular, had survived the bankruptcy and were none worse for it. I also told Fred that if we did not allow the closing to take place, we were going to have a big problem for sure as the debt service reserve was going to run out unless things dramatically changed. At least with the sale The Beach Company would significantly reduce their debt, eliminate the huge operating loss, and give the island some huge improvements that would enhance their chance to be successful long term.

In the end, Fred Figge was right because Oak Tree did file for bankruptcy and was seized by the FSLIC just before the Ryder Cup. However, I was also right because following the announcement of the Ryder Cup the island took off. Real Estate sales boomed, and the island never looked back!

A few years later, Charlie Way had a mortgage burning celebration on Kiawah at the historically significant Vandrost House. Joel, Mark Johnson, Linda Fairchild, and I were all in attendance along with Hugh McColl. At one point in the evening Hugh McColl pulled me over to congratulate me on my involvement. He said, "How many jobs do you think have been created by this loan?"

"It was Buddy Kemp's loan," I told him. "Without him we wouldn't be here celebrating." (Buddy had tragically passed away from a brain tumor in 1991.) But then to answer his question, I said I thought there were at least 1,000 jobs directly related to the loan given the ramp up in hiring at Kiawah and all the construction activity.

Hugh said, "First of all, I agree with you about Buddy, however, I disagree with you about the number of jobs. This loan has brought a huge number of wealthy people to the Charleston area, and they spend money in the restaurants, they give money to charities, and they get involved in the community. This loan has and will create tens of thousands of jobs and it will forever change this part of South Carolina for the better!"

Hugh was right. I had forgotten about the multiplier effect in Economics 101. Later that evening, as we returned to Charlotte on the bank's plane, I thought that this loan was perhaps the greatest partnership I would ever have with a group of entrepreneurs, but I would be wrong! While I would go on to have a wonderful relationship both personally and professionally with the Ways, Longs and Darbys, there would be many others!

Chapter 22

The Start of a New Decade
The Start of a New Job

As we rounded the corner into 1990 and the new decade began, I was 38 years old, and life was good except for a few missteps which I will mention later. The economy was healthy although the fed was just about to start a series of rate increases to head of some inflation that was starting to show up in the numbers. Blake was moving along in school, and by then we had been in Columbia over a year. I was starting to get more involved in the community with the Chamber of Commerce and the South Carolina Bankers Association.

Every year the Bankers Association had a legislative visit to Washington to meet with our delegation where we would discuss legislative items of interest for our industry. By then, interstate banking was being discussed even though the bill would not pass until September 29, 1995, when the Riegle-Neal Act was put in place.

As we began planning for the annual legislative visit in March, I gave Lee Atwater a call to touch base and see if we could catch up while Lisa and I were in DC. Lee said for sure and that he would be back in touch. I didn't think any more about it until we were sitting in Georgetown having just arrived for our visit and the phone in our hotel room rang. It was Lee, who had tracked me down through my secretary, Mary Willa Roper. Back then cell phones weren't that much in use, so it had taken him a little doing to find me. Phone calls with Lee were always short and to the point.

He said, "Would you like to come and visit the White House?"

I said, "Sure!"

He asked if any of my banker friends might want to come, and I suggested Joel Smith and Roger Whaley. He said to check with them and call him back with the driver's license information for everyone who wanted to come, and then plan to be at the West Gate at 11 am. I had no idea what he had planned, but I figured it was just the standard tour. When the three of us arrived at the West Gate, we were welcomed with open arms. It seemed that everyone knew Lee, and they were expecting us. It was clear that Lee had become close with all the staff regardless of their level, and they knew him in a way that was personal and warm. Lee was always taking care of the people others tended to overlook. Whether it was tickets to a BB King Concert (his favorite artist and friend), or a baseball game, or a barbeque, he was always looking out for them. Besides, they were all voters and politics was his game.

So, the reception we received was exceptional. Both Roger and Joel were impressed. Lee met us at the door and immediately gave us a tour. I remember being struck by how homey the White House was under First Lady Barbara Bush. There were pictures of family and dogs everywhere, and the staff were all like one big family. Of course, we saw all the historical rooms, and then Lee said, "Let's go sit in the Oval Office."

Pretty obviously, Lee had the run of the place. Joel and Roger were further impressed. After sitting and chatting in that great room Lee said, "Let's go get something to eat," so we went downstairs to the executive dining room which was warm and cozy much like a paneled den. I remember the other person there with a small group was Richard Darman, Director of the Office of Management and Budget. Lee said hello but then pointed us toward a different table. "Let's go sit over here away from the economic mukety-mucks." That was typical Lee, totally spontaneous and unfiltered even for someone who was Chairman of the RNC.

We sat down and had a nice meal of hamburgers and fries, Lee's favorite. Then, Lee looked at his watch and said, "Do you want to go meet the boss? He's coming in now."

We responded, "For Sure!" So we departed the dining room and headed for the rose garden. Since the three of us were there for the Bankers Association meetings we all had our suits on as well as trench coats due to the wet late March weather.

The scene we witnessed when we walked out into the garden will be forever implanted on my brain. First, it was the same picture I had seen on TV so many times with the helicopter coming in to land. But what I had never seen was the huge throng of people with cameras, who once they saw Lee came running towards us like some giant wave.

I remember asking Lee who they were, to which he responded, "The press." Then he said, "Watch this. I'm going to have some fun."

As he walked out to speak with them, he raised both hands. "Ladies and gentlemen, I am here with an important group that is about to meet with the President. I will be out to make a statement after the meeting."

I couldn't help but smile. Lee, ever the promoter, was up to his old tricks! I could envision the media begging Lee in later sessions for information about who we were. He would keep them guessing and maybe even tell a white lie about the meeting if it suited his purposes. In any event, we went inside and had a nice short visit with President Bush who was as pleasant as he could be.

It was very clear that Lee had a special relationship with the President, and for that matter, all the Bushes because he had visited the family many times at Kennebunkport. Lee never did go back out to talk to the reporters, which kept them guessing. Later that afternoon Lisa and I stopped by and had a drink with Sally and Lee at their Georgetown townhouse.

It was the last time I would see Lee in good health because he was diagnosed a few months later with an astrocytoma of the brain after passing out during a speech. His doctors initiated a very aggressive treatment protocol having radioactive seeds implanted in his brain, but he died in March of 1991. Without Lee to run the campaign, in 1992 Bill Clinton defeated George H.W. Bush in his run for re-election. In large measure Ross Perot's campaign to run as an independent split the Republican vote.

Clinton was the man Lee had said he was worried about at the Renaissance weekend in Hilton Head years earlier when the Arkansas governor was still a relative unknown. I have often wondered what would have happened had Lee remained healthy. In my mind, there is no doubt that he would have found a way to take Ross Perot out of the equation.

As we moved into 1990, I began to develop a banking relationship with an entrepreneur I had met a year earlier at the request of Hootie Johnson. George Dean Johnson was one of three sons of a much loved Spartanburg Physician. A lawyer by trade, George had been the youngest person ever elected to the SC Legislature in the early 1970s. By the time I met him he was becoming a serial entrepreneur having successfully completed several real estate deals, and along with his brother Stewart, having started a garbage collection business that they sold to Waste Management.

In early 1989, Hootie had asked me to go up to Spartanburg to see George. He didn't give me any specific instructions, but just wanted me to go see him because he believed that George would become eminently successful one day. Hootie had sent me on similar calls to meet other entrepreneurs several times already. He always cautioned me to use my own judgement, but I could always tell when he liked someone and believed in their potential. To say he had a feel for entrepreneurs would be a huge understatement.

I went to meet with George and was impressed. He had a lightning quick mind and could calculate in his head faster than most people with a calculator. He liked basic businesses that served a wide swath of the population, and he liked a business with a successful template that could be replicated over and over again.

Through the process of selling the Spartanburg garbage business to Waste Management, he met Wayne Huizenga and Dean Buntrock. By 1987, Wayne had left Waste Management and was trying to grow a small business he had purchased called Blockbuster that was in the business of renting VCR movies. At the time the movie rental business was a small mom and pop industry with negative connotations from the rental of X-rated movies. Wayne's plan was simple: come with a clean, bright, fun, family-oriented environment and brand the concept by rolling stores out in rapid succession all across the country. To do that he needed to supplement company owned stores with those of well financed franchisees.

He found such franchisees in George Dean Johnson and his partners, Craig Wall and Dean Buntrock. By late 1988 or early 1989 George had acquired franchise rights for a large territory in the Southeast that would ultimately encompass over 200 stores. To build it out he needed financing in the $100 million range, and due to the rapid rollout, he needed it fast. We started financing the stores one at a time in early 1989. By the spring of 1989, the numbers were compelling, and George was ready to roll with speed. There were just a couple of small problems.

As is the case with most new businesses you lose money until your customer base builds up, and you eventually break even, and then in the succeeding months you become profitable. In banking jargon, we call that slope the "ramp to profitability." In the case of Blockbuster stores, the ramp was unusually fast. It took 6 months to break even and then the profits would quickly swell with incredible returns. In fact, in a typical store that cost $600,000 all in to upfit and inventory, franchisees would get all their money back in two years for an unlevered internal rate of return close to 50%. The problem was that in a situation where the plan was to open about 20 stores a month, the losses from the newer stores (open less than 6 months) overwhelmed the cash flow from the older stores, so the business would show massive losses (which bankers hate). This would last until about 18 months into the process when the number of now-profitable stores began to vastly overwhelm the brand-new stores and the business would be solidly in the black.

Technology concerns were another big problem. Everyone knew that we would eventually have streaming technology that would make Blockbuster's business obsolete. The only question was how quickly? Most knowledgeable people felt that by the mid-to-late 90's we would have it. Therefore, the relative life of Blockbuster was only going to be about 7 years. In the end, it was a lot longer because movie rentals survived well into the first decade of the 21st Century, however at the time we were considering making the loan, it was definitely a big concern.

To address the two concerns within the structure of the loan, we did two things. First, we established a cash flow covenant test for every store ranked by age. For example, stores open 1 month had to be operating at a certain level of loss. Stores open 2 months had to be at a lower level of loss, then open 3 months lower again, until break even at 6 months. From that point, our covenants required them to be increasingly cash flow positive. In this fashion, as long as the glide path was in line with the ramp to profitability, we knew it was only a matter of time until the overall entity was heavily in the black. If there was a failure by any tranche of stores to meet the covenant test, we could stop funding new stores and slow the growth curve way down. To address the technology concern, we made each tranche of stores fully amortize over 5 years once they had been open 6 months. In this fashion, our loan would be fully paid off by 1995.

George and his partners accepted our terms, so we loaned them, through an entity called WJB Video, approximately $30 million in 1989 and then another $60 million in mid-1990 with the only collateral for the loan being the video tapes and the cash flow. By Christmas of 1990, the business was booming, and they were past the inflection point so that profits from the older stores had started to overwhelm the losses from the new stores, and our loan had started to pay down.

But then, when everything seemed to be working perfectly, we encountered a big problem. On January 17, 1991, President Bush started an air and naval bombardment to expel Iraqi troops from Kuwait. The bombardment lasted for 5 weeks until we invaded, after which the war was short lived. However, during those 5 weeks, General Norman Schwarzkopf was on TV every night showing missiles going into enemy buildings, and the American public was glued to the news. As a result, the video rental business went to zero, and no one knew how long it would last.

At the same time, Hugh McColl had brought in a number of credit people from the Texas bank because rates were rising and we were starting to enter a recession. The way Hugh figured it, the Texas crowd had seen the Valley of the Shadow of Death and they would be effective in getting us ahead of the curve. He was right, but as a consequence, Bill Kelly, the new chief credit officer, was all over the WJB video loan and wanted to move it to the special asset bank where workouts were being handled. Fortunately, Bill had met George and liked him. While Bill was tough, he bought into my idea to give George and his partners some time before making that call. Fortunately, as soon as the war was over by the end of February Blockbuster's business was booming again, and we were off to the races with the loan rapidly paying down.

In 1993 George and his partners in WJB sold out to the franchisor, and George moved to Ft. Lauderdale to be president of Blockbuster Entertainment. Our loan paid in full, and in 1984 Blockbuster was sold to Viacom. George and Wayne went on as partners and started a number of other businesses including Boca Resorts, Auto Nation, and Extended Stay America, just to mention a few. I was involved in the financing of many of those businesses, and in my second banking career at Wachovia/Wells Fargo, Wayne Huizenga would be a great customer and friend.

In the process of building those businesses, Wayne and George created tens of thousands of jobs and improved the communities where they operated. In the late 90s George moved back to his hometown in Spartanburg and went on to create a number of other businesses, which I helped finance, creating thousands of jobs in his old hometown, as well. On top of all that, the Johnson family put their money and influence behind an effort to transform Spartanburg. Every entity, from Wofford and Converse Colleges, to Meeting Street Academy (a school for disadvantaged children, mostly children of color), and many others greatly benefitted from Johnson Family support. George and I became dear friends and in later years following my retirement from the Bank I joined his family office board of directors.

Aside from my involvement with the Beach Company and George, there were many other great customers my team and I were fortunate enough to meet and help finance during those years in Columbia. However, while I have focused on several specific successes, there were also problems.

In the commercial banking with middle market companies, a good rule of thumb is that lending losses should not exceed one quarter of one percent of loans on an annual basis. Thus, a bank with a $1 billion loan portfolio should not lose more than $2.5 million per year. Some years would be higher, especially in recessions, and it might be zero in the good times. However, on average .25% is a good rule of thumb. Bottom line, you have to be right 99.75% of the time, or for every 400 good loans you can only have one totally go bad.

As bankers, we used to like to say that if a portfolio had no charge off's the bank wasn't making enough loans. A bank with too many charge offs was making too many. Over the course of my career, I had losses but on average, my batting average was good. Even though I had a reputation for being aggressive, and I was, based on my gains and losses I was within that acceptable range over the length of my career, and I have no regrets even with the mistakes.

One of those mistakes was a loan I made to a large rubber glove manufacturer in eastern South Carolina. They were growing in a healthy manner and making money, and then the AIDS crisis came along. As a result, their sales went off the chart, and we financed their equipment expansion. Their profits boomed, and they were making boatloads of money right up until the growth of the industry brought in foreign competitors with cheaper labor and factories closer to the rubber raw material source.

Hopelessly undercut in pricing, the company went under and had to file for bankruptcy.

I remember sitting in my office on the 19th floor looking at spreadsheets and the history of the loan as I tried to figure out how I had missed it. At that time, reviewing bad loans to learn from them was a best practice, and we even had a little newsletter called "Spilled Milk" to impart those lesson. On this particular day, Hootie stopped by my office and asked what I was doing. I told him I was reviewing a past problem trying to learn what I had missed. He asked me to give him 30 seconds on the transaction leading up to the problem, which I did. He looked at me straight in the eye and said "Yep, you missed it. Anytime something is too good to be true, it is". With that he turned on his heels and doorway. Years later George Dean Johnson would explain his theory that "Excess profits invite ruinous competition," and that is exactly what happened to the glove company in eastern S.C. Hootie was dead right.

Another situation took place at the end of 1989 after the sale of the resort assets at Kiawah to the Landmark Land Company. In early 1989, we had financed the spinoff of the assets in Harbour Towne from the bankruptcy trustee at Sea Pines to a Prudential Bache syndicated limited partnership controlled by Avron Fogleman, the part owner of the Kansas City Royals baseball team. We advanced a bridge loan to purchase the assets with the payoff coming from the funds raised by the syndication of limited partnership interests to retail investors, who would buy the shares as a dividend play. The first loan worked perfectly, and we made a large fee for a loan with a very short duration.

At the end of 1989 we made a similar loan to buy the golf courses in Port Royal and Shipyard Plantations out of the Hilton Head Company bankruptcy, this time a $30 million loan to a limited partnership controlled by Mr. Fogleman bridging the purchase until Prudential Bache could raise the investor funds to effect the sale. This time, however, there was a problem. In early December, John Riddick on Hilton Head called to inform me that the closing was not going to occur. I asked what happened because the last time I had checked the money was all but raised. John said the accountants were unwilling to render an opinion that was necessary in order to break escrow and close, so the company was going to return all the funds to the limited partners.

Hearing that news, a group of us in Charlotte, including a great attorney named Ben Hawfield, boarded a bank plane and immediately flew to Memphis, Tennessee, where we met with Mr. Fogleman. He could not have been more of a gentleman. By then it was obvious that without the accountant's opinion Prudential Bache would not release the funds to pay us off, so Mr. Fogleman agreed to let us quickly resell the property in an effort to pay off the loan. As we boarded the plane to come back to Charlotte, I thought I knew who would buy the golf courses, my old friend Charlie Way at the Beach Company who had just sold all the resort assets at Kiawah to Gerry Barton.

When I called him upon our return, I said, "Charlie, what a deal I have for you." The Hilton Head assets were established golf courses with more rounds of play, so instead of being an operating drag they were producing about 3 million in cash flow. Fortunately, Charlie liked the idea, and the Beach Company ended up agreeing to buy the assets for just short of $30 million which gave us 100% of our principal back and something approaching 80% of our interest. However, it ended up being a tough negotiation, and the strain of the talks to get to a closing gave me a case of Bell's Palsy days after the closing.

On New Years Eve, Lisa and I were at a Party at the South Carolina Yacht Club owned by our great friend JR Richardson. As the evening drew to an end, Lisa looked at me and said, "My God, what is happening to your face?" When I looked in a mirror, I saw that the entire left side of my face was collapsing. I looked like the Batman character Two Face played by Tommy Lee Jones. Fortunately, with time the Palsy went away.

On the closing day, Marc Johnson and I dove into the Harbour Town Yacht Basin and did a victory lap because we were so relieved to get rid of what, at that time, could have been a big problem for NCNB Bank. It took a few days after for the stress from the negotiation to react and cause the onset of the Bell's Palsy. Charlie Way later commented that my new name would be Teflon, due to my skill at getting out of sticky situations.

On a lighter note, at the beginning of the new decade Marc Johnson called me from Charleston where he ran the Eastern Region for me. "Guess who's in my office," he asked.

"I have no idea," I said.

"Your old friend Tom Parsell. Guess what he wants to do?"

"I have no idea," I said.

Mark told me that Tom wanted to open a restaurant in the building he had taken in trade as part of the sale of his dealership to Hendrick Automotive. Tom's thinking was that he could not find a tenant for the building so he would be his own tenant, open the restaurant and lease the space from himself. I asked Tom what made him think he could be in the restaurant business.

"Well, Suzi and I eat out a lot."

Half mocking but also half serious, I asked Mark to lock the door of his office and keep Tom inside until I could get there and talk him out of it. At that point, Marc put Tom on the phone, and he explained his plan. He and Suzi were going to renovate the space and name the restaurant Magnolias. They had agreed to partner with Donald Barrickman, a dynamic, young chef who had been incredibly successful at a restaurant called Carolinas. I knew that Tom and Suzi were great businesspeople who used excellent accounting systems to track results. Marc and I approved the loan, and Tom and Suzi went on to make a huge success out of Magnolias, then go on to do two more restaurants, all in a row along East Bay Street in buildings they owned. Blossom would open a few years after Magnolias and then Cypress a few years after Blossom. While Cypress and Blossom are no longer there, Magnolias is and has been a landmark on the Charleston dining scene for over 30 years.

As the end of 1990 approached Joel Smith came into my office with a big surprise. "Carlos, I have been promoted to be the President of NCNB South Carolina, as well as NCNB North Carolina, and I want you to head up commercial banking for both states."

I was elated! This promotion would give me 3 times my current responsibility because the commercial business in North Carolina was about twice what it was in South Carolina. Best of all, I assumed the job would allow me to stay in Columbia where Lisa, Blake and I were incredibly happy. When I said that to Joel, he looked at me and said, "Carlos, one of us has to move to Charlotte." Right away, I knew what that meant.

Chapter 23

On To Charlotte
The NCNB Culture

In the fall of 1990, when Joel told me of my promotion and my need to move to Charlotte, I was not that surprised. It had been four years since NCNB purchased Bankers Trust, and in that time they had essentially left the old Bankers Trust alone. While we were clearly part of NCNB, it was 100% the Bankers Trust management team running South Carolina with virtually no involvement from Charlotte. As time went on, I knew that there would have to be more integration of the culture, and to do that it would be necessary to move people around.

In my case, I thought it was a little unusual that it was me having to make the move rather than Joel, who was going to be President of the two banks. However, Joel was pretty entrenched in Columbia since he had always been there and had very strong political connections in South Carolina. Those political connections would be important as we began to ramp up the appeal for true interstate banking. On the other hand, I had already moved 3 times and did not have the ties to Columbia that Joel did. So, it was up to me to be the sacrificial lamb and make the move, but there was one big problem, my wife Lisa!

Over the course of our three moves Lisa had been a real trooper, suffering through two major home renovations and all the disruption that came from changing locations. In Columbia, she was in the dream home that her father helped renovate to her taste, and we had become members of her old church. Blake was settled in school, and since Lisa's parents loved keeping him, we had built in babysitting anytime we needed. She had fallen back in step with many of her old college friends and was enjoying getting reacquainted after the 8 years that we had been away.

When I explained the situation, she was shocked. Her comment was that she thought Columbia would be our final resting place, which suited her just fine. To pick up and move after such a short return to her home was unsettling at best. However, Lisa understood that it was a big promotion for me. As she had done in the past, she was once again a trooper and agreed to go, provided I made a commitment to come back to Columbia after 5 years (She would come to be very happy in Charlotte, and as of my writing this book we have now been here for 30 years.) Lisa would make one stipulation: I needed to find a house that would not need to be renovated so we could move right in and not have to live in a construction zone.

So off to Charlotte we went. I was able to find a house in the Eastover section that was essentially finished except for the interior details. So, Lisa got to pick out the moldings, wall paper and light fixtures, and in January of 1991 we were able to move. At that point, I had already been working in Charlotte for about 3 months, staying in a hotel during the week and commuting home on weekends. With the move efficiently handled by my old friends at Millen Moving and Storage, it was great to be back together as a family.

In early spring 1991, Lee Atwater passed away finally losing his fight with cancer. In the end, Lee's situation became very sad because the radioactive implants took a terrible toll on his physical condition. While the funeral was a celebration of his life, the overall mood was very somber. There were many eulogies from the political world: Dan Quayle, Carroll Campbell, Strom Thurmond, just to mention a few. Everyone was saddened by such a vibrant life being cut short.

As we moved into the spring the contrasts between Charlotte and Columbia were stark both in the community and in the bank. Starting with the community, from the beginning it was clear that Charlotte was a business town as opposed to Columbia which was all about the University of SC and State Government. In Charlotte, the Chamber of Commerce was dynamic and very much at the forefront of everything going on. The Chamber had a very capable leader in Carroll Gray, who interestingly was also a South Carolinian. Also, the pace in Charlotte was much faster than

Columbia, which was more a slow southern town.

In Columbia, the public sector led, while in Charlotte, the business sector was clearly in charge with a small group of people calling the shots. John Belk, former mayor and CEO of the Belk Department store chain; Bill Lee, CEO of Duke Energy; Rolfe Neil, chairman and publisher of the Charlotte Observer; Ed Crutchfield, CEO of First Union; and Hugh McColl, our CEO, basically ran the town. There was a can-do attitude and a vibe that the sky was the limit as far as Charlotte was concerned.

From the outset it was very clear to me that unlike Columbia where Joel did all the heavy lifting in the community, the bank wanted me to be very involved. At the time, there were two senior general banking officers in Charlotte, Ed Dolby who was the North Carolina consumer banking head and me as commercial banking head for the two Carolinas. We both reported to Joel along with Roger Whaley who was the South Carolina consumer banking head. In Charlotte, since I was the person interacting on a day-to-day basis with the business community leadership that basically ran the place, it was only natural that I take the lead. Therefore, I dove in, getting involved with the Chamber and The United Way. Also, I joined the Children's Theatre board, as well as the Discovery Place board (Children's Science Museum), in addition to the Winthrop University Foundation board. The pace was frantic, and I loved it!

Sometime after my arrival in Charlotte, in late 1991, I got a call from Joel Smith basically saying that the bank wanted me to help Pat Phillips, who was the incoming president of The Arts and Science Council. ASC was an umbrella organization that raised money for the art and science nonprofits in Charlotte, like what the United Way did with Health and Human Services. At that time, they ran an employer-based workplace giving effort similar to United Way, then used a volunteer board to allocate the funds. I assumed they wanted me to help Pat make some corporate donor calls because when Joel called, he simply said there was a meeting later that day at the ASC offices.

I headed over at the appointed time and was a little surprised that the only people in the meeting were Pat Phillips, Michael Marsicano, the head of ASC, Laura Smith who was on the ASC staff, and Mack Everette, chairman of the ASC and Executive VP at First Union Bank. I remember walking into the meeting thinking to myself that they really needed help if they had no one else available to make calls! As the meeting went on, they kept asking me what I thought about this or that, which I found unusual for someone who was just going to make a few asks for money. Then the subject turned to a campaign goal, and someone threw out $3 million, which was roughly a 30% increase over the amount raised the year before. Then they all looked straight at me and asked if I thought we could do that, to which I responded, "Sure!"

As I said it, I remember thinking that $3 million was going to be a very ambitious goal and whoever ran the campaign was going to have their work cut out for them! At the conclusion of the meeting Laura Smith turned to me and said that she would be back in touch to set up a time for a press conference where they would announce the goal. It was then that I realized I was not there to make a few calls. I was there because they wanted me to chair the campaign. As you might imagine, I was frozen with fear! I hardly knew Charlotte and didn't know the first thing about the Arts and Science Council because South Carolina didn't have anything like it!

Luckily, it turned out that Michael and Laura were fabulous organizers and fund raisers themselves. Mac Everette and Pat were wonderful partners and helped with a lot of the asking. We went on to have a very successful campaign, and in fact, raised more than $3 million. I made a lot of new friends and running the campaign accelerated my getting to know my new hometown.

As far as the climate at the bank, it was definitely different. The NCNB culture was edgy and very much in the mold of Hugh McColl, the ex-Marine. Military language continued to permeate everything. Bank functions were more like pep rallies, or locker room talks before a football game, or perhaps more like military speeches before an invasion. McColl's highest award to a teammate was a crystal hand grenade. There was a strong distaste for losing and disdain for the competition. While we would work with our competitors when it came to community endeavors like the Arts and Science Campaign, there was absolutely no socializing with the competition who McColl called, "The Enemy."

The north side of Tryon Street was our side of town, and the south side was First Union's. Wachovia had long since dropped off the radar screen as the two Charlotte banks, through acquisitions, were already almost 3X the size of Wachovia. There was a lot of competition within NCNB as well.

Given the untimely death of Buddy Kemp in the summer of 1990, there was a lot of speculation as to who McColl's successor would be. Before Buddy's death, it was clearly going to be Buddy Kemp, and there was a certain equilibrium because of that certainty.

With Buddy gone, it was clearly an open playing field and while I do not know this for certain, it seemed that Hugh stoked the fire and pitted the potential successors against each other. All that was a harsh contrast when compared to the Bankers Trust culture, which had been all about teamwork and working with each other for the benefit of the community we served. It had never been about Hootie Johnson. By contrast, the NCNB culture was molded after Hugh's persona and while we would work hard to benefit the community, winning was first and foremost, and it was not simply enough to beat the competition. At NCNB, we wanted to Kill Them!

There was also an attitude of not needing the other banks. At Bankers Trust we had been very involved in The SC Bankers Association and cooperated with the other banks at a variety of different levels. At NCNB we tolerated the NC Bankers Association, but we generally thought of it as an outdated organization. We had a clear view that sooner or later there would be interstate banking and we could be more effective at lobbying for our own interests by ourselves. All this fed a culture of inflated confidence and some might even say arrogance that was far different from what I had been used to at Bankers Trust.

What held it all together was that at the end of the day everyone knew that Hugh really loved and cared for the troops. He said it best at a speech when the crown was lit for the new headquarters building in Charlotte. He said, "We care for each other like family—in policy and everyday small gestures." At the end of the day, Hugh had a soft spot for the team, and everyone knew it and loved it.

He used to say, "We all drink from the same canteen," and that is how he operated, but like a Marine officer, Hugh always made sure that the troops were fed and watered first. Thus, the culture was a study in contrast: a dog-eat-dog environment, but under the command of a benevolent dictator. To be honest, I loved it because it was exhilarating and exciting. It was almost like we had been sheltered at Bankers Trust, and we were now at the forefront at NCNB. However, there was one worry. What would happen when the benevolent dictator, Hugh McColl, was no longer there?

As 1991 ended and 1992 began, I was settling into my job and spending lots of time in the field. During 1991, NCNB acquired C&S Sovran after being repulsed in the late 80s when Hugh had made the famous comment to Bennett Brown about, "Launching his missiles," which had been his way of saying that he would do a hostile takeover if they could not come to terms. Bennet and the C&S management team had been able to turn back the unfriendly offer, and Hugh had retrenched and not gone hostile. Hugh's offer had led to C&S doing a merger of equals with Sovran Bank in Virginia, which had proved to be a mistake because the bank ended up being full of problem real estate loans, particularly in the Northern Virginia/DC market.

The second time around Hugh was successful, given the weakened condition of C&S and the strategy he deployed to take a more "soft glove" approach. As part of that strategy, Hugh offered to change the name from NCNB to NationsBank, which was less offensive to the C&S shareholders. As a practical matter, the NCNB name had already proven to be a liability in Texas where people resented having a "North Carolina bank" in their state. Mocking phrases were coined for the NCNB acronym, "No Cash For Nobody" and "Nobody Cares Nobody Bothers." In essence, being willing to give up the NCNB name was a throwaway for Hugh, but it played well with Bennett and the C&S Board, making it sound like the deal was more of a merger of equals versus an outright takeover. As others would soon learn there was no such thing as a merger of equals with Hugh McColl.

So, we started 1992 under the banner of NationsBank with $100 billion in total assets still under the protection (or hamstrung depending upon how you looked at it) by the Reciprocal Bank Pact. Clearly, NationsBank was now a player on the national banking scene, and no one questioned that we would ultimately be a survivor in the interstate banking environment that would surely come.

Given the C&S merger and my move to Charlotte, I had a whole new management team composed of 3 old NCNB executives in North Carolina: Jim Leavelle in Charlotte, Henry Carrisson in the Triad (Greensboro), and Howard Edwards in Raleigh (the Triangle). In South Carolina, there were two former C&S executives, Stan Gibson in the Eastern Region in Charleston and John Windley in the upstate or Piedmont Region, as well as MZE Wilkins, a former Bankers Trust executive in the Central Region headquartered in Columbia.

They were a great group, and while they were all relatively new in getting to know me (except for MZE), they took to my management style and we quickly coalesced as a team. In particular, I was pleased that the former NCNB guys did not seem to harbor any ill will at a South Carolina outsider being their boss. I think they realized that my mission in life was to help them be successful, and that is exactly what I did using the same management style that had proven to be successful in South Carolina. In a nutshell, I stressed being available to my people and their customers. I continued to always answer my own phone, and I was willing to roll up my sleeves and do the hard things that I was asking my people to do. Most importantly, I continued trying to find ways to help my people make loans versus just saying no.

Of my six regional executives, one was a female, MZE Wilkins. Throughout my career I had worked hard to mentor and promote females and people of color, so after the C&S merger, I was very pleased that MZE was part of my management team as a regional executive. Each regional executive had teams of lenders in their respective cities reporting to them. In Columbia, a young African American executive, Tony Grant, was the team leader.

Tony was an up and coming executive I had mentored earlier and, in fact, I continued to mentor during my entire career with NCNB/NationsBank/Bank of America. Tony went on to do great things serving on the National Urban League Board, and as chair of the South Carolina State University board (his alma mater), just to mention a few of his accomplishments in service to community. Tony also became an entrepreneur himself starting his own very successful financial consulting practice, Grant Business Advisors, which is still in business and where his son Hamilton is now taking over. Tony is a dear friend and remains so.

The one problem as we entered 1992 was that the economy was stuck in a recession. In particular, real estate was hit hard as were a number of operating companies in certain sectors. Fortunately, after the 1991Ryder Cup Kiawah was off to the races. However, the credit team Hugh McColl had brought in from Texas was cracking down. Every quarter there were day long meetings with the credit review committee where they would review loans to send to the workout group or special assets bank.

At that time, we had a risk rating system that graded loans 1 through 10. 1 was the equivalent of US Treasuries or cash-secured, while 10 was a charge off. The 9s went to the workout group. Our credit guy was a wonderful Texan named Marvin Schiebout. We nicknamed him "9 out Schiebout" because he wanted to send everything to special assets. I resisted where I had the facts on my side because in most cases the workout group was a dead-end street for our banking relationship.

The workout group would always claim that they would rehab situations, but that was almost never the case. Besides, the group was known to make some stupid decisions that only accentuated the losses. Things like pulling the plug on well-meaning people who were simply victims of circumstance, or doing fire sales in situations where assets would bring nowhere near their full value, or focusing more on simply collecting cash in the short run versus maximizing value in the long run. In my opinion, they still operate the same way today, but a lot of people would disagree with me. Because I was good with numbers and usually had the fact pattern right, I made good arguments. I think our people respected the fact that I would stick up for them and our customers. Those day long meetings were grueling with arguments back and forth. In the end, we came through, and our losses were within the accepted range.

The merger with C&S Sovran gave me the opportunity to reacquaint myself with Harold Chandler, the banker I had competed with on Hilton Head. Harold and I had stayed in touch and, in fact, when we were approached by a group of investors in the late 80s, we had discussed the possibility of forming a new bank on Hilton Head Island. The investors felt that between the two of us, our new bank could have owned the banking market on Hilton Head. At the end of the day, both Harold and I were moving up in our respective banks, and we concluded that big bank bankers made more money than small bank bankers, and we decided to stay put.

In any case, we became reacquainted after the merger. Harold, ever the up and comer at C&S, had been sent to Washington to straighten out the problems in Northern Virginia and DC, and by 1992 he was well on his way to doing just that. In early 1992 after the merger was consummated, we had a management meeting of the senior officers of the two banks. At that meeting Harold and I had a great time catching up and sat at the same table for dinner when Hugh McColl was speaking. At the end of Hugh's speech as he left the podium, he made a point to walk buy and speak to Harold within ear shot of Ken Lewis, who at the time was the front runner to replace Buddy as Hugh's heir apparent.

Hugh said to Harold, "I understand you might be the person to replace me one day." Clearly, Hugh was making sure that all the horses in the race kept running, and I strongly suspected that his comments were intended to stoke Ken Lewis. In Hugh MColl's competitive Marine world, keeping the competitive juices flowing was part of the vibe and the culture. Harold, sometime in 1993, left NationsBank to become CEO of Provident Insurance Company and later on UNUM. Years later, he told me that he thought he was being used as a stalking horse for Ken Lewis. I think he was right.

As 1992 wore on and the country began to recover from the recession, I was getting back out in the field as much as possible to win business. In that respect, the competitive culture of NCNB, by then NationsBank, fit me perfectly. I loved taking customers from other banks and had gotten quite good at it. Our people in the field recognized this and, as a result, they constantly invited me to their markets to call on customers and prospects with them. At the time, our middle market commercial loan portfolio in the two states was about $4.5 billion and our earnings were about $50 million net after taxes, and I set out to grow those numbers. Making calls with our people was what I loved, and I went at it with gusto. As I always had, I loved the plant visits, the chances to meet new people and learn how those entrepreneurs started their companies.

During this time, while I met hundreds of company owners each with their own story, two in particular stand out. I remember them not only because they exemplify what entrepreneurs do, but also because of the impact they would have on my later life after I would leave banking.

Tom Teague was born the son of a tenant farmer in Burlington, North Carolina. He went into the Marine Corps never finishing college. By the mid 60s he was selling Yellow Page ads and had become quite good at it, so much so, that the owner of a very small truck leasing business in Winston

Salem, NC, hired him because he had sold the owner so many Yellow Page ads. Tommy began to grow the business in earnest, and by the early part of the 70s he was doing business with a number of the major companies in the Greensboro/Winston area.

One of those companies, UNIFI, was a publicly traded fiber company founded by Allen Mebane who was friends with Ken Langone, who sat on the UNIFI board. Ken is a wonderful Wall Street type whose boutique investment bank, Invemed, had helped take Ross Perot's EDS public. Ken was also a founding shareholder of Home Depot and had served on many public company boards including the New York Stock Exchange. At one of the UNIFI board meetings, Ken noticed that all their trucks were leased from Salem Leasing, a small company in Winston Salem. He questioned Allen Mebane on the soundness of having all their leasing with such a small company when trucking was critical to their business. In essence, he told Allen that they needed to fire Salem and do business with someone bigger.

Allen responded, " Ken, if you want to fire them, then you drive over to Winston and do it yourself."

Ken said, "I will," and he got in his car and drove over.

Upon arriving at Salem Leasing, he met with Tommy and asked Tommy to tell him about himself. Tommy went over his background including the part about being poor and then clawing his way up.

In typical New York fashion Ken asked, "What are you going to do if we pull all of these trucks and take them away from Salem, and you don't have a job?"

Tommy replied, "Mr. Langone, I was poor once, and I'll never be poor again. If I lose this job, I'll be up at 5 am tomorrow morning and will hit the ground running selling something."

Ken responded, "Mr. Teague, you and I are going to be partners together, who do we talk to about buying this business?"

Ken and Tommy went to see the owner and were able to work out a deal to buy Salem Leasing Company and merge it with a shell public entity Ken owned that had huge operating loss carryforwards. Salem was later taken private with Tom Teague owning 2/3 and Ken owning 1/3. When Tommy got the paperwork for the initial purchase from Ken's lawyer, he immediately picked up the phone and called Ken.

"Ken, your lawyer has made a mistake, I'm supposed to own 1/3 and you are supposed to own 2/3."

Ken responded, "Tommy, there's no mistake. The way I figure it, if you own more of the company, I'll make more money because you will have more incentive to make the most of it."

Not only was it highly successful, but it is an incredible story of Ken's generosity and his desire to help people be successful. Tommy went on to grow Salem exponentially into one of the largest truck leasing businesses in the country. He also became a major investor in PBR (Professional Bull Riding), which I financed, and he went into the bucking bull business through Teague Bucking Bulls where he ultimately owned several National Champion Bulls.

I ended up loaning Tommy the money to invest in PBR as the only non-cowboy stockholder. PBR is the national sanctioning entity that regulates bull riding in a similar fashion that NASCAR establishes the ground rules for stock car racing. Importantly, PBR also controls all the TV rights, and while originally I thought Tommy might be over his skis a little on this transaction, I knew he was good for it. In the end it was a very good deal both for Tommy and the cowboys because Tommy brought his excellent business sense to the table.

When Tommy first called to tell me he wanted to invest in PBR, I asked him what the hell did he know about the Beer Business thinking to myself that PBR was Pabst Blue Ribbon. Tommy explained that it was the bull riding business, and I told him that was even worse. The truth was, Tommy was a good businessman, and in my experience good business people have skills that are transferable across many different types of situations. That transferability was true here, and Tommy was able to help the bull riders create value and accrue some personal net worth to be secure financially after what was usually a very short career due to the physical risks associated with bull riding.

When I met Tom Teague, NCNB/NationsBank was the agent on his leasing company's large line of credit. The company was doing exceedingly well, and we were delighted to be the agent which is a prestigious role for a bank. The agent bank is essentially one that puts together a syndicate of banks to handle a large credit facility that is too large for one bank to handle on its own. I had called on Tommy a good bit because he was a large customer but also because I liked him, and we hit it off.

About the same time I was meeting Tommy, I was financing a company in Greenville for a young entrepreneur named Jack Tate. When I first met Jack in the late 80s, he was a relatively small customer with several stores operating under the Baby Superstore name. They were a place where expectant mothers could go and shop for all of their baby needs. Jack had written the business plan for Baby Superstores during his time at Harvard, and when I met him, he was essentially deploying the plan he had written years earlier. After experimenting with several store formats, Jack went to a big box model and adopted a catchy slogan, "Baby Superstores, prices are raised elsewhere but lowered here."

The combination of the bigger store format and the catchy advertising started producing huge sales numbers, so I started financing the growth of the business with a large line of credit using a similar structure I had put in place for WJB Video on the Blockbuster stores where we would track each vintage of stores against the ramp to profitability. By late 1992 when I was getting to know Tommy Teague, Baby Superstores was going gangbusters with great profits and putting up huge sales increases. It was becoming readily apparent that to keep up the growth, they needed to go public because bank debt will only go so far in a high growth scenario.

Jack's attorney was a smart young lawyer named Ed Menzie, who was also doing a lot of work for us at the Bank. Ed was also a friend who has become a dear friend as time has gone by. He and I concluded that the perfect person to help Jack take Baby Superstores public was Ken Langone given his experience with Home Depot, so we set up a meeting with Ken and Tommy.

As soon as Ken saw the Baby Superstore numbers, he knew it was a hit so they immediately began the process to take it public. On the day of the offering in September of 1994 it was an immediate success. The stock came out at 20, then went to the high 20s, and from there went to the mid 40s. A few weeks later we had the closing dinner celebration which was actually a spaghetti dinner in the tiny village of Pumpkintown, SC, where Jack Tate's home was located. Ken Langone made his Italian recipe for spaghetti sauce, and we had a wonderful celebration.

At one point in the evening Ken and I were standing in a corner by ourselves, and I asked him what worried him about the business. Ken is a very big man with large hands which he uses to gesture, and that evening he had on an apron that was splattered with spaghetti sauce. I remember as clear as yesterday how he looked down at me (since I am 5 feet 8 inches tall) and with those large hands pointed over at Jack. I fully expected some technical answer about the capital expenditure requirements of the business, the inventory turns or some other financial response, but to the contrary, he said, "You see that little guy over there," speaking of Jack. "Well, as of today he's worth about $500 million. In my experience money changes people, so let's just hope it doesn't change Jack." As it turned out, Ken's concerns over human nature could not have been more prophetic.

In the years leading up to going public, Jack Tate had been a hands-on business operator who worked long hours 7 days a week. Right after going public, he bought a Lear jet, a helicopter, and a motor yacht. Some would say he took his eye off the business. In 1996, accounting issues caused an earnings restatement. The stock took a huge hit, which resulted in the sale of the company to Toys R Us. Jack as majority shareholder got slightly over $16 per share while the rest of the shareholders received slightly over $25 per share. It was the first time I had ever seen a majority shareholder take a haircut to make the rest of the shareholders whole and to make the transaction work. I'm not sure of the rationale behind the discount other than to keep everyone else from getting a lower price and possibly suing Jack. Toys R Us filed bankruptcy several years later, and many would chalk up Baby Superstores as a missed opportunity. In any case, Tommy and Ken remained good customers and friends. Our paths continued to cross many more times over the remainder of my banking career and afterward.

In late 1991 on one of my visits along with Howard Edwards to Raleigh, NC, I met another great entrepreneur, Temple Sloan Jr. Temple was an entrepreneur across several different businesses. While still a student at Duke University, he purchased a small finance company in eastern North Carolina. He grew it to five locations then sold it, taking the nest egg and starting a wholesale auto parts distribution business called General Parts. Temple liked to say that they almost failed three times because he didn't know anything about auto parts or distribution. However, this statement was perhaps Temple just being modest.

True or not, Temple and his brother Ham were able to survive and grow the company, ultimately expanding into the ownership of their own parts stores operating under the Carquest banner. The parts stores sold to professional mechanics at the car dealers and elsewhere. By the time I met Temple in the early 90s, the business had over $1 billion in sales and was one of the largest private companies in North Carolina. Most impressively, it had a track record of increasing profits every year for 35 years!

In addition to the parts business, Temple and a group of investors owned a huge concrete company called Southern Equipment, as well as a large auto dealership called Al Smith Buick. On top of all that, Temple was a significant investor in commercial real estate. He had started and sold to CALPERS (California Public Employee Retirement System) a commercial office rental company called Highwoods some years earlier, and now Temple was building the real estate business again!

But there was one small problem: the 1991/92 recession had hit Raleigh real estate particularly hard. While Temple's auto parts business was going exceptionally well, as was the concrete company, his auto dealership business and commercial real estate investments were suffering. I was having regular conversations with Marvin Schiebout about what to do. From my standpoint, the parts business and concrete business were just fine, and I thought the other companies would eventually come around with time. When things started to turn, Al Smith Buick came back, but the real estate remained a lingering problem. The real estate issues were exacerbated by the fact that several of Temples investors had problems elsewhere, and their ability to meet the necessary capital calls was in question.

By late 1993 Temple was looking for a solution. It was about that time that he learned of something called a REIT (Real Estate Investment Trust) from his broker at Merrill Lynch. Simply stated a REIT is a publicly traded entity that pays out 90% of its earnings as dividends. It is an ideal structure for owning real estate because it uses equity investor capital as its principal funding source, as opposed to using debt. The lack of mandatory interest payments makes a REIT a more solid platform for acquiring and holding income property. For Temple, it was an ideal solution because after going public the money raised from the equity offering would essentially de-lever all of the assets making it a much more stable entity.

The only problem was that he would need about $200 million in assets to go public and Temple's holdings were much less than that. First, he went to CALPERS and talked them into selling him back the old Highwoods assets to complement what Temple and his partners already had. He was also able to talk some other developers in Raleigh into joining with them to get the asset pool over $200 million. In addition, he needed to have $60 million in bank lines for liquidity to close the equity offering.

To fulfill that requirement, Temple obtained $20 million from each of three banks, $20 million from First Union, $20 million from Wachovia, and $20 million from NCNB/NationsBank, so everything was set to go public in 1994. Unfortunately, the Friday before the Monday on which the offering was set to take place, NationsBank's Real Estate Group pulled their commitment. By then, real estate lending at NationsBank was in a totally separate specialized group separate from commercial banking. I was not supposed to make real estate income property loans unless it was owner occupied and the real estate was a plant or something occupied by an operating entity we were banking.

When I got the call Friday afternoon from Howard Edwards, he was livid. Temple's operating companies including General Parts, Southern Equipment and Al Smith Buick collectively were one of our biggest customers in Raleigh. Howard used to smoke cigarettes and I could always tell when he was nervous as he would constantly thump the ashes on a crystal ashtray in his office and it would "ding." Well on that afternoon the ashtray was going ding ding ding as Howard was thumping away. He said the real estate people backed away because they had been told by the Texas credit people not to make any more real estate loans due to all the problems we were still experiencing from the recession, even though times were getting better.

Howard said that if we didn't do something, Temple would start looking around, and if he was successful in finding another bank we would end up losing his business, which was significant. I was well aware how significant a customer Temple was. was so I asked a few questions. "Howard, am I correct that the day they close all of the debt is paid off except for the 60 million in lines?"

His response, "That's correct."

My next question, "Howard, am I also correct that the lines will be unfunded or at zero balance the day the equity offering closes?"

"Correct."

"Howard, this is my last question. Am I correct that Temple does not guarantee this loan personally and he will not own more than 5% of the resulting entity and that the management team of the new Highwoods will be independent of all of Temple's other businesses?"

Howard responded, "Correct."

I then told Howard that since I had $20 million of authority, and since we did not need to aggregate the other loans to Temple, I would use it to approve the loan so he could go ahead and issue the commitment, thereby allowing the transaction to close. The public offering went off without a hitch the following week. However, since I knew I would be criticized for making the loan our real estate experts would not make, I called Joel Smith to tell him what I had done. Joel did not chastise me, he simply said. "You realize you are not our real estate expert," to which I responded yes. He then said, "You realize our real estate experts turned this loan down," to which I responded yes. I then went on to tell Joel that while they were the real estate experts, I was the commercial bank expert and our commercial relationship was far bigger than the real estate piece by a multiple of 9 or 10 times.

Essentially, I had made a business decision to protect the relationship I had at risk, and if anyone wanted to criticize me, they were welcome to try. I would stand by my decision. Joel was a great sport, because he was never critical. He simply put me on notice that others might criticize me, but they never did. Temple Sloan and I went on to have a wonderful business relationship. Our paths crossed many times over the remainder of my banking career and afterward.

Chapter 24

Interstate Banking Arrives Along With A Personal Crisis

By 1993 the recession still lingered but was beginning to fade. Hugh and the corporate officers had moved into the new 60-story Corporate Center, and Ed Dolby and I set up shop on the former executive floor in the old 40-story NCNB Building which became the headquarters for the North Carolina and South Carolina banking groups. I occupied what was former chairman and CEO Tom Storrs old office. My son Blake, about 10 at the time, called it the James Bond Jr. office. It had huge steel double doors that would immediately slam shut upon me pushing a button and electric drapes I could close with another button. It even had a private bathroom.

Mr. Storrs must have been very security conscious because a security desk in the lobby staffed by two armed security guards controlled access to the upper floors. While I have never been particularly caught up in the trappings of office, I must admit it was nice. However, pleasant or not, I was on the road every week either in my car or on small planes.

When in Charlotte I would usually have customers in for lunch using the private dining rooms on top of the new 60-story Corporate Center. The new building was an impressive setting. People in Charlotte began to call it "The Taj McColl." Huge ceilings towered over the lobby along with a giant fresco at the entrance done by the artist Ben Long.

Ben's agents in Charlotte were two sisters, Ann McKenna and Kitty Gaston. Ann lived across the street from us, and we became good friends. She was a stylish lady with a very deep voice. There was always something going on at her house with the team of artists Ben had brought in to do the fresco. There were many drop ins with lots of wine and good conversation, and we got to know Ben during the time he was doing the work. Ben, an ex-Marine, was also good friends with Hugh. He was incredibly talented (and still is today) and full of charisma. The entourage of artists, many from Europe, was great fun to be around. We had Ben do a charcoal portrait of Lisa, since we could not afford to have it done in oil. We did have one of his assistants, Laura Buxton, an artist from England, do an oil of our cocker spaniel Chevy.

On a personal note, this was a great time in our lives. We were carefree and constantly going places. Blake was in public grammar school at Eastover Elementary where he could walk the three blocks to school every day. As had always been the case, there was much visitation from Lisa's family as well as my family. Every summer we would go to the beach for a week and have both sets of parents visit. There were also frequent trips to Lake Summit (our On Golden Pond) where friends and family often visited. Blake went back to Camp Mondamin every summer, and I always joined him for our three day father-son camping trip.

Since I was always on the road with a car phone, I frequently called my dad, who by this time was starting to be in poor health. We talked almost daily or at least every other day. He seemed to revel in hearing of my travels and the stories of the entrepreneurs I had been to see that day. On one occasion when I had to go down to check on things at Kiawah, I chartered a small private plane and paid for it personally because I wanted to take my dad to see the island. I picked him up and we flew down. It was a stunningly beautiful day. My good friend Pat McKinney met us at the airport and gave us the full tour. At that time, the island was exploding with activity in the aftermath of the Ryder Cup. I remember Dad had one of those driving caps on with the button-down bill. He seemed so fragile and small, however that day was a good day, and he beamed with enthusiasm over all he had seen. The plane flight was especially fun for him given all his time in airplanes during the war years. As I dropped him off back at the small airport several miles from Salem, we hugged, and he told me how proud he was of me. I told him the feeling was mutual.

In late 1993, I looked at my interoffice mail to see that someone had sent me a newspaper article about my former boss who had been the city executive on Hilton Head when Lisa and I moved there 13 years earlier and

I took the position of senior lender. That former boss had been convicted of bank fraud and would serve jail time. I was shocked. If anyone had asked me before reading the article if that was possible, I would have said no. The article made me reflect on the fickleness of life and how it can change. I know nothing of the circumstances that led to this person's conviction other than that there must have been a crisis of some sort in his life that led him down the wrong path. Little did I know at the time that our family was about to face its own crisis.

In early 1994, the good times seemed to be continuing. Things were rocking along at the bank, and we were getting traction on many fronts. Lisa was happy in Charlotte, and she no longer talked about moving back to Columbia. Because there had been breast cancer in Lisa's family history, she was good about getting regular checkups. Unfortunately, on one of those checkups in 1994 it was discovered that Lisa had a tumor in her right breast. It turned our life upside down. We knew time was of the essence, so we moved quickly.

Fortunately, there was a great Oncologist in Charlotte named Dr. James Boyd. Initially, we did see another Oncologist in Columbia, but it quickly became apparent that we would rely on Dr. Boyd for advice. After the pathology came back, we had a long meeting where Dr. Boyd gave us many options for treatment, everything from minor surgery, to major surgery, to radiation only, to full blown chemo.

Our heads swam with all the options. Finally, I asked Dr. Boyd if it was his wife what he would advise. He told us that he would treat the cancer aggressively with surgery and chemo. Lisa was a rock, she chose to treat the cancer as aggressively as she could. Therefore, in early 1994 we went to the hospital in Columbia to have the surgery done. We chose Columbia because we wanted to be close to her parents for support.

After the surgery, I remember sitting in her room while she was still asleep from the meds. I remember thinking about what life would be like without her, and it was just too much to even comprehend. While I have always loved my wife and tried to be a good husband, I am by no means perfect. I have a short attention span and can also have a short temper. I knew there were many occasions when I had taken her for granted. I resolved right then and there that no matter what happened, I would never, ever, take Lisa for granted again. About that time a nurse entered the room, she handed me a small handwritten note. I still have it today. It was from my attorney friend Ed Menzie. He told me that he had been to Mass that morning and said a rosary for Lisa and me. Lisa was still asleep but somehow that simple act from a friend gave me comfort that with the support of friends we would find a way to see our way through whatever happened.

When Lisa awoke, we entered a terrible period of waiting for the results of all the lymph node tests. We knew from our conversations with Dr. Boyd that if any of her lymph nodes tested positive, the probability of recurrence went up significantly. If several tested positive, it went up exponentially. I think it was a day or so before we heard the results. I stayed there with Lisa and slept in the room. When the doctor came in with the results we held our breath, and then the great news came, none had tested positive! We were so relieved, it was like a new lease on life; however, we knew there would be rough days ahead with the chemo.

When Lisa started the chemo, we knew that given her decision to be aggressive with the treatments, the process would be difficult. At first, there were hardly any ill affects, but as the weeks went by and the chemo built up in her body, it became debilitating. Aside from the loss of all her hair, there was also the sickness and the total loss of energy. With her last treatment, she was so weak she could barely walk. Fortunately, her parents. Joyce and Walker, came and stayed with us to help and take care of Blake. Aside from my worries about Lisa it was also clear that Blake was impacted by her illness. He was only 12, and I could tell it was tearing him up to see his mom so weak.

Fortunately, as each day passed after her last treatment she grew stronger. When her hair came back it came back curly which was unusual given the fact that Lisa's hair had always been straight. Our life as family began to normalize once again, except for the regular checkup dates when we would all hold our breath. We have now had almost 30 years of checkups and we have been blessed; so far with no sign of the cancer's return.

As I began to resume my normal work schedule things began to heat up at the bank. With the passage of Riegle-Neal, which essentially gave banks the power to branch across state lines and buy banks anywhere in the country, the rate of merger activity accelerated greatly, and for the next three years NationsBank would rattle off a string of acquisitions: :

Bank South, CRT (Chicago Research Trading), Montgomery Securities, Boatmens, and Barnett Bank just to mention some. It certainly looked to me that Hugh McColl was on a frantic race to achieve mass before someone else could step in.

Each acquisition followed a similar script, starting with a well-rehearsed press conference in which the two CEO's would mouth all kinds of pleasantries about the acquired company joining the NationsBank family. Shortly afterward came a giant pep rally with our new teammates where Hugh would hold forth and extend the offer to get on the "NationsBank Train." Hugh was an outstanding speaker, who could win people over in a heartbeat. He had the perfect blend of being able to fire people up like a field general or coach with all the military vernacular about "storming the hill," but he also had the ability to make people feel like he was in it with them, and he was. All his speaking was off the cuff and totally spontaneous, and he had that great gift that most great speakers have to adapt to the situation and audience on the fly. In short, Hugh was magnificent!

In most merger situations blending the cultures is critically important. In fact, when mergers fail it is usually because of culture clash. So, these giant pep rallies were in many respects the first step toward making sure that the acquired bank's key people bought in. In almost every case we would have a number of NCNB/NationsBank senior leaders attend to participate in the "Sheep Dipping" process. I was fortunate enough to be invited to participate in a number of these "introductory gatherings." They were a study in how to get people integrated into a new team quickly and Hugh was clearly the coach and the quarterback all rolled into one.

One of Hugh's favorite philosophies was that you lead from the front, meaning the leader gets down in the trenches and gets his or her hands dirty. I had already adopted this as part of my management style, but for the employees of many of these acquired banks the concept was foreign. They were used to command and control environments where the leaders sat on the top floors of their ivory towers and rarely came out in the field other than to do what we termed an occasional "Fly By" to shake hands and press the flesh. NCNB/NationsBank under Hugh was totally different and the merged employees would immediately pick up on it and loved it.

I learned a great deal from those functions, a lot of it about human nature, but more about how to inspire people to gather around a common cause. Some of the human nature lessons were that people thirst for great leadership, and while much is said and written on the subject, it is a rare commodity. I also learned that one of the key things all great leaders have is the ability to show empathy. In simplistic terms, care about your employees and make sure you show it. I made a mental note to be sure that my philosophy about win-win also translated to the employees. Since I was already operating under the golden rule that things had to be good for the customer and the bank, it was a natural extension to apply it to employees, as well. After all, everybody knows that in a service business like banking your employees are a company's greatest asset. Years later in another career with another bank that knowledge would prove to be incredibly valuable.

In addition to the lessons in team building and human nature, seeing Hugh in action made me realize I was totally inadequate in the public speaking arena. I began to work on enhancing those skills. I started writing down everything I wanted to say word for word and then breaking that down into an outline that I could hold in my head. I learned to slow my cadence down and use pauses to add emphasis where appropriate. I also learned to think a lot about the audience in advance and how my approach might best appeal to them. I also learned from Hugh that buying a new white shirt and putting it on just before a speech somehow made me feel better and more confident. In short, while I would not call myself a great public speaker, by adopting some of Hugh's techniques, I did get manage to get better.

Sometime in 1995 I was presented with an interesting new challenge. A teammate named Roger Hayes came to see me. Roger was head of Municipal Finance at NationsBank and was an NCNB early follower of Hugh McColl. At the time the municipal bond business sat in the capital markets group (part of the investment bank). Investment Banking was going through a cost cutting exercise, and there was much discussion about whether the bank should stay in the municipal bond business or not. At the time it was marginally profitable, but it served an important constituency that sat in the general bank part of the commercial bank, as opposed to the large corporate area where most of the investment banking customers were handled. Roger knew that I could be a strong ally in his effort to keep NationsBank in the tax-exempt bond business.

For me, it was a no-brainer. The tax-exempt world includes cities, counties, states, colleges, universities, hospitals, and nonprofits of all different shapes and sizes. Aside from the fact that nonprofits were an essential part of the fabric in the communities where we did business, they were easily 25% of the deposits that sat in commercial banking. My thesis was simple, if we do not take care of tax-exempt customers' bond needs, someone else would, and they would want those deposits that were the raw material banks use to extend credit.

Another factor was the nature of CFOs in the nonprofit sector. Unlike the private sector where companies can afford to pay up for talent and CFOs are usually the second most highly compensated employees, nonprofit CFOs tend to be more modestly compensated. As a result, the typical nonprofit CFO might not be as adept at navigating the capital markets and as a result they might depend upon and more highly value the advice of bankers. Thus, it was a double whammy: if we exited the tax-exempt bond business we would walk away from customers who represented one of our largest deposit bases, and we would surrender our important role in helping nonprofits access the capital markets thereby giving our role of trusted financial advisor to other banks. When I presented my case to Ken Lewis who was charged with deciding what to do with the business, he simply said, if you think it is a business we should be in, then it now reports to you and you are accountable for it. But it better make money.

For me, it was an exciting opportunity to learn something new and to take over a business that was important to commercial banking. At the time, we were essentially a nobody in the municipal bond business. We weren't even in the league table top 50, the league tables being a measure of underwriting success based on the total value of bond issuance a company either managed or co-managed. The business was breakeven at best, and while we were a leader at handling the traditional banking needs of cities, counties, states, hospitals, institutions of higher education and nonprofits, we were not viewed as a partner of choice for handling bond issuance.

The good news was there was a great group of people in the business including Roger Hayes and a young banker named Phil Smith who handled the sales team. There was also a young lady named Valerie McKernan, who was the business manager. Valerie was smart as a whip and incredibly capable in staying on top of the numbers. One of the first things I did in working with Valerie was to set up a system where we could allocate all the profits of the business back to the commercial banking markets in the field that were handling the traditional needs of nonprofit customers.

With this in place municipal finance was just like any other product that traditional bankers delivered to customers, and it gave them a vested interest in seeing that municipal finance would be successful. However, as we pursued that business, we took great care to not run afoul of a myriad of laws limiting the non-licensed bankers in the field from directly receiving incentive payments for their efforts in referring business. However, sales could be tracked under the overall umbrella of cross-selling, and that is what we did.

Once we got the accounting in place, things began to roll, and we began to move up in the league tables. In addition, there was the added benefit of the relationship enhancement that occurred when we became the trusted advisor on bond issuance for a client. Simply put, the more products we could deliver to a customer the more important we become to them and the harder it was for them to consider leaving.

In addition to the work Valerie and I did on the accounting, we also changed the incentive plan to align with the business's bottom line. Simply put, we developed a plan that would fund one level of bonuses for the municipal team if we met budget, and then higher levels if we exceeded budget, but less if we fell short. This incentive plan was essentially separate and distinct for municipal finance and walled off from the other incentive plans in investment banking.

This was an important consideration because in the world of investment banking, municipal finance was typically considered a second or third tier business, and those bankers were the last to get paid, especially in a tough year. With a clear incentive plan that tied the team's bonuses to their financial success we had everyone in municipal finance joined at the hip.

As we began to have more success, we began to attract attention from top municipal finance bankers who wanted a good platform to operate from. All of them were well aware of the "second class citizen" problem of being muni banker inside investment banking, and so our incentive structure, which walled them off from the rest of investment banking resonated with many. While a number of top bankers moved to us, one in particular was a huge win and representative of what we were trying to do.

Edward Boyles was one of the top municipal finance bankers operating in the Southeast for Merrill Lynch. He was the son of Harlan Boyles, long running and very successful Treasurer of the State of North Carolina and author of a book called, "The Keeper of The Public Purse." While being Harlan's son gave him a certain level of notoriety, Edward was a self-made man with the reputation for being a very trusted advisor to cities, counties, states and nonprofits of all types. In particular, Edward had become advisor to the City of Charleston. Unlike Charlotte, which was led by the business sector, Charleston was led by its entrepreneurial and very successful Mayor Joe Riley. Mayor Riley had singlehandedly led a renaissance of the city using cutting edge tax increment financing bonds to fund a number of public improvement projects making the city more attractive to tourism and people moving down from the North.

Today many are aware of Charleston and what a great city it is, but in those days the city was literally falling down. Nothing much had happened in the 100 years following reconstruction, and Charleston had whole neighborhoods that were literally rotting. There was a need for many infrastructure projects, and while not totally out of control, crime was an issue. Over a long period of time with a lot of hard work, Mayor Riley fixed all of that and then some as he made Charleston into the city it has become. In essence, Mayor Riley operated under a version of my win-win, with his philosophy being if it was good for the city, it would be good for its citizens.

In short, Mayor Riley was the epitome of another type of entrepreneur, one devoted to his community versus one committed to his business and making money. Along the way, like most entrepreneurs in business, he took a lot of risk, suffered much criticism, and essentially did things other people were not willing to do. The net result of his work over 40 years as mayor was a total transformation of the city of Charleston. Since I knew Joe Riley personally and had the utmost respect for him, and since I knew Mayor Riley was the best mayor in the country and that he had a very high regard for Edward Boyles, it made sense that we needed to hire Edward Boyles.

As Phil Smith and I began to court Edward, the topic of the incentive plan was front and center, and it was also the elephant in the room. Everyone knew that investment bankers were paid differently from traditional commercial bankers, and I knew Boyles had a concern about how it would work for a municipal finance banker to ultimately report to a traditional banker (me). I took the approach of putting this topic on the table right up front which was how I always handled things. As I had come to understand from long experience, in almost any decision there is usually one major issue. Whether in loan approvals or business decisions, I like to deal with the biggest problem first. Some people call this "cutting to the chase," and for me it has always been helpful to get the big concerns off the table right away. In my mind, it always seemed to take the tension out of the air and make the rest of the conversation easier.

In the case of Edward, I knew he made a lot of money, and so right up front I said, "Edward, I realize that investment bankers make more money than traditional bankers like me. My goal is for you all to make a lot more money than me because if you do, we will be making a lot of money in municipal finance for NationsBank and as a result, we will have been successful. Besides, I said, "You all are in a different kind of business that has a high risk reward ratio. Municipal finance is not an annuity business like commercial banking where we have recurring revenue from a big loan portfolio. You all start over every year, so it tends to be more feast or famine. In the good years my expectation and hope is that there will be many people that make more money than me."

There was also the concern about what might happen if investment banking had a tough year when municipal finance had a banner year. Would this diminish the municipal finance bonus plan? My response was simple, "Municipal finance's plan accrues separately based on how much money the business makes." I told him I controlled the accrual as well as how the money was spent. If anyone tried to short the accrual, it would have to be over my dead body because I had given my word that this would not happen.

For me personally, doing business this way had become part of my nature. At the beginning of this book, I talked about the importance of being able to engender trust in business and in life. I said that if you behave in a certain way long enough and consistently enough, it becomes part of who you are. For me, the simple notion of my word being my bond came through and it was an effective sales tool both with customers and employees. Being forceful, candid, and not mincing words seemed to resonate with Edward, and so we were successful in hiring him. This would be but one of many similar conversations we would have that would lead to our being able to significantly increase the talent in the municipal finance business, all the time being careful to balance the added expense of these new, highly talented bankers while preserving the bottom line.

By early 1998 things were rolling not only in Municipal Finance but also in commercial banking in the Carolinas. The fed funds rate was in the 5.5% range, which at the time was still low in relative terms. The economy was beginning to experience the dot com boom that would ultimately result in another recession, but it was still a few years away. NationsBank was one of the largest banks in the country and we had our sights set higher. Lisa was fully recovered from her treatments, and while we would still hold our breath with every checkup, every year that went by made our confidence grow. I had become incredibly active in the Charlotte community. In addition to having chaired a number of nonprofit boards, I chaired the Chamber of Commerce New Membership Campaign as well as the Charlotte Regional Partnership, which was the multi-county economic development entity. Yes, life was good, but little did we know that events were underway that would have a dramatic impact on our lives as well as my career.

Carlos Evans

Chapter 25

A New Name A New Boss

In April 1998 it was announced that NationsBank would acquire Bank of America in a stock deal that would create the largest bank in the country by total assets at over $523 billion. Interestingly, at the same time Jamie Dimon at Bank One would acquire First Chicago in a deal to create the fifth largest Bank at $230 billion. Clearly, the end game in interstate banking was starting to play out, and Hugh McColl was winning the race by creating the first coast-to-coast bank in the country. At the time of the merger announcement, it was stated that Hugh would be chairman and the 50 year old CEO at Bank of America, David Coulter, would be the president. My former boss Hootie Johnson would be the chairman of the executive committee for the merged entity.

The old NationsBank board would control a majority of the directors but only by one vote. This was a huge mistake by the former Bank of America board as that one vote effectively made the deal a takeover. There was a statement in the merger agreement that said, "It is the current intention of the board that Mr. Coulter would succeed Mr. McColl." Despite the flowery language in the press releases, all of us knew that would never happen.

By the summer of 1998, there was much excitement in Charlotte as the two banks plodded toward integrating the two companies. One of the first people dispatched to San Francisco was Hugh McColl's key lieutenant, Ken Lewis, who despite the current intention of the board language, was viewed as the front runner to succeed McColl as the next CEO. Ken was a self-made man and a tough operator, and while in many respects he tried to emulate McColl with all the military rhetoric and tough language, everyone knew he lacked Hugh's heart for the people.

In the summer of 1998, I was at the beach taking a long weekend with Lisa and Blake, as well as my mom and stepdad, and his two sons and their families. It was there that I received a call from Joel Smith that would start a feeling of discomfort inside me that would grow steadily for the next two years.

The moment Joel called I knew something was up. I could sense it in the tentative tone of his voice. By then, I had worked for Joel for over 10 years, and we knew each other well. He was a wonderful boss who pretty much gave me free reign but was always there when I needed him to back me up. I always kept him apprised of what I was doing, but for the most part, I was able to operate with great independence, which was the way I liked it. Joel started our conversation by telling me that he had been promoted to be president of the bank east of the Mississippi while Gene Taylor would be president of the bank in the West. They would both report to Ken Lewis who was coming back to Charlotte.

Joel went on to say that Ed Dolby would become president of the Carolinas bank and that they wanted me to move to Florida to be head of commercial banking for that state. My first response to Joel was one of congratulations. I knew this was a big step for him, and I was truly happy for my friend and mentor. However, secretly I had some concern because it seemed that this was another case of Hugh setting up a horse race, this time between Ken Lewis and all other comers.

It was clear that Hugh, who was approaching retirement age, was beginning to set the stage for leadership transition. The thought of that gave me pause. Under Hugh, his love for the people allowed the aggressive dog-eat-dog culture to stay in check. Who knew what would happen with him gone? The part about Ed Dolby did not surprise me either since Ed was one of the highest ranking African American executives at the company and someone deserving of a greater role. Ed and I had become good friends during the 7 years of working together in Charlotte with both of us reporting to Joel.

The thing that surprised me was the part about me. While the total consumer and commercial bank in Florida was much bigger than the combined Carolinas, the commercial bank in Florida was smaller. Through a lot of hard work over a number of years, we had achieved a significant lead in market share in the Carolinas for the commercial segment. As a result, the total loans and deposits of the commercial bank in the Carolinas was bigger than Florida's.

As I contemplated all this, I quickly realized what was going on. For years NCNB, and NationsBank had a very strong focus on diversity. It was promoted at every level of the company, especially at higher levels within the organizational structure. In fact, on more than one occasion, I had been asked by high-ranking personnel executives why I did not check the Hispanic block. Clearly, since I was 50% Hispanic due to my mother being Costa Rican that was an option. The inference by the folks in personnel was that it would help my career, and it would help them play the numbers game. For me, my response was always the same. While I was proud of my Hispanic heritage, I had always viewed myself just like everyone else, and besides, if I succeeded I wanted it to be because of my own merit and nothing else.

So when Joel told me about Ed, I told him that I understood the imperative around diversity, and had I been in his shoes I would have made the same call. The truth is I never knew who really made the call. Whether it was Joel or someone higher up. Over the years Joel and I have become dear friends and I have never asked the question because for me, the answer really didn't matter. What mattered to me was my next move. Would there be one, or no move at all?

Reflecting on my situation, I knew the offer of a new job in Florida was, in part, designed as a way for me to save face because it was being positioned as a promotion with more money. Maybe part of it was because senior management knew the potential in Florida was much greater than the Carolinas and by all rights our commercial business in Florida should have been much bigger. There may have been an element of them wanting to see if I could do for Florida what I had done for the Carolinas.

The thought also crossed my mind that maybe they just wanted me out of the way so Ed Dolby wouldn't have me operating in his shadow. I really didn't think that was the case because Ed had been a consumer banker his entire career and he really didn't know anything about commercial banking. For him to be successful, he was going to need a strong person in my role.

As I thought about all of this, I asked Joel if I had a choice. I explained that I had no problem working for Ed. I also knew he needed an answer, so I said I would talk it over with Lisa and Blake and let him know Monday. Joel said that the decision was clearly mine and that he knew I had always gone wherever he and the company wanted me to go but, if there was a problem this time, he would respect my decision.

When I got off the phone with Joel, Lisa and Blake immediately chimed in. They had both been listening to the conversation and knew that I was being asked to go to Florida. Lisa was adamant that she did not want to go. Blake was as well. While Lisa was now 4 years into her recovery from the cancer, she was still heavily reliant on the support group we had here in the Carolinas from her parents, her doctors, and our Church.

Blake for his part was a sophomore at West Charlotte High School. At the time Charlotte was busing students to achieve racial integration, and West Charlotte was a largely African American high school on the other side of town near Johnson C. Smith University. While there were excellent private schools in Charlotte, both Lisa and I were strong supporters of public education. Besides, I wanted my son to fully appreciate the diversity of the real world, and I didn't believe the real world was represented by the experience he would have at a private school.

Blake was doing exceptionally well at West Charlotte. He was in all AP classes and with Lisa's help was making excellent grades. Even though he was only in the 10th grade he was already thinking about colleges and was considering Davidson, Washington and Lee and Bowden. Florida was going to be a long way from all those places. As I reflected on the decision in front of me, I knew that at the end of the day Lisa and Blake would do whatever I felt best for my career and for the family.

However, as much as the excitement of a new role intrigued me, I couldn't ask Lisa to make another move. She had been a trooper throughout my career, even when she didn't want to make the move from Columbia to Charlotte. Blake's situation was further icing on the cake, and besides the whole thing just didn't feel right to me. As a lender, I had been taught to rely on my gut instincts. Over the years, I had proven that I had good instincts around making decisions and my gut this time was telling me to say no.

So I called Joel Monday morning and told him I wanted to stay in

Charlotte and work for Ed. Little did I know that this decision would prove to be a godsend but in ways I could not have imagined at the time. Once the decision to stay put was made, I went in to see Ed Dolby to tell him that I was looking forward to working for him. I told him I was committed to helping him be the most successful bank president in the system, and that I was committed to making the commercial bank in the Carolinas and the municipal finance business all that they could be. The whole municipal finance situation was interesting because in truth neither Ed nor Joel knew much about the business other than it reported to me. While I was responsible for the P&L, the results were distributed to the states where the customers were located.

As to municipal finance, I had my hands full keeping our team settled down as we moved toward the consummation of the merger with Bank of America. Phil Smith, Roger Hayes and Valerie McKernan came and met with me. Word was that the Bank of America municipal finance business was more than three times the size of ours based on the league tables which measured volume of deals done in the market. Based on that, their foregone conclusion was that the BofA team would run the business and our folks would report to them.

I told the team to go to LA and meet with Anthony Taddey who ran their municipal finance team. I instructed them to take all our financials and organization charts and to ask that Taddey's people have theirs available for the meeting as well. I emphasized that no one should jump to any conclusions about who would report to whom because this first meeting was just to share information. Valerie McKernan asked if I would be joining them for the meeting, and I told her I would not attend the initial round. I think Valerie thought my response was very unusual because over the three years the business had been reporting to me, I had been very directly involved in all the strategy sessions and meetings with teammates, etc. In this case, I held back because I wanted a lot more data before I sat down for a face-to-face meeting.

When our team returned from California, Valerie immediately came up to my office with all the financials. What she shared was shocking. While the municipal finance business at BofA was indeed three times our total revenue, as a business it was actually slightly less profitable.

Clearly our model of leveraging the relationships we had with government entities and nonprofits in the traditional bank was working, as evidenced by the significantly greater profit margins on the NationsBank side. It was also clear that the Bank of America model was much riskier because they were taking huge trading positions to support their underwriting business and there were significant swings in profitability from month to month based on the gains/losses in the trading book.

At the time, while municipal or public finance reported to me, a wonderful capital markets banker named Tom Houghton oversaw the trading function. When I went to Tom and showed him the numbers, I knew I had a powerful ally to support our model. Based on the strength of my discussions with Tom, I wrote a long memo outlining the case for our model and the business continuing to report to me. I proposed that the business be run on a day-to-day basis by a four-person team to include Anthony Taddey in the West, Phil Smith in the East, a wonderful banker named Curt Hagfeldt running the West Coast trading desk, and Roger Hays running the desk in the East. Valerie McKernan would function as the unit's business manager with all of them reporting to me. The response from Ken Lewis was swift and decisive. We would adopt the NationsBank model and public finance/municipal finance would continue to report to me.

As we moved into 1999 and began putting the two teams together, it was clear we had a winner. While expensive, having two trading desks seemed to make sense because the institutional investors on the West Coast that bought tax exempt bonds were different from the investors in the East. The trading team out west would report in at 5:30 am West Coast time, by which time the East Coast team would already have the pulse of the market. By 1 pm on the West Coast, their day was done, and they could go home. Not a bad lifestyle! In addition to synchronizing the two desks, we were also able to control more origination. This made us a much more relevant partner for the institutional investors that bought this paper. All in all, it was a winning combination, and we really started to move the needle.

However, after not too many months, it came to my attention that we had a problem. Sometime in late 1998 or early 1999, Phil Smith and Curt Hagfeldt came to visit me. Roger Hayes did not attend because by this time he was beginning to plan his retirement. The message from Smith and

Hagfeldt was clear: they wanted to dramatically grow the business, and to do this they needed to make an investment in rock star bankers like young Edward Boyles.

This, of course, would cost money, and at the time Anthony Taddey was the most highly compensated person in the division by a wide margin. In Phil and Curt's opinion, for them to execute the business plan, Taddey had to go to make room for the young stars they needed. Their logic was totally sound. I also found it interesting that I had two senior leaders, one from Bank of America and one from NationsBank, who were on the same page.

In particular, I was struck by Curt Hagfeldt's support. While Curt oversaw the trading desk he was a great guy and had an excellent feel for the origination side of the business. To see a legacy Bank of America guy in support of letting one of his old teammates go gave me comfort. Since this was going to be a tough conversation with Tony, in keeping with my policy of being front and center when something hard needed to be done, I told Curt and Phil that I would fly out west to meet with Tony and deliver the news.

When I met with Tony, he could not have been more of a gentleman. He was gracious in every respect. I explained it was a business decision and that the management team was all in agreement. I told him that I had the utmost respect for him and his ability as a banker. I emphasized that the decision had nothing to do with performance and that he would be given a generous severance package. It was a hard conversation to have with a good guy, but I was glad I had done it because Tony deserved that level of respect.

Little did I know that in a just over a year I would be in the same situation except the shoe would be on the other foot. However, in my case there would be no respect coming from senior management. Instead, it would be a low ranked human resources administrative person delivering the message.

As 1998 and 1999 wore on, we were hitting on all cylinders in the commercial bank and also in public finance. We were winning lots of new business, and I looked forward to the monthly P&L that charted our progress. My finance partner was a young African American lady named Jackie Brown. She would start calling almost immediately after month end when the different pieces of the P&L came in, starting with net interest income, then the expenses and loan losses, which were minimal because we were into the sweet spot of the economic cycle where most companies were doing well. I loved getting all the pieces as they came in as they gradually gave Jackie and me the full picture. Actually, since I was so directly involved in the day-to-day flow of transactions, even before the numbers came in, I could pretty much tell what kind of month we were going to have. By mid 1999, it was clear that the two businesses were going to have a shot at making a $100 million in net after tax income. I became fixated on that number for no reason other than it was a nice round figure.

At that stage in 1998, Ed and I were getting along well. On many occasions when I was out in the field, bank people would make unsolicited comments like , "You should have been named President." Whenever I heard this, I would shut it down, saying that Ed was totally deserving of the job and that had I been tasked with making the choice, I would have chosen him myself. I would remind folks that I was totally loyal to Ed, and that the best favor they could do for me was to be loyal to him as well.

While things were going extremely well overall, there were clearly storms brewing on the horizon. In the fall of 1998 as we began to approach the consummation of the merger Hugh and the team held one of their big pep rallies to start the integration process (or the sheep dipping as we fondly called it). The senior management teams of both companies attended, and I was lucky enough to be there. Hugh gave a big speech about how we were all in this together, drinking from the same canteen and so forth. I happened to be at the same table with Mike O'Neil, the CFO of BofA who would in later years become the lead outside director at Citicorp. While I didn't know Mike O'Neil, and he would certainly not know me today, I could read his body language. O'Neil was buying none of Hugh's pep talk, and he seemed very aware that the transaction was a takeover and not a merger of equals. O'Neil would not stay to be part of the new company.

By the end of 1998 David Coulter would also be gone. In the fall of 1998 Coulter emailed Hugh to tell him about a $1 billion plus exposure he had with DE Shaw, a hedge fund, that could potentially become a large loss. Word was Hugh became furious at both the magnitude of the problem and at getting the news in an email; however, the DE Shaw troubles gave

Hugh and Hootie the excuse they were looking for.

That September, at the time all this was going on, Coulter came to Charlotte and attended a Panthers game in the Bank's box. I was there that day with a bunch of the bank's good customers and prospects, and Hugh was there, as well. The body language between the two men was terrible. Hugh, ever the tough marine, did not give Coulter the time of day. In fact, I don't think he even spoke to him. Coulter, on the other hand, was like a puppet on a string. He was clearly nervous and totally unsettled.

I would later read that on the flight back to San Francisco, Coulter called Bank of America's lawyers to try and get out of the deal. They informed him that since he had been flying all over the country talking up the merits of the transaction, it would be hard to back out just because he didn't like the man on the other side. The merger was consummated as scheduled in October. Shortly thereafter, Hootie flew to San Francisco's and fired Coulter over breakfast.

I never really knew why Hootie did the firing. Perhaps it was because he was chair of the executive committee even though Hugh was the chairman and CEO. Perhaps Hugh had just had enough of Coulter and firing him was not worth his time.

With Coulter out of the way, Hugh set up his horse race again, this time between Jim Hance the CFO and Ken Lewis. I knew Jim Hance and liked him a lot. Unlike most CFO's, Jim was a people person and very involved in the Charlotte community. He was also smart as a whip with a great mind for numbers. Jim also had a great feel for the banking business and its customers—definitely not your typical CFO. Throughout 1999 Hugh would put them on stage together in front of the team for management meetings. Ken Lewis's body language on stage around Hance was terrible. Ken wouldn't look at Hance or even acknowledge his presence. I was embarrassed for Hance who always handled himself well.

In the winter of 1999/2000, I was hunting quail at The Oakland Club, an old timey gun club where Hootie was the president. It is old school and a wonderful place, and I am a member today. I was there as the guest of another member, Ronnie Wrenn, who happened to be Hootie's son-in-law, married to Hootie's daughter, Sally, who was also a dear friend.

Hootie was there with several guests, but I dreaded running into him because I had a feeling he was going to ask me about Hance and Lewis. At

Oakland, the custom is to have a drink before dinner in the front parlor of the old house. After we mixed our drinks, sure enough Hootie asked me to step into the next room because he had something he wanted to ask me.

I was totally in terror. If I told him I liked Hance, I thought he would be mad because everyone in the company knew he and Hugh were leaning toward Lewis. If I lied to him, he would sense it, so my goose was cooked either way. When he asked the question, I simply decided to tell him the truth.

As I had suspected, the question came right away. "Carlos, tell me what you think of Ken Lewis and Jim Hance. Who would be the better CEO?"

I paused for a second then said, "Clearly Ken Lewis has more operating experience because he has been on the banking side his entire career. However, Hance might lack the operating experience, but he totally understands the business. He's also more of a people person, everyone likes him more than Lewis both inside the bank and in the Charlotte community."

With that comment I knew I had crossed the line. Hootie was a big man who still had the neck of the blocking back he'd been in college. When angered the veins would stick out in his neck, and they were definitely on display right then. He said, "Damn it, Carlos, this is not a popularity contest! The next CEO doesn't have to be a rock star like Hugh McColl!" With that, he got up and walked off.

Of course, I already understood what Hootie was trying to tell me, that CEO's do not have to be cut out of the same cloth and that the next CEO didn't need to be like Hugh McColl. Different types for different times. However, I also knew that the old NCNB dog-eat-dog culture under Hugh was one thing, but that under Ken it would be something else. That worried me, especially since, after the encounter with Hootie, I knew for sure that McCall's successor would be Ken Lewis.

As we rolled into 2000 what I knew was becoming more obvious inside the company as well. There were a number of Ken Lewis sycophants rising to key roles, nowhere more prevalent than in the commercial bank. These were hard young men who tried to emulate Ken's tough guy persona. From my perspective, they were total amateurs, and listening to them was like hearing fingernails on a chalkboard. I had no respect for them as people or for what they knew about banking. In the case of commercial, they were at the segment level which was top of the house and where they were supposed to design strategy. They had none of the foot soldiers reporting to them since all the people including me and my people reported up through the state presidents organization. In my case, I reported to Ed Dolby, who reported to Joel, who reported to Ken Lewis. However, while I did not report to them, these Lewis sycophants were powerful. They were setting the course for my business, and that concerned me because ultimately I would have to execute whatever strategy they chose.

I could say a great deal about how misguided these people were and give example after example. One excellent example was their disregard for Greenwich Associates, the foremost authority on how corporate and commercial middle market customers viewed their banks. Our contact at Greenwich was a partner named David Fox, who I considered to be the foremost authority in the business.

Every year Greenwich did a major survey with thousands and thousands of interviews where they would measure market share by state and score the banks on a variety of metrics. They were eminently qualified, and their information was incredibly accurate. Anyone who did not listen to David Fox and his team was a fool, however the Lewis Disciples labeled them as consultants and had no regard for their information.

One of the first things the segment team came up with in 2000 was a strategy to bifurcate commercial into two segments, one named Growth for the smaller, fast-growing companies and one named Strategies for the bigger, more complex companies. The idea was to match skill sets with customers. It sounded good in concept, but the practical negative implications of this strategy were numerous. First, assigning bankers to either Growth or Strategy and also allocating customers to one group or another created terrible turnover with almost half the bank's customers being assigned to different account officers. Second, it created a caste system within commercial banking because a large size customer was a badge of honor. With this change, the Strategy teams viewed themselves as being more important. In addition, Growth relationship managers who had grown accounts from small businesses into a much bigger businesses now had to surrender those success stories to someone on the Strategy team, and as a result the bank lost huge amounts of institutional memory.

Last but not least, big customers in smaller towns where there weren't enough big customers to have a local Strategy officer were covered remotely from perhaps as much as 100 miles away. Our CEO customers hated turnover, and therefore they hated these changes, as we came to learn from the Greenwich surveys. It proved be a killer for the business, and I was losing a lot of sleep worrying about it. I had argued as strenuously as possible as I tried to point out all negatives, but the segment team went forward anyway.

In addition to some of my concerns about the overall direction of the business, I was also beginning to have some issues with Ed. As we began the process of budgeting for the next year, Ed wanted me to step up for a huge growth number that was unheard of in commercial banking. The increase he wanted was high teens or maybe even 20%. While I had been putting up big numbers and Ed knew he had a horse he could ride, the number I was being asked to commit to was unreasonable if not unsafe.

Everyone knew that growing a loan portfolio was a balance between growing too much or not growing enough. Overly rapid growth meant a bank was taking too much risk; however overly slow growth meant they were playing it too safe. In my case, the number I was being asked to produce was too risky and I spoke up about it in the right way. Over my 28 years in the business, I had always spoken my mind, and if I didn't agree with something I would say so. However, at the end of the day everyone knew that once a decision was made, I would salute and move into execution mode, and that was what I would have done with Ed. However, I could tell that Ed did not like my disagreeing. I guess he expected me to just salute on day one and not express my opinion.

Aside from my nagging concerns with the way we were running the business and the leadership at the top, by early 2000 we were rolling along, and I was having one of the best years in my 28-year banking career. Life was good at home as well as we were beginning to plan for Blake going off to college. With the help of our minister Bill Wood, he was accepted at Davidson College just 20 miles up the road and a fabulous school! My dad was becoming more and more feeble, which was a concern.

A year earlier, I had put a small addition on his and Dorothy's small house that would give them a little more room and a second bathroom. I now spoke to Dad every day as I made my travels around the two states and beyond in support of the public finance business. Every summer we returned to Lake Summit (On Golden Pond), and the time there would help re-energize me. Little did I know that very soon I was going to need all the energy I could get.

Carlos Evans

Chapter 26

The Night of the Long Knives, The Lewis Purge

The Night of the Long Knives, otherwise called the Rohm Purge was a period in German History in 1934 when Adolph Hitler basically eliminated any dissenters by killing anyone that questioned his leadership. I am by no means saying Ken Lewis was like Adolph Hitler, but he was someone who eliminated dissent and those who weren't on his team. He certainly wasn't the first to do it, because the idea of consolidating power and cleaning house to make room for your own team has been a strategy in Corporate America for a long time.

My instincts had been telling me for some time that bad stuff was about to happen. So, when Joel Smith came to me in June of 2000 to tell me he was retiring to become the Dean of the Darla Moore School of Business at the University of South Carolina, I immediately knew what was up. At the time, Joel didn't give me the full story on his departure, but I told him that no one would leave such a high ranking (and paying) position in banking to become the dean of any school. I also told him that from my point of view this was the beginning of a scorched earth elimination of people, and I would be next.

Joel said that wasn't the case because he had discussed my situation with Ken, and I wasn't on the cutting board. I told him I didn't believe it would play out that way. That evening, I went home and told Lisa what had happened, and that I was next. Her response was that I was far too valuable because the customers and bankers were loyal to me. Besides, she said, "You're having a great year. Surely they know that."

I said, "None of that matters!"

I really was having a great year, and I had a loyal following of customers and employees. I knew that both customers and employees felt they could count on me, that there was a bond of trust, and that working for me or doing business with me was a win-win. I knew those things were worth a great deal, but by that point I could see that the culture within the bank had changed in such a way that none of it seemed to add value, at least as far as the people in charge were concerned. That change in culture had made me miserable, but interestingly, I was still loyal to the company.

By early July people started not showing up at work. I would often ask, "Where is Jerry?" I would just get a sheepish look that I knew meant Jerry had been fired. I also noticed that during this time Ed Dolby was totally avoiding me.

By mid-July, I got the call from an administrative person in personnel on a Friday afternoon. "We would like to meet with you. Do you have some time?"

My response was, "How about right now. I would like to do this sooner rather than later." When I went into the windowless room there was one person with a small stack of papers. He had an embarrassed look on his face. I said, "Rob, I know this is not your doing and you're just the messenger. Don't feel bad. Let's just get on with it."

He said, "Your services are no longer needed.

"Might I ask why?"

"You can ask, but we don't have to tell you."

I shrugged. "Okay, so let's review the severance package."

My package was the standard at the time, one month of salary for each year of service up to a maximum of 18 months. He also shared with me a press release which had been prepared about my retirement. Presumably, they thought this would be important to me as a way to save face.

I said, "Let's just call this what it is, you guys are firing me!"

My only concern at that stage was insuring that all my restricted stock would vest. Rob said it would. My last comment was that I would work out my two-week notice, and my last day would be two weeks from then. I told Rob that I had seen many people leave in the night, and I was not going out with my tail between my legs. They could count on me to transition everything smoothly and make sure things were left on an even keel. I would in no way create trouble or try to undermine management.

My only concern in staying was to ensure that customers were taken care of because there were many transactions in mid-stream. He said fine, and that was it.

As I worked through the two weeks, I didn't say a word to anyone about the circumstances of my departure, but the word got out. I received hundreds of handwritten letters and notes from employees and customers. I still have all of them today. They were a great source of strength to me in a difficult time. One in particular from my old friend and teammate, Mark Johnson, summed it up. Mark wrote, "Today's news has been most distressing. I am certain you will go on to even greater successes, but an unjust end has come to an era. An era you created by treating people fairly and with humanity, carrying the company flag in the darkest hours when it would have been easier to join the masses in condemnation. Being loyal to your associates and your superiors, unflaggingly I might add. Most importantly, always trying to create the win-win situation for our clients and stockholders. You will be sorely missed, and it is now our job to pick up the mantle and try to carry forward the ideals you instilled in many people throughout all corners of the bank."

Lisa was also a rock, as was Blake, who by this time was old enough to fully understand what was going on. I got many calls from customers. They all wanted to know where I was going and they wanted to move with me. I told everyone that after 28 years in banking maybe this was a sign from above that I needed to do something different with my life. For years, with the bank's consent, I had invested in real estate with my good friend and partner Jim Bradshaw. While just a small portfolio of commercial properties, I thought that could keep me busy. To say I was disheartened would be a huge understatement. I had given my all to the company for 28 years, to its customers and employees. At the time my dad was getting weaker and weaker; one consolation was that I could spend more time with him.

About a week into my two-week notice, I received a call from Ben Jenkins, Vice Chairman of First Union Bank, the big competitor down the street. Ben and I had crossed paths over the years mostly in the late 80s when he was president of First Union's South Carolina bank. Ben said, "We heard what has happened to you, and we would like to talk."

I said, "Ben, I'm flattered, but I'm not sure I want to get back in banking. Besides, my father is on his last legs, and I need to focus on him. Can I get back in touch with you after I leave, go be with my dad, and have some time to process all this?

His response, "We want to talk with you and will wait to hear from you".

The Friday of my last day, I stayed until 6 pm as was my custom. All afternoon I packed up my office. The place was a ghost town with no one there and it felt like a funeral home. After 28 years playing at a high level, I had a huge collection of deal toys or tombstones as they are called. They are given as a remembrance to all who participated in a deal. Each one was a reminder of a successful transaction coming to closure and all the people involved. The memories came flooding back.

However, in that moment, I was shaken from my sadness and self-pity as I realized that I had been good at what I did. My team and I had helped so many entrepreneurs, cities and counties, nonprofit hospitals, colleges and universities with bond transactions and loans. I thought about my dad and his early lessons about doing the best that one could do. I knew that I had done my best possible job, and there was no shame in my departure.

At that moment there was a soft knock on my door. It was the two security guards from up front. I half jokingly said, "Well, I guess you guys are here to show me the door."

They said, "To the contrary, Mr. Evans. We want to see if you need any help taking all this stuff to your car. We want you to know that it would be an honor for us to help you. Most people don't think we have a clue as to what's goes on, but at our desk we screen every call coming in and we see what's going out. The way we figure it, you're the hardest working person on this entire floor and the only one really doing something to take care of customers."

It was one of the highest compliments I had ever had or have ever had since, and with that, they helped me load things up.

That last week in the office before packing up, I sent a long memo to Ken Lewis, Ed Dolby and the head of HR, Steele Alphin. I copied Hootie and Hugh McColl. Truthfully, the email was primarily for Hugh and Hooties benefit. My concern was that people would make things up about my performance, and I wanted to set the record straight. Attached to the memo was a long spreadsheet comparing financial performance for the 11 commercial divisions in the Bank of America system with my Carolinas being one of the 11. The numbers showed that I was #1 in revenue growth through July and #1 in net income growth, having grown profitability by 18% over 1999. In addition, associate turnover, an important measure of employee satisfaction was over half the average for the rest of the commercial banks. Finally, public finance had moved up the ranks in the league tables from not even in the top 50 to #9. The combined businesses were on track to make well over $100 million in after tax income for 2000.

Hugh McColl sent me a very nice letter dated August 23, 2000, which I still have today. It read: "Dear Carlos, Know that I share your disappointment in the outcome of the recent management shifts in the company. You have done a good job for us for many years, and I personally appreciate it. I also appreciate the personal help you gave me in solving a number of business problems that were presented to me by customers.

"My guess is you won't stay retired very long and that you will find something rewarding to do. I encourage you to do that. I will say that I was disappointed that you resigned from all your public jobs. While in most cases you represented the bank, there is no doubt that what people really wanted was Carlos Evans, his energy, his drive, and his determination to see the job through. I hope you will reenter the public arena soon. We need your help.

"If I can be of any help in talking with anyone for you, I will be glad to do so.

"Know that I care. Kindest personal regards, Sincerely, Hugh McColl Jr."

That letter gave me great comfort. Hugh McColl was a total class act. Over the course of my time with NCNB, NationsBank and then Bank of America I learned a great deal from watching him: How to inspire people; how to roll up your sleeves in support of community; but mostly, how to be tough minded but to still have heart.

Hugh's reference to my community involvement was a result of the decision I made to resign from all the boards I was involved in, which were many. Back in those days some nonprofit board slots were reserved for the biggest employers in the community. In my case I was there representing Bank of America. Since I was no longer with the company, I felt it appropriate that I step down. Lisa and I had been involved in so many things in Charlotte over 10 years. With my departure from the bank, we decided from that point forward to focus our community efforts on our home state of South Carolina, even though we were Charlotte residents.

As I sat at home and contemplated my next move, I became focused on my health and exercise. After 28 years of sitting behind a desk I had put on a few extra pounds, and I had gotten soft. I began exercising 2 to 3 hours per day and quickly got back into shape. About that time, Jim Bradshaw and I started planning a second self-storage facility on Hilton Head. We had one already open, and it had been very successful. I began to think that investing in real estate would be an ideal thing for me to do. Besides, I would be on the payroll for another 18 months, so our overhead was covered.

As the days rolled by dad's situation worsened. Toward the end of August, he went into the hospital, and I went to Florence to be with him. When I arrived my brother and sister were there. It was painfully clear that this time he would not bounce back. Over the years Dad had wrestled with Diabetes, a heart condition, as well as several other health issues. Now, his system was essentially shutting down. That evening I told my sister and brother to go home and come back in the morning, and I would spend the night there with Dad.

I wanted to talk to him about my situation, which he was unaware of. In some ways, I was searching for answers on what l should do with the rest of my life. As I sat on his bed and explained to him the circumstances of my firing, I held his hand. By this time, Dad was so weak he could not talk, but it was clear to me that he understood what I was saying. I could see it in his eyes. When I got to the part about the call from the bank down the street and the possibility of a job offer but my uncertainty about what to do, I could feel him squeezing my hand. The fire in his eyes was unmistakable. I knew right then what I was going to do. I went from being totally unsure to being 100% full speed ahead, not just to get back into the banking business but to get even!

The next morning my sister came back to the hospital to relieve me so I could go to my mother's house and get a shower. In the hour I was gone dad passed away peacefully.

Upon our family's return to Charlotte after the funeral in early September, I called Ben Jenkins to tell him I was ready to talk. Ben was in the middle of moving from Virginia back to Charlotte to be president of the general banking group, which was consumer banking, small business, business banking, commercial banking and real estate lending—basically everything other than corporate banking and investment banking. We met for breakfast at his hotel in SouthPark. It was a very relaxed conversation.

Ben started out by saying that Ken Thompson, the new CEO who had succeeded Ed Crutchfield, was in the middle of a major overhaul of the bank in the aftermath of the disastrous acquisition of The Money Store. There were also serious problems with the integration of two recently purchased banks in Philadelphia and New Jersey. Ben said that he and Ken had discussed my situation and they wanted to talk to me about coming on board as the commercial segment leader for the whole entity. Unlike, Bank of America, which was running a functional business model with business segment leaders reporting to state presidents, First Union still used a market model with commercial leaders reporting into 40+ market presidents who reported to 5 state presidents. While they weren't prepared to go fully functional, they wanted more consistency of execution, thus they needed top of the house guidance on strategy and how the business was run.

The commercial segment role was a new job, and Ben wanted me to take it. I realized of course that in the segment role I would not have the foot soldiers reporting to me because they would report up through the market president organization where the state presidents reported to Ben. Ben could sense that not being on the front line gave me pause, so he said that in his version of matrix management, the segment job would have plenty of power.

I told Ben that I was not an egomaniac and that my management style had always been collaborative, so I felt I could work with the market presidents. I also told him I was flattered they would think of me, but I wanted to be sure I was the right fit for the job. I gave him a list of information I would like to see before making a decision that included financials on each commercial team, organization charts, etc. He agreed and so the rest of our conversation over breakfast was about family and life in general.

At the conclusion, Ben looked me in the eye and said, "I have one more question. How are you going to feel about competing against your former teammates down the street?"

My response was, "If I chose to do this, I will be their worst nightmare!" Ben said, "I like that."

A day or so later, I received a package of information from Ben. From what he gave me, it was obvious that the First Union commercial bank was incredibly inconsistent with huge divergence in performance from team to team. I quickly digested all the information and called Ben back.

I said, "Ben, I'm willing to take the job if you will give me two things which I have to have if I am going to be successful in doing what you want. First, I have to have absolute control over the incentive plan for commercial banking, both the design and everything about it. I will work with the state presidents to allocate the dollars, but I have to have absolute say over the end result." I told him that in my experience people did what you paid them to do, and that if my job was to create consistency and high performance, I needed control.

He immediately responded. "You have it. What's the second thing?

"I have to have one of my direct reports in each state, a banker who reports directly to me and not to the state presidents. They will have a dotted line to the presidents and will be a strong right arm to them. They will help in running the commercial business with the market presidents to insure credit approval consistency, consistency of pricing on loans, etc." I explained to Ben that in today's world credit structures had become much more complex and the market presidents did not have time with all their responsibilities to be experts on structures.

Ben said immediately, "You've got that as well."

"Then I'll take the job."

Ben said, "Wait a minute, don't you want to know what your pay will be?"

I said, "Ben, why don't you just pay me what I was making in my old job." I told him what it was, then added, "If you don't like it, just pay me whatever you want. I'm ready to go to battle!!"

With that, we had an agreement. Ben said he wanted me to meet Tom Pacer who ran wholesale banking for him which included commercial, business banking and Real Estate. Ben said the meeting was more of a formality but that I would like Tom. He said, "Let's shoot for you to start on October 1st."

I said, "Fine with me!"

300

Chapter 27

New Team, New Uniform, Same Game

When I showed up at First Union in early October 2000, I was prepared for a cultural change. However, I did not have a clue how big the change would be. First, my new office was very small, located in an old building across the street from the headquarters. The building looked like a power substation and the area more like a cost accounting center than a bank. Compared to my old James Bond Junior Office it was a night and day difference. However, that was fine with me because I had already decided that my new world would contain nothing of a personal nature. No deal toys, no personal items, just a desk, a computer and one picture of Lisa and Blake. There would be no more collection of stuff that made moving a painful hassle. Aside from the clutter, I didn't want any distractions. I was going to war, and I wanted to be incredibly focused, so anything that was a distraction was dispensed with.

More than the difference in offices, however, was the immediate difference in the culture of the company. They were all so nice, too nice. Make no mistake about it, First Union was a big $250 billion company, and up until NationsBank's acquisition of Bank of America which made it decidedly bigger, it had been neck and neck between Ed Crutchfield and Hugh McColl. Probably because First Union's roots went back to rural North Carolina (and in the case of one of the big predecessor banks, Northwestern, those roots even extended to the mountains of North Carolina), the company attitude was rather folksy, almost like living in a small town.

Everyone spoke to each other in the hallways, people were friendly, and there was none of the "dog-eat-dog, storm the hill" environment that existed down the street. Because all the acronyms were different, the first presentations were like listening to a foreign language. Another big difference was the commitment to diversity and, in particular, females. While Bank of America had a similar commitment, it was clear that First Union was much further along. Gwen Whitley, the head of human resources for the general bank, soon became a strong ally.

In addition to the bank's commitment to diversity, there was also a much stronger commitment to technology. When I showed up, everyone was walking around with laptops and first generation devices that were the predecessors to Blackberrys. Technology was everywhere. The bank felt like a Western North Carolina Google campus with everyone trying out the newest hardware, meeting in groups in common spaces and sharing information.

Perhaps most important, First Union had a remarkable openness to change and willingness to accept other ideas. To some extent, the bank had been wounded by the Money Store acquisition and the botched integration of their mergers with northern banks. In some respects, they were in awe of the old NCNB, now Bank of America, and they had a huge curiosity about how we did things down the street. As I have thought about it over the years, I think that curiosity about BofA was part of their culture, not just their circumstances. The bank had a sense of humility that made them willing to learn from others. It was a good thing and a trait that would allow me to implement change swiftly and with staggering effect. There was a world of difference between First Union and the old NCNB in terms of their willingness to adopt best practices even those that were not their own. This contrasted with the know-it-all attitude down the street and, as I would learn 8 years later, at Wells Fargo.

Early on, one of my old teammates down the street asked me what it felt like to make the move. I said it was like playing for a pro football team for 28 years and then moving across the country to a new team. The stadium was different, the cheers were different, the uniforms different, the plays different. But make no mistake about it, once the whistle blew, it was the same game. And in my case, the whistle had blown and the game was on.

After a few short days, I figured out that working within the market president system was going to be my biggest problem. It was ingrained in the DNA at First Union, and in some respects resembled like the old feudal system in Europe. The bank's territories were broken down into markets, each one ruled by a baron or a baroness who ran that market in totality. It was their individual fiefdom, and everything in it reported to them, except corporate banking and investment banking which had been recently organized along functional lines. Those Lords then reported to a king or queen in each state (state president).

The state presidents actually ran multiple states, except for Florida, and they were incredibly powerful. Of all the 5 State Presidents (New York/New Jersey; Pennsylvania/Delaware; Mid Atlantic; Carolinas which included Georgia; and Florida) I learned from Tom Pacer that Bob Helms, the state president of Florida, was the most powerful among all of his peers.

Right out of the chute, I decided to go see Bob. By then, my commercial executive for Florida, a man named Howard Halle had been named. While Howard would report directly to me, he would work closely with Bob as his "commercial expert." I decided it would be good to have dinner with both of them so off to Jacksonville I went on a Sunday evening.

I remember the dinner like yesterday. Bob Helms was from Western North Carolina, and standing about 6 ft. 5 inches tall, he towered over my 5'8": He was incredibly quick with an air of confidence borne out of many years of experience, and he did not mince words. He asked about my background, I told him my history and was straight up about the fact that I had been fired.

He said, "I don't like the fact Howard is reporting to you. Why should we listen to you?"

I showed him the spreadsheet of the summary financial results for the 40+ commercial teams reporting to regional presidents and then up to the states. The numbers (meaning key banking metrics such as return on assets, return on equity, growth rate and others) were all over the place. I then showed Bob the bonuses for those team leaders. There was absolutely no correlation between pay and performance, and the delta between the top teams and the bottom teams was huge. Interestingly, most of the top teams were in Florida.

I said, "Bob if we are going to get consistency there needs to be more central oversight." I added, "Deal structures are becoming more and more complex. We need to develop more consistency of structure and pricing if we are to be more competitive. From my seat in Charlotte, I will see much more deal flow than Howard sees. If he has constant access to me, he will have the benefit of my information to feed into all your pricing and structure decisions. As good as you all are, you 're missing on too many good deals because you all don't have a broad view of what the competition is doing. When I was at Bank of America my commercial business was three times the size of First Union's in Florida. I want to help you get to that place. Besides, I said, this is going to feel like Howard reports directly to you, and as practical matter he will since he will be in Jacksonville with you next door, and I'll be in Charlotte. We'll jointly do his annual performance evaluation as well as his annual salary review and bonus.

Bob smiled and said, "I already knew all that. I just wanted to see what you would say." Then he added, "Ben Jenkins says you're a good guy and that's good enough for me."

Bob Helms ended up being my strongest advocate among the fiefdoms, and Howard Halle ended up being one of my best, if not the best, commercial banking executive. Bob and I became good friends, but unfortunately, he died shortly after his retirement. He was a fine man, an excellent leader, and an outstanding banker.

After my trip to see Bob, I went on the road with Tom Pacer who introduced me to the other state presidents. I especially valued his introductions in the Northeast in New Jersey/New York and Pennsylvania/Delaware, two markets I knew little about. What I did know was that those areas were suffering from the botched integration of CoreStates and First Fidelity, both banks that Ed Crutchfield had paid big premiums for, betting they could be quickly integrated with cost savings realized sooner rather than later.

Because they had been rushed, the conversions had been a mess with countless errors in customer statements, lost deposits and other problems that resulted in customer dissatisfaction and attrition. Since Tom Pacer was from the Northeast, he knew those markets well and was a great help to me with all the introductions. He was a good man, and he retired early the following year following the merger with Wachovia.

In Pennsylvania/Delaware the commercial executive was Vik Dewan and in New Jersey Alicia Scharf. Both were great people, and Tom Pacer was instrumental in helping me pick them as well as steering me through the maze of all the other strange faces. Tom was a good guy and an able banker, however very early on, it became apparent that Ben Jenkins was a hands-on numbers oriented leader and as a practical matter, I really reported to him.

In addition to getting a buy-in from the state presidents, I knew I had to get a total overhaul of the incentive plan finished and in place before the end of the year. The current incentive plan was a total mess, a point-based system measuring product sales that was supposed to correlate to profitability but did not. I did a survey of the field to find out what they liked and didn't like. Everyone hated the plan including the people who were making a lot of money with it because they knew it was unfair.

I worked with a compensation specialist named Tracy Kidd to devise the new plan. Tracy was an outstanding partner. In later years she was unjustly singled out by the regulators as part of the Wells Fargo fictitious account problem, even though she had been in HR at the time. She arrived on the scene as the HR person in consumer banking years after the flawed comp plans had been put into place by her boss, Carrie Tolstedt. There was no way Tracy could have been responsible, and I would love to argue that point with anyone who knows the fact pattern and history. Personnel people do not create the incentive plans. They take their direction from the business lines, and in the case of Wells Fargo, the line of business leaders were Supreme Dictators.

In any case, Tracy and I crafted a plan that tied funding to PTPP at the top of the segment. PTPP stood for Pre-Tax Pre-Provision Net Income, basically how much money we were making before reserves. While the overall pool was arithmetic and funded based on top of the house results, I would allocate the funding across the States and regional teams based on a variety of factors including performance-to-budget, and good sound judgment.

For example, an office might have a huge, extremely profitable customer that got sold unexpectedly in mid-year, which would create a hole so large it couldn't be filled. There was also a knockout clause for bad behavior. In other words, if someone had a great year financially but they did bad things (not being team players, making new bad loans, giving terrible customer service, etc.) their bonus could be significantly reduced and, in some cases, taken to zero. At target for PTPP (which was basically the top of the house budget) the plan would fund a pool that would, on average, allow us to pay bonuses consistent with market compensation for all our job families. At levels above target, the plan would over fund all the way up to 150% of target, but it was a two-edged sword because at levels below target the pool would be reduced by as much as 50%.

There was also a multiplier for exceeding the return on asset goals. ROA is a key measure of earnings quality, measuring how many dollars are brought to the bottom line based the assets or loans made. For example, a loan book of $25 billion with a net income after taxes of $250 million would have a 1% ROA, the return high performing banks aspire to equal or beat.

The catch to all of this was that I wanted a fence around our incentive plan in commercial with me controlling the accrual. That way, I could tell people that come "hell or high water" if we made this much money we would have this pool of dollars generally available for bonuses. This would create Hugh's "We All Drink From The Same Canteen" scenario, which I found very effective but only if I could back it up. To Ben Jenkins's credit, he immediately understood what I was trying to do. After reading the proposal he looked at Tracy Kidd and asked, "Tracy do you think this will work?" She responded yes, and that was it. We were approved, and a few days later I signed all the supporting written documentation for distribution to the field.

With the incentive plan done, I turned my attention to establishing a baseline for where we were and called David Fox at Greenwich Associates. Like most consultants/advisors Greenwich had menu of what they could provide, everything from a top of the house view, which was cheaper, to the "Full Monty" state by state. I told David I needed the Full Monty because I was in a foreign land and I needed the best map I could get.

Unlike my prior job where I knew every customer in the Carolinas like the back of my hand, all the bank employees, and where I understood all the things we had been doing consistently for many years, now I was flying blind and needed intelligence. David said it would take he and his partner Don Rafferty a few weeks to compile all the data then they would come to

Charlotte to share the results and their observations.

When David and Don came to meet with Ben and me, they were very straightforward. David said we have good news, and we have bad news. I said, give us the bad news first, to which they responded you are incredibly inconsistent, your delivery and execution is weak at best, you are not differentiated at all. Your people are not viewed as being credit relevant. I said, none of this surprises me.

I then asked for the good news. David quickly said, "You have no way to go but up." He smiled, then said, "Actually there is a glimmer of hope." He said that while we had a weak "Lead" share of business, we actually had a pretty high "Do Business" share. Lead share means the bank identified by CEOs as their most important, their go to lender. Lead is the status all banks aspire to. Do Business share just means you have your foot in the door and the companies use you for one or two products. The good news in a high "Do Business" share is that if you can distinguish your bank and bankers you can move up because you are already in the door. Ben and I went on to establish a strong relationship with David Fox and Don Rafferty,. They were our eyes and ears and helped guide our efforts for the "Wachovia Years."

After our meeting with David Fox, I went back down to my little office. I was encouraged, knowing that if we could dramatically change how we were executing I could move us up in the number of lead relationships and in so doing dramatically improve overall profitability. I also knew where this new business could come from, right down the street from my old friends at Bank of America who had the going away Lead share. Not only could I significantly improve profitability, but I could have my revenge and "pound of flesh" as well.

I knew there was a lot of work to do, and that I needed to get out to the field in every state and change the message. Unlike my old jobs where I was able to move the needle through my own personal efforts, I was now in a role where I had to do it through others. The good news was that Ben Jenkins had put me totally in control and I liked that. I had a clean sheet of paper and the opportunity to run the railroad the way I wanted, based on the knowledge and experience I had accumulated over 28 years.

But before I did anything else, I needed to engage more deeply with the credit process at First Union even though it was largely driven by the credit teams.

Spurgeon Mackie, a highly experienced good guy, was the chief credit officer for Ben Jenkins's part of the bank. I met with him to share my views on the credit process, which I will explain in more detail below. Wanting to have a common agreement and for us to be in sync, I told Spurgeon the credit process should be a partnership between the line of business and his people. On the ultimate go-or-no-go decision his people were the general partner with final say so, and the line of business was the limited partner. On the pricing decision the line of business was the general partner and his people the limited partner. However, both sides needed to be at the table in loan discussions. Spurgeon was in agreement in concept. We both knew that going from concept to execution would take time and in cases, be bumpy.

I then asked Spurgeon if I could attend the workout meetings. He was surprised that I would even be interested. In fact, I think my whole interest in the credit process was new to him because before me the First Union management folks had basically left that up to his team. From my perspective, the best way to learn how credit people think is to see how they handle problem loans. By late 2000 we were starting to see some problems due to the dot com recession, and the next several months were a great learning opportunity for me. Basically, I learned that Spurgeon and his team were good credit people, and they were receptive to more line involvement as long as we understood they had the final say so on yes or no.

After reaching agreement with Spurgeon, I quickly undertook and effort to get the message out. When we went out to the field, we had meetings in every state that included all the commercial teams and the regional presidents and state presidents. While I was still not a good public speaker, I had improved a little with practice. My message was simple. I started with my golden rules. You are in charge, never let customers feel like you are only a messenger. Only do deals that are a win-win. If a deal wasn't good for the customer and the bank don't do it. We were only successful if our customers were successful. Be responsive, answer your own phone. Respond quickly even if it is a no. A slow no was the kiss of death. Try to be creative and find a way to do deals. We only made money when we made loans. A lot of risk could be mitigated with proper structure.

I also told them that entrepreneurs were the backbone of our free enterprise capitalist system. Our job was to help them be successful, and we helped them by providing capital to fund growth. If we did our jobs right everyone benefited through the creation of jobs and the rising tide scenario. We were losing to many deals over credit and pricing. Our people were not viewed as credit relevant because they were abdicating their responsibility in the process to the credit officers and underwriters. There needed to be dynamic tension between the line and credit. It was a partnership and both points of view had to be at the table. If the process was one-sided the engine would sputter and stall. If credit had too much control, commercial teams would not make enough loans. If the line had too much control, the bank would make bad loans. But if both groups were at the table as a team the engine would run smoothly, and we would start winning. Working properly the partnership with credit was a beautiful thing, and it was sacred.

I then gave them my too nice speech. "Folks, the truth is that you all are too nice. You lose deals and just say, 'Okay team, let's try to win the next one.' You all need to have a stronger distaste for losing. You need to want to beat the competition and you should want to beat them every single time not just most of the time. In fact, you should want to crush them. If you let them eat at the table, it's your food they're eating. When you lose a deal, you need to have a postmortem. You need to analyze what went wrong, what you could do different to win. If we can change what we're doing, we can be successful, and by being successful all of you can prosper together financially with our new incentive plan. Here it is and here's how it works. We are all in this together! I am in it with you, and I want to be in it with you to help you win." I then used one of Hugh's old lines "Winning is fun, but when you can do it with friends it becomes extra special. I want this to be extra special for all of us!"

Then I gave them the punch line. "Here is the Greenwich data for lead share for all our markets and for your market in particular. The bad news is we have a long way to go. The good news is that we know whose business we want to get and it's Bank Of America's. The further good news is that I have their playbook and can help all of you every time you are going up against them. If you will call me every time we are putting a term sheet on the table in competition with them, I can help you craft a proposal that will win. When you call, if I am in the office, I will answer the phone. You will not go through a secretary or switchboard and people will not have to track me down. I will be there for you every time 24/7. On weekends, Holidays, anytime. I know what makes them tick, and I know their weaknesses. ."

The people started to believe. I could see it in their eyes! By early 2001 we were starting to get traction. I was bringing in a lot of business myself in the Carolinas where I had many contacts, like George Dean Johnson, Tom Teague at Salem Leasing, Tom Parsell the Charleston restaurant owner just to mention a few. Many of my contacts were big customers, $200 to $300 million relationships that were extremely profitable with high ROAs in the 1.5% to 2% range, the kind of business the bank made $ 3 to $5 million a year on.

I was keeping score, or as one might say, tracking kills like a hunter. I had a nice round figure of $100 million in mind. Since banks sold at a multiple of 10x earnings, I figured if I could move a $100 million in after tax earnings from Bank of America to First Union, I would cost them $1 Billion in shareholder value. I figured that would be my pound of flesh. I was obsessed and it drove me.

I was still bound by a non-solicit agreement covering Bank of America employees that had about four months to run. Not only was I going to take their customers, but once the non-solicit expired, I was going to take their best people as well. The non-solicit said I could not call their employees, but plenty of them were calling me. I was like a man on a mission, totally driven and focused on inflicting as much damage as possible for what they had done to me.

Despite my anger, I was loving my work. It was clear to me that Ben Jenkins and Ken Thompson were good people. They were great leaders and fully supported me in all I was doing. They were also not figureheads; they both got their hands dirty and understood banking in all its aspects. They would go with me to call on customers anytime I wanted...especially when it was a Bank of America customer. They were good at it, and I loved having them involved.

We were starting to do a lot of customer entertainment events. One in particular was at the famous Merion Golf Club in Philadelphia where one of our state presidents was a member. In early 2001 we were able to arrange a customer/prospect entertainment event involving afternoon golf followed by a seated dinner with speakers. The next morning we played another 18 holes followed by a seated luncheon with prizes for the best team and individual scores.

That first year of the event, sporting legends Jack Whitaker and Jim Nance were the two speakers. Both men have encyclopedic memories encompassing all kinds of significant sporting history, everything from horse racing, to the Olympics, to golf. Their chemistry was wonderful. It was one of the most memorable evenings I can remember. Both Ken and Ben were wonderful hosts. The customers and prospects loved it. The bank had moved beyond its integration problems in the Northeast and we were starting to inflict heavy damage on our competition. Little did I know that things were about to change in a big way yet again!

Carlos Evans

Chapter 28

A New Name, Another Culture

Toward the end of April 2001, it was announced that First Union would be acquiring Wachovia and taking Wachovia's name. It was positioned as a merger of equals with 9 directors from each bank on the new board for a total of 18. Bud Baker, CEO of Wachovia, would become chairman and Ken Thompson would be the CEO. The new bank would become the fourth largest in the country with total assets of about $330 billion with roughly $72 billion coming from the old Wachovia and $258 billion coming from First Union. Bud Baker cut a good deal for the Wachovia senior leadership because the agreement called for 60% of the top jobs to go to First Union people and 40% to Wachovia leadership even though First Union was over 3 times the size of Wachovia.

When I first heard of the deal, I knew instantly that it was a match made in heaven. First Union would get a new name and a fresh start ridding itself of the First Union moniker which had been soiled by the terrible Money Store acquisition and the integration problems in the Northeast. Wachovia would merge with a much bigger bank that would allow its name to survive and give the new company mass that the old Wachovia had been unable to achieve. As I would later learn, the two companies would also be a good cultural fit.

While a match made in heaven for the two companies, I knew the merger would probably make me the odd man out. As is the case in any merger, cost savings and synergy are code words for job elimination, which is always part of the deal. In this case, the cost saves were projected to be $1.3 billion so I knew a number of high-ranking jobs from both companies would be lost. Having only been on board about 7 months, I went to see Ben Jenkins. I said, "Ben, I know there will be many job cuts as part of this transaction with many coming from the First Union side. I have enjoyed my time here, and I want you to know there will be no hard feelings if I don't end up with a seat. I understand how mergers work, and since I'm the newest kid on the block my presumption is that this job will probably go to someone from Wachovia."

Ben was very quick to say that he and Ken had discussed my situation. They were both very pleased with what I was doing. More importantly, they wanted me to have a role in the new company and were planning for me to stay in my role as the commercial segment head. Ben said that Tom Pacer would probably retire which would mean I would report to a new wholesale executive from Wachovia, Walter McDowell, who would report to him. I shared with Ben how appreciative I was to have a seat and promised to make sure he and Ken's confidence would be justified.

I went away from the meeting more committed than ever to the two of them, knowing that many former First Union and Wachovia people who had been there much longer than me would not have a seat. I went home and told Lisa that it looked like I would be able to have a place on the combined new team and continue in my current role. She said, " I knew they would never let you go." Her vote of confidence made me more committed than ever.

The combination of the two banks ended up being an excellent cultural fit. Wachovia, like First Union was wedded to the state president/regional president model. Like First Union, there were very definitely Barons and Baronesses at Wachovia, however there had been a matrix organization with segment roles for a longer period so their people were already comfortable with the shared management concept. Also, the Wachovia line leadership was incredibly credit relevant, and they were already using a partner model to deliver credit with equal line involvement similar to what I was trying to implement at First Union. This would help me get roles aligned faster and bring about change quicker through the First Union ranks.

While both banks had a very nice, lower key approach full of camaraderie and teamwork, the Wachovia culture had just a little more edge around doing business, which fit with some of the other changes I was trying to make. Walter McDowell proved to be a good partner. He was a very experienced corporate banker who totally got everything I was trying to do.

In the end, while there was much discussion about which operating systems we would use in the go to environment for the loan platform, deposit platform, treasury management, etc., the basic business model ended up being what I was already running. As far as the systems selection it was a "best of breed" selection process as was the whole integration. It was very refreshing to see two different teams come together from two different companies and choose how to do things based on what made the most business sense. The people were courteous and respectful of each other and while there were certainly some merger politics in play, the whole decision-making process was largely about what was best for the new company.

I found myself contrasting the approach with the "My Way or the Highway" model largely used down the street. I also thought about the huge differences in culture. It was obvious to me that there would have been no way a merger between the old NCNB culture and either Wachovia or First Union would have worked. In the case of Wachovia and First Union, however, they fit well together largely due to the collegial cultures that existed both places.

As 2001 came to an end we were really starting to kick into high gear because we weren't experiencing any of the normal disruption associated with a merger. In fact, the data we were getting from David Fox and his team at Greenwich suggested that our scores were getting better and better across most performance attributes that CEO's value. In fact, David's comment was that they had never seen a merger go so smoothly. We were also winning more and more new customers. To increase emphasis on new customer acquisition I worked with my head of marketing, a wonderful man named Craig Veazey, to come up with a new program.

From my first day at First Union, I knew I had to instill more of a killer instinct in the people. We needed a much stronger bias toward winning and a distaste for loosing. I also knew that we had to significantly improve our win/loss ratio when competing for new business. Wachovia had a better record on this front, but even they were nowhere near where we needed to be. Going back to my early days as a branch manager I knew it was important to track both the volume of new business as well as its quality (as measured by profitability).

Craig and I came up with the concept of tracking new customer acquisition in a new fun way by calling it the "Animal Hunt." Clearly, I was in the hunt for Bank of America's customers, and we were starting to make meaningful progress toward my $100 million net income after taxes goal, (representing my $1 billion pound of flesh). To get all our people in the game, we decided to put new customers into 3 categories. Rabbits were customers worth $10k per year up to $100k. Elephants were customers with annual profitability between $100k and $500k. Red elephants were the really big new customers acquired with annual profitability in excess of $500k. Craig and I toyed with representing the new customers as "kills" which would have been consistent with NCNB military culture. I decided to opt for a softer approach and something more consistent with our kinder, gentler culture so we decided to call them "captures."

As we settled on the plan, we decided to engage a young lady named Amy Beerman in the process. Amy would be responsible for all the graphics and the tracking. We decided early on that we didn't want the contest to be "blood sport." In keeping with our culture to not be dog-eat-dog we decided that the prizes would be a fun trip rather than money, so there would be no confusion with the incentive plan. Prizes would be awarded to the top 5 relationship managers in each category as well as the top 5 overall. This would allow the relationship managers in small markets to be in the game since their access to elephants and red elephants was limited but the rabbits were plentiful.

Because we wanted the administrative assistants in the game since they provided all the support while the relationship managers were out calling on customers, we included them if their man or woman won. The winning relationship managers with their spouse/partners would go on the trip along with their administrative assistants and their spouse/partners. Thus, there would be roughly 40 couples attending: 5 relationship managers and 5 assistants from each of the four categories plus their spouse/partners. Also attending would be Ben Jenkins and me, as well as the commercial banking executives.

As Craig, Amy, and I talked through trip options, we quickly settled on New York City during the Holidays. We would depart on a Friday right after lunch, stay at the Ritz Carlton on Central Park, go to dinner and see plays on Friday night then have a wonderful seated dinner on Saturday in a restaurant overlooking the tree at Rockefeller center for the tree lighting. The budget was about $2,500 per couple with all expenses paid by the bank. Ben Jenkins did not bat an eye when he approved the budget because he knew exactly what I was trying to accomplish.

I will never forget that first trip at the end of 2002 and the faces of many of the administrative assistants from small towns. Many had never been to New York, nor had they experienced something so nice. Clearly, from that first year on I knew I had everyone in the game and that there would be serious competition across all our relationship teams every year. There came to be story after story of administrative assistants literally pushing their bosses out of the office to go make calls on new customers because they wanted to win. However, it was all in good fun and in keeping with the Wachovia culture. The Animal Capture theme complete with graphics and regular monthly reporting made it that way.

As the game got underway, we used our customer profitability tracking system to audit the true realized value of the new relationships our managers were bringing in. With very few exceptions people were being honest about the value of what they were "capturing". The byproduct of this competition was a cultural shift to an aggressive, sales oriented "let's win" culture. As a result, the impact on our competitors and notably Bank of America was significant. In addition, the lift to our financial results was stunning!

In April 2002, Ben Jenkins penciled a note to Ken Thompson along with our financial results through the first quarter. The note to Ken Thompson said, "Remember Carlos in your prayers every night." Ken Thompson sent the note to me along with a handwritten personal note on his stationary. It said, "Carlos, I'm not praying for you cause you don't seem to need it. Great, great work!!!" I still have both notes today. The financials showed that in the first quarter commercial segment earnings were $75 million after taxes, an increase of 65.4% over the prior year and 53.2% ahead of budget. We were on a run rate to make over $300 million in net income after taxes, a return on assets of close to 2% for the business, and we were just getting started.

Aside from the commercial segment, Ben Jenkins had given me two additional functional businesses to run where all the foot soldiers reported directly up to me. The government and institutional banking business was transferred to me through my five commercial executives at the end of 2000 before the Wachovia Merger. It was business I was very familiar with given my experience at Bank of America where all nonprofits were in the commercial bank and where public finance (Phil Smith) had reported directly to me.

This business at First Union was about $5 billion in loans and deposits and about $75 million in earnings. Unlike Bank of America where it was handled in the markets by dual purpose bankers, at First Union it was functional with nonprofit specialty teams in each state only handling the needs of governments, nonprofit hospitals, colleges and universities, YMCA's, etc. It was a great business at First Union because the combination of specialty teams distributed in each state and market gave customers the best of both worlds: bankers who understood the specific needs of tax exempt customers along with relationship managers who were in the field where the customers were.

While the public finance team sat in the investment bank and (like Bank of America's had been in the beginning) was clearly broken, the core banking teams were very effective and working well. While we had many great people in this business, Mara Holley in Georgia and Mike Hanna in Florida were both exceptional members of the group. Mara sat in Atlanta and had a team of bankers who were all truly professional. Mike Hanna worked in Florida and reported to Howard Halle. Both were well connected politically, personally knew every elected public official as well as everyone in the healthcare and higher education business in their respective states. They were both forceful and highly outspoken in a good way. Both would rail on me about the public finance business being broken and how it was affecting our government business. I told them Rome hadn't been built in a day, and if they would give me time, I would fix the broken business, even the parts that didn't report to me.

Aside from the government and institutional banking business, Ben also gave me the indirect auto finance business after the merger with Wachovia. This was also a business I was familiar with from my early days at Bankers Trust. Auto finance handled the floor planning and equipment financing needs of car dealers but, more importantly, bought the retail consumer auto loans that were made at the dealerships then sold to banks.

This was a business with about $5 billion in floor plan loans and another $5 billion in consumer paper. While a good business, it was marginally profitable making about $50 million per year but with a return on assets of only about .5%. The business reported to a Wachovia banker named David Stevens, a good man who over the next few years helped me chart a course to improve the profitability.

So as 2002 wore on and the economy recovered from the dot com bust, life was good. I was running three businesses that on a combined basis would make about $425 million after taxes, and I was making a real contribution at the new Wachovia. I loved the people I was working for and the team I was working with. Things were good at home as well. Lisa was approaching 9 years of being cancer free, and Blake had entered his freshman year at Davidson in 2001 and was now a sophomore. While Lisa and I felt a sense of void as empty nesters, we enjoyed our quality time together.

While there were many weekend trips up to Davidson for football games and basketball games with Blake, we also made a lot of trips back down to South Carolina to see friends. There were many weekend trips to Charleston, Hilton Head, and Columbia. While we were clearly Charlotteans having been in North Carolina for over 10 years, South Carolina was still home, and so many of our friends were there. In keeping with our commitment to do more for nonprofits in our home state, I joined the Spoleto Festival USA board as well as the Medical University of S.C. Foundation board. Ultimately, I chaired both boards, doing my best to help organizations that would have a meaningful and positive impact on our lives and the lives of others.

By the end of 2002 in addition to helping take away a number of Bank of America customers, I was also having great success in helping to move talent from Bank of America since my non-solicit had long since expired. The list included Kendall Alley, who would become regional president in Charlotte; Stan Gibson, president of Bank of America's South Carolina bank, who would become my Carolinas commercial executive; Morrison Creech, who would later have a very senior position in wealth management/private banking; and Will Howle, who would end up as the #2 in consumer banking at Wachovia and would eventually become the head of consumer banking in North America at Citicorp.

These folks were all part of a never-ending string of people I helped bring over to the new Wachovia, and all made a meaningful contribution. However, as successful as I was at moving customers and moving talent, one person had eluded me. Phil Smith, the head of public finance who had reported to me when I was down the street, was doing great things as Bank of America moved up into the top five in the public finance league tables. Whenever I ran into Phil in airports, which happened rather often because we both traveled frequently, I would ask him if we could talk. His response was always the same, "I'm flattered and miss working for you, but now is not the time."

Nevertheless, I was undeterred, and I kept asking. I found the entire situation at Bank of America very interesting. I knew I was doing a lot of damage, stealing both customers and employees, but there was no word from down the street other than the feedback I got from the employees I was stealing which was, "What you're doing is really starting to hurt." It seemed as if the higher ups were either unaware or didn't care. Either way it suited me because their failure to go into damage control mode just made my job easier.

At the end of 2001, Ed Dolby, my former boss at Bank of America, had "retired". Sometime later, Bill Wilson, the person who replaced me as commercial executive for the Carolinas was let go. He was a good man, and I felt sorry for him. While I knew none of the specifics or circumstances surrounding either departure, I suspected that it was because of the damage I was inflicting. I was obsessed, but not in a good way. While the obsession clearly drove me to achieve a good outcome for Wachovia, there was also a dark side to it. I didn't realize at the time, but it was affecting my personality. It probably wasn't visible from the outside, but inside it wasn't good.

At every turn I was looking for ways to hurt Bank of America. One example occurred when my good friend and former customer Ronnie Wrenn came to me to say that Bank of America was calling his loans and asking him out of the bank. Ronnie, who was also Hootie's son-in-law, had a company called Starboard that for years had done well exporting salted codfish from Alaska into Portugal. Ronnie, like most entrepreneurs, had built the business from zero. He had started working in a seafood restaurant in college and had started wholesaling fish with one truck right after graduation.

At a point, he figured out that he could rent crab boats in Alaska (the ones you see on the reality show deadliest catch), which lie idle in the summer, and use them to catch codfish. The fish would then be salted and shipped to Portugal where salt cod is one of their staples. The problem with the business was the time lag between processing and getting the fish to market. It took too long, and in that time many variables could impact his profits, including foreign exchange fluctuation, prices in the market which were subject to dumping by the Russians, and Portugal's highly complex import tax system that could change on a dime.

During one particularly difficult period, all those variables went against Ronnie's company, and he booked a loss for an entire year. These uncontrollable variables caused Ronnie to make the decision to shift back into a domestic wholesale seafood distribution business. The problem was that Bank of America refused to give him the time to see it through.

By the time Ronnie came to see me, he had exhausted every avenue in his attempts to get Bank of America to work with him. Despite the fact he had never been late on payments, not only were they not working with him, but they had turned his loan over to the workout group that was imposing huge penalties and fees totaling about $360 thousand. While the workout group was legally entitled to impose those fees, I felt it was wrong. I have always believed that when good customers hit hard times, we should work with them to make their turnaround easier. Bank of America was doing just the opposite.

In the case of Ronnie Wrenn, I knew that the big C for Character was impeccable, and that Ronnie would never leave anyone holding the bag. I also had confidence in Ronnie's entrepreneurial instincts and faith that he would be successful in transitioning back to a domestic seafood distribution business. History would prove that I was right because Ronnie's business is now being run by his son Holt and is incredibly successful. However, at the time all of that was not so clear. What was clear to me was that Ronnie had that thing all entrepreneurs have—the ability to overcome obstacles and roadblocks and the persistence to somehow find a path to make things work. They also had to be fearless, with high energy and enthusiasm for what they were doing, and Ronnie had plenty.

When Ronnie came to see if I would pay Bank of America off, my immediate response was yes. However, there was one small, or not so small catch. I told him that the only way I would make the loan would be if Bank of America would waive the $360,000 of penalties and fees and furthermore that they would have to agree to this by Friday, just two days away. Ronnie, who had just gotten a glimpse of daylight, saw his window closing. He said there is no way they are going to do that.

I told him, "Yes, they will, because your loan is in the workout group and all those guys care about is getting paid. In their world, they will be heroes even though they will be waiving a lot of money." My parting comment was, "Ronnie, I won't do it unless they waive the $360,000. Your company needs this money to effect its turnaround, which is critical to my loan being paid. Besides, they didn't earn it in the first place. To push someone just because you can is just not right."

The truth was, I was going to make the loan anyway even if they didn't waive the fees, but I wanted Ronnie to be convincing. That afternoon Ronnie called elated, he said they agreed to the waiver. I told him they would have their check Friday, and we delivered. Ronnie delivered as well. He went on to turn the business around, slowly at first but gaining momentum as he went. We are dear friends to this day and often laugh about the story even though it was not so funny at the time.

I tell this story because it was emblematic of the way I was operating back then. Any time I could inflict damage or do something that would hurt the team down the street I did. My efforts were not limited to the Carolinas because I was now doing it through my people up and down the East Coast. Anytime we had an opportunity with one of their customers, I was all over it. I would get on a plane and fly anywhere anytime to sit down and explain to entrepreneurs why we were a better choice as a financial partner. The $100 million I had been working on was in the rear-view mirror, and I was working on the next $200 million. My people loved the support and I loved the "Revenge." However, I came to realize that I had taken the whole thing too far.

For several years Lisa and I had made it a habit to spend New Year's at Spring Island with friends. We would invite three or four couples and have a wonderful long weekend. Usually, we would have dinner at the River House the first night. The River House dining room is very small and intimate. Maybe 5 or 6 tables complete with a fire, which makes it cozy.

That evening, Ken Lewis, the CEO and chairman of Bank of America was there with his wife Donna and another couple. Their table was directly across from ours in plain sight. The more I drank the more I thought about my firing. I was boiling inside.

When their table got up to leave, Ken walked by and said hello to Lisa. He then looked at me and extended his hand, saying, "Oh Carlos, I didn't realize you were there." The way he said it made me see red because we had been sitting just a few feet apart all night. In that instant, something inside me snapped. As I shook his hand, I pulled him closer and whispered in not so kind words that I was on a mission to take all their business.

My comments led to an exchange of words. I was totally out of line and knew it the moment the words left my mouth. In an instant, it was over, but I would not sleep all night. I knew I had been wrong and more importantly, I knew I had to call him and apologize. I also knew I had taken the revenge thing too far. It was changing my personality and not in a good way.

The next morning my good friend Neel Keenan and I talked. Neel agreed that I needed to call. I knew it was the right thing. I was able to find the number for the cottage they were staying in. When I called, Donna, Ken's wife, answered the phone. I apologized to Donna and told her I wanted to apologize to Ken, and my hope was that he would accept it.

Ken got on the phone, I explained to him the anger I had been harboring over being fired for no reason after being loyal for 28 years. I told him that there was still no excuse for my behavior, and that I was sick inside over it. While it would not undo what I had done, I was hoping he would accept my apology. He paused for a second and then said he could understand where I was coming from, and he accepted my apology. That was it. When I hung up the phone, I felt a huge release. Ken had been a total gentleman in the conversation, and I will be forever grateful for that small gesture. For me, a giant dark cloud had been lifted, and while I was still sorry for what I had done, I could move on. The negative energy that had invaded my life was gone. I would still be as competitive as ever and focused on winning, but it would be without revenge in mind. I was finally free.

Carlos Evans

Chapter 29

The Wachovia Championship

By 2003 the merger integration was in the rear-view mirror, and Ken Thompson was looking for ways to put the Wachovia brand on the map. At the same time Johnny Harris, president of Quail Hollow Golf Club, had been working to bring a major golf tournament to Charlotte. To do that, he needed a major corporate sponsor.

While Bank of America was probably the logical choice, they had recently purchased the naming rights for Panther Stadium (now known as Bank of America Stadium). Also, with the Taj McColl looming over downtown Charlotte, they really didn't need additional exposure.

Wachovia, on the other hand, was in a different place, and Ken Thompson took the bold step of putting our name on the tournament. It was a match made in Heaven because Johnny Harris and Quail Hollow would make it a first rate stop on the tour.

Many of the pros in the first year said it felt like a major event in its first year. The golf demographic made a perfect fit for our bank, and it benefited my business, as well as the corporate bank, the most. It is a known statistic that most CEO's play golf because the sport is often an excellent opportunity for business development and for getting to know people.

When asked about the rationale for sponsoring the tournament, I described it like this: When entertaining a customer over dinner, you could either take them to a restaurant or invite them to your home. Inviting them to your home was far more effective because it was much more intimate, and golf was a little bit similar. A bank could invite customers to any professional golf tournament, but when the tournament carried the bank's name, it was more intimate and more special, a totally different customer entertainment experience.

Another major benefit was that all earnings from the tournament were contributed to First Tee, a nonprofit educational outreach program for youth. This allowed the bank to do a lot of good and a generate lot of goodwill at the same time. In some respects, the tournament was an extension of what my business was already doing every year at Merion. Jim Nance had become a fixture at our event in Philadelphia, and it was a favorite event for both customers and prospects alike. The Wachovia Championship had even more appeal and we used it effectively as a business development tool.

By the middle of 2003 the new Wachovia was rolling. With Ken and the board's approval, Ben Jenkins and CeCe Sutton, head of consumer banking, moved quickly to do de novo branching in New York City. While the real estate was very expensive, the numbers coming out of these new branches was explosive. After opening, they were growing at a rate that was 10x what our normal branches did.

We had also opened a commercial banking office in New York City at Rockefeller Center. I began making frequent calls in the city with members of my team. Visiting customers and prospects in New York and for that matter, anywhere north of Washington, DC, had always been interesting. For some reason, businesses seemed to welcome the softer (maybe even kinder, gentler) southern touch. I also always attributed this to the fact that we came across as being on the same side of the table with them versus being across the table.

I also found that giving up the vendetta I had been pursuing with Bank of America helped return me to my roots where helping customers be successful had been my focus. I'm not saying I ever lost that motivation because my first question was always whether I could create a win-win. However, there is no doubt that for a time I was driven by the notion of inflicting punishment on Bank Of America.

Now, re-centered on my primary original motivation to help businesses grow and be successful and to create win-win situations, I felt refreshed, rejuvenated and even more motivated. Upon reflection, I think I was better at my game and more effective in helping my people.

In September of 2003, Walter McDowell became president of the Carolinas banking group, and I was back reporting directly to Ben. The truth was it had always felt like I reported to Ben anyway. Then, in October 2003 it was announced that Bank of America was acquiring Fleet/Boston, giving the combined bank almost $1 trillion in assets, more than double the size of Wachovia.

It had been no secret that Ken Thompson had been trying to buy Fleet, but Bank of America had been willing to pay more. Shortly after the announcement Ken Thompson asked me what I thought about going de novo to California. The first words out of my mouth were something I'd heard Hugh McColl say, "It's a bridge too far." It was a well known military phrase that meant you don't want to outrun your supply lines. I suggested to Ken that he think about Texas. I didn't give the conversation another thought. Little did I know that his wheels had already been turning before he spoke to me.

Late one Friday afternoon in December of 2003 just before Christmas, I received a call from Ben Jenkins. "Carlos, Ken and the Board have decided to go de novo into Texas. Do you know any Texas bankers we could hire to run the new bank?"

I said I knew a few, but it might take me some time to track them down. I said I would make a few calls and get back. When we hung up, I immediately wrote down two names, Guy Bodine and Bill Wilson. Both had been Texas bankers when NCNB acquired First Republic in the government assisted deal. I knew both well, and furthermore, knew they were great people. Like me, they had been chewed up in the dog-eat-dog world down the street and had not survived. I went to work calling directory assistance and got the number for Guy at his ranch.

When I called Guy's number, he picked up on the first ring and was somewhat surprised to hear me on the other end. I said, "Guy, what are you up to?"

He said, "I'm sitting here talking to Bill Wilson because we're planning to start a new bank."

I said, "Well, that's interesting because I've been trying to track him down as well, can you put me on the speaker phone?" Once he had put me on speaker, I said, "Since you guys are planning to start a bank, why don't you start one for us?"

I explained to Guy and Bill that I was calling on behalf of Ken Thomson CEO of Wachovia and Ben Jenkins Vice Chairman. I told them we had decided to enter Texas on a de novo basis, and I felt like the two of them were the perfect leaders with Guy serving as president reporting to Ben, and Bill serving as commercial banking executive reporting to me. I hadn't discussed titles with Ben, but knowing both bankers it seemed like the right fit.

I went on to tell Guy and Bill that we were trying to replicate what had been a huge success in New York City, and we were prepared to invest a huge amount of capital to insure our success in Texas. I also said that there would probably be acquisitions along the way, but we wanted to jump start the whole process. It would be a much grander start up than a stand-alone community bank. Guy and Bill said they were both interested in talking further. I suggested a possible meeting in Charlotte after the new year since it was almost Christmas Eve.

When I hung up the phone, I was full of myself. They would be the perfect two leaders, and Ben was going to be impressed with how quickly I was able to line things up. I called Ben and relayed the results of my call, but instead of congratulations, there was a pause before Ben said, "Carlos, Ken wants to get on this right away. Can they come next week?"

I said, "Tuesday is Christmas Eve."

"We'll send the bank plane and have them back in plenty of time."

Right after I hung up with Ben, I called Guy back and told him that Ken and Ben wanted to move on this right away. We would send the Bank plane to get them Sunday and have them back Monday. They agreed, and as they say, "The rest is history." Guy and Bill came to Charlotte, and Ken and Ben loved them and immediately made a deal to hire them as I had proposed. They would prove to be great leaders and the perfect combination to jump start our efforts in Texas, which would be just as successful as our entry into New York.

As I had predicted, by June of 2004 it was announced that Wachovia would buy SouthTrust headquartered in Birmingham and creating a $464 billion asset bank. The acquisition gave us a huge presence in Birmingham and all of Alabama, bolstered our lead consumer bank market share in the Southeast, and gave us additional branches in Texas to support what Guy and Bill were already doing there. Since SouthTrust was a strong commercial bank, even though they were only 15% the size of Wachovia at just over $50 billion, their commercial bank grew us over 30% to just over $30 billion. For most of the remainder of 2004 I spent lots of time in Birmingham helping to integrate the bank, calling on customers, and helping to make our new teammates and customers feel at home. The SouthTrust acquisition was a successful one because the culture of the two banks fit, and Birmingham, a Southern city like Charlotte, was a great place to do business.

As we rolled into 2005, we were growing like a weed in the commercial business as well as the government and institutional banking business. David Fox was giving us great grades in his survey at Greenwich, and we were steadily moving up in lead relationships. I still had problems with our public finance effort, but the traditional government and nonprofit business was doing great despite our not being a real player in municipal finance. I ran into Phil Smith yet again on one of my frequent plane trips to Alabama (Phil is a die-hard Roll Tide alumnus). I reiterated that we had a spot for him, to which he responded, "Now is not the time." I put him on the back burner because I had other things on my mind.

Our indirect auto finance business known as Wachovia dealer finance was growing and making money. However, its return on assets was marginal at .5% versus the stated goal of 1%. At the time, we only competed in the super-prime-credit spectrum lending to consumers with credit scores of 750 or higher. In that space, losses are minimal to nonexistent, which is why the ultra-conservative old Wachovia had been there. The problem was that the competition was cutthroat in that space so spreads (the difference between what the bank can borrow money at then lend to the customer at) were paper thin at around 1%, leaving very little room to cover losses as well as salaries and overhead.

I knew it wasn't a sustainable business model so I asked David Stevens to look at how we could buy deeper into the credit spectrum, not all the way down to sub prime (the riskiest borrowers) but the level below prime, called "near prime," where the spreads were better. David and I concluded that there were two paths. Either we could build our own scoring models and credit platform, or we could buy someone that already knew how to approve credit in the space without losing their shirt.

We quickly concluded that it would take too long to build our own model (models are based on years and years of loss history) so we started looking for a company to buy. We found one we could buy for a $100 million, but the business was a piece of trash. It had been around for only 4 years and was just starting to make money. Their track record was rocky at best, and we concluded that inheriting someone else's problems was not a good idea. In the end the company was further evidence of how costly it would be for us to "build our own." We went back to the drawing board.

In early summer of 2005 an offering landed on my desk. It was either from Goldman Sachs or one of the other big New York investment banks. The name of the company was Westcorp, and they were squarely in the near prime space. David Stevens thought the company might be too big of a bite because they were publicly traded, with over $20 billion in loans. The punch line was that they were on track to make over $400 million and a return on assets in excess of 2%. They were 8 times more profitable than Wachovia dealer services which was making 50 million. As I pored through the numbers, I became more and more impressed. Their operating record was both exceptional and consistent with earnings increasing steadily every year. I got to the back of the book and saw that they had a savings and loan charter with 19 branches in Southern California! I became so excited my hands shook as I called Ben Jenkins. "Ben, I have it, this is it! This is how we improve the profitability of Wachovia dealer services, and best of all, it gets us to California!"

From that point forward the rest of the summer was consumed with due diligence on Westcorp. There were three trips to Irvine California with 60 or more people to pore over the numbers and all aspects of Westcorp's business. Since I was on point for the transaction I was there for every trip. There were many naysayers because by that point in the economic cycle folks had started to talk about the next recession and how consumers, who were over leveraged, were going to bear the brunt. Everyone pointed to auto loans as the possible epicenter of the problems, but no one pointed to residential mortgages.

The more I met with Ernest Rady, the founder of Westcorp and owner of over 50% of the shares, as well as Tom Wolfe, the CEO, the more convinced I was that it was a good deal, even at 10 times earnings or $4 billion. The company had a very sophisticated approval model. They would handicap loan applications based on the make, model and type of auto or truck to adjust for historical resale values. Their model also handicapped whether the vehicle was to be used for business or just to get around. Their experience showed that work vehicles were more likely to pay because borrowers needed them to survive. Their favorite collateral was the Ford F-150 pickup truck.

Westcorp was a magnificent company, well regarded and valued by all their dealer customers. Best of all, they were a perfect fit with our dealer group. We could offer all their dealer customers floor planning and capital equipment loans in addition to buying their super prime car loans, which Westcorp didn't bid on due to the very thin spreads. We would offer their deeper buy into near prime paper to all the Wachovia dealer customers. Their people appeared to be very compatible with ours, and except for the fact that Westcorp's top management hated the idea of centralizing certain support functions like marketing, compliance and HR, it would be a good fit.

As I made my case to Ken and the board, it became obvious that Bob Kelly, Wachovia's CFO didn't like the deal. I ran scenario after scenario to the downside, and he kept asking questions. I'm not being critical, because $4 billion was a lot of money and folks were beginning to talk recession. I'll never forget late one afternoon when Ken Thompson came down to my office. He said, "Carlos, we're going to do your deal. I just want you to know that and not be discouraged. You need to keep answering all the questions and just keep doing what you are doing."

His words gave me the confidence to keep my head down and keep plowing forward. I went back to Irvine one last time for another dose of due diligence. I went far back into history to look at auto paper performance in prior recessions. The history showed that in recessions losses would go up, but Westcorp's losses had been manageable through the past two recessions.

Furthermore, in the aftermath of recessions, they made a lot of money in near prime loans because in the panic many banks had pulled back and spreads had widened dramatically. It gave them an opportunity to become more selective and buy better quality paper due to less competition. Even though I did not know it at the time, my downside scenarios would play out just that way. When the recession finally came in 08/09, Westcorp, which by then was Wells Fargo dealer services, would rain money even though it didn't report to me after the acquisition of Wachovia by Wells Fargo.

Wachovia shareholders approved the Westcorp acquisition in January of 2006, and upon consummation of the deal in March the combined Wachovia dealer services reported to me as a separate functional business. David Stevens, the wonderful banker who had helped me engineer the transaction had to take a back seat to Tom Wolfe the CEO of Westcorp who would run the combined business. David was a real team player throughout the process because he did everything he could to make the transaction happen knowing that he wouldn't be CEO of the combined entity given Westcorp's size. I had the utmost regard for him and still do today.

Almost before the transaction closed, we made the decision to establish two commercial banking teams in California, one in LA and another in San Francisco, which would be the headquarters. I sent my best commercial banking executive, Howard Halle, to San Francisco to lead the charge. We were winning across the board in our base commercial business, and I knew we could be successful in California. I was right .

That same May when I was up to my ears in due diligence, Blake graduated from Davidson. Lisa's parents came for the graduation. We were all so proud of him. Davidson had been tough. At his freshman orientation we had been advised by the president that all of the students were used to making As in high school, which was what had gotten them to Davidson ,sometimes called the Ivy League of the South. At Davidson, many of those same students would make C's and B's. Davidson, true to the president's promise, had been academically demanding. Blake had been successful in making it through and would soon go to work for Carolina First, a smaller bank in Greenville. I bristled with pride that my son had not squandered his education like I had, and he was now going to be a banker.

That summer we often went up to Lake Summit as a family. Blake came up from Greenville only 40 minutes away. We have many fond memories with Lisa's parents, and it was a great way for me to escape from all the due diligence pressure.

By early 2006 we were getting traction everywhere. I was running two functional businesses in government banking and dealer services that were making about $750 million per year, and I had responsibility for the commercial segment under a matrix arrangement with the state presidents. That business was making another $600 million per year, for a total of about $1.35 billion.

As time had passed, the matrix had come to feel more and more like a functional business. As I had told Ben 6 years earlier the deal structures and pricing were becoming more and more complex, and as a result, the presidents were deferring to my commercial executives and me to make those calls. In addition, we were the ones engaging with credit to make things happen and get approval. Everyone also knew that we controlled the incentive plans, so it had come to feel more and more like a purely functional business.

At the same time, the state presidents and regional presidents were very helpful in winning new customers. They were highly visible in all the markets and were happy to weigh in where they could help. They were very effective in certain situations, and we had a good partnership. It was a total team approach.

As far as taking the final step to go functional, I never rocked the boat with Ben Jenkins to lobby for change. I didn't have to because plenty of rocking was coming from my counterpart in the consumer bank. Segment executive Cece Sutton was running arguably the best consumer bank in the country. The University of Michigan was regularly giving her consumer bank the best customer service scores across the land. As one of the highest-ranking females at Wachovia, she was incredibly powerful, deservedly so. She was pushing all the time to go functional, so I just sat back.

In the spring of 2006, I knew the pressure was mounting on Ken Thompson to do something. The year before, we missed on the acquisition of MBNA, again to Bank of America. As a result, Bank of America was now over $1 trillion, while following the Westcorp acquisition, we were about half that size but incredibly well thought of and delivering high quality earnings.

In the fall of 2005 Ken Thomson and I were invited to a golf outing that Ken Langone (one of the funders of Home Depot) and Tommy Teague's partner in Salem Leasing had every year at his home in Cashiers, North Carolina. Included were a number of Wall Street types including Jimmy Dunne, CEO of Sandler O'Neil, and Ed Herlihy, one of the lead attorneys at Wachtel Lipton and arguably the best bank M&A lawyer in the country.

That first day Ed and I were paired together. Ed is a wonderful man and one of the most knowledgeable people on the planet when it comes to the financial services industry.

At one point, Ed commented, "I hope your boss knows that the world is passing you by." It wasn't a high-pressure statement, just an observation that the game of interstate banking was playing out and others were establishing true coast-to-coast franchises. Others, especially Bank of America, had been more aggressive on deals like Fleet and MBNA. Ken Thompson was a great guy, but Herlihy's comment underlined to me that he must be under incredible pressure.

In May of 2006 at the Wachovia Championship, it was announced that we would be buying Golden West, a $125 billion savings bank owned by Herb and Marian Sandler. Only a very small group of people had been involved in the due diligence including the new CFO, Tom Wurtz who had replaced Bob Kelly. Having had no involvement, I was totally surprised by the deal, but I wasn't surprised at not being included, since residential mortgage lending was not in my purview.

As I looked at it, at a high level at least on paper the deal made sense. Wachovia's loan portfolio of about $400 billion was 60% commercial and corporate loans and only 40% consumer loans. In the part of the bank for which I was responsible, we had about $100 billion and the corporate and investment bank had about $150 billion for a total of $250 billion. The consumer bank had about $150 billion. The acquisition of Golden West with its $125 billion in consumer mortgage loans would bring us close to 50-50. As a rule, commercial and corporate loans (which tended to have lumpy exposures) were riskier than consumer loans where the exposures were more granular.

At the time everyone thought that residential mortgages were the safest asset class, and no one was predicting the blow up in home prices that would come later. The Sandler's had navigated two prior recessions relatively unscathed. Their average loan to value was about 70%, very low for a mortgage company, and they were not sub prime since their customers had good credit scores. Their primary product, the "Pik a Pay Mortgage," was very much like the reverse mortgages Tom Selleck advertises today. Properly used, there is nothing wrong with the product.

What was hidden from plain view was a ticking time bomb called,

"Human Nature" that I am not sure anyone would have picked up on, but I will explain in more detail later. Therefore, while I was a little surprised by the small group doing the due diligence, the acquisition was not that surprising especially since it gave us a major presence in California with over 100 branches. I'm not saying it wasn't a mistake, because it was. What I'm saying is that the mistake was hidden from plain view since, at the time, no one imagined we would have the collapse in home prices that we had. Even the small group of people who finally figured it out didn't do so until much later in the next year when they started shorting the stock of mortgage insurance companies.

As I will try to explain in much greater detail, even as bad as the Golden West deal ended up being, in and of itself, it should not have caused Wachovia to fail.

Carlos Evans

Chapter 30

The Coming Storm

After the announcement of the Golden West acquisition, my businesses continued to power along. Somewhere around the time of the Westcorp acquisition, Ben gave me a promotion to wholesale banking executive which meant I had responsibility for all the wholesale businesses in the general bank including commercial banking, business banking (companies with $1 million to $10 million in sales), government and institutional banking, Wachovia dealer services, as well as commercial real estate. While promotions and titles were never that important to me, I was now running a $2 billion earnings machine, and it was humming. My peer in reporting to Ben was CeCe Sutton who ran the consumer bank and was first among equals in Ben's operating world since the branch system made about $2.5 billion per year. In total in 2006, Wachovia would make about $7.7 billion, up over 15% from the prior year. In the fourth quarter alone, we would make $2.4 billion or close to $10 billion annualized. The stock had risen to over $50 per share, and in 2007 we would increase our dividend to 64 cents per quarter or $2.56 per year for a dividend yield in excess of 5%.

Sometime in 2006 I got a call from Ken Thompson asking me to chair the United Way Board in Charlotte, stepping into the line of succession behind the current chair Ned Curran, his successor, Graham Denton, and the next in line. I had been very involved in United Way in the 90s but had stepped down when I left Bank of America. By this time, I was very involved in South Carolina nonprofit work in keeping with the promise Lisa and I made to commit more to our home state. At that point, I was in the succession chain to become chair of the Spoleto Festival USA board as well as chair of the Medical University Foundation board, both located in Charleston.

Around the time, Lisa and I also purchased a second home in downtown Charleston in the Historic District that we renovated, and we spent a lot of time there on weekends. We purchased the house because between the two boards we were going back and forth a lot so it seemed to make sense. Although I was staying pretty busy with these two nonprofits, when Ken called I immediately said yes. I thought the world of Ken Thompson and would have done anything he asked. Also, my time in the chairman's seat at United Way would not start for four years until 2010 or so I thought!!

In 2006 we continued making great progress in all my businesses. One of the only hiccups was a scare with the old Westcorp management team that I had to deal with. While we had a great relationship with Ernest Rady, the former owner who became the largest individual shareholder of Wachovia Stock after the sale, Tom Wolfe, the CEO of Westcorp was having problems with our desire to institute central reporting for certain support functions like human resources, marketing and compliance. By that point, Ernest was on the Wachovia Board and had a better understanding of how big companies are run, but Tom was having real problems giving up total control.

I woke up one night worried that he might walk away, and while he had a non-compete, his loss so early in the integration process would have been a blow. Ben Jenkins and I discussed the situation and concluded that the best way to prevent that from happening would be to sweeten the compensation scheme. With that in mind, I worked with my old friend Tracy Kidd to develop an additional package over and above the Wachovia stock and bonus plan that would fund a large deferred comp pool for Tom and the senior officers if they stayed for 5 years and met their business goals. It was pre-funded, and they got to invest the dollars in a series of funds. They key was they could see the money every quarter when they got their statements, a constant reminder of what they would be walking away from if they left. With the Westcorp management team stabilized, I was then able to focus on the other businesses.

By 2007, we were hitting on all cylinders. Wachovia dealer services was having great success delivering the near prime product to the old Wachovia dealers and we were achieving great success in delivering floor planning, cash management, and super prime paper to the old Westcorp dealers.

Commercial banking and government banking were doing great as well. Our regular checkups with David Fox and the team at Greenwich Associates showed that were #1 in the country in middle market client satisfaction and we were #1 in lead relationships on the East Coast . We were also starting to get great traction in our Texas and California expansion markets. Howard Halle and Bill Wilson as well as Guy Bodine were doing an excellent job leading those efforts. While we were only the fourth largest bank in the country we had moved up to number 3 in middle market business share ahead of Citicorp but behind the coast-to-coast franchises of JP Morgan and Bank of America. We were on a roll, and I was having the time of my life doing what I loved—helping entrepreneurs grow and do what they do best, creating jobs and supporting the economy along the way. Every week would take me on travels all over the country to meetings with my teammates and customers. Little did I know what was just around the corner.

Sometime in the middle of 2007 I made a large purchase of Wachovia stock. The cost was in the high 7 figures, and I borrowed much of the purchase price on margin. I thought I was being smart since the dividend yield by that time was in the 7% range, so it would more than cover the interest on the loans. Besides, I had great confidence in Wachovia because I had clear line of sight to the businesses I was running, and we were putting up spectacular numbers. It was a huge mistake and defied the biggest rule in investing, "Don't put too many eggs in one basket."

Despite the huge business I was running, I was still in the little office on the middle floors of the Wachovia Building. Having done the big office thing earlier in my career, I really didn't care about having a bigger office. I had a wonderful assistant in Sandra Medlin who did a fabulous job booking my airline flights and getting me where I needed to be when I needed to be there. I had all I needed, and life was good. I was working hard but had plenty of time for family and special weekends in the mountains at Lake Summit.

By fall 2007 there were signs that not all was well. The end of the third quarter saw a huge flight to quality in the bond markets, and credit spreads widened dramatically. In layman's terms widening credit spreads indicate that investors are becoming more and more risk averse, thus requiring higher and higher yields to justify perceived credit risk. In a nutshell, in '07 people knew that something bad was going to happen; they just didn't know exactly what it would be.

Also in late fall of 2007, I got the call I had been waiting for. Phil Smith at Bank of America was ready to talk. After my departure from Bank of America, Phil and the municipal finance team once again reported to the investment bank. In addition, the wall I had put up around the old municipal finance incentive plan was no longer there. As part of the broader capital markets group, Phil's incentive plan was about to be reduced to take care of people in the more glamorous businesses like high yield and equity that were having a terrible year. Phil's business, on the other hand was having the best year ever. The flight to quality had caused municipal bonds to perform extremely well. Phil was incredibly frustrated that his people were going to be under-compensated, and I knew that we had the opportunity I had been looking for.

I went upstairs to see Ben Jenkins and told him what was going on. Ben was 100% supportive and we immediately flew to Darien, Connecticut, to have dinner with Phil who lived there and commuted into New York City. We made a deal to hire him as the head of government and institutional banking as well as municipal finance. The government and institutional piece was easy since that reported to me. The municipal finance part was going to be more difficult since that reported up through the capital markets group. It took me three months to work out the compensation and reporting with my peer in capital markets, but in the end we were able to get it done. Phil came on Board at the end of March 2008 and immediately hit the ground running taking municipal finance bankers away from Bank of America. It was easy pickings as they were incredibly dissatisfied with what had happened to their pay. While I was excited about stealing Phil away and delighting in the revenge element, my real excitement came from the knowledge that I was getting a great athlete who could make an incredible positive impact on part of my business.

In 2007, despite the turmoil in the capital markets, Wachovia earned $6.3 billion down from $7.8 billion. Almost all the drop was in the corporate and investment bank which was roiled by the blow up in the capital markets.

Almost all the money made was in my business, CeCe Sutton's consumer bank, and the wealth management/asset management business under David Carroll. All three of those businesses were very stable with granular earnings from huge numbers of customers. We ended the year with shareholder equity of $76.8 billion and Book Value of $37.66 per share, and we were the #1 consumer bank and middle market bank based on customer satisfaction scores. Also in 2007, Wachovia significantly increased its community development lending and outright contributions and donations in the communities where we did business. We were an outstanding corporate citizen in every respect. Wachovia's loan portfolio of roughly $500 billion was highly diversified with the exception of the Golden West portfolio of $125 billion where roughly 60% or $75 billion was in first mortgage home loans in California. Unfortunately, there, in California, was the ticking time bomb.

As mentioned above, by the fall of 2007 with the turmoil in the capital markets, I was aware that we were going to have a recession. Having been through 4 serious recessions in my career I knew the signs, and my businesses were on storm alert. The signs were pretty clear—widening credit spreads, business momentum beginning to soften across multiple industries, slowing housing and construction markets, lower corporate profits and in some cases losses. All this was taking place with gathering speed.

In a bank, since our loans are not traded securities, we use a risk rating system that, at the time, was basically 1-10 with shades of grey in between. A 1 would be the highest quality credit either secured by cash or T-Bills, and a 10 would basically be a total charge off. In between, we had 5.2, 5.5, 5.8, etc. Since we received regular financial information on all our customers as required under the loan agreements, we constantly monitored and reevaluated the ratings all the time. One of the first signs of bigger problems was a negative grading migration in the portfolio, i.e. 5s going to 6s then to 7s, etc. By late 2007, we were watching the portfolio like a hawk.

By 2007, Spurgeon Mackie had retired, and Mike Carlin was my chief risk officer. Mike was an outstanding credit guy. He was all over the details and very conservative but also fair and reasonable. By that I mean if I had sound rationale for why we should do something that went against his original conclusions, he would listen, and if persuaded, adjust his opinion accordingly. I don't mean to imply that Mike was easy because he was not.

However, that is what you want in credit people. The best are tough in granting approval but also willing to change their mind if the circumstances warrant. A good example of the way Mike and I worked together was a deal we did for Anschtuz Entertainment Group called LA Live. The loan was for infrastructure supporting their new LA Live project in Los Angeles. It was a tough deal because unlike most loans we did not have a first mortgage on the underlying assets. However, we could get a pledge of multi year income streams from the parking revenues associated with the underground parking for the Staples Center as well as naming rights revenue for a multitude of sponsorships, signage etc. Working with Howard Halle our commercial executive in California, we were able to make the deal work, and Mike rolled up his sleeves to help us figure out a way to make the loan safe even without hard assets as collateral. We were all excited to attend the opening ceremony as the governor spoke, and Phil Anschtuz rewarded us with some handsome deposits for our help with the project.

Thus, by 2008 we were having many wins like the one at LA Live and helping to make things happen for entrepreneurs by creating the win-win. At the same time, aware that the cycle was a bit long in the tooth, we were being careful and monitoring things closely. Being more conservative, Mike was the perfect partner for me in this regard since I tend to be aggressive and always try to find ways to do business. From my perspective, we were a case study on how the partnership with credit should work, and by that point we had institutionalized the partnership across the entire commercial bank. Even as 2008 wore on and things started slowing down, our portfolio was holding up extremely well with little if any sign of problems. One of the reasons for that was that, with Mike's help, we had been careful. Staying away from risky situations and saying no when there was too much risk or any doubt whatsoever, about the big C (Character).

One such "no" came in early 2008. We had been approached by Don Sterling, owner of the LA Clippers, for a $100 million unsecured line of credit. A litigation attorney by background, Mr. Sterling had made his fortune years earlier in real estate. He was incredibly wealthy and almost all the big West Coast banks were extending him lines. He had stolen the

Clippers years earlier for a song and it was just one of his many holdings. Clearly, his financial position supported the loan, so we issued a term sheet.

However, in our due diligence we came across public transcripts from a trial where Sterling was being sued, and there was a lot of commentary, some from Sterling himself, about his treatment of women. When I read the transcripts, I immediately knew we could not make the loan. Howard Halle, my commercial executive, agreed even though we had already issued the term sheet. In keeping with my habit of being with my people when we had to deliver bad news, I flew to California to have dinner with Howard and Don Sterling. It was the one and only time I ever failed to make a loan after delivering a term sheet (which is non-binding). Non-binding as they may be, term sheets are sacred, and a bank usually does not issue one unless they are willing to make the loan. When we delivered the message, Mr. Sterling pressed for more specifics. I simply said that in our due diligence we determined that a relationship was not a good match for him or us and simply left it at that. It was a good decision and emblematic of how careful we were being well before the recession hit.

In early April, Ken Thompson announced a stock issue to raise capital. At the time the shares were trading in the mid $30s so it was highly dilutive, and we issued more shares than most people thought necessary to see the economic problems through. I asked Ken in a conference call why were we diluting ourselves so much. His response was ominous but also very thoughtful and sincere. "Carlos, I view my role as CEO, captain of this ship, to be almost sacred. While I have many responsibilities, one of my primary roles is to make sure we have enough liquidity and capital to see our way through periods of financial uncertainty. We are in one of those periods and I believe what we are doing is necessary to weather the storm so the ship can come through."

I was almost embarrassed at having asked the question. I was worried about all those shares I had purchased and what the dilution would do to the stock price which was already well below my cost. Clearly, what Ken did was the right thing. Unfortunately, in my opinion, the board would totally mishandle the situation from that point forward and essentially seal Wachovia's fate with their actions.

By that point in 2008, hedge funds were actively shorting stocks they felt were vulnerable. They were feeding on any company with residential mortgage exposure and any kind of bad news story. Clearly, Wachovia had a bulls-eye on its back with the "Pik A Pay" loans. Even the name sounded terrible for the times. As everyone knows, banking is a business based on confidence. Little did I know that the board was getting ready to drag the Wachovia name through the mud in what I believe ended up being a public relations nightmare.

First in early May, they stripped Ken of his chairman's role. That drove the stock down from the mid $30s to the mid $20s. Then in early June they fired Ken, the one person who could have saved us. At the time I believe the board was looking for a scapegoat because they were worried about their own skins. In their minds, firing the guy at the top conveyed that they were taking action, but I believe in the end it was the thing that destroyed us.

The second round of bad publicity pushed the stock down into the teens, after which the board left the bank drifting like a ship lost at sea for almost 5 weeks run by Lanty Smith, the lead outside director and new board chair, who was not a banker but a textile guy. Finally in July, they hired Bob Steel who also wasn't a banker but an investment banker, but by then the die was already cast. We had lost roughly 60 days of valuable time when, I believe, Ken Thompson would have been doing something.

As to what Ken might have done, I believe the answer could have been one strategy. In order to raise cash and put us in the strongest liquidity position, we could have increased the interest rates on our certificates of deposit. Sometimes called hot money, certificates of deposit, move to whichever bank is paying the highest rate since many of the participants in that product are smaller depositors below the FDIC insured $250 thousand limit. As a result, they are not so concerned with safety and soundness because they are covered by the insurance. Certificates of deposit have maturities usually 1 or 2 years out, so the money is tied up and an early withdrawal carries a penalty. While the bank would have sacrificed forward earnings by paying up for those deposits, it would have been a small price to pay for survival.

The savings and loan industry did this a lot in the '91 recession, and while ultimately it didn't save the industry as a whole, it did keep many of them in the game. I believe Ken Thompson would have been doing everything humanly possible to save us in those intervening 6 to 8 weeks when we were rudderless. He had basically made that pledge during the equity raise call. I believe the constant negative press from the board's multiple actions made us easy prey for the shorts so they could just keep piling on. Ken did make a bad decision on Golden West, but as I have already said, the fatal weaknesses were not totally clear at the time the acquisition was made. Everyone on the board approved the acquisition including Lanty Smith so it was not just Ken. In my humble opinion, they wanted to make him the scapegoat for a decision they all made. Unfortunately, their actions only served to shine a spotlight on Wachovia's vulnerability and exacerbate the problem much to the glee of the shorts.

By early summer with Ken's departure announcement, we were in a crisis mode. I was flying all over the country to keep our customers settled, and we were having good results with that. In particular, I went to Florida several times to meet with the State Treasurer, Alex Sink who had been my teammate in the old Bank of America days. The state of Florida had over $3 billion on deposit with us. They were one of our largest government banking clients.

Like all governments, their deposits were secured and backed by treasuries so they were safe regardless of amount. I went anyway to make sure Alex was comfortable that we were adhering to the collateral agreements. Alex never wavered and we never wavered on our obligations. I am proud of the fact that during this volatile period we never failed to fund a loan commitment or do what we had committed to do for our customers. While hot money would move, especially large institutional deposits in excess of what was insured, by and large our customers stayed with us out of loyalty for all the years of good service.

By mid-summer, I was operating at a frantic pace to keep our employees focused and spending tons of time with customers. The pressure on me was incredible especially given my mounting losses on the stock. By this time, I also knew full well what the ticking time bomb was. For years, the family home had been the consumer's most sacred asset. No one ever considered the possibility that the price of their home might drop significantly below the amount of their mortgage. That had never happened before because homes had mostly appreciated. Well, home prices had also never doubled year-to-year the way they had in California where the worst was about to happen because houses in California were about to drop 50%.

Two years earlier, during the Westcorp integration on one of my many visits to Ervine I looked at townhouses that were selling for $1 million when one year earlier they had been selling for $500 thousand. That same townhouse in Charlotte would have been worth $350 thousand.. Seeing those houses brought to mind Hootie's statement years earlier that when things seemed too good to be true, they were usually not true.

In the case of the townhouse, it wasn't worth $1 million and would revert back to $500 thousand. In the case of Golden West since their average loan was 70% of appraised value (in this theoretical case let's say the townhouse loan had been made on an appraised value of $1 million), they now had a $700 thousand dollar loan on something worth $500 thousand. If the customer stopped paying and they had to foreclose and resell, their loss would be $200 thousand plus expenses or roughly 30% of the original loan amount.

I kept running the math in my head. If 100% of the loans in California defaulted and went to foreclosure, 30% of $75 billion would be $22.5 billion. Surely, 100% of the loans would never default because that would be a total meltdown and would never occur. If 50% defaulted and went to foreclosure the losses would be half that or $11.5 billion but that would occur over perhaps 3 to five years. I knew that my business, CeCe's business, and David Carroll's business was grinding out $7 billion per year in consistent sustainable earnings. Over three years that would be way more than enough to offset the losses. And that would assume the corporate and investment bank would not return to profitability in that time.

Granted that quick analysis did not take into consideration other parts of the country where Golden West had 40% of its loans, but in those areas, values did not drop nearly as much and therefore people would not have been as inclined to cut and run like they did in California. Call it human nature, call it being more attached to home and family. Call it buying for shelter and not for speculation.

For whatever reason the defaults were just not nearly as bad elsewhere. The bottom line was that under just about every scenario I ran, I was pegging the max loss number at about $15 billion over a three-year period, and we had the base earnings to deal with it in our three core businesses.

Even though the actual losses are very difficult to determine because they were obscured by the Wells Fargo merger accounting treatment, I believe they were actually close to that $15 billion number. In the end, while our losses were severe, I believe we could have powered through. Also, I know for a fact that other banks with loan problems greater than ours managed to survive. They simply did not have as much bad press. In the final analysis, none of the math mattered because we were dealing with a crisis in confidence and the board's actions put us in play.

That summer was a blur. In July, I was running on adrenaline during the day, and when I staggered home late at night I would collapse from exhaustion. To compound my problems, the United Way was in a crisis over the CEO's compensation. Without getting too technical, years earlier the Board had given the CEO a retirement plan which had been expensed and run through the P&L every year as deferred comp, however, they had not taken money out to actually fund the plan. When they finally did, it was over $800 thousand in one year because it represented multiple years of expenses. That is what showed up in the 990 (the public document all nonprofits must file) and it caused her total comp to be well in excess of $1 million. That, along with aspects of her management style triggered a crisis of confidence in the United Way. The Charlotte Observer was all over it and there were headlines every day, which caused the current board chair and the-next-in-line to step down. While I hadn't been on the board when the CEO's comp plan was structured, and I wasn't expecting to be board chair until 2010, it now fell in my lap.

All this pressure along with my mounting financial woes prompted me to sit down with Lisa one night. She was well aware of the problems at the bank and United Way since it was playing out in the paper every day. While she knew we owned a fair amount of Wachovia stock, she has always left the details of our finances to me. Despite all the problems at work and the United Way, what bothered me most was my poor decision on the stock and the result that I had let my family down. While our marriage had always been a true equal partnership, like most couples, we divided up certain important tasks. I had failed on one of the most important things I had been entrusted to do, and like a giant weight on my back, it was literally crushing me with guilt. It had gotten to the point where I would get sick at night, was unable to eat and felt like throwing up.

I told her that we were going to lose an incredible amount of money if the bank failed. I told her while not destitute, we would have to change a lot about our lifestyle, especially if the bank got sold and I ended up out of a job. I told her that the pressure was crushing me, and now this thing with United Way had been laid in my lap. I was thinking about telling them I just couldn't do it. The person who had asked me, Ken Thompson, was no longer at the bank. Besides, people would understand the pressure I was under at work and the many different directions I was being pulled in.

Lisa gazed at me with a calm, determined and loving look. She said softly, "Well, we started out with nothing 30 years ago. I can do nothing again. You don't worry about us, you just go do whatever you think is right."

The moment she said it, the weight of the world came off my back. I knew exactly what I was going to do. I would say yes to United Way because I had made a commitment. The fact that Ken was no longer at the bank had nothing to do with it. The fact that I was under a lot of pressure at the bank had nothing to do with it. I had made a promise and I needed to keep my word, or else I was like one of those people who stopped paying their loans. From that point forward, I knew that whatever hand I was dealt I could handle it.

The fact was the problems were really just starting to mount both at the bank and United Way. Wachovia would ultimately be forced to sell, and I would go months not knowing if I would still have a job. The United Way board chair seat would get hotter. I would be sued personally by an aggressive plaintiff's attorney with service delivered to my home on a Sunday morning just before church by two armed police officers in two separate police cars as a means of intimidation. There would be long days and nights ahead full of pressure and bad publicity where I would need to be strong, focused and thoughtful. But the moment Lisa said what she said, none of that mattered. No matter what came, I knew we could make our way through it because she had my back.

That August, Ben informed me that I would be joining the Bank's management committee. By then, we had already made the decision to go functional with the commercial segment, so all the foot soldiers would be reporting directly to me which is how I had wanted it from the beginning. I should have felt like I was on top of the world, however the world was crumbling around me. By then, Bob Steel was running around trying to find M&A solutions which was what everyone else, including Hank Paulson and Tim Geithner, was doing. The byword of the day was to marry everyone up, make the big banks even bigger, force Bank of America to buy Merrill Lynch and Countrywide, force JP Morgan to buy Bear Stearns, and ultimately Washington Mutual Savings Bank (WAMU). I would later find it interesting that the biggest criticism of that period was that we allowed these big banks to attain "Too Big To Fail" status. At the time, no one questioned those mergers because we were in a crisis, however, they definitely exacerbated the "Too Big" problem, which would ultimately be all people would talk about.

As Bob Steel focused on an M&A solution, we looked at many different combinations. At one point, we talked about merging with Goldman Sachs who needed a bank partner because they were running out of cash. We also talked with Citicorp, Morgan Stanley and others. Much to my shock, they even considered selling Wachovia dealer services for $2 billion, which would have been just plain crazy. After the melt down Wachovia dealer services made close to $2 billion in a single year.

The whole place was like a circus with everyone running around trying to do deals. For my part, I stayed focused on the business, our employees and our customers, putting one foot in front of the other every day. Customers and employees were scared as the world melted down around them. I figured the best thing I could do was stay at the helm, steady as she goes, and make sure we were performing our basic function of making loans and taking care of needs. We did all that and we did it well even through the worst financial storm in modern history.

The second week in September, a group that included Ben and I went to California on the bank's plane to wave the flag and be with customers and employees. While there, the TARP program was announced, which was essentially a way to prop up the banking system by injecting capital into every bank in the country. Everyone had to take it, whether they needed it or not, so no one was singled out or painted as being "weak."

Our stock recovered mightily on the day of the announcement. By Monday the following week, the stock fell back again as Congress started arguing over the legislation. The stock fell further as the debate went on. A week later, on Wednesday September 24, Ben and I were having dinner with David Fox and Don Rafferty from Greenwich Associates. We were in the dining room at Quail Hollow Club where Ben was a member. It was a celebration of sorts since the year before Wachovia had been named the best middle market bank in the country in their annual awards for customer service scores.

Ben's phone buzzed, he stepped out to take the call. When he returned his face was ashen. He told David, Don and me that $300 billion WAMU had just failed and was being sold to JP Morgan Chase. It would be announced on Thursday morning. I had been aware of WAMU's problems. Unlike Wachovia, their entire portfolio was residential mortgages where with us, the Golden West assets only represented 20% of our loans.

Ben said that the WAMU announcement would likely kick off a chain of events and we would be next. I found it incredulous that a savings bank thousands of miles away that was so different from us could impact us in the most profound way. After all, we had what they did not have—three core businesses consistently grinding out $7 billion per year in earnings. While I was right on that last part, I was wrong on the not affecting us part and it would happen right away. In fact, it happened that weekend, just two days from our getting up from the dinner table.

Chapter 31

The Weekend at the Adoption Agency

On Friday, I was advised that there would be three banks running due diligence to buy Wachovia over the weekend. Wells Fargo, Citicorp and one other I never heard from. Mike Carlin and I were asked to be available all weekend. It was handled in that matter of fact way. There was no explanation as to why they were pulling the plug. As far as I could tell, we weren't running out of cash even following the WAMU announcement. Sure, big institutional money had moved around, which I am sure strained our cash position, but our core customers were hanging with us. I knew that because I was talking to them every day with and through our people.

I have since called this time the "Weekend at the Adoption Agency." It was like our family was being forced into adoption by the FDIC, and we had no say so over who the new parents would be. We also had no assurance that we would not be broken up and separated from each other. In short it was terrible. People who knew very little about our company were pulling the strings, and it was frustrating. All they knew was that we had this problem with Golden West. They had no clue that the other parts of the bank were alive, well, making lots of money, and in fact, very healthy.

That Friday night was grueling. I think Mike and I were on the phone until 3 am. The first call early in that evening had been with the Citicorp people. They asked just a few questions because from the start it was clear that they had an FDIC backstop so they weren't digging deep. From the questions I could also tell they didn't have a clue about middle market banking. They were an international retail bank and a corporate and investment bank. I knew if they bought us, it would be a nightmare because they didn't know my business.

The Wells team, on the other hand, was sharp and on their game. On the phone was Dave Hoyt, head of all wholesale banking. At Wells, wholesale was not only everything in my world but the corporate and investment bank as well. Also on the call were Hoyt's chief lieutenant, Tim Sloan, who would later become CEO; wholesale chief credit officer Dave Weber; and Mike Johnson, head of corporate banking. There were also a few others, but Hoyt, Sloan and Weber were the principal participants.

Their questions were knowledgeable and to the point. We reviewed asset quality statistics for every portfolio as well as the trends over time. I shared with them that we had been on "Storm Alert" for over a year anticipating the recession and had been downgrading credits at the first sign of any issues. We dug into the specific credits that were problems, but they were few and far between. Clearly, we had our business under good control. We also reviewed our huge letter of credit book that supported our government and institutional banking business. They were impressed that the book was largely investment grade.

I have been dealing with credit people my entire career, and I can tell when they are comfortable. I could sense it on the phone by their questions and their overall tone. We went through the largest credit exposures of which there were many. Mike Carlin and I knew these names backwards and forwards. We could recite up to the minute financial information as well as details and the fact pattern associated with each credit. At the conclusion of the call, the two Daves and Tim said they loved our business. They said it looked just like theirs, and they were comfortable with it.

At the end of the call, I went and woke Lisa. I told her that I thought Wells would buy us for between $16 and $18 a share and that we would at least salvage something. I awoke early in the morning because I wanted to go to my office and listen in on the corporate and investment bank due diligence call. While I would not be a participant, I knew the Wells side would be the same cast of characters as the night before. On the way in, I stopped by Ben Jenkins's house to tell him about the call the night before. I told him it went well, that I believed Wells liked everything they heard about our wholesale businesses in the general bank, and that I thought they would buy us for between $16 and $18 per share. He said he already knew that because Dick Kovacevich had called Bob Steel. I told him to keep his fingers crossed because I didn't think that day's call would go as well.

My feelings about the Saturday call were correct. The Wachovia corporate and investment banking business had its share of problems. The capital markets blow up in 2007 caused that year to be only slightly profitable due to losses on a variety of fronts. 2008 so far had been a disaster with further markdowns in securities and loan losses associated with "hung" syndications. (A syndication is where a bank makes a big loan and plans to sell off chunks to get its exposure down.) Depending upon the type of security and the priority in the pecking order of payment some securities are much riskier than others.

In Wachovia's case since we had been an active participant in the capital markets, the positions were complex. Since the Wells team did not have an investment bank, a lot of our positions appeared new, different and difficult to understand. Not that Hoyt, Sloan and Weber weren't smart; they were some of the sharpest credit minds I had ever met, but to understand this complex basket of exotic deals was going to take time.

As the call went on, taking up the entire day, it became more and more apparent to me that the Well's team was getting increasingly uncomfortable. Just as I had sensed comfort and confidence the night before I was now sensing discomfort, worse yet fear of the unknown. At the end of the day, I got back in my car totally exhausted and deflated. The high from the night before had been reversed. I was now in the depths of depression.

As I drove home, I passed Ben who was taking a walk to relieve the tension. I rolled down the window and he looked in. "How did it go". I told him that I had worked with credit people all my life and I knew when they weren't comfortable, and there just wasn't enough time for them to get their arms around all the exposures. I said "Ben, they're not going to do this deal."

His face showed his disappointment. Ben Jenkins had put a lot of his bonuses his entire career in something called deferred compensation, which like an IRA is a tax efficient way to save. However, in a Wachovia bankruptcy, his deferred comp would be just like any other unsecured credit, meaning it would be wiped out, a total loss for Ben on many years of savings. I could tell he was concerned, and I was concerned for him despite my own problems. He had been a great boss and unlike me, he was at the end of his working career.

When I got home Lisa and I had dinner. I was exhausted so I went to be bed early. The next day I learned that Dick Kovacevich had called Bob Steel to tell him Wells was out, confirming what I had been feeling the day before. On Sunday, Lisa and I went to church as we always did. I said a silent prayer asking God for strength because I knew I was going to need all I could muster to lead our people through the changes that lay before us. Sunday was a gloomy day, but I tried to take walks in the neighborhood to keep my mind off my troubles. Besides the problems at the bank, I had been dealing with a number of United Way issues.

In late August we announced the firing of the prior United Way CEO, which kicked off the lawsuit. As the new board chair, I also announced formation of an independent committee of people from all walks of life in Charlotte to review what had gone wrong and what changes needed to be made in the governance of United Way to insure problems would not happen again. Bob Sink, a well-known community volunteer and also an outstanding lawyer with Robinson Bradshaw was chairing the committee. Mac Everett another outstanding community volunteer agreed to serve as interim CEO.

It was a critical time in the United Way calendar because of the fund raising campaign that took place in the fall of every year. A lot of health and human service organizations were depending on us to fund them, and I was also full speed ahead in trying to find a new permanent CEO to replace Mack once we got through the campaign. Because of the high visibility of United Way in Charlotte we were holding press conferences weekly to detail the steps we were taking to right the ship.

By this time, I was also holding constant conversations with our lawyers and insurance providers because of the lawsuit. It was complicated because we actually had three separate policies: one for general liability, one for any discrimination claims brought against United Way, and one for the board. Since the plaintiffs' attorney on the other side was bringing actions that involved all three policies, any settlement was going to be complex at best.

On my walks I was thinking about all of these issues as I tried to plan the steps we needed to take to restore confidence I was also trying to think through what I needed to do at the bank next week. For weeks on end, because of the turmoil, I had been having regular calls with all my teammates to make sure I was constantly accessible to them. On these calls, I would answer any questions they had, and I constantly reinforced that the most important thing they could do was to take care of our customers and take care of each other. The message had been getting through because despite all the turmoil our people had been executing flawlessly in an environment full of distractions and fear. In fact, despite Wachovia's failure I was full of pride for what these folks were doing each every day. In short, they were magnificent to a person.

On Monday morning it was announced that Citicorp would buy Wachovia in an FDIC assisted deal that limited the losses Citi might be exposed to in the transaction. It was clear to everyone that the FDIC was perhaps more worried about Citi than they were about us, and for whatever reason they felt putting us together with government assistance would be good. Crazy as it sounds, that is what they were thinking.

I was deflated because I knew the Citi people did not have a clue about our business. That view was reinforced when a very senior Citi person called to talk but asked none of the in-depth questions Hoyt and his team at Wells had asked. It was what I called a "Howdy Doody call," and it made me sick. Despite my feelings, I needed to show confidence to our people, which I did my best to do.

On Tuesday, Phil Smith called to tell me that the municipal finance trading desk had just had its best month ever. A week or two earlier he had promised the team that if they stayed on track for the month, he would treat them to pizza and beer at the pool hall down the street. He said, "Carlos you know that Citi has a huge municipal business. They're #1 in the league tables and all their trading is in New York City. All the people I was going to take out for a beer are going to get fired, and they know it."

I knew he was asking for my opinion on what he should do. I told Phil that we needed to take the trading desk for beer and pizza anyway. A promise was a promise. They had delivered and we needed to deliver. After work that afternoon, we all went down to the pool hall. It was somber. I gave my best pep talk and told everyone to hold their heads high. They shouldn't jump to conclusions about what Citi would or would not do, I told them. I would be a strong advocate for them and no matter what happened, Phil and I would do our best to help each and every one of them.

We were proud of how they had continued helping cities, counties, states, colleges, nonprofit hospitals, and others get their bond deals done despite the fury of the storm. I told them that their teammates on the commercial side of the bank had been doing the same thing for entrepreneurs, and that we were all in this together. Somehow, we were all going to see it through.

On Wednesday and Thursday, I had many more conversations with teammates who knew that the Citi deal was going to be tough. Over the course of those four days, I was amazed that while there had been an LOI (Letter of Intent) announced on Monday, it had not been followed up with the merger agreement announcement which meant a true contract had not been signed. I would later learn that under the terms of the agreement the wealth management/asset management business (essentially David Carroll's world) was being spun off as a separate company owned by the existing Wachovia shareholders. All week a Citi team of accountants camped in Charlotte wrangling over how the cost of our real estate and overhead (essentially lease expenses and cost allocations) would be split between the two entities.

I found it stunning that on a deal this big where they were basically buying Wachovia for $1 per share with a government backstop, they were arguing over pennies. Crazy, but that is what occurred. Friday morning when Wells Fargo came back to the table with an unassisted deal (clearly superior to the government assisted deal) at what was roughly $6 per share, Citi had still not signed a definitive agreement (contract). That whole week the Wells team never put their pencils down, and they finally got their arms around the corporate and investment bank risk. Citi's haggling over pennies and their failure to quickly sign a definitive agreement was eventually their downfall and Wells Fargo's gain.

While the letter agreement said Wachovia would not solicit or sign any other offers, under N.C. Law as a N.C. Corporation, the Wachovia board was obligated to entertain other offers that were better. By this time, we were all cheering for Wells Fargo. Our little bit of exposure to the Citi folks had made it clear to all of us that they were not the best choice.

Over the weekend, it became clear that Vikram Pandit, CEO of Citi, was going to fight. That left us, our depositors, and customers in limbo. If Citi prevailed, we were covered by the FDIC. Until Wells actually closed on the purchase on December 31st, who would be covering our depositors, who were insured through FDIC Insurance only up to $250,000? It was a huge uncertainty at a time when depositors wanted certainty.

Dave Hoyt called me over the weekend and asked if I had any loans I could pledge to secure a line of credit from Wells to cover us if there was a run on the bank. I reminded him of the high quality government and tax exempt loan portfolio. He said that would be perfect and to get him a list of the $20 billion in loans on Monday. I reflected on the conversation and wondered why in all the running around about selling Wachovia dealer services for a paltry $2 billion, no one had thought about seeking what Dave was proposing to do, a simple loan with collateral. As it turned out, we didn't need it because by mid-October the FDIC had gone to unlimited FDIC Insurance, and Hank Paulson was finally able to get the Tarp approved by Congress. The combination of those two things settled the markets down. Either of those two things would have saved Wachovia.

For the remainder of October my time was spent in meetings with the people at Wells beginning to plan for integration. In their model, business banking and Wells Fargo dealer services would report in to Carrie Tolstedt in the community or consumer bank. Real estate would report functional up to Tim Sloan as would commercial and government banking as well as asset based lending and corporate/investment banking. I remember one meeting with John Stumpf, the incoming CEO who would replace Dick Kovacevich, who was retiring. In the meeting John asked me about the dealer business, telling me it was a business Wells had gotten out of years earlier.

The implication was that Wells was smarter than Wachovia, so why should they keep this business now? He said it in a very nice way, but I got the message. I explained that Wachovia, due to the lack of profitability in the super prime space, had considered getting out as well, but we were able to find Westcorp. I explained that it was a great company, and it was getting ready to rain money in the current environment when others were pulling away. Fortunately, John listened, and Wells stayed in the business and made a lot of money in the ensuing years.

Aside from the conversation with John, I had to make many presentations to the integration teams on my areas of responsibility. The corporate and investment bank leadership wanted me to combine my presentation with theirs, so we appeared like one wholesale unit, which was how Wells ran the business. I declined because I didn't want my numbers mixed with theirs. We were making lots of money and they weren't. In the end, few of the Wachovia corporate banking leadership survived the merger.

I even had many questions about whether I would survive. In every merger, there is a little bit of the buyer having all of the answers. The only time when it was different was in the Wachovia merger when it had been about looking at both ways to do things then picking best. Given the strong culture at Wells, it was clear that they were in charge, and while they were polite, there was a little bit of a "know it all" attitude driven by many years of incredible success under the leadership of Dick Kovacevich. Little did I know it at the time, but this aspect of the Wells culture would come back to haunt them in the most profound ways.

I didn't realize it at the time, but my constant interaction with the Wells team was a sort of interview to see if they were going to keep me. For my part, it was very clear that Dave Hoyt and Tim Sloan were very smart people and outstanding bankers. From day one it was obvious that both had come up through the ranks, and I felt that early on we all saw eye-to-eye about how to run the business with few exceptions.

Their bigger concerns were over the corporate and investment bank. It appeared that they were seriously considering whether or not to stay in the investment banking business. I lobbied hard to stay in because I knew our customers needed those services. Fortunately, in the end they chose to stay in the business, which has been a good thing for them overall.

As November rolled around, I was getting very concerned about whether I would have a job. I knew I had to keep working to try and regain our family's financial footing given all the losses from Wachovia which was trading in step with Wells Fargo based on the 1 share for 5 share exchange. The current price of Wells at that point was about $14 per share and going lower, much lower since Wells would finally bottom in early 2009 at between $6 and $8.

Lisa asked one day about all the Wachovia options I had been given as compensation through the years. I told her she could consider it play money because the options were worthless. In order for them to be worth anything, based on the exchange rate, Wells would have to trade over $200 per share and it would never see that price.

On one of my "interviews" with a staff support person I was asked directly what I would do if Wells didn't give me a job. My response was, "A smart person once told me the truth never hurts. Well, ma'am, if you do not give me a job, I guess I will just have to put myself out for hire. I did a lot of damage once before, and I know I can do it again since I'm only 55 years old. One of your competitors will pay up for that, but it's not what I want to do. My preference is to stay right here and help you hold onto our people and our customers. However, my family needs me to keep working, and I need to make a lot of money these last years of my career to try and recover some of my losses."

Her eyes got very big. She knew it wasn't a threat, I was simply telling the truth.

Aside from my own financial worries, I was also worried about my people. The commercial and government business was finishing its best year ever. Based in the funding methodology we were on track to fund a pool of bonuses 150% of market. The Wells team was walking a legal tightrope because technically they could not intervene in Wachovia decisions until after the merger. Bob Steel was thinking about a zero for everybody. I argued that our people had earned it ,and that they deserved it based on their financial results and according to the bonus formula. Besides, I told Tim Sloan, if we paid them nothing, we would put them greatly at risk as many competitors were calling trying to get them to jump ship. Ben Jenkins also lobbied on our behalf. Finally, the decision was made to fund at 75% which was half of what the formula said. Despite the haircut, in my mind, it was a victory for my people.

Finally, on November 7, 2008, I received a letter from Linda Tanner in HR. I still have it today. They offered me a job in the new combined company at a salary higher than what I had been paid at Wachovia. I would also be paid a generous and fair bonus for my work in 2008 and a retention payment staggered over two years in order to keep me on the ship. If I walked, I would lose the retention payment, but I had no plan of walking. Best of all, I would receive a generous stock option grant shortly after the first of the year like all the other Wells executives with the strike price based on where Wells was trading at the time of the grant.

Since the stock was trading so low, I knew I could make a lot of money on those options if we were successful in combining the two companies.

I signed up and was fully committed to that goal. I would report to Tim Sloan, and my title would be Executive Vice President in charge of the Wells commercial banking business east of the Mississippi, as well as the government and institutional banking business nationwide, and municipal finance. Phil Smith would continue to report to me. I would go on the Wells Management Committee, and I would move upstairs to the 40th floor in the large corner office right beside where Ken Thompson used to sit. I went home and told Lisa that I could now see the pathway to how I could earn our family out from the hole I had dug. It would be a long march uphill, but at least now I had the means to get there. In typical form Lisa said, "I knew they would not let you go!!" We hugged, and for the first time in months I had a glimmer of hope.

Chapter 32

The Death of Wachovia

Over the last thirteen years since Wachovia was forced to sell, I have wrestled with two questions. First, could Wachovia have survived? Second, should Wachovia have survived? Let me be frank that I did better personally because of the merger with Wells. My compensation and financial health, which were highly skewed to the value of Wells stock, recovered faster under Wells, and from a professional point of view even though my role was slightly smaller in scope, for the most part, I had a very fulfilling time there.

The city of Charlotte and also the State of North Carolina also fared well. Wells did not reduce the number of employees in Charlotte, and in fact, there are more Wells employees in Charlotte today than there were in the time of Wachovia. Wells has also been a good corporate citizen continuing the philanthropy that we all benefitted from during the time of Wachovia. However, with regard to the question of whether the country and economy are better off or not, that is a much more involved question. In the short summaries below I will try to offer my thoughts as I have pondered both questions over the years.

As to the question of whether Wachovia could have survived, my response is absolutely yes. First there was the strength of the core earnings power of the bank apart from Golden West. My businesses, which earned about $2 billion per year, continued to earn at that level and much higher after the forced merger. In particular, the dealer finance business alone made close to $2 billion in the aftermath of the financial crisis. The commercial/middle market bank continued to grow and produce handsome profits as did government and institutional banking. Wealth management continued to produce steady and growing profits, as did the #1 customer service rated consumer bank in the East.

While dissecting a company's earnings can be difficult, and while some may take issue with exactly how much the old Wachovia contributed to Wells Fargo's earnings after 2008, the simple facts are that the combined Wells Fargo with Wachovia produced steadily increasing earnings from 2009 on, and by 2011 the bank was making consistently in excess of $20 billion after taxes with a return on assets of close to 1.5%. To put that into perspective, the best bank in the country, JP Morgan Chase, in the first quarter of 2022 produced core earnings excluding unusual items of about $10 Billion for an ROA on an annualized basis approaching 1.2%. It is arithmetically impossible for the new Wells, subsequent to acquiring Wachovia, to have produced a 1.5% ROA unless Wachovia was producing about half of the $20 billion in earnings.

As far as the losses in the Wachovia Golden West book, which were pegged at approximately $30 billion at the time of the merger, I don't believe the actual losses were anywhere close to that. Unfortunately, it would take a team of forensic accountants looking at all the numbers in the succeeding 10 year period after 2008 to determine what the actual losses were due to the merger accounting that was utilized. As mentioned earlier, since the markdown was taken against the book value of the loans, a great percentage of future payments accredited into yield and not recovery, so if a good portion of the $125 billion legal balance was ultimately collected against the $95 billion book balance it would have showed up in the yield and net interest income.

In the years after 2008, Wells Fargo had one of the highest net interest margins of any bank in the country between 3.75% and 4%. The yield accretion mentioned above suggests to me that the actual losses on the $125 billion portfolio were nowhere close to $30 billion. As far as what were they actually, no one will probably ever know, but I think it safe to say that it was perhaps closer to the $15 billion I estimated in the examples I have given previously. Either way, whether it was $15 billion or $30 billion, I believe Wachovia had the core earnings power to make it through and the bank had enough capital to survive. Besides, I know for a fact that many banks in much worse shape than Wachovia did survive.

Next, on the question of liquidity, while I don't know what was going on in corporate treasury and just how dire the cash situation was leading up to the weekend at the adoption agency, I do know that Wachovia survived until the merger on December 31, 2008, with little support from anyone. Also, we know that one week after the weekend at the adoption agency, Tarp was passed as was unlimited FDIC Insurance. Either of those two actions (especially raising the FDIC cap) would have stemmed any run on the bank because it had that effect with plenty of other banks that were in worse shape than Wachovia.

As to the more important question of whether Wachovia should have survived, I don't feel I am equipped to answer that, however it is incredibly thought provoking on many different fronts. I do have the following observations:

1.) Forcing the sale of Wachovia only served to make the biggest banks in the country bigger. It gave us another $1 trillion plus bank in Wells Fargo to go along with JP Morgan Chase, Citicorp and Bank of America. I am not saying that it's a good thing or a bad thing because there are many angles to that question. I am saying, however, that the biggest criticism coming out of 2008 was that we had too many institutions that were, in fact,' Too Big To Fail.'

2.) Forcing the sale killed an institution that had the number one rated consumer bank based on customer service scores and the number one rated commercial/middle market bank.

3.) Forcing the sale killed an institution that had the best corporate culture I have ever worked in, a culture based on customer service, teammate mutual respect, openness to other ideas and ways of doing things, and collaboration across lines of business, not to mention giving back and service to the communities everywhere we did business. There was not an ounce of greed inside the Wachovia culture.

Even Golden West did not make subprime risky loans. Their underwriting required that borrowers have good credit scores, even though the loans had flexible repayment characteristics in much the way reverse mortgages have today. Flexibility in and of itself is not evil and can be appropriate in the right circumstances. If there was any greed at play in the lending at Golden West, it was evidenced by the speculative borrowers in California who elected to stop paying when the value of the home declined below the mortgage balance. They took the easy way out versus fulfilling their moral and legal obligation to honor their debts. The acquisition of Golden West by Wachovia was not borne out of greed but by Wachovia's desire to serve more customers and bring our extraordinary service levels to the West Coast.

4.) Killing Wachovia destroyed equity value for the Wachovia shareholders because the 5 for 1 exchange of stock effectively put them in the position of never being able to get more than 20% of their money back. This affected widows, orphans, retirement plans and many people at the end of their careers who did not have the opportunity to recover their investment like I did.

5.) Killing Wachovia exacerbated the fear factor prevalent at the time, and that fear factor was never stemmed by the forced merger approach taken by the regulators and the people in charge. In fact, even the TARP did not stem the fear. It was only the lifting of the FDIC cap that restored a sense of confidence.

6.) Killing Wachovia ultimately caused a strong culture to be tainted by the well-publicized flaws in the Wells culture where almost all the unauthorized new account activity was in the West in the legacy Wells Fargo consumer branches.

7) Killing Wachovia caused roughly half of a $1.3 trillion institution (the legacy Wachovia side) to be on the sidelines and unable fulfill a bank's fundamental role helping businesses grow by growing loans. This has essentially been the case during the past several years when Wells has been under a regulatory mandate not to grow their balance sheet.

While I feel sure there are many pluses the regulators would offer as the benefits of the forced merger and death of Wachovia, my only question would be that in retrospect, knowing all we know today, was it worth the negative aspects of what we got? However, I would also be the first to admit that I am Monday morning quarterbacking, and when people are in the heat of battle, it is difficult to see the long-term implications of the decisions being made.

In any event, when December 31, 2008, came and Wachovia went away, there was hardly a tear shed for what had once been a great institution. Instead, the name was thrown on the junk pile along with Bear Stearns, Lehman and others as symbols of greed and excess. From my perspective,

Wachovia was anything but that, and I was in the know because I was on the inside. I did, in fact shed a tear and there will forever be a question in my mind about what could have been.

Carlos Evans

Chapter 33

Wells Fargo A New Culture

After a brief period of mourning the death of Wachovia, it was straight back to work full speed ahead. There was no time for anything but business because I had many things on my mind and balls in the air. The good news was that I had come full circle back into a functional line of business model where all of the foot soldiers reported to me , just as it had been during my time at Bank of America. At Wells, the functional model had been in place for many years. In my mind, this was a big improvement over the market president organization that had been in place for most of my time at Wachovia.

The Wells bankers I reported to, Tim Sloan and Dave Hoyt, were first rate, and I would say that there wasn't a dime's worth of difference in how we viewed running the business. They were very kind to me and gave me plenty of latitude to make my own decisions as to people and credit. As head of the middle market bank in the East, my loan authority was significantly increased to $250 million, and the loan authority of all my direct reports in the commercial banking executive roles rose to $50 million.

On the people front I picked up two new direct reports from the Wells side. Marybeth Howe was a great banker in Detroit with responsibility for Michigan, Ohio, and Indiana. Paul Kalsbeek in St Louis had the middle part of the country and was a great banker as well. Aside from those two all my other direct reports were the same as they were in the Wachovia days, including Phil Smith who was running the combined municipal finance and government and institutional banking business nationwide. I was also successful in bringing Howard Halle back from California and putting him in his old role as commercial banking executive for Florida. My one disappointment on the people front was that Guy Bodine and Bill Wilson in Texas no longer reported to me because Texas was part of the West. I tried my best to find roles for them, but since they were not going to leave their home state, my options were limited.

While there was much to like about my new boss, Tim Sloan, and his boss Dave Hoyt, who ran all the wholesale businesses and was effectively responsible for $10 billion of Wells Fargo's earnings (essentially 50% of Wells Fargo's overall financial results), there were some early signs of a potentially fatal flaw in the Wells culture.

Wells Fargo in many respects had grown out of Minneapolis based Norwest Bank that had been led by Dick Kovacevich, a highly regarded CEO who engineered the merger of equals between Norwest and Wells in June 1988 to create a $200 billion bank. The headquarters had moved from Minneapolis to San Francisco, and the new company took the Wells name. While Paul Haven the CEO of Wells became Chairman, Dick Kovacevich the president and COO really ran the company. Many of the old Norwest executives moved with Dick to San Francisco and took senior positions in the combined company.

Dick, in many respects was like Hugh McColl, very outspoken and loved by the troops in the field. Kovacevich was also a great banker and very much involved in running the bank at all levels. He spent a lot of time in the field with employees and customers, and while he believed in a decentralized operating structure, he was very hands-on about everything. Under Kovacevich, Wells adopted a mantra of "run it like you own it," which in my opinion was a great way to run a big company, as long as there was some level of centralized oversight. Dick Kovacevich essentially was the oversight factor because he was incredibly involved and "in the know" about everything going on in all the businesses.

Under John Stumpf, the CEO after Kovacevich, "run it like you own it" morphed into something slightly different which was, "You stay out of my business, and I will stay out of yours." Since Stump (in my humble opinion) was a 50-thousand-foot guy as opposed to Kovacevich who was hands on, there were no checks and balances if a major business started straying off course. This dynamic was somewhat similar to Bank of America after Hugh McColl retired, when without Hugh to check the dog-eat-dog, winner-take-all culture the bank morphed into something else and became every man or woman for themselves.

In particular, people were either afraid or unwilling to speak up, so they just parroted what they thought the leadership wanted to hear. Culture corroded in that manner created a situation where the leader could believe that things were just great even though "Rome was burning." Ultimately, this kind fatal flaw in a culture is the leader's own making because the tone is set from the top, and the leader is responsible for the culture. Any culture without candor and without leaders who promote and encourage people to speak up even when their view differs from the leader's is flawed from the start and will fail.

Wells Fargo under Kovacevich had an incredible sense of confidence that mirrored the confidence of its leader. However, while Dick certainly exhibited significant confidence, in my few interactions with him, I also always sensed his humility. However, without Dick at the helm, the confidence became borderline arrogance, and nowhere was that on display more than in the merger integration with Wachovia. Unlike the First Union/Wachovia merger integration that involved the sharing of different models and processes, and the careful choosing of the best ones, with Wells it was essentially "our way or the highway."

The one exception was the government and institutional banking business combined with municipal finance where they chose to implement the model we were running under Phil Smith. All in all, however, Tim Sloan was a great boss, and since we pretty much saw eye to eye on how to run the business and how to lend money there was very little friction and almost no drama which suited me fine. After the events of the "weekend at the adoption agency," I was ready to get back to the basics of helping customers grow their business and create the win-win. So that is what I did.

By early 2009 we were hitting the ground running on all fronts having transitioned to the Wells model with the regional commercial banking offices (RCBOs) reporting to the commercial banking executives who reported to me. We never missed a beat through the transition as we were steadily growing the business and enhancing our overall profitability along the way.

One casualty of the Wells purchase of Wachovia was our relationship with Greenwich Associates, which was borne out of the disdain the Wells people had for consultants. Interestingly, I never viewed David Fox and his team as consultants but more as partners and advisors. Since the Wells team pretty much thought they had all the answers about how customers viewed them, the partnership with Greenwich fell by the wayside, and I was unable to get any interest from San Francisco in using them.

Neither did they want to continue my focus on customer acquisition which had been so productive during the Wachovia years. Aside from those two things, however, it was pretty much business as usual, and I fell right back into my old habits of spending a great deal of time in all the markets calling on customers with our people.

In addition to my responsibilities at the bank I was also knee deep in all the problems at United Way. By early 2009 we were moving at light speed to implement all the recommendations to improve governance coming out of the task force led by Bob Sink. All in all, there were 30 or so recommendations, including a stipulation that all the prior board members would step down over a two year period so that by 2010 a total turnover in the board was completed. This was necessary in order to restore confidence in the agency, and it ultimately meant that I would step down as well.

Nevertheless, the threat from the lawsuit against United Way and me personally lingered, and it took several years to get to a point where we could finally settle it. The fact that I was the only person who had context for all the issues involved in the suit required me to remain engaged with our lawyers in trying to resolve the matter for another year after I had stepped down as board chair. In addition to revamping governance and the United Way board, we also recruited a new CEO. In the end, we selected Jane McIntire, the former CEO of the YWCA, one of the agencies United Way supported. Jane was a dynamic leader and the perfect person to start the process of rebuilding confidence and trust.

In addition to working with United Way in 2009, Lisa and I spent time ramping up our involvement with nonprofits in South Carolina, where I would eventually become chair of the Spoleto Festival USA board and the Medical University of S.C. Foundation Board. Both activities took us to Charleston a great deal; we would come in on a Thursday night, attend board meetings Friday morning, then have a nice long weekend at our home there.

There were also many trips to Lake Summit on weekends where we would entertain friends and family. Both Charleston and Lake Summit provided a great escape for what was a very hectic schedule during the week, with business travels that had become even more demanding, including frequent trips to San Francisco to "Report In."

All in all, life was good as I was enjoying my interactions with Tim Sloan and Dave Hoyt. In addition, there was the added benefit that with Wells Fargo's growing earnings the stock price began to dramatically recover, and I could begin to see that one day the stock options I had been given in joining the team would have real value and allow our family to recover some of our losses in Wachovia's stock.

By the end of 2009 things were finally getting back to normal. With the problems at United Way resolved I could focus 100% of my time and effort on business. On January 1, 2010, I opened the Charlotte Observer to see that I had been named as one of the people to be thankful for in Charlotte during the past year.

The article read "At a time when his bank, Wachovia was in distress then gobbled up by Wells Fargo, executive Carlos Evans was neck deep in another crisis, chairing the board of United Way of Central Carolinas—possibly the most thankless job in town. In many people's minds the venerable charity was badly tainted in 2008 by revelations that its board approved more than $1.2 million in pay for the then-CEO Gloria Pace King. The double whammy of the pay scandal and the fall's financial crisis sent UW donations into a nose-dive, forcing big cuts in funding for its 90-some member agencies. For months Evans was its chief apologist/spokesman/reformer, badgered by journalist and assailed by an angry public. Yet when he steps off the board today, he leaves a new executive director, Jane McIntire, a new and smaller board, and giant steps along the path toward regaining community trust in the agency. Evans recalls how former Wachovia CEO Ken Thompson asked him back in 2006 or 2007 to get in line to be the board chair. "If I'd known then what I know now," he says, "I would do it again. While an incredibly difficult experience for me, the time going through the crisis at United Way was also very rewarding. Over the course of my career I have always encouraged people to get involved and to take up leadership roles in community. My feelings then and now are that aside from just doing the right thing, community service is a great way to sharpen and improve one's leadership skills. As I have explained many times to up-and-coming management talent, at work, people follow you because they have to. They know you control both the carrot (ability to pay) and the stick (ability to fire). In the community, they don't have to follow. Creating followership on nonprofit boards is the ultimate leadership challenge because you no longer have the leverage of the carrot or the stick. You have to build followership on your own merits. One of the best ways to build followership is to mentor and help other people, especially women and minorities, to rise up through the organization. Much like in my business dealings, if people sense that you have their true best interests at heart, they will be drawn to you. One of the best ways to show your people you are that way is to pick people and nurture them in a way that others can see. Especially when they are people who might be otherwise disadvantaged. If you do that often enough and long enough, it becomes part of your persona, and people will trust you to always behave that way."

In early 2010, I was asked to be one of the presenters at the first ever Wells Fargo investor conference. It was amazing to me that Wells had never done investor meetings, but in the past, they had always taken the position that they let their numbers do the talking. I thought it had been another sign of a little arrogance creeping into the culture. That silence contrasted with Wachovia where we were on the circuit every quarter talking with the analysts, and I was used to making regular presentations as the head of one of the large business lines.

I remember very clearly sitting in the large meeting room beside my boss Tim Sloan, while Carrie Tolstedt, the head of the community/consumer bank presented. All she talked about was the dramatic increases in the number of new checking accounts the bank had opened. There was zero mention of the profitability or the value of the business being booked. As I heard her raving about the numbers, I remembered past conversations with senior leaders of Wachovia consumer where I would ask about profitability. The response was always the same; they told me they were only measured by the number of widgets they produced, much like a manufacturing company. Apparently, no one on that side of the bank was measured by a profit and loss statement. I found it remarkable since these were senior executives running big territories.

I leaned over and whispered to Tim Sloan, "Why no mention of the profitability and relative size of these accounts?"

He whispered back, "Carrie is the best consumer banker in the country. Keep quiet."

To be very clear, at that point I had no clue about the problems with unauthorized account openings that was building inside the Wells Fargo consumer branches. All I knew was that to only measure the absolute number of account openings without regard to the quality or size of the deposits being generated made absolutely no sense. I reckoned back to my days as a branch manager where the monthly activity reports took into consideration both the number of account openings and also the size. I also knew from my experience with the animal hunt that it was necessary to factor in size and absolute levels of profitability for new customers, and also that managers needed to check behind their people to make sure they were reporting correctly.

So, despite the chiding I received from Tim Sloan about Carrie's presentation, I knew from a pure business point of view that it didn't make sense. As it turned out, it was even worse than I thought. The consumer bank put so much weight on each branch employee meeting their quota of checking account openings that people who fell short would not qualify for a bonus. Simply stated, it was a terrible way to run a business and totally unfair to the employees. Years later in 2016, some two years after my retirement, when I learned what was going on I reflected on that day at the investor conference and Carrie's presentation.

Wells would go on to suffer incredible negative repercussions from the whole episode, and while much negative publicity would occur touting the harm to customers, the real loser in the whole matter was Wells itself. If I understand correctly, branch managers were opening checking accounts with $10 from a customer's savings account and waiving all the service charges and minimum deposit requirements. It's been reported that in almost every case, the branch managers would have spoken with bank customers who had said something like, "Let me think about it." Clearly, such responses did not indicate that the customers had given authorization, however the branch managers would proceed with the account opening.

Even though service charges, fees and minimum deposit requirements were waived and the customers were not harmed, it was still a violation and was particularly problematic given the number of unauthorized account openings. It has been reported that the number was in excess of 2 million accounts opened in that manner. If that number is even close to accurate, Wells was the big looser because it costs a bank about $250 per year to keep a checking account open due to the cost of producing and mailing statements, reporting, doing the accounting etc. etc.

Thus, Wells would have been losing about $500 million per year on 2 million $10 accounts. Just plain stupid and bad business. The bigger sin was that they had an unfair incentive plan that drove otherwise honest people to do bad things, and thousands of young branch employees lost their jobs as a result. Worse yet, the arrogant part of the Wells culture and the "We Have All the Answers" attitude caused them to push back on the regulators and dig a deeper hole for themselves as opposed to doing a total Mea Culpa the way we did at United Way.

Two years after my retirement when Tim Sloan became CEO, I wrote him a long email of congratulations, but I also advised him that they needed to clean house with the board in order to clear the slate. Knowing the Wells organizational structure the way I did, it was clear to me that Tim had nothing to do with the missteps in the consumer bank, but the Board and ex-CEO John Stumpf certainly did because those violations occurred under their watch. Tim wrote me a nice note back, but it was clear to me he would not take my advice. Sadly, his inaction is what I believe ultimately cost him his job. Tim had been a great banker, and it was an unnecessary shame that he ended his career by stepping down.

In retrospect, it was obvious to me that the hubris of the Wells culture would not let them own up to their huge mistake. Rather than fessing up and cleaning the slate, it cost John Stumpf his CEO job and then Tim Sloan his CEO job several years later. It should have cost the entire board their jobs because they were in charge when the incentive plans were put in place, and they were at fault for failing to recognize the deeply flawed way in which the consumer bank was being run.

Sometime in 2010 I received a call from Phil Smith that gave me great pause. By then our government and institutional banking business under his leadership was beginning to hum along. In addition, the municipal bond business was making huge progress and steadily moving up in the league tables. Therefore, Phil's call took me by total surprise because the moment I picked up the phone I could tell he was worried.

Phil said, "Carlos, as you know, we've been working down our exposure to Puerto Rico."

"Yes," I replied, "last time I looked we had about $300 million of exposure and we want to take that number lower."

The phone was dreadfully silent. Finally, Phil spoke again, "Your numbers are right except for one problem. Years before I got here, back when public finance reported up through the Wachovia investment bank, we did a $500 million bond deal that is maturing this summer. When the deal was done, we took $50 million and sold $450 million to institutional investors, but we also gave a put to the investors allowing them to sell the bonds back to us as maturity approached. Therefore, our exposure isn't $50 million, it's actually $500 million since we might have to buy back all those bonds."

I gasped at the number because this would mean we had $750 million at risk to a credit that was beginning to have problems. While the Puerto Rico Port Authority was arguably a better credit than Puerto Rico itself given its different revenue streams tied to the cruise ship industry and shipping in general, it was a staggering amount of money to have out to an instrumentality of a struggling government. Phil and I concluded that the only thing we could do was to start underwriting a new bond issue without a put to refund the old one, and we had to hope we could put a high enough yield on the new bonds that greed would take over and people would buy the paper. That is exactly what we did, and we all let out a huge sigh of relief when the refunding issue successfully sold out. Phil continued to reduce our exposure to Puerto Rico so that by the time I left the bank, we were pretty much clear of any risk. For me it was a valuable lesson in something all bankers should know, which is when the principal value of a bond or loan is at risk of loss, no amount of yield can make you whole.

In early 2011 Tim Sloan was promoted to be the CFO of Wells Fargo. For me, it meant that I would now report to the person who was running the commercial bank West of the Mississippi. All my direct reports would remain the same, so there was absolutely no change in my responsibilities. However, it created a significant change in the working relationship because my new boss was no longer Tim Sloan.

The first sign of a problems came when the guy in the West didn't choose Mike Carlin to be the new chief risk officer for commercial banking. Instead, he chose a crony of his. I remember many occasions on credit approval calls where it would become immediately apparent by his questions that the new senior credit officer had not read the package. This is a cardinal sin in management. People worked long hours to prepare documentation for credit approval, and to not read the material in advance was a total disregard for that effort. In addition, answering questions which have already been addressed in the material wasted everyone's time since on many of these calls there were 6 to 8 people on the phone. Aside from the new senior credit officer being not experienced enough, Mike Carlin now had to report to this individual, which was humiliating at best since, in my opinion, Mike could run circles around him and everyone knew it.

This was but one of many personnel decisions that would ensue in which old Wells Fargo cronies were chosen for important roles, and capable leaders from the Wachovia side were passed over. For me, since I had been clear with Tim Sloan and Dave Hoyt about my intent to work for only 5 or 6 years after the merger, while working under this new leader was painful, I could deal with it. My time at Wells was getting shorter and shorter every day that went by. However, it was difficult to watch what I thought were bad decisions being made every day, and to make matters worse, it became clear that the new leader resented my being there. I thought the whole thing was totally ridiculous, since everyone knew I was not a threat to him, and my time was limited. Everyone also knew that my only interest was in making our business better and in taking care of the employees and customers that we depended on. Nevertheless, the arrogance that was very much part of the Wells culture came into full view with this new leader, and to some extent made my last three years there less enjoyable.

During 2012 and 2013, I spent a lot of time in the field growing our business. I was also by this time chairman of Spoleto Festival USA and the Medical University of S.C. Foundation so there were many visits to our second home in Charleston, and of course, Lake Summit. Wells Fargo's earnings were skyrocketing because of all our successes, and as a byproduct the stock was also skyrocketing. By early 2014 I began to think seriously about retirement. I put a stake in the ground in my own mind and decided that I wanted to leave the week before Memorial Day so Lisa and I could go to Charleston and enjoy the full 17 days of Spoleto Festival in my last year as chair, but I kept all of this to myself.

In March of 2014, my boss came to Charlotte. We had dinner, and after the meal, he asked when I was thinking about retiring. It was an interesting moment because I knew that had been the real reason for his trip. I said that when he told me what my bonus and stock grants would be for that year, I would tell him what my plans were. I said I needed to know what my resources were before I could make any decision on retirement. At Wells Fargo, bonuses and stock grants were usually approved by the board in March and paid out at the end of March or by mid-April.

He responded that he couldn't tell me because they weren't yet approved by the board. I said, "Come on, you know the Wells board is a rubber stamp. The bank just finished its best year ever, so the board isn't going to refuse the recommended bonuses and stock grants. Besides, if they don't approve it for some reason, I won't hold you to the number."

At that point he told me my bonus and stock grant would be the same as the previous year.

The truth was, throughout this conversation I simply didn't trust the man to do the right thing. If I had told him I was leaving, I felt sure he would have shorted me on my compensation. After he gave me the number, I told him I would retire the week before Memorial Day.

The next part of the conversation became very interesting. He told me that the bank wanted to retain my services in a consulting capacity by giving me title, a stipend, and an expense account. They also wanted to give me a big sendoff party in Charlotte. I could easily see through the scheme because this was all about trying to buy my credibility with the employees and customers.

I responded, "While I'm flattered and honored by your offer," (a lie) "However, I don't want to compromise myself because there are boards I may have the opportunity to serve on, and if I'm on the Wells payroll I can't be objective in giving customers financing advice," (the truth).

"You sure you don't want the retirement party?" he asked. "There are many people who would want to send you off in style."

I told him, "I'll tell them all goodbye in my own way. If you want to do something to honor me, make a gift to my alma mater, Newberry College." Of course, they never did

That was it. The meeting ended, and I left feeling energized about the next chapter in my life. I also felt good that I was leaving on my own terms, unlike the experience at Bank of America in August of 2000.

In truth, as early as the summer 2011 the working relationship with my new boss had reached the point where I considered leaving. I received a very attractive offer from Citicorp to head up their North American commercial banking business. It was a very attractive offer with a lot of money and stock. I still have the offer letter and look at it to this day and sometimes wonder, what if? However, during this period Lisa's father, Walker, became very ill. The combination of me needing to help Lisa as we took care of her father coupled with my loyalty to the team I had built from the old Wachovia, many of whom were still there with Wells, gave me second thoughts. At the end of the day, I chose not to take the job. While part of me wanted to go back to war against the arrogance at Wells just as I had done 11 years earlier when I was fired from Bank of America, the other side of me said I needed to remain loyal to the team I had built.

Besides, I knew in my heart that despite all the promises they were making, I felt like Citicorp really didn't understand the middle market business and that getting them to make all the changes necessary to compete would be a long uphill battle. In the end, I turned to offer down and decided to devote my remaining years to taking care of my team and building the business for Wells despite some of the issues I was having with management. In retrospect, it was a good decision as Lisa's father passed away in late August 2011, and not taking the new job gave me the time I needed to support her and her mother Joyce, who by that point was also suffering from dementia.

In the remaining two months I traveled extensively and said my goodbyes to employees and customers. On my way out the door I sent a letter to all my teammates telling them what an honor it had been to work with them through the good times and the bad, especially the stress that had come in 2008. The week before Memorial Day in May 2014, I quietly walked out the door excited about the next chapter. I thought about my father and the encouragement he had given me on his deathbed when he had told me not leave my career too soon or on someone else's terms.

His encouragement had made a huge difference in my life because I had enjoyed a full second career at Wachovia/Wells Fargo. I also knew, as he had trained me, that I had done my absolute best. I knew that because of my efforts and the efforts of my team members, jobs had been created, communities had benefitted and that many of the entrepreneurs I had helped along the way had been able to realize their dreams. In short, I was leaving totally fulfilled!!

Carlos Evans

Chapter 34

Reflections on Banking and on Corporate Culture

After 17 days in Charleston for Spoleto Festival, Lisa and I headed to Lake Summit to recharge and reflect. When we checked our mail on our way back through Charlotte there were many letters of congratulations from teammates, customers, and friends. Reading all those letters which I still have today gave me a much greater appreciation for how fortunate I had been to have a first career at Bankers Trust/NCNB/NationsBank/ Bank of America and then a second shot with Wachovia/Wells Fargo.

During the time Lisa and I were in Charleston, three of my friends, Charlie Way the developer of Kiawah, Joel Smith my old boss from Bank of America, and my dear friend Tom Anderson head of the Medical University Foundation held a little retirement party for me. In attendance were about 50 or so entrepreneurs who I had worked with through the years. I was humbled by the group because they reflected what I had devoted my life to over some 41 years. As I saw each one of them, memories flooded back of deals, and the many opportunities to create jobs and do good as a byproduct of working with them to create the win-win. In my brief comments I told them that for 41 years I had been lucky to have the best job on the planet.

I told them that serving entrepreneurs had been both an honor and a privilege, and that throughout my career there had never been any confusion about who we were there to serve and who was the most important cog in the wheel. Without entrepreneurs who put up the risk capital and their commitment of time, energy, reputation, and talent as they risked it all, there would have been no loans and no transactions. Without transactions there would have been no new jobs created and there would have been no rising tide that raised all boats. I asked the question: Are banks important? By all means yes, I said, but only to the extent that we understood our role which was to add a little oil to the wheel.

Entrepreneurs themselves, are the wheel. They were during my career, and they will be in the future. That evening, as Lisa, Blake and I left the party, I felt incredibly fulfilled for the second time in a few short months. I knew that I had worked in an honorable profession. I also realized I was just one of many people working hard every day in the banking field. I also reflected that the banking profession somewhere along the line, either justly or unjustly, had acquired a bad reputation. I decided to file that away for future consideration.

Following Spoleto, Lisa and I retreated to Lake Summit where we spent three weeks, the longest time ever without having to go anywhere else. Days were spent taking long walks, bike rides along the flat dirt road that circles the lake, and paddling my kayak up and down the lake with no predetermined destination in mind. Stunning views of the mountains surrounded the lake in every direction.

During these three weeks I had plenty of time for thought and reflection. As I thought about my career, I knew that I had been but one of many people doing the same thing in the banking industry. I also knew that most of my peers were essentially performing the same role and approached the business the same way, working hard to help their customers. If that was an accurate assumption, then why did the industry have such a bad rap? Everyone knew that coming out of 2008 banking had a terrible reputation.

Essentially, the predominant school of thought was that bankers were the problem and that their greed had created the Great Recession. Even Wachovia, a bank that had a wonderful legacy of doing the right thing, had become tainted with this stain of greed and avarice. As I thought about all this, I concluded that it had to be the result of the corporate cultures exemplified by some of the big banks at a time when they had become highly visible for all to see.

In many respects, I view corporate culture as the personality and character of an institution. A company with a flawed culture is just like a person having a bad personality trait or a flawed character. With an individual, a flawed personality trait or character will sometimes lead to bad things happening, and the same is true of corporations. But even if bad things don't happen, those flaws will inhibit or preclude the individual, or institution, from reaching their full potential.

Every person knows individuals who fit that mold of falling short of what they could be because of a personality or character flaw. We also know of individuals who might not be the smartest people in the room but who achieve great success because of outstanding personality and character traits.

As I thought about the personalities and character of the companies I had worked with over the years—Bankers Trust, the old NCNB which became NationsBank, then Bank of America, and Wachovia which became Wells Fargo—I reflected on the stark differences. Bankers Trust and Wachovia were cultures rooted in a set of values based on helping the people we served, the communities and states we served, as well as valuing teamwork, mutual respect, and collaboration. NCNB/Bank of America and Wells Fargo were cultures largely derived from the influence of a strong individual leader, and while workable for a period of time became unsustainable.

Another great example of that scenario is GE, which under Jack Welch appeared to be a powerhouse but under subsequent leadership became something else. I think many students of high performing companies would argue that having a good strong appropriate corporate culture is one of the keys to success. In the case of Bankers Trust, it was a smashing financial success, and when it merged with NCNB the shareholder returns over a long period of time were exceptional. Since I invested in Bankers Trust Stock through our 401k, much of what our family has today goes all the way back to that success. In the case of Wachovia, we put up incredible numbers up until the crisis in 2008, and I have already described how I feel about that whole event. I put Wachovia in the category of "Sometimes Bad Things Happen To Good People." It had perhaps the best corporate culture I ever encountered, but in the end was it put out of business. In the case of Wells and Bank Of America, while many of their leaders would argue that they had a great culture, the facts would prove otherwise. I sold all my Wells Fargo stock and options in 2014 at $55 per share, and while it has traded somewhat higher for short periods, it has essentially been a dead asset through one of the greatest bull markets in history. In the case of Bank of America, I sold all my stock in 2005 at $55 per share (55 must be my lucky number), and it likewise has not consistently returned to that level in 16 years. Another dead asset. Some might blame the poor performance on the financial crisis, but I would point to JP Morgan Chase which has significantly outperformed the market in that same period of time.

Many would argue that stock price is not the only measure of a company's value and contribution to society, and I would agree. However, as a bank that is competing in what is essentially a service Industry, I would argue that customer service is another key measure. On that score, I would only simply say that since retiring I have had the honor and privilege of serving on a number of boards of middle market companies. These companies do business with all the banks including Wells and Bank of America. I would describe the service, or business execution of these two banks as schizophrenic at best. I believe their lack of consistent performance goes all the way back to their flawed culture, namely the absence of a burning drive to create the win-win and do what is right, not just for the bank but for the customers as well. I can only hope that these two banks will eventually get it right. Between them, they control close to 20% of the nation's deposits so the country needs them to get it right. Entrepreneurs need them to get it right.

Fortunately, in the case of entrepreneurs, they have other options in the many up and coming regional Banks like South State Bank and Comerica, which are getting it right. My guess is that a thorough study of middle market share would show that Wells and Bank of America have given ground to their smaller competitors. This would be another indicator that something has been off at these two institutions.

In some respects, what happened at my two former employers happens all the time in business. As companies in any industry get larger and larger, it becomes harder for them to maintain the personal touch and deliver their products or services in a customer-centric way. It seems the bigger a company becomes, the more rules they tend to put in place. These rules may be an attempt to protect financial results, but they also tend to stifle the entrepreneurial approach which originally made the company great. While it no doubt creates greater management challenges, big banks can maintain high level service and execute in a personal manner. I know this, because I did it inside a big bank over many years.

While the above discussion of cultures is not intended to imply that Wells and Bank of America display the level of greed and flawed cultures exemplified in the failure of Bear Stearns and Lehman Brothers, the fact is that most of the big banks have done little to portray themselves in a more positive way. As a result, the industry has been painted with the same broad brush and unfortunately, while most bankers are honest, hardworking people who strive to take care of their customers, the negative connotation and perception created by a few flawed characters persists and unfortunately taints the business as a whole.

As I thought of all these things during my final week "On Golden Pond," I realized that my time for trying to do something about it was done. I also realized I needed to get on with the next chapter of my life, and while it was not in my nature to sit on the sideline and quietly retire, I had no clue what I might do next. I did, however, leave after those wonderful three weeks at Lake Summit suntanned, rejuvenated, energized, relaxed and excited about what the next chapter would reveal!

Carlos Evans

Chapter 35

A New Career On The Back Nine

When Lisa and I returned to Charlotte, I went to work on my personal affairs taking care of many things that I had neglected. We redid our Wills, and I also activated a family LLC which I established in 2000 when my dad died to hold some of the investments I had made over the years. For some time, I'd had the idea of forming family business with Blake where we could make investments together in operating companies as well as in real estate, mostly with people we knew where we would be investing side by side with capable operators.

At that time Blake was working in Charlotte for Sun Trust Bank and living with us at home to save rent, so we could easily confer on potential investment opportunities and make decisions together. Blake has an incredible mind and is an excellent assessor of risk. Unlike his dad, he tends to be more on the conservative side, so we make a good combination.

In addition to the new opportunities, I had a portfolio of existing real estate deals mostly on Hilton Head Island where I had co-invested with my dear friend Jim Bradshaw. Those investments consisted mostly of small commercial income properties including some retail, office, warehouse, and several medical office buildings. By far the biggest investments were two large mini warehouse or self-storage facilities on Hilton Head, and we were getting ready to start a third in Bluffton.

Thus, much of that summer of 2014 was spent doing the legal and accounting work necessary to set up this new entity with my son. We named it Salem Capital LLC after Salem Crossroads where my dad's country store was located and where my brother and I had spent every summer as teenagers working in tobacco. As the fall approached Lisa and I were also making frequent trips to Charleston given my involvement with Spoleto Festival USA and the Medical University of S.C. By this time, Lisa was also starting to get involved with nonprofit work in South Carolina in keeping with the commitment we had both made some years earlier.

By early fall things also began to heat up on the board front when I was approached by two former customers to join their Boards. One was George Dean Johnson in Spartanburg who had been a large customer both at Wells Fargo and Bank of America. George and his family have many investments in hotels, apartments, self-storage, industrial warehouses, and private equity, as well as an auto finance company called American Credit Acceptance. Aside from being a great businessman, he is also a dear friend, so when he asked if I would serve, I immediately said yes. The other offer came from Temple Sloan in Raleigh, former chairman of the executive committee of Bank of America and also a very good customer and friend during my time at both Bank of America as well as Wachovia/Wells Fargo.

Temple's family and his brother Ham's family own three separate companies that operate nationwide. National Coatings and Supplies is in the auto paint distribution business; American Welding and Supply is in the industrial gas business; and Warren Oil Company is in lubricants. All three companies have significant employee stock ownership, so they are all managed with the governance infrastructure of public companies. Given my knowledge of Temple and his family, I immediately said yes to his offer as well.

I knew that one of the side benefits to be gained from my service on the boards for the Johnson and Sloan Families would be the opportunity to learn from both men. They are two of the smartest entrepreneurs and businesspeople I have known, and over the years I have come to know and respect their families as well. In both situations, their sons and daughters are now taking over the businesses, and they are great people as well.

In both cases when the offers were extended, I never asked about directors fees. The truth is I would have done both for free, and at the time I wasn't aware that these particular companies would pay directors. All I knew was that I wanted to be part of their team, and I could learn a lot from both men. Aside from the personal relationships, I felt like it would be good to once again be part of something that would give me the same sense of working to create the win-win. Now, it would be more from an owner's perspective, but the sense of satisfaction would be the same, the sense of knowing that the company was creating jobs and helping people fulfill their dreams.

As I would later learn, there would also be opportunities to co-invest with both families which could be financially attractive. By serving on both boards, I have had the honor and privilege to be part of enterprises that have created thousands of jobs. For my part, since both family business models involve using a lot of bank debt, I have hopefully added some value by helping to structure loan packages designed to achieve the best outcomes.

Perhaps more important than the business involvement has been the friendships that have grown as a result. While both men were good friends and customers during my banking years, the relationships have only strengthened through my board involvements. In fact, during the dark days after I was fired from Bank of America, both George and Temple along with Tommy Teague and Charlie Way were the first to call to offer their support and willingness to do business with me when I landed at Wachovia. Their support and encouragement were key to my being able to land on my feet.

In fact, in my darkest hours over the weekend after I had been fired, George Dean Johnson sent me a personal handwritten note. I still have it today. It read, "Dear Carlos, 1.) Thank you for being our friend, banker, constructive critic and partner. 2.) We want to support you in any venture or business where you want us involved. 3.) We admire you as a person and as a businessman. 4.) This is a great opportunity for you and your family. Embrace and welcome change. It is hard to do. 5.) Focus on Blake and Lisa. 5.) We are loyal to you." It was signed, "George."

Little did I know in those trying times during August of 2000 that just as George said in his note, it would end up being a great opportunity, and I would have a second bite at the apple with Wachovia and Wells that would lead to a much larger role and the opportunity to have significantly greater impact in my chosen field. One thing I know for sure, however, is that the support from friends like George, Temple, Charlie and Tommy are what enabled me to get through to the other side. Their statements of loyalty and support along with my faith and steadfast support and encouragement from Lisa and Blake are what got me through.

As to faith, there is a brief story that pretty much sums up my feelings about how one navigates the low points in life. It is called "Footprints In The Sand."

One night I dreamed I was walking along the beach with The Lord. Many scenes of my life flashed across the sky. In each scene I noticed footprints in the sand. Sometimes there were two sets of footprints, other times there was one set of footprints.

This bothered me because I noticed that during the low periods of my life, when I was suffering from anguish, sorrow or defeat, I could only see one set of footprints.

So I said to The Lord, "You promised me Lord, that if I followed you, you would walk with me always. But I have noticed that during the most trying periods of my life there has only been one set of footprints. Why when I have needed you the most you have not been there for me?"

The Lord replied, "The times when you have seen only one set of footprints was when I carried you."

I think that little story pretty much sums up my view of faith with one caveat. Early in my life during my youth there were certainly times when I was feeling abandoned. However, somewhere along the line my faith grew to the point where that feeling of abandonment was no longer there. Even in darkest times of my life, I have been comforted by the knowledge that He is there for us. In my case, the combination of that faith along with support from family and friends has made all the difference. So when given the opportunity to help those who had helped me, of course I said yes, with pleasure.

Shortly after joining the Johnson Management board as well as the Sloan Family boards, I was asked by Temple to consider joining the Highwoods Board in Raleigh N.C., where Temple was the chairman and lead outside director. Highwoods is a REIT listed on the New York Stock Exchange that owns large office buildings mainly in the Southeast. At the time the company was run by Ed Fritsch, who was also the incoming chair of NAREIT which is the national association for the REIT industry. After interviews with Ed and the other member of the management team at Highwoods, the chairman and I were invited to join that board, and as of this writing, I am now the lead outside director.

Ally of the Entrepreneur

In early 2016 through James Macleod, a friend from Hilton Head Island I was invited to meet the CEO Sykes Enterprises. Headquartered in Tampa, Florida, Sykes is a third-party customer service outsource provider. Chuck Sykes is the CEO and son of the company's founder, John Sykes, who started the business in Charlotte. In my early years at NCNB Sykes had been a customer before they went public and listed on the NASDAQ, so I knew the history of the company well. By the time I met Chuck in 2016, Sykes was a totally different business with over 60,000 employees and call centers around the world. After additional interviews with the other board members, I was invited to join the Sykes board as well. Given my background, I initially chaired the finance committee. Later, I also chaired the special committee which ultimately led to the sale of Sykes to Sitel, a privately owned French company, at a significant premium above the average trading price before the sale,

In 2016, a headhunter, who had been referred to me by my old Wachovia boss Ben Jenkins, offered me the opportunity to join a Goldman Sachs fund board. The fund was a 40-Act private fund raised and managed by a team of specialty lenders who run a similar public entity traded on the New York Stock Exchange under the symbol GSBD. After interviews in New York with management, I was invited to join that Board, which has since merged with the public entity where I now serve as a board member. The fund makes leveraged middle market loans under the Business Development Company (BDC) business model. Since I spent my entire career lending money in the middle market space this board has been a great fit for my skill set. More importantly, my involvement in the fund world has been a great learning experience as has the exposure to the management team at Goldman Sachs who are exceptional. Unfortunately, due to over regulation banks can no longer make leveraged loans so an entire industry of specialty BDC lenders has been created. I have since joined 3 other BDC fund boards. I have enjoyed being a participant in this activity as a Board member where I am hopefully adding value.

While some might say being on two private family office boards and three public company boards is too much, I have not found it a burden. Over the length of my entire baking career, I was bombarded by a constant flow of numbers and information on a much larger scale, and in the case of the two family boards, they were businesses that I was already intimately familiar with. Since I had been their banker before retiring, the learning curve was very short and easy even though the businesses are complex. As to the public companies, the four quarterly meetings for each company per year are no problem for someone who was used to constant travel all over the USA. So, while I stay busy there is plenty of time for personal enjoyment and other projects. However, on a positive note, my board involvement has given me the sense of belonging to groups of people who are working to build enterprises where I can make a contribution based on the knowledge I accumulated through my years in banking. I love the pace, and I love staying in the flow. I welcome every financial report and enjoy the interaction with the two families and board members at the three public companies. I cannot imagine what my life would be without these associations, involvements, and the sense of being part of these capable teams of people all working to do something of value.

Aside from the for-profit board work, in 2017 I ended my term as chair of the Medical University Foundation board. At a retirement celebration on August 18, 2017, I was presented with the "Order of The Palmetto" for distinguished service to the State of South Carolina, recognizing my work at the Medical University Foundation but also Spoleto Festival USA. My dear Friend Tom Anderson, executive director of the Medical University Foundation, presented the award representing MUSC, as did my friend Charlie Way representing Spoleto Festival USA. It was a special evening for Lisa, Blake and me, one that I will never forget.

Aside from the board work my life "On The Back Nine" has also been full of special projects. In 2015 Lisa and I purchased an old beach house at Debordieu Beach just North of Georgetown, South Carolina. While it had been lovingly constructed in the early 80's by its only owners, the house needed a lot of work. Since the sellers were well into their 90's when we made the purchase, much recent maintenance had been left undone. The renovation project occupied most of 2015 and 2016, but our family has thoroughly enjoyed the use of the house since. It is a special place where one cannot help but appreciate the majesty of God's creation on the beach and in the inlets, marshes, and creeks. It has also become a special place for friends and family to gather. We go there often as an escape from the hustle and bustle in Charleston since it's only an hour and 15 minutes north of the city.

Sometime in late 2017, I began to think about buying some land where we could grow pine trees and also have a place to hunt turkey's and ducks. My son Blake and I are avid bird hunters as is my brother Andy. I had learned something about growing pine trees through my board work with the Johnson Family since they have substantial timber holdings. Aside from the investment appeal, I also thought it would be a good way to spend more time with my brother Andy. While Andy, Melba and I had always remained close, I tended to see Melba more since she now lived in Charleston while Andy was in Florence. With my mother having passed away, our trips to Florence were infrequent at best. My thinking was that if Andy and I owned the farm together, we would see each other more, and it would be a great way to entertain our friends who also enjoy the outdoors.

My brother Andy is a wonderful man. He had to get married when he was in high school and was never able to go to college, however, while in his 50's, Andy was able to get his college degree online. He had to do the work at night after his day job, just like my father who had gotten his high school degree by going to night school. The day I attended his graduation I told him that his accomplishment made anything Melba and I had done pale in comparison. I was so proud of him that day as were my sister and mother. Aside, from being a hard worker and a good husband, father and family man, Andy is also a great cook, good storyteller, and as we say in South Carolina, he has great Bubba skills. I knew Andy would be the perfect partner to have in this new adventure with the farm.

Andy and I first started looking around Georgetown since my thinking was to have something close to the beach so we could stay at our beach house on hunting trips with friends. As we looked at properties it became more and more apparent that land was too expensive so close to the coast. We began to expand the search, and I saw a listing online for some property in Marion County about 20 minutes northeast of Florence. It was 215 acres with a small one-bedroom cabin, but it had a duck impoundment and a small pond next to the cabin. Andy went out to visit and called very excited. His comment was that the property was perfect for what we wanted and that I needed to come see it ASAP. Blake and I were at the Beach, so we decided to go by on our way back to Charlotte.

When we visited the property, it was clear that Andy's assessment was dead on. It was perfect, and the cabin could be easily expanded to add a great room with a fireplace off the kitchen as well as a second bedroom, bunk room, and a second bathroom making it able to sleep 6 or 7 quests. In researching the surrounding land, we might have an opportunity to purchase three additional 100 -acre tracts, all owned by cousins of the sellers.

Lastly, the icing on the cake was that the property was an hour and 20 minute drive from the beach and only 2 hours and 15 minutes from Charlotte. Since we would be in Charlotte mostly during hunting season, the proximity would be a big plus. So, Andy and I quickly purchased the property, then later we acquired the three additional 100-acre tracts giving us a total of 515 acres. We started construction on the cabin right away and built an equipment shed, and we had everything ready for that first hunting season.

We named the farm Salem for where our dad's store had been, and we named every landmark after places we had frequented as children and teenagers during those summers working in tobacco. The crossroads on the property where four roads come together became Salem Crossroad, and the different tracts of land received the names our uncles—the CC tract for Uncle Cedric, The Son and James tract after our uncles Son and James. The Hinds place for our grandmother's side of the family. Then there was Walnut Hill, Miss Gerts and Over The Swamp for different tracts of land that our uncles had farmed, as well as a Special Place for our Uncle Punk and of course The Creek. The House was named Evans Grocery after our father's store.

While Andy and I were hard at work to get things ready for that first fall season I also began to do some heavy research on our lineage and the Evans Family. My curiosity had been peaked by information I'd gotten from my cousin Chan Joye, who had studied our genealogy over many years. From Chan I had learned that our ancestors were originally from Wales, settling first in Pennsylvania then moving south before the Revolutionary War. In South Carolina, they started in Marion County before eventually moving across the Pee Dee River sometime after the Civil War into what is now Florence County near Salem Crossroads . As Chan and I began to share emails and phone calls, I learned that the farm Andy and I had just purchased was only 3 miles from Catfish Creek, in a section of Marion County otherwise known as the Welsh Neck which had been the Marion County home of our ancestors. The more I read and learned, the more I became fascinated by the coincidence of our purchase of the farm, it's location and proximity to where my father's side of our family had their start.

I also learned that many of our forefathers (26 of them to be exact) fought with General Francis Marion otherwise known the Swamp Fox. His secret encampment was just 10 miles downriver on the Pee Dee from our new farm on Snows Island. There he ran his operation to harass the British keeping Lord Cornwallis from marching north and trapping General Washington from the rear.

Much has been written through the years about the Swamp Fox, but I had no idea of my family's involvement and how important the residents of the Welsh Neck had been to General Marion in supplying needed food, supplies and manpower to conduct his operations. While I could go on and on, the most important thing I learned was just how difficult the fight to achieve our independence had been for our forefathers. Great sacrifices were made in the interest of freedom against monumental odds by a small group of people who one might say were the country's first entrepreneurs.

While most of them were farmers living off the land, they had risked everything to come to this country in the first place and then risked it all again to achieve independence. Those who supported the cause of independence would have lost their land, their livestock and in many cases their lives if their cause had failed. All of us owe much to those early Americans, and my awareness of that heavy debt is the reason I have no patience with people who dishonor our flag and our country. Such behavior fails to recognize the sacrifices of those who once gave so much.

Since finishing the farm, we have enjoyed many good times with friends and family. It is a gathering place where we can sit outside by the fireplace, look up at the stars and again marvel at God's creation. We cook steaks or other simple meals, then get up early in the morning and sit in a duck blind where we relish the sunrise. It is also a place where Andy and I can think about our ancestors and their sacrifices and honor them in our own way.

Since completing the renovations, we have planted many live oak and cypress trees on the property. I love visiting and with each trip I am always surprised at how much they have grown. I wonder if Andy and I will be fortunate to live long enough to see them touch overhead and create the alée they will one day form. While Salem is a very simple place, I think it is my favorite place in the whole world.

Chapter 36

The Last Chapter Or Is It?

By spring of 2019, I had settled into a rhythm of enjoying my board work, managing our family investments with Blake and spending quality time with Lisa at the Beach, in Charleston, at the farm and traveling with friends in between. While I had never been subject to depression, I was experiencing some melancholy feelings as I wondered if this was the last chapter in my life. I was 67 years of age and would be 70 in 2021. I was still very healthy and active and by no means out of energy, yet I couldn't help wondering if there could be another adventure, project or opportunity. Since I have always been comforted in the knowledge and belief that God has his plan for me, the feeling was not so much one of unhappiness but more just pure curiosity.

Reflective thoughts make us aware of our blessings, and I was very aware of mine, one of which has been a wealth of great friends. I'm talking about true friends, not just acquaintances, but people I care about and who care about me. It is said that a person is blessed if they have a handful of true friends. That makes me especially blessed because I have several handfuls.

Unfortunately, some are no longer living, and not a day goes by that I don't think of them. I feel they are in a better place, but they serve as a constant reminder of how lucky I am to still be doing what I am doing surrounded by people I love.

Thinking back to Bankers Trust, there was David Rhodes, who passed away around 60, who taught me credit and how to lend money, and Bob Durant, who died in his 50s from cancer and who taught me much about human nature and how to judge character.

Three other people stand out, who were all with me for a long time before passing unfortunately at a too young age. Tom Parsell, who was the entrepreneur Chevrolet dealer turned restauranteur and the owner of three of the most successful restaurants in Charleston—Magnolias, Blossom and Cypress. Tom was one of the first people who lined up behind me and moved all his business to Wachovia during those dark days when I had been fired from Bank of America. After Lisa and I moved to Columbia in 1987, we frequently visited Tom and his wife Suzi and our families vacationed together.

Tom was a true Renaissance man. A passionate outdoorsman, he was also an avid wine collector, an artist/painter, and he also grew orchids. We shared a common passion for business and the stock market, and Tom was a great mentor for our son Blake, who he took on tours through the wine cellar and kitchens and educated on the economics of running restaurants. Tom and Suzi were very involved in nonprofit work and all aspects of the Charleston community, and along with Hank Holliday were founders of the Charleston Wine and Food Festival. Tom and I spoke by phone almost every day.

In early fall of 2007, I was seeing customers in Florida when my cell phone rang just before dinner. My dear friend and fellow Wachovia teammate Helen Pratt Thomas told me Tom had been killed in a tragic car accident. I was stunned and heartbroken. Not a day goes by that I don't think of Tom and wish I could still talk to him.

Doug Seigler, old KA friend from Newberry College died of throat cancer in his early 60s. We had made a covenant back at Newberry when we both pledged different fraternities that we would stay fast friends, and we did. Doug had been our family's attorney for our various home purchases as we moved during the early years of my career. We stayed in touch regularly as we both shared the love of hunting and all things outdoors. In the final stages of Doug's cancer, we were able to take several memorable trips together, one to Edisto Beach to go shrimping and one to Lake Summit where we kayaked, and Doug was able to enjoy some sun and take in the beautiful mountains surrounding the lake.

By far my favorite recollection of Doug was a trip we took during the late stages of his cancer to go duck hunting at George Dean Johnson's

Lowcountry plantation, Pon Pon. George was kind enough to give us the run of the place for one night and a morning duck hunt. By then, Doug was very weak, and his neck had become deformed by the cancer, causing his head to slump on his shoulder. His food was fed through a tube since he couldn't swallow. The night before the hunt, Doug was throwing up blood, and his brother Harold lobbied to cancel the hunt given his condition. Doug would have none of it. He insisted, "Damn it, Harold, we came to go duck hunting and we're gonna do it!"

The next morning, as Doug and I sat in the blind together, we both knew it was the last time. The sun rose on one of those cold, totally bright January mornings, and it was spectacular. Lots of wind came up, which made the shooting sporty. On the first flight of ducks, I shot and killed one. Doug missed. On the next flight, the same thing happened. On the third pass I shot a double and the lab picked up two since Doug had missed again. By this point, he was running out of strength and could hardly get his gun up as. I distinctly remember saying a silent prayer and asking The Lord to please let him get one.

On the next pass I didn't shoot because I wanted to spot for Doug. Now I'm not saying I believe in miracles, but sometimes things happen. In that instant Doug found the strength to get his gun up and straighten his neck just enough to make two clean shots. Doug had a double. I said a silent prayer of thanks. Almost immediately, another pass of ducks came, and I watched in amazement as two more fell.

Doug looked at me and smiled, "Well, we came to go hunting, and we did. Let's give these birds a rest and head in." That was the last time I saw him alive, but I think of him often and relive the many fun times we had.

Sterling Laffitte was the young banker from Estill whose father, Monk, was on the Bankers Trust board of directors. Sterling, his wife Linn, Lisa, and I became fast friends during our time together in Hilton Head. Sterling lived in Estill and ran the family bank there, but he visited Hilton Head almost every weekend because his family had a vacation home there. Sterling and I shared a common passion for snow skiing, so we took a number of vacation trips to the mountains of North Carolina and Wintergreen in the early years and then later out west to Vail and Snowmass. Sterling was also my personal banker. He financed every house we ever owned other than the first one I bought next to Elden Walker on

Brockwall drive. Like Doug, Sterling was diagnosed with throat cancer even though he never smoked a day in his life. Also, like Doug, he had a long battle with the disease but finally succumbed. One of my last recollections of him was an afternoon quail hunt where Lisa, Jim Bradshaw and I joined Sterling and Linn at his farm in Estill. It was a beautiful fall day, and we had a wonderful time, concluding with a fire in his fireplace and an after-hunt bourbon. Like, Doug and Tom, I think of Sterling often and always smile when I do.

I also think of my dear friend Lee Atwater. His star shone brightly for a short 40 years….much too short. I remember the fun times we had and I chuckle when I think of all the mischief. Also, my dear friend Charlie Way who lived into his mid 80s and who was one of the first to reach out to me in my time of need when I was fired by Bank of America. He would call every day to check on me in that tough time and was helpful in recommending to Ben Jenkins and Ken Thompson that they hire me. Charlie passed away last summer from lung cancer, and I often think of our Kiawah adventure.

So, in late Spring of 2019, I was thinking, as I so often did, of many of these people whose lives had been cut short and how lucky I was to still be in the game and doing exactly what I wanted. I resolved that if indeed my days of achieving new things and climbing new peaks was at an end, then it was a good place to be, and I should count my blessings for all I had been given. However, like so many times before when I least expected, things began to happen. It all started with my phone ringing.

It was my friend Tommy Teague from Salem Leasing . Since my retirement, Tommy and I had stayed in touch with frequent hunting trips and visits to Charleston and our beach house. From time to time, Tommy would ask me to look at companies he was considering buying, but on this occasion, he was asking me to help a friend of his named Dan Calhoun.

Dan and his brothers owned a tortilla company in Winston Salem, and in Tommy's opinion, they were about to make a mistake by selling the company too soon. He asked if I would look at their numbers and talk to them, and he gave me Dan's phone number. I called Dan and asked him to send me three years of financials and any other information he deemed relevant.

After receiving all the data, I reviewed it and called Dan the next day.

Dan told me that his parents had been missionaries to Mexico. As a result, he and his brothers had been raised down there, were fluent in Spanish, understood the culture and had a love for the Mexican people. Upon moving back to the US, they ultimately founded La Tortilleria, selling tortillas to Hispanic workers.

Like all great entrepreneurs, seeing the rapid growth of the market for Hispanic foods in North Carolina, they re-named the business, calling it Purple Crow Foods, adjusted their business model and became wholesale food distributors selling to small Hispanic grocers called bodegas.

From their very modest beginning, and like most entrepreneurs after suffering through several near-death experiences, their business was starting to hit stride. For 2019 they were on track to do $90 million in sales, and for the past 3 years their top and bottom line had shown 12-15% growth. Dan shared with me that they were under a letter of intent with three days remaining to sell the business for a handsome profit to a private equity firm in New York. Dan asked if I thought he was making a mistake, but I told him I couldn't discuss that with him because I didn't want to get sued for contract interference.

However, I did tell him that instead of selling the entire business, he should consider the alternative of bringing in a strategic partner. This would allow the brothers to sell part of the business, but it would leave them in control and they would still run the company. Hopefully, the strategic partner could bring growth capital and other resources to enable the management team to dramatically grow. This type of transaction would allow them to possibly create more value for themselves by participating in the growth of the business into the future.

Dan asked if Tommy and his partner Ken Langone would be that strategic partner. I told him that due to the LOI, I could not discuss that, but based on the numbers I was looking at it was my opinion that they could find a strategic partner. Dan confided in me that he was under a lot of pressure to do the right thing for his brothers, that the sale was more money than any one of them had ever seen, and that while his brothers would follow his lead it would be a tough call to walk away. I explained that since there were only 3 days left under the LOI, there wasn't enough time to have a deal on the table from a strategic partner, so to some extent they would have to take a leap of faith if they chose not to take the private equity deal.

Dan asked if I thought Ken and Tommy would be willing to meet with them. I said I thought they would, however there could be no talk of buying their company, only a conversation to share philosophies.

After getting off the phone with Dan, I put together a long memo to Tommy and Ken describing the business and the opportunity, understanding that the brothers would have to walk from the current LOI before any serious conversations could occur. I shared with Ken and Tommy my view that it was a great business, that the brothers were honest, hardworking people who had built something special, that they had an incredibly loyal employee base and loyal, highly diversified customers with no single sales concentrations to any one entity, that the brothers had a great core set of values borne out of their faith and service ethos that they had inherited from their missionary parents. The brothers treated everyone, employees, and customers alike as family, and there was a sincere commitment to creating the win-win. Best of all, it was my opinion that there was also a huge runway for growth, both through geographic expansion and penetrating the existing customer base to a greater extent.

We had a call, and Ken and Tommy asked a lot of good questions culminating with how much of the purchase price could be leveraged. To Ken's surprise, I told him that in my opinion the investor's needed to use 100% equity and no additional leverage to make sure the business was not over-levered and was positioned for growth. Tommy and Ken bought into my assessment and Ken agreed to immediately fly down from New York so he and Tommy could meet with the Calhoun's, with the understanding that there would be no discussion of buying the business. The meeting was held next morning, but I couldn't attend due to one of my board meetings. The chemistry with Ken, Tommy and the Calhoun's was excellent, and the brothers decided to take that leap of faith and let the LOI expire.

After the expiration of the LOI, I went into high gear. Working with Ken and Tommy, we hired KPMG to do a quality of earnings review. Ken also got his old friend Ed Herlihy at Wachtel Lipton to represent them in the purchase of a majority controlling interest. Blake and I agreed to make an investment on Ken and Tommy's side of the transaction through Salem Capital. Essentially, I agreed to shepherd the effort through closing and then post-closing, to go on the Board which would be composed of the three brothers and three people from Ken and Tommy's side (Ken Langone's son Bruce; Al Carey, former CEO of Frito Lay and PepsiCo North America; and me).

After due diligence, we went from a handshake to a closing at the end of August in 2019. We never had an LOI or purchase and sale agreement, which was amazing because today contracts and legal documents seem to govern everything.

Since closing, the business has taken off, and we have never looked back. In 2020 sales grew about 20% despite Covid. The business finished 2021 up another 15-20% with a total top line of over $125 million. In 2022, the business exceeded $200 million. To position for the future, we are doubling our warehouse capacity in Winston Salem and adding cold storage so we can enter the protein business. Best of all, we have added many jobs essentially doubling the number of people we employ, many of whom are honest, hardworking Hispanics who are trying to build a better life for their families.

Last but not least, the company has retained its sense of combining food, fun, faith and family and weaving that into everything they do to create positive outcomes for all their constituents. For my part, I have worked with Dan and the management team to incorporate more process into everything they do including financial reporting and corporate governance. Fortunately, I have been able to share knowledge from the other boards I am on to help Dan and his brothers as they work through this transition.

In the Spring of 2020 Covid hit, and the sales at our restaurant division that sells to small Mexican restaurants came to a full stop. Despite the drop in the restaurant division, sales to the small grocers grew even stronger. Given the impact on the restaurant side, we were advised by our banks that we could access the PPP loan program of forgivable debt through the SBA. Dan started the application process but halfway through started having second thoughts. While it would have been almost $2 million in free money, Dan knew we could make it through because the drop in sales in the restaurant division had been largely offset by the sales to the grocers. His misgivings were borne out of the fact that by taking the money we might be getting in front of someone who needed it more. After discussing with Ken, we made the decision to not take the funds. From my chair, I marveled at Dan's honesty, integrity, and selfless approach to things. We all believe it was the right call.

My involvement with the Calhoun brothers and Ken and Tommy has been incredibly exciting and rewarding. Best of all, I know in my heart that my mom is smiling down from Heaven as we undertake this work. While she worked hard to obtain her American Citizenship and loved this country, in her heart she was still a Latin and loved everything about the Hispanic people and her heritage. Knowing that I am doing something in my own way to try and help her people would make her very, very happy. I am half Hispanic, and that makes me happy as well.

You might be questioning some of what I have said above, because isn't investing supposed to be about making money? Yes, it is. However, along with making money comes the power to make a difference in people's lives. The Calhoun brothers know this as do Ken, Tommy, the other board members, and I know it. While we all want to make money, we also subscribe to the Calhoun brothers' philosophy that as a successful growing company serving Hispanics, part of our DNA and our mission is to make that positive difference in how we take care of our people and our customers.

As 2020 progressed and the story of Purple Crow and the Calhoun's brothers was still being written, my phone rang again. The Hannon Family are dear friends we have known for over 30 years. They lived next door to my aunt Tita in Gastonia. Steve Hannon is a very successful Orthodontist, and he and his wife Suzy have 5 children. I could tell many stories of fun times together in their kitchen with Suzy's mom Dorothy making meatballs and happy times at 5 of their children's weddings. They are a wonderfully generous family, and they support many good causes. One is Holy Angels, a special place that takes care of special needs children.

The Hannon Family migrated to North Carolina from Pittsburgh including Suzy's parents and Steve's sister. Steve is an entrepreneur, coming to Gastonia after dental school with nothing and starting his own practice. He now has Four locations, and his two oldest twins, Justin and Stephanie, are both Orthodontist and in the practice with him.

When the phone rang that day, it was the Hannon's youngest son, David. I had visited with him at one of Dorothy's meatball-making sessions when he told me about a startup he was involved in called CareCard. I expressed an interest in learning more and that was the purpose of his call. I basically learned that CareCard is a startup version of GoodRX, which is a discount prescription app. It basically allows the app user to go online and shop prescriptions at nearby pharmacies for discounts, real time for real value. Since David already had the app up and running with agreements already in place with the nation's largest pharmacies, his new challenge was finding the seed capital to fund his launch and fund marketing to dramatically grow his user base. While David's pro forma numbers were compelling, what really struck me was his desire to serve underserved segments of our society who are often disadvantaged by the high prices they have to pay for prescriptions given the lack of transparency and their own lack of knowledge.

His game plan was to target the African American and Hispanic communities as the largest disadvantaged segments of the population. The whole time he was talking I thought of my mother and her lifelong effort to help other people, especially those less fortunate who struggle day to day. I immediately knew this was something I wanted to get involved with, however, since I was investing with my son Blake, I told David that I needed to confer with him.

The next morning after talking to Blake, I called David and told him that we were in as seed round investors. Furthermore, I told him that I would get on the phone and call some of my friends who I thought would have an interest.

David was elated with the show of support, but my guess is that he thought my efforts to raise additional dollars would be met with limited success. After hanging up, Blake and I went to work and spent the better part of the summer raising capital. As it turned out, we were able to raise most of the money he needed to close out the first round. CareCard was now up and running, and I was excited about the prospects for the future and the opportunity to do well while doing good! Since helping David raise the necessary funding, Blake and I have also tried to serve as a kitchen cabinet as he works to build his business and create the right governance and reporting process appropriate for a company with outside shareholders.

After wondering in the spring of 2019 if my time of new adventures was over, life has been a whirlwind. In addition to my work with Purple Crow Foods and CareCard, I also chaired a special committee of Sykes

Enterprises (NASDAQ: SYKE) which resulted in our agreeing to sell the company to Sitel Corporation in an all-cash deal for approximately $2.4 billion dollars. I also co-chaired the search committee to find the next General Director of Spoleto Festival USA to replace Nigel Redden who guided the festival effectively over many years.

Despite the activity, there has been plenty of time for friends and family, which is my favorite way to spend time. I stay busy, but I look forward to each day since I love what I do. On more than one occasion I have thought about how I have come full circle. I started out as a banker who tried to help entrepreneurs, and now I have become one myself. It's certainly not where I thought I would be when I started down this road, but it's a place I am comfortable with. Given my faith, I believe that all of us are put on this world for a purpose. In my case, I often think of that little boy on a stool in his dad's country store crunching numbers to try and reconcile all the power company bills with payments. I take great satisfaction in my belief that I am doing exactly what God put me on this earth to do and I am enjoying every minute of it.

Who knows if there will be another chapter, but somehow I think there will! In fact, Tommy Teague just called. He has a minority owned trucking company he wants me to look at. I have looked at the numbers, and it appears to be a promising growth opportunity. I am excited!